Revolutionary
Multiculturalism

THE EDGE:
CRITICAL STUDIES IN EDUCATIONAL THEORY

Series Editors Joe L. Kincheloe, Peter McLaren, and Shirley Steinberg

---

Revolutionary Multiculturalism

Pedagogies of Dissent for the New Millennium

Peter McLaren

■ WestviewPress
A Division of HarperCollinsPublishers

Copyright © 1997 by Westview Press, A Division of HarperCollins Publishers, Inc.

Published in 1997 in the United States of America by Westview Press, 5500 Central Avenue, Boulder, Colorado 80301-2877, and in the United Kingdom by Westview Press, 12 Hid's Copse Road, Cumnor Hill, Oxford OX2 9JJ

Library of Congress Cataloging-in-Publication Data
McLaren, Peter, 1948–
    Revolutionary multiculturalism : pedagogies of dissent for the new millennium / Peter McLaren.
        p.   cm.—(Edge, critical studies in educational theory)
    Includes bibliographical references (p.   ).
    ISBN 0-8133-2570-6 (hc).—ISBN 0-8133-2571-4 (pb)
    1. Critical pedagogy—United States.   2. Multicultural education—United States.   3. Postmodernism and education—United States.
I. Title.   II. Series.
LC196.5.U6M35   1997
370.11´5—dc21   97-15178
                                                                                   CIP

The paper used in this publication meets the requirements of the American National Standard for Permanence of Paper for Printed Library Materials Z39.48-1984.

10   9   8   7   6   5   4   3   2   1

To Jenny,
an eternal constant in a sea of chaos

Responde tú . . .

Tú, que partiste de Cuba,
responde tú,
¿dónde hallarás verde y verde,
azul y azul,
palma y palma bajo el cielo?
Responde tú.

●   ●   ●

Tú, que tu lengua olvidaste,
responde tú,
y en lengua extraña masticas
el güel y el yu,
¿cómo vivir puedes mudo?
Responde tú.

●   ●   ●

Tú, que dejaste la tierra,
responde tú,
donde tu padre reposa
bajo una cruz,
¿dónde dejarás tus huesos?
Responde tú.

●   ●   ●

Ah, desdichado, responde,
responde tú,
¿dónde hallarás verde y verde,
azul y azul,
palma y palma bajo el cielo?
Responde tú.

*—**Nicolás Guillén***

Contents

Foreword

In summer 1995 a small group of teachers from across the state of Missouri gathered for a three-week seminar. One of the participants was a white woman, a first-grade teacher from a small town outside of St. Louis. For the first time in this town's history, significant numbers of African Americans were moving into the community, and, correspondingly, African American children were attending formerly all-white classes. Another participant was a black man majoring in black studies. Choosing to become a junior high teacher in order to transmit the cultural heritage he valued, he was committed to sustaining the process of empowerment that had shaped his identity. The class also included the chair of the math department at a community college in central Missouri. She taught a year-long remedial class in mathematics in which students who had always failed or barely passed math were helped to think and reason mathematically. The results of her work were dramatic: People who came in for two-year technical degrees realized they had the ability to become physicists, chemists, and engineers instead of service workers. Those who attended the seminar were a motley crew—people who taught high school French and art and junior high social studies. What brought us together in this seminar on multicultural education was a commitment to the empowerment of all students, to social justice, and to education for a revitalized and inclusive democracy.

There is an epistemic shift occurring in the United States. There is a great deal of attention, and rightly so, on right-wing militarists and the prevalence of divisive, fearful appeals to isolation and group privilege. Many groups are calling for us to back away from pluralism and diversity: groups on the right who are opposed to feminism and to justice for racial minorities as well as liberals who contend that affirmative action has succeeded or that a continued focus on diversity is either a luxury we can no longer afford or a force that has become dangerously divisive. The attacks on affirmative action, the resistance to continued inclusion of women and people of color in all aspects of American life, are fueled not only by the right but also by people on the left who are weary of the struggles of coalition politics, of finding ways for groups that are genuinely diverse to work together within institutions to build and implement programs in communities, schools, and businesses.

While there are many who are resistant to feminism and affirmative action, there are also people throughout the country who are still deeply committed to diversity, to democracy, to respect for all people. Within this group, which includes the teachers who chose to spend three weeks of their summer studying multicultural education, there is a sustained commitment to pursue the work of inclusion; to understand ever more clearly the economic, political, and cultural barriers to social justice; and to understand how we can genuinely share power and move from mere critique to strategies for building and transforming schools, economic systems, and community life.

It is in this horizon, in the reality of an epistemic shift, that the work of Peter McLaren matters. The cultural left and new social movements are critical of capitalism and its effect on community, as are adherents of the New Right within Europe and the United States. On the left and the right, there is a call for community, a critique of capitalism, and an attempt to sort out the structures, the values, that can help us live well. Given the contested terrain of what counts as community, the work of McLaren is essential. He helps us understand and sort out the various dimensions of the tasks facing us as educators—discovering with our students the nature of the injustices that shape our lives, actually seeing, shaping, and furthering processes of emancipatory subjectivity and group identity. Schools are a critical site in the evocation of a culture of empowerment, and McLaren helps us understand both the imperative and the complexity of this task.

McLaren's work is valuable for three reasons. First, he articulates the ways in which post-Fordism affects and is transforming education within the United States. He helps us see the ways in which our work as educators is being affected by the increasing disparity in access to valued resources, the increasing division between classes within the United States and throughout the world. Second, he not only brings sustained attention to forms of repression and oppression but analyzes as well the sites of resistance, the movements where students, workers, and communities are creating and sustaining forms of individual and group identity that challenge the imperatives of a consumer economy. Third, McLaren struggles with the monumental task of solidarity among marginalized groups. He helps us recognize the differences in forms of oppression and resistance experienced by women and by different racial groups and the differing focus of those concerned with environmental issues, those who highlight issues of class, and those who highlight disability issues. McLaren holds true to a critical analysis of the way in which we can genuinely engage these differences. We begin with our particular identities, but through the process of understanding those identities critically and through the painful process of interacting with people from other social locations, our identities as women, as people of color, as members of different social strata, are themselves changed, expanded, and transformed. McLaren helps us understand what it takes to create structures of solidarity and accountability that, so unlike the community structure of the New Right, are not dependent on homogenization for cohesion, not dependent on the exclusion of difference or the instrumentalization of women for group identity and social order. McLaren's work reflects an awareness of how the pedagogical practices that enhance this form of group identity are themselves in the process of being formed. He helps us see where we are learning how to listen to each other and work together as well as points out the ways in which we still need to revise our pedagogical and political practices.

Although I would hesitate to say that these times are more challenging than other periods of history, they are our times and our challenge. The crises of capitalism, racial oppression, and sex discrimination are clear and acute, yet the answers are elusive. No single social movement has all the answers. Feminism is necessary, but more than feminism is needed. We need ecologically sustainable forms of agriculture and industry, yet more than ecological awareness is needed. Racial justice is crucial, yet more than racial justice is required. The dimensions of oppression are multifaceted, and a thorough understanding of social injustice requires an integration of critiques by feminists, people of color, postcolonial theorists, ecologists, and analysts of class exploitation. And yet even if transnational capital were to disappear tomorrow, collapsing because of its own contradictions, what would take its place? What are just and ecologically sound ways of organizing agriculture, industry, schools, and politics? The answers, the creative vision of what a new world would look like, are vague and elusive. Our critique is far more definitive than is our vision of a just world. The New Right can here apparently offer more—a concrete vision of a past world of social harmony. We know that the world of family values lauded by the right, the world of harmony and order, was actually a system of violence and social control in which racism flourished and women were controlled and limited in their fundamental rights as citizens and as human beings. And yet, what vision can we offer?

Here the work of McLaren helps us. In this difficult time of relatively clear critiques and vague answers, in the absence of a compelling shared vision on the left, he points to the work of educators. At this time we are tilling the ground, sowing the seeds of fundamental social change. It is not yet clear what shape our vision will take, but in his description of what we can do now, we find a description of the processes that allow that vision to emerge. First, we can continue to elicit the voices of all groups and keep these voices in critical dialogue. McLaren models this in his own writing, in his attempt to understand all segments of new social movements and the cultural left. He also challenges us to examine the ways that we can bring our students to see the differences among them, to be open to working together in diverse communities, and to learn to look for, and listen to, the voices of those not represented in their own neighborhood or school. Second, he demonstrates the ways in which we as educators, with our students, can uncover the forms of oppression that limit and constrict our lives. From this matrix of mutual respect, of intelligences grounded in community—and here is the key point—of critique and envisioning enlivened by critical engagement with people from other communities, we are living out the processes that will produce a vision of renewed institutions and community structures. We are supporting students who know their history and political locus, who can think critically and creatively, who can engage difference, and who can discover that differences—while always challenging and often painful—are the means of deep insight and new vision.

Peter McLaren matters. Read him, argue with him, and let yourself be challenged by him to fan the flames of resistance, take seriously the conflicts in our own cultural and education practices, and together take on a self-critical responsibility to keep open the doorway to hope.

Sharon D. Welch
University of Missouri–Columbia

Series Editors' Preface

Revolutionary Multiculturalism contains the type of scholarship that we were hoping to publish when we conceived The Edge Series with Peter McLaren for Westview Press several years ago. In this book, McLaren grapples with questions of identity and agency at the end of the twentieth century, with its mutating forms of racism and dehumanizing post-Fordist economy. How do we begin to rethink ourselves, to reconceptualize our identities in these changing and hostile times? How in the midst of so much hate and despair do we keep hope alive? How do we move beyond critical pedagogy's traditional concern with critique to a new form of critical transformation? Where do we begin the process of creating democratic educational spheres? What role might teachers play in this process?

Such questions are central to McLaren's work. As he observes race, ethnicity, and class as they intersect with pedagogy in contemporary Los Angeles, he sees a new manifestation of American education's traditional efforts to regulate and socialize new immigrants. Such observations are important to those of us concerned with social justice and critical pedagogy, for the Californian present may provide insight into the American future. They also move McLaren to rethink and expand traditional notions of multicultural education to encompass the effects of economic globalization, new patterns of emigration, international corporations, and the combined influence of these factors on identity formation. This new global reality opens questions of hybrid identity formation or *mestizaje*—complex considerations that hold no immediate answers.

The new multiculturalism that McLaren develops in this work moves beyond traditional liberal pluralist versions. In this new critical multiculturalism, McLaren explores notions of privilege as well as issues of oppression. With these notions in mind he plunges headfirst into the new scholarly discourse on whiteness, connecting the formation of white identity to the social realities of the late twentieth century and the reconceptualized multiculturalism he has theorized. Such conceptualization is a compelling view of whiteness and its effects on the contemporary cultural landscape as well as the profound social consequences its construction holds for the non-white. Few approaches to racial politics in Western societies provide such profound insight into the "way race works" than the exploration of whiteness McLaren lays out in this work.

All of McLaren's efforts take place in a context of passionate commitment to social justice and radical democracy. Understanding that any discussion of multiculturalism that occurs outside the parameters of power relations is doomed to be a naive celebration of consensus and tolerance, McLaren proposes a pedagogical corrective that appreciates the impact of marginalization and suffering—of, in his words, the "hierarchies of subordination" under which the oppressed live. Thus, the radical democracy McLaren advocates in his book is noisy, accepting of differences, and always suspicious of universal claims to truth. Indeed, McLaren is at his best when imagining the specificities of his democratic vision.

With these ideas in mind we proudly welcome Peter's book to our Westview series—a series that would not be possible without the important vision of editors Dean Birkenkamp and Jill Rothenberg. We are ever appreciative to those individuals who support the work of scholars such as Peter McLaren.

Joe L. Kincheloe
and Shirley Steinberg

Introduction:
Fashioning Los Olvidados
in the Age of Cynical Reason

The price of freedom is death.
—Malcolm X (El Hajj Malik El Shabazz)

We don't want to be around that ol' pale thing.
—Malcolm X (El Hajj Malik El Shabazz)

El deber de cada revolucionario es hacer la revolución.
—Che Guevara

This is a book about hope, written with all the detachment that rage can afford and with the purpose of challenging social and educational policies and practices manufactured in this era of cynical reason. As the millennium draws closer and my time on this earth stretches within a whisper of half a century, I look back at my twenty-five years as an educator and social activist with few regrets. Yet I must confess a world-weariness has overtaken much of what I thought was my inviolate resolve, a feeling of anger and despair about living and dying in these new times, at this current and painful juncture in world history. I try to hide my despair and rage toward the system from my students, many of whom yearn to find in my writings some hard and fast ways to permanently dismantle structures of oppression that imprison the spirit and harden the hearts of so many of our brothers and sisters in struggle. It is perhaps a piquant irony that those commenting on what they consider to be my youthful style and determination don't realize that my motorcycle jackets, flannel shirts, and faded jeans serve less as a "retro" fashion statement or pathological addiction to the 1960s than as a sartorial cover for a heavy soul.

Despite the present social conditions that beset us, I am not in a perpetual state of dismay, forced to camouflage a secret despair. In my darkest hours I have on more than one occasion been graced by what could be described as a momentous shimmering of the human spirit, a slight breaking free from the deep inertia of this planetary soul. Occasionally light splinters the darkness in various shapes: a nascent social movement attempting to unite the barrios; a hip-hop message that becomes a rallying cry for social justice in a community under siege; a million black men marching to Washington; a hundred thousand marchers striding down Cesar Chavez Avenue to protest Proposition 187 with a resolve so formidable that you could feel electricity in the air; hundreds of high school students in East Los Angeles defying their teachers and walking out of their classrooms to show their solidarity with the anti–Proposition 187 activists. Even a simple pedagogical act, such as a group of students trying to undo the image of the Mexicano as California's demon poster boy by confronting white racists in one of my seminars, is enough to drive a tiny wedge between despair and cynical resignation.

Spaces of hope do appear, but rarely by historical accident. Sometimes they occur in the momentary indecision of the marketplace, sometimes in a rare paralysis of hate in the menacing machine of capital; but whatever the reason, these spaces need to be strategically seized. Spaces of hope offer encouragement to the forces of justice, but they are not sufficient in themselves. Spaces—often private—must be made public. They must be expanded from spaces into spheres—from personal, individual spaces and private epistemologies into public spheres of hope and struggle and collective identities.

Where do those of us living in this vaunted Western democracy stand as a nation? Look around you, dear comrade; look inside as well as outside, for the outside is really a mirror of who we are as a people. The Dickensianizing of postmodern megalopolises like Los Angeles (the enhancing of the personal wealth of the few who live in places like Beverly Hills at the expense of the many who live in places like Compton or East LA) is not a natural historical event (there is nothing natural about history). It is a politically contrived dismemberment of the national conscience. And it is comfortably linked to global economic restructuring.

One of the largest Latino-owned companies in the United States, International Garment Processors, washes, inspects, tags, and ships denim garments for Levi Strauss of San Francisco and finishes denim clothing for the Gap, Sasson, Liz Claiborne, and Guess. Located in El Paso, Texas, where it pays its workers $6.00 an hour, the company is moving to Ensenada, Baja California, Mexico, where it will pay its workers the same rate as other *maquiladoras*: $1.25 an hour. Because of the North America Free Trade Agreement and the gradual elimination of clothing tariffs, companies are moving to places where it is easier to exploit the most vulnerable of the global population.

Sustaining a meager existence is becoming frighteningly more difficult with the passage of time for millions of Third World peoples as well as First World urban dwellers, including millions of inhabitants of the

United States. Global capitalism is excluding large numbers from formal employment while the poor, trapped within post-Fordist arenas of global restructuring and systems of flexible specialization, appear to be less able to organize themselves into stable and homogeneous social movements. Standardized forms of mass production in which companies retool and keep production costs down in order to keep competitive in the international marketplace are now disappearing. Economies of global efficiency are sidestepping the ability of nation-states to mediate the control of money and information.

Labor markets are growing more segmented as full-time workers are replaced with part-time workers who are unable to secure even meager health or dental benefits. The days of high-wage, high-benefit mass production manufacturing are receding into the horizon as the First World bids farewell to industrialized regimes. Yet manufacturing has not completely disappeared from the United States. In Los Angeles, where I live, you can witness the Latinization of the Southland's working class; Latino/as now make up 36 percent of Los Angeles County's labor force in manufacturing (the nation's largest manufacturing base). And the exploitation of these workers continues to increase.

California governor Pete Wilson has joined a list of governors attempting to drop a state requirement that counties provide general assistance programs for poor families. Wilson also wants poor people who can't provide safe environments for their children to put them up for adoption. Since in Wilson's view poverty is obviously a condition suffered only by those who don't try hard enough to be financially secure or even rich, it only follows that families who are not economically secure don't deserve to have children.

Stock options go up in companies that downsize and lay off thousands of employees. It used to be a sign that a company was in trouble when it laid off large numbers of workers. Now it's an indication of strength, making stockholders proud. Companies are increasing their outsourcing, turning routine work over to affiliated companies and outside agents and thus decreasing costs entailed in employing full-time white-collar staff and making their employee structure more "cost effective." Cutting costs is everything as business moves farther away from even a peripheral engagement with the world of ethics. In fact, capitalism has made ethics obsolete. The buying and selling of labor power is all about aesthetics, and although aesthetics does share a hinge with ethics, the latter is subsumed by reification's terrible beauty.

Assets of the world's leading 358 billionaires exceed the combined annual incomes of approximately half the population of the globe. The war on poverty has given way to the war on the poverty-stricken—a war that is about as mean-spirited as wars can get. The average worker has to do without the luxury of a decent living because improving conditions for the majority of the population would cut too deeply into the corporate profitability of the ruling elite. Rarely has such contempt for the poor and for disenfranchised people of color been so evident as in the hate-filled politics of the past several decades.

For over a decade, a San Francisco Bay area drug ring sold tons of cocaine to Los Angeles street gangs—the Crips and the Bloods—and transferred thousands of dollars in drug profits to the FDN (Fuerza Democrática Nicaraguense—the Contras), which was run by the U.S. Central Intelligence Agency (Barrs 1996). The U.S. fight against the Sandinista government from 1982 until 1986 thus helped to put crack cocaine in the streets of major U.S. cities at a time when the government was conducting a war on drugs throughout the country. While Nancy Reagan posed for photographs with a "Just Say No" sticker, the U.S. government was allegedly facilitating drug deals in the streets of South Central, Los Angeles (Barrs 1996), an area where a number of my graduate students happen to teach in the public schools. One could assume that the Central Intelligence Agency considers expendable those African American and Latino/a neighborhoods where crack cocaine is used.

According to Gary Webb, crack cocaine is "a product so hellishly desirable that consumers will literally kill to get it" (1996, 17). That the cocaine brought into black LA during the 1980s was rumored to have been linked to the cocaine cartels of Columbia, the Central Intelligence Agency, and the FDN is perhaps not so surprising. But don't ask the government to take any responsibility for spawning the major crack markets. In fact, the CIA has been denying the story. The urban poor have always been easy for the government to write off—and for the average white American to write off as well—especially in African American and Latino/a neighborhoods. It's been a proud democratic tradition in this country to hate the poor.

In 1996 the Crenshaw district of Los Angeles witnessed growing grass-roots protests and candlelight vigils surrounding reports that the CIA directed drug sales in the South Central area of the city. The growing number of protesters hasn't been this impressive since the aftermath of the Rodney King beating. The fact that a disproportionately large number of African Americans are serving prison sentences on drug charges creates a scenario that reads more like a war on black communities than a war on drugs (Connell 1996). CIA director John Deutch came to Watts in November 1996 to speak to the people of South Central (mainly, the media people who were assembled there), no doubt worried that the controversy might damage the agency's funding efforts. Not many people were fooled by the disinformation efforts by Deutch, or by what cynical critics may assume is the CIA's house organ, the *Los Angeles Times* (which had previously run a three-part series on the CIA drug connection and pronounced it unfounded). It was hard for the people of South Central to swallow the idea that an agency that is believed to have toppled foreign governments and assassinated political figures could be impartial enough to investigate itself. As an example of the agency's ability to police itself, Deutch cited a successful attempt at clamping down on some agents' misuse of credit cards. The comparison was ludicrous and only increased the agency's lack of credibility. Of course, suspicions of CIA-sponsored wars against people of color are nothing new, especially in the international arena. What quickly comes to mind is the 1954 overthrow of Jacobo Arbenz's government in Guatemala and the Bay of Pigs operation directed at Cuba in the 1960s; the military coup against President João Goulart's government in Brazil in 1964; the U.S. invasion of the Dominican Republic in 1965; the overthrow of Allende's government in Chile in 1973; the "dirty wars" in Argentina and Uruguay in the early 1970s; the counterinsurgency activities in El Salvador, Guatemala, and Nicaragua in the 1980s; and the bailouts of Mexico's Partido Revolucionario Institucional (PRI) governments in 1976, 1982, 1988, and 1995.

Americans are continuing the democratic tradition of hating the poor and then, as if to assuage their guilt, suddenly feeling pity and donating a turkey to a food bank on Thanksgiving or some used clothing to unemployed war veterans. Yet charity does tend to stigmatize the receiver and elevate the giver. Sincere acts of charity are commendable, but random giving is not a substitute for an eradication of the causes of poverty, which seems to be traceable to advanced capitalism. The vast majority of Americans still continue to scapegoat immigrants, especially undocumented workers, and to seek salvation in increasingly more vociferous and politically demonic ways in this era of the promise of bond markets and "fast" capitalism. As fiscal resources move from inner cities to outer cities, from postwar suburbs to postmodern suburbs or white-dominated "edge cities," marginal living conditions for people of color will become more and more the norm.

The greed and avarice of the U.S. ruling class are seemingly unparalleled in history. Yet its goals remain decidedly the same. Michael Parenti writes:

> Throughout history there has been only one thing that ruling interests have ever wanted—and that is *everything*: all the choice lands, forest, game, herds, harvests, mineral deposits, and precious metals of the earth; all the wealth, riches, and profitable returns; all the productive facilities, gainful inventiveness, and technologies; all the control positions of the state and other major institutions; all public supports and subsidies, privileges and immunities; all the protections of the law with none of its constraints; all the services, comforts, luxuries, and advantages of civil society with none of the taxes and costs. Every ruling class has wanted only this: all the rewards

and none of the burdens. The operational code is: we have a lot; we can get more; we want it all. (1996, 46)

As long as the small-business lobby and other interests tied to capital successfully derail health care reform whenever the issue raises its disease-ravaged face, as long as the bond market continues to destroy public investment, and as long as business continues to enjoy record-high profits, acquisitions, and mergers (with the aid of corporate welfare) at the expense of wages and labor, prosperity in the United States, like its administration of social justice, will remain highly selective. And we all know who benefits from such selectivity. To remain in a state of political paralysis or inertia is to aid and abet the sickening suburbanization of the country—a suburbanization driven by a neoliberal agenda designed to serve whites. Working under existing rules established by the National Labor Relations Act and the procedures carried out by the National Labor Relations Board, unions are being deprived of their right to organize, and this is contributing in no small way to wage decline. The situation reflects only too well what Parenti calls his "iron law of bourgeois politics": When change threatens to rule, rules are changed (1996, 248).

Residents of the United States do not have a natural disposition to swindle the gullible, to target the poor more forcefully than an F-16 fighter locks onto an enemy hunkered down in the sands of Iraq, to scapegoat immigrants and fashion them into *los olvidados* (the forgotten ones). The current evisceration of public protection programs, shamefully absent enforcement of environmental standards, rising health insurance premiums, drastic declines in salaries for working people, erosion of the primary-sector proletariat, and steady increase in the numbers of chronically unemployed have catapulted the United States onto a tragic course toward social decay and human misery—a course that is far from inevitable.

It is possible that in a half century, whites will be a minority in the United States. As they continue to feel that their civil society is being despoiled and to blame immigrants for their increasing downward mobility and the disappearance of traditional American values, whites fall prey to the appeal of reactionary rhetoric and a Fascist politics of authoritarian repression (Sunker and Otto 1997). This is especially true in a time when whites continue to feel removed from their ethnic roots and undergo what Winant (1994, 284) has called "a racializing panethnicity as 'Euro-Americans.'"

The kindling of fascism lies in the furnace of U.S. democracy, waiting for a spark to ignite a firestorm of state repression. Previous firestorms have occurred in the Watts rebellion of August 1965, the civil rights movement, and the antiwar movement of the 1960s but also in more current forms such as the Los Angeles uprising of April 29, 1992, and the

East LA high school walkouts of 1995 over Proposition 187. We don't get many firestorms because, as Parenti (1996) has so presciently noted, fascism is already here on low flame, and it burns just fine with the occasional stoking from reactionary governors such as Pete Wilson.

The citizenry of the United States has been sold a damaged bill of goods in the Republican Contract with America. Parenti captures its ideology perfectly:

> The GOP socioeconomic agenda is not much different from the kind pushed by Mussolini and Hitler: break the labor unions, depress wages, impose a rightist ideological monopoly over the media, abolish taxes for the big corporations and the rich, eliminate government regulations designed for worker and consumer safety and environmental protection, plunder public lands, privatize public enterprises, wipe out most human services, and liberal-bait and race-bait all those opposed to such measures. (1996, 42)

The task ahead for those of us who wish to reclaim the dignity offered by true justice is to revivify democratic citizenship in an era of diminishing returns. It is to create critical citizens who are no longer content in occupying furtive spaces of private affirmation but who possess the will and the knowledge to turn these spaces into public spheres through the creation of new social movements and anticapitalist struggle.

Record numbers of disaffected white youth are joining citizen militias and white supremacist organizations at a time when black churches are burning in the South and when cross-burnings are occurring at an alarming rate across the nation in Louisiana, Georgia, Pennsylvania, Oregon, Maine, southern California, and elsewhere. As white youth search for identity in their lives, many are able to find meaning only in relation to their capacity to hate nonwhites.

The struggle in these new times is a daunting one. While some postmodernists adventitiously assert that identities can be fluidly recomposed, rearranged, and reinvented toward a more progressive politics in these new "pluralistic" times, I maintain that this is a shortsighted and dangerous argument. It would take more than an army of Jacques Lacans to help us rearrange and suture the fusillade of interpolations and subject positions at play in our daily lives. My assertion that the contents of particular cultural differences and discourses are not as important as how such differences are embedded in and related to the large social totality of economic, social, and political differences may strike some readers as extreme. Yet I think it is fundamentally necessary to stress this point.

We are not autonomous citizens who can fashionably choose whatever ethnic combinations we desire in order to reassemble our identity. Although the borders of ethnicity overlap and shade into one another, it is dishonest to assert that pluralized, hybridized identities are options available to all citizens in the same way (Hicks 1991). This is because class, race, and gender stratification and objective constraints and historical determinations restrict the choices of some groups. The division of labor linked to political organization and the politics of the marketplace regulate choices and often overdetermine their outcome (San Juan 1995). Identity is more than the ideological trafficking between nationality and ethnicity; it is the overlapping and mutual intereffectivity of discourse that is configured by the social relations of production. In other words, nationalism, ethnicity, and capitalist circuits of production can be seen as moving into a shared orbit.

Rather than stressing the importance of diversity and inclusion, as do most multiculturalists, I think that significantly more emphasis should be placed on the social and political construction of white supremacy and the dispensation of white hegemony. The reality-distortion field known as "whiteness" needs to be identified as a cultural disposition and ideology linked to specific political, social, and historical arrangements.

One of the themes that will be emphasized in the chapters that follow is the need to incorporate, yet move beyond, the politics of diversity and inclusion when discussing multicultural education. The discourse of diversity and inclusion is often predicated on hidden assumptions of assimilation and consensus that serve as supports for neoliberal democratic models of identity.

Neoliberal democracy, performing under the banner of diversity yet actually in the hidden service of capital accumulation, often reconfirms the racist stereotypes already prescribed by Euro-American nationalist myths of supremacy—stereotypes that one would think democracy is ostensibly committed to challenge. In the pluralizing move to become a society of diverse voices, neoliberal democracy has often succumbed to a recolonization of multiculturalism by failing to challenge ideological assumptions surrounding difference that are installed in its current anti–affirmative-action and welfare "reform" initiatives. In this sense people of color are still placed under the threshold of candidacy for inclusion into the universal right to self-determination and interpolated as exiles from U.S. citizenship. After all, as a shrinking minority, whites are running scared, conscious of their own vulnerability, and erecting fortresses of social regulation while they still have the power to do so. Todd Gitlin declares:

> The Republican tilt of white men is the most potent form of identity politics in our time: a huddling of men who resent (and exaggerate) their relative decline not only in parts of the labor market but at home, in the bedroom and the kitchen, and in the culture. Their fear and loathing is, in part, a panic against the relative gains of women and minorities in an economy

that people experience as a zero-sum game, in which the benefits accruing to one group seem to amount to subtractions from another. Talk about identity politics! These white men, claiming they deserve color-blind treatment, identify with their brethren more than their wives or sisters, or minorities. (1995, 233)

Of course, one of the most hated groups among the poor here in the Southland are the Mexican migrant workers. Stereotyped as *crimmegrants,* they have become the object of xenophobia par excellence. Ron Prince, one of the architects of Proposition 187, remarked: "Illegal aliens are a category of criminal, not a category of ethnic group" (cited in Gómez-Peña 1996, 67). Guillermo Gómez-Peña comments on the imbrication of borders as a perceived crisis effect by white Americans:

For many Americans, the border has failed to stop chaos and crisis from creeping in (the origin of crisis and chaos is somehow always located outside). Their worst nightmare is finally coming true. The United States is no longer a fictional extension of Europe, or the wholesome suburb imagined by the screenwriter of *Lassie.* It is rapidly becoming a huge border zone, a hybrid society, a mestizo race, and worst of all, this process seems to be irreversible. America shrinks day by day, as the pungent smell of enchiladas fills the air and the volume of quebradita music rises. (1996, 67)

The process of "Mexicanization" has struck fear into the hearts of the Euro-American who views this inevitability as an obdurate political reality. And this fear is only exacerbated by the media and anti-immigration activists. As Gómez-Peña notes,

Now, it is the "illegal aliens" who are to take the blame for everything that American citizens and their incompetent politicians have been unable (or unwilling) to solve. Undocumented immigrants are being stripped of their humanity and individuality, becoming blank screens for the projection of Americans' fear, anxiety, and rage. . . . Both the anti-immigration activists and the conservative media have utilized extremely charged metaphors to describe this process of "Mexicanization." It is described as a Christian nightmare ("hell at our doorsteps"); a natural disaster ("the brown wave"); a fatal disease or an incurable virus; a form of demographic rape; a cultural invasion; or the scary beginning of a process of secession or "Quebequization" of the entire Southwest. (1996, 66, 67–68)

I remember the bestial hate mongering among whites after the anti–Proposition 187 march in East Los Angeles in 1994. The size of the crowd—approximately 100,000 protesters by some estimates—instilled such a fear of a brown planet that many white Angelenos fervently took to the streets in anti-immigration demonstrations. Too much "difference effect" resulting from the borderization phenomenon has created among previously stable white constituencies a type of fibrillation of subjectivity—a discursive quivering that eventually leads to a state of identity collapse. Wreaking havoc on the social landscape by creating a spectacular demonology around African American and Latino/a gang members, welfare queens, undocumented workers, and gays and lesbians, members of the professional-managerial class made up primarily of cosmopolitan whites have tried to convince white America that its identity is threatened and that white people now constitute the "new" oppressed. Can anyone take this claim seriously, coming as it is from the most privileged group in history?

In addition to decentering the homogenizing and domesticating currents within multicultural education, this book is an attempt to address the aforementioned issues surrounding the construction of ethnoracial identity, in particular the invention of whiteness. I believe that an emphasis on the construction of whiteness will help put a different and important focus on the problems surrounding identity formation at this particular juncture in our history. When North Americans talk about race, they inevitably refer to African Americans, Asians, Latino/as, and Native Americans to the consistent exclusion of Euro-Americans. I want to challenge the prevailing assumption that in order to defeat racism we need only to put our initiatives behind the inclusions of minoritarian populations—in other words, of nonwhites. I want to argue instead that we need also to put our emphasis on the analysis of white ethnicity and the destabilization of white identity, specifically white supremacist ideology and practice. As David Roediger notes, "Whiteness describes, from Little Big Horn to Simi Valley, not a culture but precisely the absence of culture. It is the empty and therefore terrifying attempt to build an identity based on what one isn't and on whom one can hold back" (1994, 13).

This book follows the work of critical multiculturalists in attempting to unsettle both conservative assaults on multiculturalism and liberal paradigms of multiculturalism; the latter, in my view, simply repackage conservative and neoliberal ideologies under a discursive mantle of diversity. In undertaking such a project, I have tried in a modest way to advance a critical pedagogy that will service a form of postcolonial hybridity.

It is true that the concept of hybridity has been used in a powerful way to counter essentialized attempts at creating monolithic and "authentic" forms of identity (McLaren 1995; Hicks 1991). However, Coco Fusco rightly reminds us: "Too often . . . the postcolonial celebration of hybridity has been interpreted as the sign that no further concern about the politics of representation and cultural exchange is needed. With ease, we lapse back into the integrationist rhetoric of the 1960's, and conflate hybridity with parity" (1995, p. 76). Since not all hybridities are equal, we must attach to the term an ideological tacit nominal qualifier (Radhakrishnan 1996). In making this assertion, Ragagopalan Radhakrishnan provides us with an important qualification. He maintains that we should distinguish between a metropolitan version of hybridity and postcolonial hybridity. Whereas the former is a *ludic* form of capricious self-styling, the latter is a *critical* identitarian mode. Metropolitan hybridity, notes Radhakrishnan, is "characterized by an intransitive and immanent sense of *jouissance,*" whereas postcolonial hybridity is marked by a "frustrating search for constituency and a legitimate political identity" (1996, 159). Metropolitan hybridity is not "subjectless" or neutral but is a structure of identitarian thinking informed by the cultural logic of the dominant West. Postcolonial hybridity, in contrast, seeks authenticity in "a third space that is complicitous neither with the deracinating imperatives of Westernizaton nor with theories of a static, natural, and single-minded autochthony" (162). It is within such a perspective that educators are called to create *una pedagogía fronteriza.*

Revolutionary multiculturalism as a point of intersection with critical pedagogy supports the struggle for a postcolonial hybridity. Gómez-Peña captures the concept of postcolonial hybridity when he conceptually maps what he calls the New World Border, "a great trans- and intercontinental border zone, a place in which no centers remain. It's all margins, meaning there are no 'others,' or better said, the only true 'others' are those who resist fusion, mestizaje, and cross-cultural dialogue. In this utopian cartography, hybridity is the dominant culture: Spanish, Frangle, and Gingonol are *linguas francas*; and monoculture is a culture of resistance practiced by a stubborn or scared minority" (1996, 7).

The tension between multiple ethnicities and the politics of universal justice is the urgent issue of the new millennium. How are educators to approach this question with a politics both progressively critical and optimistic? William E. Connolly calls for an *ethos* of critical responsiveness as a response to the inherent paradoxical and relational character of the *code* of universal justice. He notes:

> As a movement struggles to cross the magic threshold of enactment, it may introduce a new right onto the register of justice. It thereby exposes retrospectively *absences* in a practice of justice recently thought by happy universalists to be complete. If and as the new movement becomes consolidated into a positive identity, it too becomes sedimented into settlements of the newly configural pluralism. And its presumptions, too, may now constitute a barrier to the next drive to pluralization. (1995, 185)

Unlike the *codification* of justice, an *ethos* of critical responsiveness is not grounded in transcendental or ontological principles. In fact, an ethos of critical responsiveness *exceeds* justice by recognizing that there is never any justice without absence. Consequently, an ethos of critical responsiveness becomes *uncodifiable* in calling into question the complete closure of any grand narrative or universal principle through proclamation, divine fiat, or rational consensus. While the practice of justice is ethically indispensable, it must exist in dissonant independence with an ethos of critical responsiveness.

Connolly notes that the ethos of critical responsiveness maintains that diversity is never irreducible to basic proclamations, rules, commands, or laws. Rather, diversity is always contingent and relational, and to think of it as a solid ground is to do it an injustice (Connolly 1995). Consequently, "the ethos and the code coexist in an asymmetrical relation of strife and interdependence" (Connolly 1995, 187). The point that needs to be made in relation to Connolly's call for an ethos of critical responsiveness is that identities should never be naturalized or transcendentalized because there is always a fleeting, fugitive, and contingent quality to identity. Connolly notes that "cultivation of critical responsiveness grows out of the appreciation that no culturally constituted constellation of identities ever deserves to define itself simply as natural, complete, or inclusive" (1995, 188).

If we challenge essentialized identities from the dialectical perspective of code and ethos, we still are left with the question of how to fashion coalitional and collective subjects of history that can and will work together from the perspective of a common ground of struggle rather than a common culture. Of course, this is the challenge posed by this book, a challenge that is directed at the formation of postcolonial hybrid subjects engaged in a struggle to transform the condition of life and labor.

I believe that research in multiculturalism and critical pedagogy must congeal more visibly around the central theme of developing a political economy of historical agency. In this way criticalists can further develop a language that better speaks *to* people, not only *about* them, with respect to what it is possible to become in a world that violently enlists one's identity in order to render such an idea ludicrous. It is important to always remind our *compañeros y compañeras* who participate in the struggle (*la lucha*) of liberation from white patriarchal capitalist exploitation that they must never cease to resist new forms of consumption and desire that are put before the basic needs of the people. One example of determination is that of the *soldaderas* of Mexico, the working-class women of the Mexican Revolution who fought alongside their *compañeros* on the battle lines.

To know ourselves as revolutionary agents is more than the act of understanding who we are; it is the act of reinventing ourselves out of our overlapping cultural identifications and social practices so that we can relate them to the materiality of social life and the power relations that structure and sustain them. Yet those among us who cynically persist in resisting and avoiding antiracist, antisexist, and anticapitalist struggle not only douse the flame burning at the heart of democratic struggle but forfeit the only hope for social justice. Critical pedagogy is ultimately a dream, but one that is dreamed in the wakefulness of praxis. This is because an individual cannot say he or she has achieved critical pedagogy if he or she stops struggling to attain it. Only sincere discontent and dissatisfaction with the limited effort we exercise in the name of social justice can assure us that we really have the faith in a dialogical commitment to others and otherness.

Critical pedagogy, as I am formulating it in this book, attempts to reengage a social world that operates under the assumption of its collective autonomy and so remains resistant to human intervention. Critical pedagogy, in this sense, remains committed to the practical realization of self-determination and creativity on a collective social scale. When I think of critical pedagogy as a practice of liberation, I think not only of Paulo Freire, Augusto Boal, Rosa Luxemburg, Judi Barri, Che Guevara, and Malcolm X, for example, but also of Emiliano Zapata. Blessed by Nahuatl shamans, Zapata was a spiritual warrior who struggled to protect the sacredness of the land and freedom from oppression. Like Zapata, critical educators need to wage nothing less than war in the interest of the sacredness of human life, collective dignity for the wretched of the earth, and the right to live in peace and harmony. Critical pedagogy speaks to specific forms of intelligibility and critical rationality, but it is also about the history of the soul. It speaks to the voiceless and the peripheralized, the marginalized and the excluded. It is mythopoetical in that it is linked by the pulse of memory to the history of liberation struggles throughout the globe.

The struggle for critical subjectivity is the struggle to occupy a space of hope—a liminal space, an intimation of the antistructure, of what lives in the in-between zone of undecidability—in which one can work toward a praxis of redemption. That space can't be taken for granted, and it won't be found in the fetishism of normative plurality or ethnic absolutism, or in the politics of liberal consensus. It can be created only if we take the struggle over the social division of labor as seriously as we do the struggle over meaning and representation.

A sense of *atopy* has always been with me, a resplendent placelessness, a feeling of living in a germinal formlessness where places—countries, cities, streets, buildings, houses, pubs, plazas, ideas, thoughts, feelings—gesture to me, sometimes even beckon me, yet always glide past me like some eerie opium-induced object that quickly fades to black. I recognize now that I have never left the concerns of my early work, which dealt with ritual identity, with liminality, with a *regio dissimilitudinis*, with being betwixt and between, with crossing thresholds, with living in the margins. Such indeterminancy is greatly despised by Enlightenment thinkers, which is why I have always felt an outsider to the academy and which is why my work has so often been received by the guardians of Truth as a form of outlawry. I have been folded into the creases of legitimacy, and it is in the margins that my creative agency has been formed. I cannot find words to express what this border identity means. All that I have are what Georges Bataille (1988) calls *mots glissants* (slippery words).

Living in Los Angeles is like being encysted in a surrealist hallucination. Yet as I look at the city from this café window, things don't seem that bad: Kid Frost pulsates through the airwaves; a 1964 Chevy Impala cruises the street in all its bravado lowrider beauty; the sun is shining bountifully on brown, black, and white skin (albeit prematurely aging the latter); my gas tank is full and the ocean is reachable before the heat gets too heavy and the streets get too packed. I'll take Olympic Boulevard toward Venice, searching for that glimmer of light in the eyes of strangers, seeking out that fertile space to connect, picking through that rag-and-bone shop of lost memories, and seizing that splinter of hope at the fault line of the impossible where the foundation of a new public sphere can be fashioned out of the rubble of concrete dreams.

Notes

For a better sociological understanding of Los Angeles, I am indebted to the work of Rudy Torres.

References

Barrs, Rick. (1996). "The Real Story About How the Use of Crack Cocaine Exploded in South-Central." *New Times*, September 12–18, 9.

Bataille, Georges. (1988). *Inner Experience.* Albany: State University of New York Press.

Connell, Rich. (1996). "2,000 Protest Alleged U.S. Role in Crack Influx." *Los Angeles Times*, September 29, B1, B4.

Connolly, William. (1995). *The Ethos of Pluralization.* Minneapolis and London: University of Minnesota Press.

Fusco, Coco. (1995). *English Is Broken Here: Notes on Cultural Fusion in the Americas.* New York: New Press.

Giroux, Henry. (1993). *Border Crossings.* London and New York: Routledge.

Gitlin, Todd. (1995). *The Twilight of Common Dreams: Why America Is Wracked by Culture Wars.* New York: Metropolitan Books.

Gómez-Peña, Guillermo. (1996). *The New World Border.* San Francisco: City Lights Books.

Hicks, Emily. (1991). *Border Writing.* Minneapolis: University of Minnesota Press.

McLaren, Peter. (1995). *Critical Pedagogy and Predatory Culture: Oppositional Politics in a Postmodern Era.* London and New York: Routledge.

Parenti, Michael. (1996). *Dirty Truths.* San Francisco: City Lights Books.

Radhakrishnan. R. (1996). *Diasporic Mediations.* Minneapolis and London: University of Minnesota Press.

Roediger, David. (1991). *The Wages of Whiteness.* London and New York: Verso.

Roediger, David. (1994). *Towards the Abolition of Whiteness: Essays on Race, Politics, and Working Class History.* London and New York: Verso.

San Juan, E., Jr. (1995). *Hegemony and Strategies of Transgression.* Albany: State University of New York Press.

Sunker, Heinz, and Otto, Hans-Uwe, eds. (1997). *Education and Fascism: Political Identity and Social Education in Nazi Germany.* London and Washington: The Falmer Press.

Webb, Gary. (1996). "Unholy Connection." *New Times,* September 12–18, 10–24.

1 Writing from the Margins: Geographies of Identity, Pedagogy, and Power

**Peter McLaren
and Henry A. Giroux**

The excess of language alerts us to the ways in which discourse is inextricably tied not just to the proliferation of meanings, but also to the production of individual and social identities over time within conditions of inequality. As a political issue, language operates as a site of struggle among different groups who for various reasons police its borders, meanings, and orderings. Pedagogically, language provides the self-definitions upon which people act, negotiate various subject positions, and undertake a process of naming and renaming the relations between themselves, others, and the world.

Educational theory is one of the discursive faces of literacy, pedagogy, and cultural politics. It is within theory and its concern with the prohibitions, exclusions, and policing of language along with its classification, ordering, and dissemination of discourse that knowledge becomes manifest, identities are formed and unformed, collective agents arise, and critical practice is offered the conditions in which to emerge.

At the current moment of dominant educational practices, language is being mobilized within a populist authoritarian ideology that ties it to a tidy relation among national identity, culture, and literacy. As the cultural mask of hegemony, language is being mobilized to police the borders of an ideologically discursive divide that separates dominant from subordinate groups, whites from Blacks, and schools from the imperatives of democratic public life.

Current attempts at providing a language for examining the process of schooling, for conducting research in educational settings, and for gaining greater access to a more critical understanding of the social, cultural, and political dimensions of learning have been less than satisfactory. In fact, they have been gravely inadequate, especially in this current era of postnational identity formation and the globalization of capitalism. Educational research needs a new theory that takes seriously how language and subjectivity intersect with history, power, and authority. The absence of such a theory is evident not only within the domain of mainstream research on schooling but also in the failings of critical educational theorists. As a group, we have failed to develop a comprehensive understanding of language, identity, and experience and their relation to the broader power-sensitive discourses of power, democracy, social justice, and historical memory. It is true that feminist, poststructuralist, and postmodern theories have greatly expanded how we understand the relationship between identity, language, and schooling; but all too often these discourses collapse into a dehistoricizing and self-congratulatory emphasis on articulating the specifics of ethnographic methodologies and the ideological virtues of asserting the importance of naming one's location as a complex discursive site. As essential as these theoretical forays have been, they often abuse their own insights by focusing on identity at the expense of power. Language in these texts becomes a discursive marker for registering and affirming difference but in doing so often fails to address how they are related within broader networks of domination and exploitation. In part, this may be due to the ahistorical quality of this work. Lacking a historical context, they fail to engage the political projects that characterized older versions of critical pedagogy and end up failing to locate their own politics and its value for larger social, political, and pedagogical struggles.

In effect, by downplaying the importance of the historically constructed relationship between language and power, critical educators have failed to develop a discourse that articulates issues of identity, place, pedagogy, and history with a language of vision and public life. (This is developed in Giroux, *Border Crossings*, 1992, and McLaren, *Critical Pedagogy and Predatory Culture*, 1995.)

The first section of this chapter outlines the current crisis in critical pedagogy which we describe as an inability to move beyond a language of critique and domination. In the second section we examine the relation of language to the formation of subjectivity and praxis and try to persuade the reader that the choice of language we make as educators in describing, interpreting, and analyzing social reality is a crucial factor in educational and social change. In the third section we move from a discussion of how language works to socially construct and mediate reality, and how language interacts with experience to shape subjectivity, to the current debate among critical educators regarding whether or not the language of radical educational theory is too abstruse and impractical. Lastly, we outline provisional elements of a critical pedagogy for classroom use that offers the potential for helping to create an active, critical citizenry of learners in the current age of postmodern media knowledges.

Critical Pedagogy and the Crisis Within the Language of Theory

Radical pedagogy as it has been developing in both England and the United States for the last decade has drawn heavily upon particular forms of political economy, ideology critique, and cultural criticism. Its main task—and important achievement—is that it has challenged what can be loosely termed the ideology of traditional educational theory and practice. Traditional educational research attempted the paradoxical feat of depoliticizing the language of schooling while reproducing and legitimating the cultural and political authority of dominant groups. In opposition to the traditionalists' attempt to theoretically suppress important questions regarding the relations which obtain among knowledge, power, and domination, critical educational theorists were able to develop new theoretical languages and modes of criticism to suggest that schools were largely (though not exclusively) agencies of social, economic, and cultural production. At best, public schooling offered limited mobility to members of subordinate classes but, in the final analysis, served primarily as a powerful instrument for the reproduction of capitalist social relations and the dominant legitimating ideologies of ruling groups.

In spite of its success at developing insightful theoretical and political analyses of schooling, radical educational theory suffered from some serious flaws, the most significant being its failure to move beyond the language of critique and domination. That is, radical educators remained mired in a language that linked schools primarily to the ideologies and practices of domination. In this view, schools were seen almost exclusively as agencies of social reproduction, producing obedient workers for industrial capital. Radicals generally dismissed school knowledge as a form of bourgeois ideology, and often portrayed teachers as being trapped in an apparatus of domination that worked with a relentless precision and lockstep certainty.

Of course, the reproductive model of schooling became more and more sophisticated theoretically over time. Critical theorists used it to explore the role schools have played in capital accumulation, ideological legitimation, and production of knowledge necessary to carry on the increasing demands of a changing capitalist society. But, while the theory was extended to a set of wider concerns such as gender relations and the political economy of publishing, its underlying logic did not change. It still provides a model in which everything operates within and in response to the logic of capital. Put bluntly, the reproductive theory of schooling has in some instances become a reactive mode of analysis, one that repeatedly oversimplifies the complexity of social and cultural life. It ultimately ignores the need to create a theoretical discourse that transcends the imperatives of possibility within existing capitalist configurations of power. The major failure of this position has been that it prevents left educators from developing a programmatic language in which they can theorize *for* schools. Instead, these radical educators have theorized primarily *about* schools. Writing off schools as agencies of domination, they have seldom concerned themselves with trying to construct new, alternative approaches to school organization, curricula, and classroom social relations.

Radical educational theory has been burdened by more than the language of critique. It has also failed to explore and develop a number of important concerns that are central to a critical theory of schooling. First, as a group we have failed to develop a public philosophy that integrates the issues of power, politics, and possibility with respect to the role that schools might play as democratic public spheres. Most radical educational theorists have been so caught up in describing the reality of *existing* schools that they have failed to take up the question of what it is that schools *should* be. Lacking any substantive vision, most radical theorists have ignored the task of developing the foundation of a progressive public philosophy as a referent for reconstructing schools as democratic public spheres. In this case, educators have failed to construct a programmatic discourse for providing students with the knowledge, skills, and values they will need, not only to articulate their own voices, but to understand these voices and encourage students to transform themselves as collective social agents.

Second, radical educational theorists as a group have eschewed trying to develop a theory of ethics that can either justify our own language or legitimate the social practices necessary for defending a particular vision of what schools might become. Caught within the paradox of exhibiting moral indignation without the benefit of a well-defined theory of ethics and morality, we have been unable to move from a posture of criticism to one of substantive vision. We are caught on a shifting ground regarding ethical principles that inform such a discourse. We have rarely discussed what the moral referents might be for defending particular social and cultural practices, nor do we have a clear sense of what values need to be defended in the interest of an emancipatory vision of schooling.

Third, radical educational theory has been unable to analyze schools as sites which actively produce and legitimate privileged forms of subjectivity and ways of life. We have failed to analyze how subjectivities are schooled, how power organizes space, time, and the body, how language is used to both legitimate and marginalize different subject positions, or how knowledge not only mystifies, but also functions to produce identities, desires, and needs. In effect, as Philip Corrigan (1987) has pointed out, there is no moral and political discourse in radical education theory that interrogates how existing social forms encourage, disrupt, cripple, dilute, marginalize, make possible, or sustain differentiated human capacities that extend the possibilities that individuals have for living in a truly democratic and life-affirming society and world.

Fourth, radical educational theory has vastly underplayed the importance of redefining the actual roles that teachers might play as engaged critics and intellectuals in both the classroom and as part of a wider movement for social change. Teachers have been worked on but not included as self-determining agents of political and pedagogical change. For example, we have rarely addressed the role that teachers might play in alliance with parents and others as part of a wider educational and socio-political movement. Such alliances between teachers and the parents of Black, Latino, and low-income white children have been widespread during the Reagan-Bush era. For example, in Chicago parents joined with teachers in creating the Parent Equalizers of Chicago, headed by Dorothy Tillman. As a result of this movement, hundreds of parents were educated about the workings of the school system, how to get actively involved in the schools, and how to get elected to various levels of policymaking boards. These parents got rid of the Mastery Learning Reading Program, created Local School Improvement Councils, and have played an active role in promoting school criticism and educational reform. This is exactly the type of movement that radical educational theorists need to take into account when we write about present-day schools and the role of teachers. We have to be alert for signs of potential change in the schools, in the direction of greater democracy.

Language and Reality: Conceptual Underpinnings

In order to address some of the problems we have underscored in the previous section, we want to focus on the need for a more comprehensive theoretical language that is capable of conceiving schools as complex sites which cannot be understood solely within the modalities of reproduction or resistance theory. Part of the project of transforming our understanding of schooling is how we talk about the process of schooling itself. This, in turn, involves a struggle over the theoretical and ethical vocabulary we employ in analyzing how schools work and function in our society. We want to argue that the purpose of developing a critical language of schooling is not to describe the world more objectively, but to create a more ethically empowering world which encourages a greater awareness of the way in which power can be mobilized for the purposes of human liberation. Critical educational theory needs a language that understands how experience is produced, legitimated, and organized as a central aspect of pedagogy. We need to examine language and its production as a form of historical argument; furthermore, we need a language that is critical about its own mechanisms of authority. The critical educational language which we envision is one in which difference is seen as a site of both affirmation and remaking, as a negotiated and complex critical practice in which the possibility of democratic public life becomes a central referent of both critique and possibility.

To better understand schooling as a culturally complex, political enterprise is to recognize the social nature of language and its relationship to power and forms of knowledge. This relationship is critical for understanding the limitations of the way we currently interpret the role of schooling in our society. But before we explore this issue, it is important to know something about the way in which language functions as a mediator and as a constitutive factor of what we take to be reality. The first point we wish to emphasize is that language constitutes reality rather than merely reflects it. Language in this case is not conceptualized as a transparent window to the world but rather as a symbolic medium that actively refracts, shapes, and transforms the world. That is, language is the primary medium through which social identities are constructed, collective agents are formed, cultural hegemony secured, and emancipatory practice both named and acted upon (Fraser, 1992). Language is not some conduit to an immutable order of coherence and stability but is generative of the reality which it evokes and to which it speaks. It is the *arche syncope*, which means that language is always distorted and distorting; it invites rather than resists a variety of interpretations and readings (Parker, in press). Knowledge in this view is a social construction, which means that the world we inhabit as individuals is constructed symbolically by the mind (and body) through social interaction and is heavily dependent on culture, context, custom, and historical specificity (McLaren, 1988, 1989). What this means, according to Richard Brown, is that we must give up the bifurcation of the literal and objective from the metaphoric, symbolic, and subjective. Brown (1987, p. 118) has pointed out that "the realities to which symbols refer are also symbolic—that is

. . . they are intended by human actors and within some shared frame of vision." For Brown, as for us, this suggests that words are not signs for things, but rather things are signs for words, since there is no social reality that is not experienced through a social matrix of discourse. While language is not the only source of reality (clearly there is a non-discursive world outside of language), it is largely through language that meaning is created.

This means that there is no ideal, monolithic, autonomous, pristine, or aboriginal world which can be understood outside the social nature of language and to which our social constructions necessarily correspond. There is always a referential field in which symbols are situated and this particular referential field (e.g., language, culture, place, time) will influence how symbols generate meaning. As Bakhtin (1981) has noted, language is always populated by other people's meanings, since it is always "shot through with intentions and accents" (p. 293). Consequently, language is unqualifiedly intersubjective. Language stamps the world with a social presence that is never neutral or unproblematic. Language does not reflect an untarnished image of reality "out there"; whatever image or object or event it attempts to render, it does so through refraction and distortion. This amounts to saying not that knowledge is always false but rather that it is never complete. We can say, therefore, that language produces *particular* understandings of the world: i.e., particular meanings.

When meaning is produced through language unreflectively to the extent that it gets sedimented into common-sense knowledge—which we call ideology—it tends to masquerade as "fixed truths" or "existing facts" about the social world, as if such facts were immune to particular relations of power or material interests. Language, however, is always situated within ideology and power/knowledge relations that govern and regulate the access of particular interpretive communities to specific language practices. And this is no less true of the language that we, as educators, employ in order both to understand theoretically our own work with students and to teach them. Meanings of any event or experience are only available through the language selected by the particular interpretive community wishing to render such events intelligible. Language is always located in discourses or families of ideas and the range of discourses is always limited or "selective" since the dominant culture has legitimated and made available certain discourses while discrediting and marginalizing others. The space of meaning is always a colonized space in which necessity has already been inscribed by cultural codes and the broader field of political, economic, and social relations. Language can therefore be used to frame and legitimate different readings of the world. It is both a symptom and a cause of our cultural understandings.

Radical educators have come to recognize that it is not the truth that sets us free but an understanding that truth constitutes the effects of narrative engagements with the world; the truth is never independent of the reading and writing practices we use to arrive at it—to speak it. The truth—like facts—is not antecedent to our interpretive schemes. The truth depends on which vocabularies of interpretation have provisional dominance and a contingently held authority. There is no single discourse or discursive community that holds the franchise on truth. Discourses are not auto-regulatory, self-initiating, or self-functioning. There is no reality in itself that is not at the same time a reality as-we-see-it. Reality conforms to and results from the critical languages we use to describe it. There is no original point-by-point correspondence of language to "true" descriptions of the world. The very possibility of discourse presupposes a multiplicity of interpretations, a logic of supplementarity. If there is no self-present alignment of representation and the way things "really" are, then all of our descriptions are vulnerable to re-descriptions and recodifications, displacements, and re-readings. If this is the case, then every reading is also a misreading. If truth is subordinate to its effects and if all of textual reality can be placed *sous rature*—including our visions of liberation and emancipation—then it seems to us that we need to abandon our truth claims and a language of interpretation purged of distortion and direct our efforts at challenging those narratives that justify one percent of the population controlling the lives of the rest by exploiting their labor and by colonizing their capacity to resist—to dream or to think otherwise.

Language and Subjectivity

An important point about language, emphasized by Richard Brown and others, is that the language we use always implies a partisan political "advocacy of realities"; it always acts as a form of "persuasive symbolization"—that is, it always acts *rhetorically* (Brown, 1987, pp. 97–117). The idea here which Brown is stressing is that *truth* is not independent of the political and linguistic processes and purposes by which it is evoked. In other words, truth cannot be named outside of its rhetorical dimensions. In this sense we can agree with Robert Scholes that language in some sense always contains an aspect of violence and alienation in that as part of the process of naming reality it separates human beings from that, the thing, that is named (Scholes, 1985, pp. 111–112). Moreover, every time we use language, we engage in a highly partisan socio-political act. Using language is partisan and political because each time we use it, we embody how cultural processes have been written on us and how we in turn write and produce our own scripts for naming and negotiating reality. We both produce language and are produced in it. We can claim no diplomatic immunity from the consequences of the language we employ. Identity largely resides within the rhetorical dimensions of language, that is, within the political and linguistic processes by which it is summoned into being (Brown, 1987, p. 81). The language we use to read the world determines to a large extent the way we think and act in and on the world (Volosinov, 1973).

If it is true that we make sense of social reality through language which is always replete with a range of discourses supported by material interests and forms of social power, then it follows that through language we are produced as *subjects* (i.e., provided with available subject positions or points of view). Following this, it can also be said that language helps constitute subjectivity, which is often constructed out of a multiplicity of subject positions (see the excellent discussion of subjectivity in Weedon, 1987). We use the term "subjectivity" here as distinct from identity because subjectivity permits us to acknowledge and address the ways in which individuals make sense of their experiences, including their conscious and unconscious understandings, and the cultural forms available through which such understandings are either constrained or enabled. The term "identity" on the other hand implies that there is a fixed essence that exists independently of the range of discourses made available to individuals. That is, the term identity suggests a unitary, self-constituting sovereign subject whose autonomous, primordial characteristics are pre-discursive in nature, allegedly constituted outside of language, history, or power. Karl Racevskis underscores this point when he writes:

> Identity is what is naturally given and is therefore considered a possession, yet it is also that which possesses the individual. If, on the one hand, identity is constituted by a personal experience and an individual history, it is also inevitably a product of the otherness of cultural, social, and linguistic determinants. As the individual reconstructs and reflects upon an imaginary identity, he/she cultivates an illusion of conscious control that only serves to occlude the aleatory and contingent nature of this imaginary essence. (1988, p. 21)

In this context, identity is imaginary (in the Lacanian sense) and, according to feminist theorists such as Luce Irigaray, such a construction of the self is invariably and unavoidably male (see Whitford, 1988). Jane Flax (1990) points out that even in postmodernist theories certain patriarchal dispositions are produced. She is worth quoting:

> In postmodern philosophies woman is often still utilized as the other or as mirror for Man; when she exists at all, it is as the repository for the qualities Man has denied to himself and now wishes to reclaim. Woman's speech is constricted by these rules—or she is (and may remain) silenced. As Irigaray

so aptly puts it, woman is "for them—but always according to him—essentially an-archic and a-teleological. For the imperative that is imposed on them—but solely from the outside, and not without violence—is 'enjoy without law' . . . when that strange state of 'body' that men call woman's pleasure turns up, it is gratuitous, accidental, unforeseen, 'supplementary' to the essential." (Flax, 1990, p. 226)

Subjectivity, on the other hand, suggests an individual presence without essence. It underscores the contingency of identity and the fact that individuals consist of a decentered flux of subject positions, highly dependent upon discourse, social structure, repetition, memory, and affective investment to maintain a sense of coherence in a world of constant change.

Subjectivity is more than memories we have quarried or fears we have quarantined in the vaults of our unconscious. It is more than our proclamations about others or assertions about ourselves. As we define it, subjectivity is a process of mediation between the "I" who writes and the "I" who is written, the "I" who speaks and the "I" who is spoken. Subjectivity is sheathed in countless layers of discourse that simultaneously encyst and unfold us, ensnare and release us. Our subjectivities are given birth through our participation in worldly events, through our sensuous orientation to and embodiment in a world informed by social relations and determinant processes of production. Language and subjectivity inform our practical consciousness in which the "I" is always dependent upon a "we," and always contingent upon historical and social localization and the ensemble of social relations constituent of the larger social totality. We prefer the term "subjectivity" because it stresses the fact that a subject position is a standpoint taken up by a speaker within a discourse which may be affirmed or opposed to the positions taken up by other speakers. Discourses are invested in material and institutional forms and governed by discursive practices which, after Foucault, refer to the anonymous historical rules that govern what can be said and what must remain unsaid, who can speak with authority and who must listen (see McLaren, 1989, 1995). From the perspective of schooling, a discourse can be defined as a "regulated system of statements" that establish differences between fields and theories of education (Smith & Zantiotis, 1989). Since discourses emerge from and are constitutive of particular configurations of power, they are necessarily tied to an ideological position. Discourses are ideological not simply as reflections of an economic base, but in their effects of power. As such, they may be considered in themselves material practices. Discourses locate history not in the register of a universalized notion of truth, but rather in that of signifying practices (Kaplan, 1987, p. 23). Such signifying practices are taken up with a politics of location or from the positionality of the individual which is informed by race, class, gender, sexual orientation, and other social and cultural determinations.

We usually consent to assuming subject positions which are familiar to us and in which we feel comfortable. It is through the textual grammar of discourse (i.e., the rules by which meanings are generated) that we constitute ourselves as a polity and we also note, along with Richard Brown, that "transformation of the grammars of a polity is a definition of revolution" (Brown, 1987, p. 128). We argue that discourses do not totally cement identities or subjectivities but produce a range of subject positions around which subjectivities tend to cluster and/or resist each other (Donald, 1985, p. 344).

Language, Experience, and Praxis

The importance of language resides in the fact that it is through language that we both *name* experience and *act* as a result of how we interpret that experience. This is important not only for researchers attempting to understand the process of schooling but also for students who are attempting to critically analyze their everyday experience. *The struggle over how to name and transform experience is one of the most crucial issues in critical pedagogy and the fight for social change.* This struggle is, in part, influenced by the struggle over language and how it is employed. As a socially organized and culturally produced human practice, language never acts on its own but only in conjunction with readers, their social locations, their histories, and their subjective needs and desires. Only when we can name our experiences—give voice to our own world and affirm ourselves as active social agents with a will and purpose—can we begin to transform the meaning of those experiences by critically examining the assumptions upon which those experiences are built. Using language in specific ways can help to constrain or enable particular forms of behavior. This can be seen in the language used by critical ethnographers and action researchers who, having theorized the dominant culture as imposing oppressive constraints on their subjects under study, have often worked to change the oppressive features operating within their research sites rather than simply describing them. Without a theory of domination, researchers often consider their sites as value neutral and choose to act as disinterested, "objective" observers. As Marx has noted: "The weapon of criticism cannot, of course, replace criticism of the weapon, material force must be overthrown by material force; but theory also becomes a material force as soon as it has gripped the masses" (cited in E. San Juan, 1995, p. vi).

Educational researchers who are able to name social injustice often extend their role of researchers to that of social activists. But if the concepts of domination and oppression are not part of a researcher's vocabulary, then it often follows that the researcher's analysis will likely remain disinterested, neutral, and devoid of social criticism. Language traffics in power through its ability to accommodate, produce, and resist historically specific configurations of power. As a dominating practice, language usage implicates itself not merely by naming the world so as to support relations of oppression and exploitation, but also through its unwillingness to interrogate the constructed nature of its own categories and the selective visions it embodies in its own social geography. The language of mainstream educational theory often becomes in this instance an oppressive totalizing system precisely because it is incapable of interrogating its own discursive production of the real and the social relations it both constructs and sustains, relations which often deny rather than enable a life without exploitation and human suffering.

Krystyna Pomorska writes that predicating or naming constitutes the nucleus of the creative power of language and that in "predicating or naming, we create the reality" (cited in Brown, 1987, p. 127). The nature of the language we use determines *how we make sense of our experiences and the type of social action we choose to engage in as a result of interpreting our experiences*. It also determines the range of possibilities we have to organize our social world, to develop new forms of sociality, and, as teachers, new forms of pedagogy. If experience is largely understood through language, and language shapes how we see and act with and on the world, then it follows that experience itself does not guarantee truth since it is always open to conflicting and contradictory interpretations. That is, our experience is not some fixed or fluid essence, or some concrete reality that exists prior to language, waiting to be reflected by language. Rather, experience is constituted by language (Weedon, 1987, p. 85).

Experience—"events and behaviors occurring in social formations" (De Lauretis, 1987, p. 42)—is highly constitutive of subjectivity. Since language enables us to interpret our experience then it follows that language is also constitutive of subjectivity. We have noted that experience does not speak for itself, outside the frames of reference (discourses) associated with the language we select *or are given* in order to make sense of that experience.

Given that we lack an immediate identity with ourselves, we affirm the admonition of Lévi-Strauss, who wisely proclaims in *Tristes Tropiques* (1973): "to each reality we must first repudiate experience" (cited in Sarup, 1996, p. 37). The serious issue here deals with *the ways in which we have been inserted into language both as teachers and students*. To reflectively situate ourselves in discourse—in language—is to historicize our role as social agents. *If we think only those thoughts which we already have the words to express, then our presence in history remains sta-*

tic. Part of the state of this crisis is reflected in the unavailability of subject positions in which students are permitted to practice forms of radical critique and engage in social practices informed by a commitment to establishing a more democratic social order.

Teachers and students are given subject positions in language which govern their range of perspectives in interpreting the world. Access to particular forms of subjectivity is also regulated by the act of reading itself, in addition to institutionalized social relations and power relations which often provide the context for privileging certain readings on the basis of race, class, and gender. Take the example of gender-constructed subjectivities; as Chris Weedon points out, dominant discourses of female sexuality define sexuality among women as naturally passive and construct definitions of femininity which privilege a woman's subordinate role in the social order (Weedon, 1987, p. 36). Women's interests are subordinated to the interests of men through the exercise of patriarchical discourses. On this note, Leslie W. Rabine remarks that "the very structures of Western language exclude women and can function only through the silencing of women and the repression of feminine sexual desires" and that our future existence depends upon "overcoming androcentric structures of subjectivity" (Rabine, 1987–1988, p. 21). If subjectivity is structured by language, then the struggle becomes developing new forms of subjectivity and language which can integrate themselves into social struggles (p. 21). This oppression through language is no less true of the authorial discourses found in school classrooms than those found in medical consulting rooms, courts of law, or theories of schooling. Our subjectivities are constructed in language through the play of discourses and the subject positions which we consent to assume. Discourses cannot be understood outside the institutional patterns, forms of transmission, social practices, and material interests which inform and sustain them. Language, in itself, is not naturally gender-specific but the subject positions we assume within certain discourses are indeed gendered and are supported by patriarchal social and institutional power (Weedon, 1987, p. 173).

Texts create *particular* meanings and modes of understanding that need to be investigated. In our classrooms, we are beginning to recognize the paucity of texts of women's historical resistance to patriarchy (which amounts to the very silencing of women) *which has deprived students of the history of alternative resistant subject positions which illustrate the non-natural status of current gender norms* (Weedon, 1987, p. 170). Weedon's warning is important: "While we need texts that affirm marginalized subject positions, however, it is important to be constantly wary of the dangers of fixing subject positions and meanings beyond the moment when they are politically productive" (p. 172).

What Weedon is stressing is that all texts (and we are using the term "text" to mean various representations such as institutions, classrooms, behaviors, and social practices) need to be understood in their historical, political, and cultural specificity. That is, no texts are *meant* the same way by readers who occupy different contexts, at different historical junctures. For instance, it is wrong to assume that the readings engaged in by women and men, or the affluent and the poor, are homogeneous. Addressing this point, Tony Bennett acknowledges the reiterative and already coded status of knowledge production. Bennett cuts across the notion of the unique, unitary experience of reading meaning by arguing that subjects approach a text with already coded perceptions of what he calls "reading formations," comprising a set of discursive and textual determinations which organize and animate the practice of reading (Bennett, 1986; see also summary in Kaplan, 1987, pp. 26–27). These reading formations may, as Bennett notes, be shaped by the dominant codes that govern the popular text or by subcultural codes such as feminism, trade unionism, Marxism, Moral Majority thinking, white supremacist thinking, etc. In some cases, the reader refuses the offered position and denies interpolation and there may also be an ideological discrepancy in relation to ethnicity. The question for educators may be summarized as: To what extent do conventional schooling practices duplicate the already constructed reading formations of teachers and students?

So far in our discussion it appears that the die is cast, that the "language game" has fixed us as students, teachers, and researchers as subjects "always already spoken" by discourse rather than permitting us to become social agents actively contesting the prison house of language and capitalist social relations of production. In order to break free from the prison house of language as students, teachers, and researchers, we need to understand that reality is not co-extensive with the categories of discourse, since failing to do so means limiting social change to the permutations of discourse within the same set of categories (Whitford, 1988, p. 120). Allan Megill reminds us that "if one adopts . . . the view that everything is discourse or text or fiction, the *realia* are trivialized. Real people who really died in the gas chambers at Auschwitz or Treblinka become so much discourse" (1985, p. 345).

Luce Irigaray and Cornelius Castoriadis urge us to struggle for change within the social unconscious or symbolic order itself; we need to believe that "radical transformations in the social imaginary *can* take place, and [a] new and previously unimaginable configuration [can] take shape" (Whitford, 1988, p. 121). It is in the arena of the social imaginary that critical pedagogy as a form of cultural politics can make a necessary intervention. In recognizing that individuals are produced through the clash of conflicting discourses and subject positions, critical pedagogy *can help us to critically interrogate those discourses,* allowing us to develop a sense of "critical agency." Agency, in this case, refers to the ability of individuals to analyze subjectivity, reflect upon subject positions they have assumed, and choose those which are the least oppressive to themselves, to others, and to society as a whole.

What this means pedagogically for critical educators is not easy to articulate. For students this means teaching them to read texts as languages constructed through the ordering of particular codes which name and legitimate reality and social identities in specific ways. Students need to learn how to read not as a process of submission to the authority of the text but as a dialectical process of understanding, criticizing, and transforming. They need to write and rewrite the stories in the texts they read so as to be able to more readily identify and challenge, if necessary, how such texts actively work to construct their own histories and voices. Reading a text must be a way of learning how to choose, how to construct a voice, and how to locate oneself in history. This amounts to intervening differently in one's own self formation and the self formation of others. Since discourses which work through language lead to particular social and institutional practices, a knowledge of the discourses that inform our subjectivities can lead to the construction of new forms of subjectivity, social relations, and institutional arrangements more hospitable to equality and social justice. For teachers and educational researchers this means being able to recognize the limitations which mainstream social theory has placed on the way we understand schooling and its relationship to the wider society and how this has shaped our subjectivities as intellectual actors engaged in naming and producing a particular view of the world.

We all speak from complex subject positions, which amounts to saying that we can never escape ideology or the effects of discourse. Subject positions, as we have noted, grant us the illusion of being temporarily fixed as autonomous authors of meaning and agents of social practice. The point is not to lament our lack of total autonomy but to actively engage in forms of "critical agency" by learning how to negotiate, translate, resist, and transform power arrangements and interests which are legitimated by uncritically assuming particular subject positions. What we are guarding against here is the overdetermination of language in the production of the social subject. As Richard Johnson notes, we must take seriously the notion of political will and the discursive self-production of subjects (Johnson, 1986/87, p. 69).

The issue, of course, is how through the language of educational analysis teachers have become produced as social subjects and how this affects their roles as researchers and instructors. Once educators recognize the manifold ways in which they are produced through language, they can start to provide for their students a critical language that will help them to become conscious of their own self-formation. In the next section we wish to describe more specifically some prevailing problems with the language that presently constitutes radical educational theory.

Language and the Primacy of the Political Project

Language is always constructed with respect to the specificity of the audience it addresses and should be judged not only in pragmatic terms but also with respect to the theoretical and political viability of the project it articulates. It is not primarily the complexity of language which is at issue but the viability of the theoretical framework it constitutes and promotes. Moreover, the relationship between theory and practice is multifaceted and complex. Simply put, theory in some instances directly informs practice, while in others, practice restructures theory as a primary force for change. In some cases theory (in the more limited sense of the practice of producing narrative and rhetoric) provides the refuge to think beyond current forms of practice so as to envision that which is "not yet." Privileging practice without due consideration of the complex interactions that mark the totality of theory/practice and language/meaning relationships is not simply reductionistic but also a form of theoretical tyranny. Disconfirming theory in this way becomes a form of practice that ignores the political value of "theoretical discourse" within a specific historical conjuncture. That is, rather than examining the language of theory as part of a wider historical moment of self-examination, the language and politics of theory is merely reduced to an unproblematic concern with clarity rather than the problematizing of certainty itself. The intimacy of the dialectic between theory and practice is reduced to an opposition between theory and complexity, on the one hand, and practice and clarity on the other. This is the mark of a vapid, pragmatic, anti-intellectualism whose leveling tendency occludes the role of language in constructing theory as a historically specific practice that makes politics and praxis possible as part of an engagement with the particularities and problems of a given time and place.

Within the present historical conjuncture, with its appeal to universality, its totalitarian view of history, its ethnocentric embrace of culture, and its celebration of greed and individualism, the questions to be asked about language and theory might begin with the conditions necessary to develop forms of theoretical practice capable of retrieving history as the discourse of the Other, reclaiming democracy as a site of struggle within a wider socialist vision, and developing a radical ethic that rejects finality and consensus for the voice of difference and dialogue. At the present time, theory offers the opportunity for a discursive practice whose identity and political value can only be understood in particular circumstances, informed by the historical conjuncture that gives it meaning. As Bruce Robbins puts it, the real debate over theory is about both the specific ideological content of various theoretical discourses and the "circumstances that give these ideas their limits and their cogency" (Robbins, 1987/88, p. 9). At issue here is whether the language of theory works in the interest of making the familiar strange, acknowledging difference as the basis for a public philosophy that rejects totalizing theories which view the other as a deficit, and providing questions that the dominant culture finds too dangerous to raise. What many "radical" educators forget is that the importance of language as a theoretical practice derives from its power as a critical and subversive discourse. To judge theory next to the simple yardstick of clarity more often than not represents a specific theoretical discourse incapable of reflecting on its *own* practice within the present historical conjuncture, a practice that has more to do with a defense of the status quo than it does with a viable politics of theory, language, and schooling.

In addition to arguing against the concern for clarity over that of the political project that language seeks to illuminate and expand, we also are wary of the new poststructuralist discourses which often fetishize the text at the expense of those whom its analysis is supposed to serve. We would like to make clear at the outset that the type of critical language that we are advocating does not endorse, as do deconstructionists such as Derrida, the position of anti-referentiality (the denial of the possibility of presence, perception, and also experience, which is implied in the claim that we never experience anything because we encounter only deferred traces of things, that is, only a structure of infinite referral or pure differences in which there are only traces prior to any entity to which they refer). Similarly, we do not wish to erase the world by arguing that reference is simply a mirage of language. This is not the same as arguing for unmediated perception or to claim that the world is not textualized by relations of power and interest; rather, it is, in the words of Robert Scholes, to assert that language *accommodates reality as much as constructs it,* that "human language intervenes in a world that has already intervened in language" (Scholes, 1985, p. 112). We are in no way suggesting that poststructuralist and deconstructive social theory in its totality is to be rejected. Such a position is ludicrous and fails to understand many of the important theoretical gains made by various proponents arguing from these perspectives. We are especially impressed with the poststructuralist argument which asserts that there are no grand theories with which to justify social practices as neutral and apolitical—that is, outside of ideology and beyond historical specificity and struggle. Moreover we fully endorse those deconstructive and poststructuralist approaches which suggest that the Enlightenment conceptions of knowledge, truth, objectivity, and reason are the effects of asymmetrical forms of social power.

Our main concern with the poststructuralist legacy and its various eruptions in literary criticism, drama theory, and elsewhere in the academy is the way in which it denies the viability of political work by enacting the discourse of profound skepticism. Its overall lack of a public philosophy, its lack of organic connections to a wider public sphere, its suffocating emphasis on a narrow notion of textuality, its domination by intellectuals from elite schools, and at times its suffocating pedanticism make it less a threat to the established configurations of power than an unwilling ally. There is a domesticating element in its practice, an elitism that threatens to suffocate its most important theoretical insights by cutting it off from those who are really oppressed, and a smugness that substitutes academic convention for real substance and action. There is a certain politeness that governs this discourse that domesticates its potential for advocacy, a narrowness of vision that feeds the very society it claims to oppose. Robert Scholes speaks to some of these issues:

> For the generation whose sensibilities were shaped by the sixties, the anarchistic irreverence of deconstruction holds a profound attraction. For those who still remember the slogans of the past well enough to think of themselves as having sold out, as having been co-opted by the establishment, the verbal or textual posture offered by deconstructive discourse is almost irresistible. Its appeal is so strong because it allows a displacement of political activism into a textual world where anarchy can *become* the establishment without threatening the actual seats of political and economic power. Political radicalism may thus be drained off or sublimated into a textual radicalism that can happily theorize its own disconnection from unpleasant realities. (Scholes, 1988, p. 284)

Within the context of higher education in the United States, deconstruction has narrowed the range and substance of resistance by displacing older categories of oppression such as class, gender, and race (Giroux & Simon, 1988; McLaren, 1995); similarly, it has undermined the notion of agency at a time when many subordinate groups are trying to locate themselves as part of a wider social movement for cultural, economic, and political justice. It is with this sentiment in mind that Barbara Christian writes:

> The new emphasis on literary critical theory is as hegemonic as the world which it attacks. I see the language it creates as one which mystifies rather than clarifies our condition, making it possible for a few people who know that particular language to control the critical scene—that language surfaced, interestingly enough, just when the literature of peoples of color, of black women, of Latin Americans, of Africans began to move to "the center." (1987, p. 55)

Developing a Discourse of Critical Pedagogy and Critical Literacy

In this final section we attempt to offer an outline of an approach to teaching which takes seriously the question of knowledge production through language and experience. Critical pedagogy takes as one of its most fundamental aims an understanding of how the socially constructed and often contradictory experiences and needs of students might be made problematic so as to provide the basis for exploring the interface between their own lives and the constraints and possibilities within the wider social order. Traditionally, radical educators have emphasized the ideological nature of knowledge (either as a form of ideology-critique or as ideologically correct content to get across to students) as the primary focus for critical educational work. Central to this perspective is a view of knowledge that suggests that it is produced in the head of the educator or teacher/theorist and not in an interactional and primarily cultural engagement expressed through the process of writing, talking, debating, and struggling over what counts as legitimate knowledge. Within this perspective, the production of knowledge is limited to what goes on outside of the classroom, and the ways in which teachers, students, and texts interact to produce particular readings and forms of knowledge are generally ignored. In contrast, a critical theory of schooling needs to acknowledge that the pedagogical process itself represents an important aspect of the production of knowledge in classrooms. This is crucial not only in order to understand how students actively draw upon their own cultural resources in order to produce meaning, but also because it theoretically legitimates the various forms of investments that students make in the learning process itself. Pedagogy itself is not merely concerned with transmitting knowledge; it is primarily concerned with how knowledge is productive of both meaning and affect, how it comes into being as a cultural currency that resonates and extends the interests that both teachers and students legitimate within the context of the classroom.

The type of critical pedagogy of language and experience that derives from the productive and interactive processes that make up the classroom encounter is fundamentally concerned with student experience in a threefold sense. First, the concept of student experience is validated as a primary source of knowledge and student subjectivity is seen as a multilayered, often contradictory repository of meanings. In this perspective, experience and subjectivity do not collapse into the humanist notion of the integrated ego as the source of all actions and behavior (although this position has tended to avoid looking at how memory and history work to provide some sense of fluid continuity to the self). Similarly, if student experience is viewed as constituted out of difference and rooted in contradictory discursive and nondiscursive practices, then both the experiences that students bring to schools and the cultural forms out of which they are produced operate within tensions that are never closed or unassailable. The concept of the subject that emerges from our view of student experience as a terrain of struggle is articulated by Larry Grossberg:

> This "post-humanistic" subject does not exist with a unified identity (even understood as an articulated hierarchical structure of its various subject-positionings) that somehow manifests itself in every practice. Rather, it is a subject that is constantly remade, reshaped as a mobilely situated set of relations in a fluid context. The nomadic subject is amoeba-like, struggling to win some space for itself in its local situation. The subject itself has become a site of struggle, an ongoing site of articulation with its own history, determinations and effect. (1986, p. 72)

Second, such a pedagogy attempts to provide students with the critical means to negotiate and translate critically their own particular lived experiences and subordinate knowledge forms. This means assisting students in analyzing their own cultural meanings and interpretations of events so as to illuminate and intervene into the processes by which they are produced, legitimated, or disconfirmed. Student experience is the fundamental medium of culture, agency, and identity formation and must be given preeminence in emancipatory curriculum. It is therefore imperative that critical educators learn how to understand, affirm, and analyze such experience. This means not only recognizing the limits and possibilities which inhere in the cultural and social forms through which students learn how to define themselves, but also learning how to engage student experience within a pedagogy that is both affirmative and critical and which offers the means for self and social transformation. (These issues are more fully developed in Giroux, 1988, and McLaren, 1995.)

Third, a radical discourse of pedagogy needs to incorporate a viable theory of critical literacy, one which in this case focuses on the interests and assumptions that inform the generation of knowledge itself. This is particularly important for developing a pedagogy, as Paulo Freire would put it, for both reading the world and reading the word (see Freire & Macedo, 1988).

School texts are, for the most part, the products of the interests that inform dominant social and cultural groups. Critical literacy attempts to destabilize the constellations of reified facts and to defamiliarize the domesticating myths which often serve to legitimate existing relations of power and privilege among dominant groups. Texts are interrogated for what they do not say—for their "structured silences"—as well as for what they do say. To operate from a position of critical literacy is to recognize that knowledge never speaks for itself (see Giroux, 1987; Lankshear and McLaren, 1993). Even the alleged great works of literature do not transcend history or the contextual specificity of the discourses which generated them; to argue that these works deserve to be universally conserved regardless of the particular characteristics of the students whom the curriculum is intended to serve is to fail to make this recognition. That is, knowledge must not be presented as inexorably given and self-justified by its academic valoration through the ages but must be approached as a form of production with a view to the socially constitutive nature of both readers and texts. In this way educators can come to understand why, for instance, the high-status knowledge of classic literary works has become the only kind of knowledge deemed immutable and sacred enough to warrant its inclusion in the proposed "national" curriculum and why the subjugated knowledges of economically disadvantaged groups, women, and minorities are insistently denigrated.

A pedagogy of critical literacy must do more than interrogate and demystify the interests that inform dominant Eurocentric knowledge forms; it must also include and bring to the center of the curriculum those forms of knowledge that constitute the spheres of the everyday and the popular. These are forms of knowledge which constitute student experience; they are also part of those wider cultural formations and social relations that promote forms of exploitation unmatched historically in this country. Mass and popular knowledge is deconstructed as part of a critical theory of teaching and learning. Educators need to acquire more knowledge about how students invest themselves in such mass and popular knowledge forms; they need to understand how such knowledge forms and "structures of feeling" operate through various circuits of power: their production in the economy, their legitimation in the mass market, and their appropriation by students. For critical literacy to be effective, it must be embedded in the concrete lived conditions of the students themselves. In this regard, it is especially important to explore the connection between student alienation and classroom resistance to new narrative forms currently being constructed in the domain of the popular. A critical literacy situates itself in the intersection of language, culture, power, and history—the nexus in which the subjectivities of students are formed through incorporation, accommodation, and contestation. The struggle is one that involves *their* history, *their* language, and *their* culture. What makes literacy "critical" is its ability to make the learner aware of how relations of power, institutional structures, and models of representation work on and through the learner's mind and body to keep him or her powerless, imprisoned in a culture of silence. In fact, a critical perspective demands that the very ideological process of language itself be interrogated.

A pedagogy of language and of experience means teaching students to read both the word, image, and the world critically, with an awareness of the cultural coding and ideological production involved in various dimensions of social life. This means, as Robert Scholes points out, teaching students to read, to interpret, and to criticize. In reading we produce a text *within* a text; in interpreting we create a text *upon* a text; and in criticizing we construct a text *against* a text. To read the world and the word means understanding the cultural and generic codes that enable us to construct words into a story—stories we can tell in our own words, and from different points of view. To interpret means being able to thematize and generalize about the narratives that constitute social experience: in short, it means to be able to tease out the hidden assumptions and motives that structure our everyday cultural system of values. In other words, it refers to grasping the ideological elements of our social world. To criticize means to understand the construction of social life as a particular mode of production which can be analyzed alongside other cultural texts which speak to other modes of ethical discourse and forms of sociality from which students can be called to ground their social action in the world.

In sum, what a critical pedagogy of language and experience attempts to do is to provide students with "counter-discourses" or "resistant subject positions"—in short, with a new language of analysis—through which they can assume a critical distance from their more familiar subject positions in order to engage in a cultural praxis better designed to further the project of social transformation. We need to assist students to inquire into the historical specificity of the production of their own subject positions and modes of sociality and their place in today's hegemonic network of social power. Power, as we have seen, is exercised through forms of subjectivity, which means that the subject positions which we assume uncritically and without a knowledge of more progressive alternatives can lead to the production of oppressive social practices. Of course, developing a critical pedagogy of language and experience for use with students can only follow from the development and employment of a new theoretical language for educators who wish to further their critical understanding of how schools work within the context of the larger society, and how they help to construct the subjectivities of the students who spend time within their walls for a significant portion of their young lives.

Clearly, critical pedagogy has performed an important service by illuminating through a language of critique conditions involving schools, the wider society, and the exercise of cultural power that might otherwise remain obscure or hidden. Its major ideological and political service has been to unravel the manner in which schools reproduce the logic of capital through the ideological and material forms of domination that structure the lives of students from various class, ethnic, and gendered groups. But in order to move beyond simply changing our opinion of schooling through a disclosure of schooling's oppressive conditions, it is necessary to embrace a different language of theoretical analysis which is capable of radically reshaping our very understanding of the school/society relationship. To achieve this, the hermeneutical net from which our current understandings of schooling are drawn must be restrung in order to capture a greater contextual understanding of the relation of schooling to economies of privilege and circuits of power at work in the larger society. A transformation of the oppressive dimensions of schooling must be preceded by a transformation of the language we use to speak about, and therefore comprehend, interpret, and criticize, the process and purpose of schooling.

Students as Cyborgs

While it is true that no language of theory has a privileged relation to reality, we want to emphasize the importance of pushing and reconfiguring the boundaries of the languages we use to understand the social life of the classroom and larger society in order to confront critically the new forms of literacies that are remaking both students and teachers within postmodern cultural contexts. Literacies are not just about language but also refer to the effects that cultural politics and social relations of power have upon the act of interpretation and the generation of meaning.

Jane Flax (1990, p. 222) writes that

> Like the use of languages, interpretation of meaning is not a purely private or unbounded process, but the rules may be so much a part of the game that it is hard to bring them to consciousness. Nor can the rules be understood solely within or generated by language because language and discursive rules both reflect and are located within complex contexts of social relations and power.

In attempting to provide an analysis of postmodern texts of identity, postmodern theorists (who are predominantly male) have failed to deconstruct their own acts of repression that, as part of a phallocentric textual economy, have marginalized or obscured women's acts of agency and mastery (Flax, 1990, p. 215). Critical pedagogy needs to develop modes of deconstructive analysis in which discourses of women do not depend on the congruences between what patriarchy assigns to women and the pervasive social meanings associated in our culture with being female.

One of the challenges we see in constructing a language and politics of representing social life and transforming our relations within it consists of examining new technologies, systems of significations, and reading practices that make few appeals to current standards of rationality. We are referring to the emergence of postmodern media knowledges (i.e., computers, television, film, interactive video, MTV, etc.) or information technologies that instantaneously transform our affective investments in discourses of desire and identity. These new information technologies have collapsed the boundaries between machines and human subjectivities, creating what Donna Haraway (1991) refers to as "cyborg" identities. Consider the fact that students are increasingly making what Bill Green and Chris Bigum (1993) call "cyborg couplings" outside of the classroom through inhabiting the cyberspace of Nintendo games, computer technology, VCRs, and MTV (Kincheloe and Steinberg, 1997). This digital ecosystem produces contexts which are indeterminate and contingent instead of being anchored in biological or human time. Each school day students are ripped out of this techno-cocoon and placed in a 19th-century world of linear time and print technology. How can teachers provide a language of analysis to help these young cyborgs gain a critical understanding of their own techno-identities and how their desires have become constructed within the current proliferation of technocultures (Giroux & McLaren, 1992)? Teachers require a critical language for students who are growing up in cyberspace, one that provides the opportunity for them to engage existing media literacies while "simultaneously making use of its technological advances" (McRobbie, 1992, p. 147). How can such a language be developed? How can we begin to map the more fluid boundaries of the postmodern self as constituted within new technologies and virtual realities that represent *in themselves* historically and culturally discrete systems of producing race, class, and gender relations (see the work of Lankshear and Peters in Giroux et al., 1997)? How can educators develop a language that does not textualize social reality such that they palliate the ground of historically concrete social relations from which real rebellion and resistance might occur?

In the symbolic realm there are many disparate sites and possibilities for struggle. Yet the world of concrete social relations and the unequal distribution of power and privilege that inform them are not simply texts to be analyzed but formations that must be resisted, ruptured, and transformed. In short, we need a critical pedagogy of language and experience in which the categories of understanding differences and otherness do not prohibit other differences from being named. We need a language that can help serve as an instrument for the student's discursive self-shaping and as a means for producing a collective political subject. This language is one that must be simultaneously engaged by students, deployed in strategic ways by teachers and cultural workers, and transformed in the interests of developing greater educational, political, economic, and cultural justice.

References

Bakhtin, M. (1981). *The dialogic imagination: Four essays,* M. Holquist (Ed.). Austin: University of Texas Press.

Bennett, T. (1986). Texts in history: The determinations of readings and their texts. In D. Attridge, G. Bennington, & R. Young (Eds.), *Post-structuralism and the question of history* (pp. 63–81). Cambridge: Cambridge University Press.

Bowles, S., & Gintis, H. (1986). *Democracy and capitalism.* New York: Basic Books.

Brown, R. H. (1987). *Society as text: Essays on rhetoric, reason, and reality.* Chicago: University of Chicago Press.

Christian, B. (1987, Spring). The race for theory. *Cultural Critique, 6,* 51–63.

Corrigan, P. (1987). In-forming schooling. In D. W. Livingstone (Ed.), *Critical pedagogy and cultural power.* South Hadley, MA: Bergin & Garvey.

De Lauretis, T. (1987). *Technologies of gender.* Bloomington: Indiana University Press.

Donald, J. (1985). Troublesome texts: On subjectivity and schooling. *British Journal of Sociology of Education, 6*(3), 341–351.

Flax, J. (1990). *Thinking fragments: Psychoanalysis, feminism, and postmodernism in the contemporary West.* Berkeley: University of California Press.

Fraser, N. (1992, Winter). The uses and abuses of French discourse theories for feminist politics. *Theory, Culture, and Society, 9,* 51–71.

Freire P., & Macedo, D. (1988). *Literacy: Reading the world and the word.* South Hadley, MA: Bergin & Garvey.

Giroux, H. A. (1987). Educational reform and the politics of teacher empowerment. *New Education, 9*(1/2), 3–13.

Giroux, H. A. (1988). *Schooling and the struggle for public life.* Minneapolis: University of Minnesota Press.

Giroux, H. A. (1992). *Border crossings.* New York: Routledge.

Giroux, H. A., & Simon, R. I. (1988). Popular culture and critical pedagogy: Reconstructing the discourse of ideology and pleasure. *Cultural Studies, 2*(3), 294–320.

Giroux, H. A., & McLaren, P. (1992). Media hegemony: Towards a critical pedagogy of representation. In J. Schwoch, M. White, & S. Reilly (Eds.), *Media knowledge: Readings in popular culture, pedagogy, and critical citizenship* (pp. xv–xxxiv). Albany, New York: State University of New York Press.

Giroux, H., Lankshear, C., McLaren, P., & Peters, M. (1997). *Counternarratives: Cultural studies and critical pedagogies in postmodern spaces.* London and New York: Routledge.

Green, W., & Bigum, C. 1993. Aliens in the classroom. *Australian Journal of Education, 37*(2).

Grossberg, L. (1986). History, politics and postmodernism: Stuart Hall and cultural studies. *Journal of Communication Inquiry, 10*(2), 61–77.

Haraway, D. J. (1991). *Simians, cyborgs, and women.* New York and London: Routledge.

Johnson, R. (1986/87, Winter). What is cultural studies anyway? *Social Text,* pp. 33–80.

Kaplan, E. A. (1987). *Rocking around the clock.* New York and London: Methuen.

Lankshear, C., & McLaren, P., eds. (1993). *Critical Literacy: Politics, Praxis, and the Postmodern.* Albany, New York: State University of New York Press.

Lévi-Strauss, Claude. (1973). *Tristes Tropiques.* London: Cape.

McLaren, P. (1988). Language, social structure and the production of subjectivity. *Critical Pedagogy Networker, 1*(2/3), 1–10.

McLaren, P. (1989). *Life in schools.* Albany, NY: Longman.

McLaren, P. (1995). *Critical Pedagogy and Predatory Culture.* London and New York: Routledge.

McRobbie, A. (1992, May). The *Passagenwerk* and the place of Walter Benjamin in cultural studies: Benjamin, cultural studies, and Marxist theories of art. *Cultural Critique, 6*(2), 147–169.

Megill, A. (1985). *Prophets of extremity: Nietzsche, Heidegger, Foucault, Derrida.* Berkeley: University of California Press.

Parker, Stuart (in press). *Reflective Teaching in the Postmodern World: A Manifesto for Education in Postmodernity.* Buckingham, PA: Open University Press.

Pomorska, K. (1980). The overcoded world of Solzhenitsyn. *Poetics Today, 1*(3), 163–170.

Rabine, L. W. (1987–88, Winter). *Ecriture Feminine* as metaphor. *Cultural Critique,* No. 8, pp. 19–44.

Racevskis, K. (1988). Michel Foucault, Rameau's nephew, and the question of identity. In J. Bernauer & D. Rasmussen (Eds.), *The final Foucault* (pp. 21–33). Cambridge, MA: MIT Press.

Robbins, B. (1987/88). The politics of theory. *Social Text, 6*(3), 3–18.

San Juan, E. (1995). *Hegemony and Strategies of Transgression: Essays in Cultural Studies and Comparative Literature.* Albany, New York: State University of New York Press.

Sarup, Madan (1996). *Identity, Culture and the Postmodern World.* Athens, Georgia: The University of Georgia Press.

Scholes, R. (1985). *Textual power.* New Haven: Yale University Press.

Scholes, R. (1988, Winter). Deconstruction and communication. *Critical Inquiry, 14,* 278–295.

Smith, R., & Zantiotis, A. (1989). Teacher education, cultural politics, and the avant-garde. In H. Giroux & P. McLaren (Eds.), *Schooling, politics, and cultural struggle.* New York: SUNY Press, pp. 105–122.

Steinberg, S. R., & Kincheloe, J. L., eds. (1997). *Kinderculture: The Corporate Construction of Childhood.* Boulder, CO: Westview Press.

Volosinov, V. N. (1973). *Marxism and the philosophy of language.* New York: Seminar Press.

Weedon, C. (1987). *Feminist practice and poststructuralist theory.* New York: Basil Blackwell.

Whitford, M. (1988). Luce Irigaray's critique of rationality. In M. Griffiths & M. Whifford (Eds.), *Feminist perspectives in philosophy* (pp. 108–130). Bloomington: Indiana University Press.

2 Liberatory Politics and Higher Education: A Freirean Perspective

In loving memory of Paulo Freire
1921–1997

I suggest those who have not read Amilcar Cabral's works on the struggle in Guinea Bissau take up the task of reviewing them. I am much impressed by his works, as well as those of Che Guevara. Furthermore, both shared a mutual respect for the other. It was in Guinea Bissau where the two met for the first time. They kept silence, observing one another. I would call it a revolutionary love with clasped hands (even though Amilcar was short and Guevara was an extraordinary specimen of a man). They both shared a love based on the revolution. And what was most interesting of all, they did many similar things—like being eminent pedagogues, great educators of the revolution.

*   *   *

It is a shame—since our North American cousins have unspeakable interests in this regard—that we continue to live in Latin America without knowing each other.

*   *   *

I myself was a university professor for a long time, long before the coup in Brazil. But the professor I have become is not the professor I was. It couldn't be! It would be horrible! Even exile played an important part in my reeducation. It taught me that radicalization is a fundamental course and enabled me to go through different experiences as a university professor in different parts of the world: in Latin America, in the United States, in Canada, in Europe, in Africa, and in Asia.

*   *   *

I remember in 1968 young people rebelled all around the world without coordinating themselves. Students in Mexico in 1968 were not telephoning young people in Harvard, or Columbia, or Prague, or Brazil. Nevertheless they carried out more or less the same movement. It was impressive. I also remember that communication between world universities was nonexistent, and it was unbelievably easy for dominant classes to repress world wide movements.

—**Paulo Freire in *Paulo Freire and Higher Education* (1994)**

42

We are living the hallucinatory wakefulness of nightmare reason. It is a time in which U.S. culture and history threaten the autonomy of the human spirit rather than exercise it. Henri Lefebvre (1975) warns that during this present historical conjuncture we are suffering from an alienation from alienation—that is, from a lack of awareness that we exist in a state of alienation.

Educators and cultural workers in the United States living in this twilight of reason are facing a crisis of democracy. The democratic aspiration of U.S. schooling and social, cultural, and institutional practices in general have been carried forth to an unheralded present moment in what retrospectively appears to have been an act of bad faith. The consequences of such an act for future generations are only faintly visible and are bathed in an ethos eerily reminiscent of earlier swindles of hope. The "democratizing" imperatives of private enterprise, wage labor, free trade, and other fundamental axes for the new capitalist world system ushered in by the third industrial revolution of computer technology have shrouded individuals in a web of promotional logic patterned by the conquering dynamism of Eurocentrism. Colonization has gone transnational and corporatist (Miyoshi, 1993). As Jacques Attali (1991: 120) warns, "From Santiago to Beijing, from Johannesburg to Moscow, all economic systems will worship at the altar of the market. People will sacrifice for the gods of profit." We live in an age in which desires, formerly tilted inwards, are now constructed on the surface of bodies like pathologically narcissistic tattoos that reflect lost hope and empty dreams—forfeited identifications turned into grotesqueries, unable to escape the circuit of deceit and despair constructed out of capitalist relations and rationalizations and new modes of social regulation that produce not persons or individuals, but subjects.

Capitalism carries the seeds of its own vulnerability and frailty even though its cunning appears inexhaustible and its mechanisms of production and exchange irreproachable and unchallenged. Its vulnerability is, ironically, the most steadfast and dangerous precondition for its further development. So long as it has bourgeois universal reason and the epistemic privilege of science as its spokesperson and Eurocentrism as its cultural anchor, and whiteness as its foundation of cultural calculability, its very constitution as a discourse of power within an increasingly homogeneous "world culture" needs to be challenged by popular movements of renewal within a polycentric cultural milieu.

Educators in the United States have no special immunity to these conditions but bear a signal responsibility to understand them and, in turn, help their students to do the same. Students are particularly vulnerable in these dangerous times, as they are captured in webs of social and cultural meaning not of their own making, motivated to remember in specific ways, and silently counselled through advertisements, the media, and religious and political "others" to respond to the logic of commodity fetishism as if it were a natural state of affairs. Teachers and students together face New Right constituencies of all types and stripes, in particular, fundamentalist Christians and political interest groups who are exercising an acrimonious appeal to a common culture monolithically unified by a desire for harmony in sameness.

The past decade has witnessed unprecedented levels of struggle over the meaning and deployment of racial "difference," culminating in the Tuesday, November 8th 1994, wide margin of vote (59% to 41% margin overall; 78% Republican, 62% Independent, 36% Democrat) in favor of Proposition 187 in California. The measure is designed to restrict public schooling, welfare, and nonemergency medical services for those persons who are unable to prove their legal immigration or nationality status in the United States. The measure originated with Orange County political consultant Robert Kiley; his wife, Yorba Linda Mayor Barbara Kiley; and Ron Prince, an accountant who had been unemployed for three years and who recently was forced to file for bankruptcy.

As a blue-eyed Anglophone Canadian from the Great White North, who was issued a green card in 1985, I have little fear of being targeted by the measure, since the campaign ads and rhetoric surrounding the measure were clearly focussed on the southern state border, with Mexico. Marking an historical moment unparalleled in modern Californian history, 8 November 1994 is a day that henceforth shall live in infamy. For this moment signals not only the resurfacing of fascism but also the complete and utter villainization and demonization of the Latino/a immigrant in a manner so ferocious that even the most militant and cynical Raza have been caught unprepared. What is at hand is not simply a further backward step in the sad but steady erosion of ground won by decades of civil rights activism, but rather the triumph of cultural apartheid and the inquisition of the colonial mind. Racial authoritarians have defiantly sloughed off their white cocoons, transformed now into full-blown racist terrorists, whose symbolic projection was captured the morning after the vote in the Governor's cutting of prenatal care to undocumented immigrants, mostly Mexicana. A moment of struggle is at hand that has a special political valency and ethical potency. When the law of the land is trotted out as a cover for a form of ethnic cleansing, we need to act. It is plainly time to push western civilization up against the wall and demand that democracy live up to its name.

What is remarkable is that in this dislocated climate of victimization, a spirit has risen up to strike back at the white fangs of gringo injustice: we are witnessing a resurgent *indigenismo*, bolstered by the example of the Zapatistas; the new youth *movimiento* that has seen thousands of Raza youth take to the streets in school walk-outs; the discontinuous histories of the powerless that have coalesced into a new recognition of the plurality of Chicano/a-ness; new forms of self-creation through an engagement with the social memory of Chicano/a struggle; and the political mobilization and systematic cultural activism of Latino/as, often in concert with other groups. And professors in places like California State University, L.A., and U.C.L.A. have committed themselves to positions of civil disobedience, and to offering to start up sanctuary schools, should the measure finally be implemented. It is obvious that Proposition 187 is another blow to the very meaning of public education, another assault on the public sphere as a place for the practice of equality for all individuals, even the strangers in our midst, regardless of their legal status.

For educators and cultural workers, this current historical moment refracts through a series of unstable standpoints which represent a broad canvas from which to frame our struggle for liberation; it is a bold summons to re-examine our commitment to the forging of history, rather than just its representation, translation, or interpretation. As nihilism and despair begin to impose their own inevitability we need to construct a counter-memory, a counter-discourse, a counter-praxis of liberation. It is a time that calls us to examine how we, as cultural workers, have been invented by Western culture within the process of colonization and the formation of Eurocentrism. It is a time to examine how we, as citizens committed to public education and the rights of children, can allow ourselves to be positioned as INS agents in universities and schools.

The call for the educator and cultural worker to act is not a call for a new Chicano/a centrism or subaltern collectivity centering around the return to Atzlán—a treasurehouse of Chicano/a authenticity waiting to be unlocked—for any centrism, be it Afrocentrism, Eurocentrism, phallocentrism, gabachocentrism, or androcentrism, obeys an epistemology hospitable to myths of originary unity, an unsullied historical time, and an eternally stable racial self around which a redemptive narrative of heroic struggle pivots; such centrisms are themselves often infected by and complicitous with Western codes, assumptions, and conventions. Rather, it is a call not merely to challenge our strategies of representation but to dismantle the ineffable structures of terror that pervade both the politics of the public and the popular, that are inextricably bound up with global economic developments, and that form the structural unconscious of the United States.[1] I am talking here about discourses of power and privilege and social practices that have epistemically mutated into a new and terrifying form of xenophobic nationalism in which the white male Euro-American becomes the universal subject of history.

Such a dilemma points to a necessary displacement of the United States as the center of analysis and the development of a more inclusive, global perspective. It suggests, too, that as critical educators for social justice, we must no longer advance our view of what it means to be American on the corpse of another culture once we have destroyed it and ransacked its leftover symbols; nor can we view ourselves as disinterested chroniclers, as detached entertainers, as agents who operate in a realm outside the messy web of ethics and politics.

We practice our craft within expressive culture, but such a culture needs to be located within a systemic entity known as global capitalism. As such, we never leave its circuits of subordination, of commodification, of simulacra. Educators, especially, need to politicize their readers against the violent thrall of capital, to menace their social apathy and haunt their "comfort zones" like a surly stranger. The educator as social agent needs to challenge the white media's attempts to commodify black rage, Latino/a militancy, and Asian resistance, and to resist its attempt to hellify the lifeworlds of subaltern populations as it continues to establish an equivalence between youth of color and full-throated deviancy. In a society in which prison has become the most realistic educational alternative for African Americans and Latino/as, the educator as activist cannot stand on the sidelines and hide in the false binarism of objectivity/subjectivity. Rather, the educator must assume a standpoint from which, as Paulo Freire asserts, to read both the word and the world.

Without much of an economic base to work from in our inner cities, we are faced with strategies and tactics of diversion from conservatives who try to focus the blame for social problems on the breakdown of family values. Interestingly and perhaps terrifyingly, a July *Los Angeles Times* poll of 1,500 people nationwide suggests that the political influence of culturally divisive groups associated with the Democrats (feminists and gay activists, for instance) cause more concern to voters than the religious right. In fact, more people see the breakdown of moral values as the root of social strife in the United States than they do economic constraints. Within such a right-leaning climate, it is not surprising that some conservative school districts in Los Angeles are denying hungry students breakfast programs because such programs are viewed as "anti family." In other words, starving is good for young students' characters. A Los Angeles program to help black inner-city youths through organized golf attempts to counter the behavior of youth who sport the bad, black L.A. Raiders fashion with the cultural capital of a good white sport.[2] Whiteness has located itself in those discourses of the public and the popular in such a way (whiteness is everywhere and nowhere) that our definition of the normal and the commonsensical has been colonized. If we do nothing to contest the Republican initiative that will place the children of those on social assistance in orphanages, how will we be able to resist when the initiative calls for forced sterilization? Or internment camps for illegal Latino/as? We need to remember that few spoke out when Jewish students were forced out of German universities or when Jewish faculty were expelled.

In such circumstances, we as educators need to move beyond a notion of multiculturalism as liberal pluralism because pluralism always has an ideological center of gravity which rarely gets defined for what it is: liberal pluralism as the politics of white supremacist patriarchal capitalism. This is the same pluralistic society whose system of capitalism is paying its workers in underdeveloped countries salaries which amount to little more than slave wages. Not to mention its own sweatshops in New York and elsewhere. It is the same system that calls for the privatization and corporatization of education and signals the end of public education as we know it. It is hard to develop the form of class consciousness necessary for contesting current conditions because, as Brosio has noted, after Jameson, the current postmodernist culture, "characterized by disconnected and decontextualized images," and its "celebration of randomness, heterogeneity, and claims of unprecedented complexity," does little more than to "reinforce the difficulty in understanding the, as yet unrepresentable, capitalist totality" (1993: 480). This situation enables Newt Gingrich to call on the ghosts of Father Flanagan and Whitey Marsh to provide us with the moral fortitude to struggle on in the name of truth and justice, and Mortimer B. Zuckerman, editor-in-chief of *U.S. News and World Report,* 12 December 1994, to proclaim that U.S. immigration policy discriminates against Europeans and that the "standard of living in a California jail is higher than that in many Latin American villages" (p. 123).

The forms of ethical address which have been constructed by the sentinels of our dominant political, cultural, and educational systems— even under cover of abstract endorsements of diversity—are bent on draining the lifeblood out of difference by installing an invisible ideological grid through which appeals to normalcy, decency, and citizenship may be filtered and differences extorted into reconciliation. They are effectively limiting the range of meanings which are being stockpiled in the name of democracy. E. D. Hirsch wants to reduce culture to a paraphrasable core of necessary ideas; the English Only movement desires to ontologically and epistemologically fix the relationship between citizenship and language so that "real Americans" won't be bothered anymore by the babel of foreign tongues; educational reformers under the sway of marketplace logic are implored to get youth off the streets and into the declining job markets where they can then be conscripted into the corporate wars with Germany and Japan.

Insinuated into grand narratives of progress, these contestable sets of assumptions and social practices effectively reproduce the systems of intelligibility that further the interests of the privileged and powerful.

Against the backdrop of the global underclass, the growing influence of neoconservatism and neoliberalism in political life in general and education in particular, and the struggle for democracy, exists the work of Paulo Freire, one of the great revolutionaries of our era. Freire's name encrypts the contested encounter among capitalism, schooling, and democracy, and his work is traversed by a call to rethink the concepts of education and liberation. The feeling evoked by reflecting upon Freire the scholar and Freire the activist can be partially captured by the words that Theodor Adorno used to describe Walter Benjamin: "Anyone who was drawn to him was bound to feel like the child who catches a glimpse of the lighted Christmas tree through a crack in the closed door" (Adorno, 1967: 230). Freire's life and work inspires a love that is reserved for those revolutionaries whose lives mirror the struggle for justice in their writings.

It is important to make clear that Freire's work cannot be articulated outside the diverse and conflicting registers of indigenist cultural, intellectual, and ideological production in the Third World. The "Third World" is a term used most advisedly here after Benita Parry and Frantz Fanon to mean a "self-chosen phrase to designate a force independent of both capitalism and actually existing socialism, while remaining committed to socialist goals" (Parry, 1993: 130). As such, it offers a starting point for a critique of imperialism and "retains its radical edge for interrogating the Western chronicle."

Of course, one of the powerful implications surrounding the distinction between First and Third Worlds involves the politics of underdevelopment. Andrew Ross (1989) describes the classic model of underdevelopment as one that benefits the small, indigenous elites of Western developed nations. Foreign markets such as those in Latin America provide a consumption outlet for the developed nations of the First World so that they are able to absorb the effects of a crisis of overproduction in the core economy. According to Ross, the peripheral economy (Latin America) underproduces for its domestic population. He reports that "The economic surplus which results from peripheral consumption of core products is appropriated either by core companies or by the domestic elites; it is not invested in the domestic economy of the peripheral nation" (1989: 129). Of course, what happens as a result is that the domestic economies of Latin America fail to possess the productive capacity to satisfy the most basic needs of most of the population. This is because "the only active sector is the one that produces commodities either for the indigenous elite or exotic staples for the core metropolitan market" (Ross, 1989: 129). The contact between Latin America and foreign capital certainly does encourage peripheral economies to develop, but such development—if you can call it that—is almost always uneven and consequently such contact forces the peripheral economy to under-develop its own domestic spheres.

When there is economic dependency, cultural dependency often follows in its wake. However, the capitalist culture industry is not simply superstructural but constitutive in that the masses—in both First and Third Worlds—do not simply consume culture passively as mindless dupes. There is often resistance at the level of symbolic meaning that prevents the culture industry from serving simply as a vehicle of repressive homogenization of meaning (Martín-Barbero, 1992; McLaren, 1995). According to Ross (1989), the elites of the peripheral nations are the first to acquire access to Westernized popular culture, but because of the limited access of the indigenous population to the media, the media generally serve to encourage affluent groups to adopt the consumer values of the most developed countries. The elites basically serve in a supervisory capacity when it comes to the cultural consumption of the indigenous peasantry. However, the continuing ties of the peasantry to their own ethnic cultures do help them become less dependent on Western information. Foreign mass-produced culture is often interpreted and resisted at the level of popular culture, and we must remember that cultural values of the First World can also be affected by contact with the cultures of less developed countries. And, further, not everything about contact with Western culture is to be shunned, although the emergence of a new, transnational class appears to have all the ideological trappings of the older, Western bourgeoisie. For instance, my own contact with Brazilian feminists has revealed to me that oppositional feminist critique in the United States can be successfully appropriated by Brazilian women in their struggle against the structures of patriarchal oppression, structures which can permit men to kill their wives if they suspect them of infidelity on the grounds that their "male honor" has been violated.

The image of Freire that is evoked against this recurring narrative of the decline and deceit of Western democracy and the cultural hegemony of developed nations is a distant voice in a crowd, a disturbing interloper among the privileged and powerful—one who bravely announces that the emperor has no clothes. Ethically and politically Freire remains haunted by the ghosts of history's victims and possessed by the spirits that populate the broken dreams of utopian thinkers and millenarian dreamers—a man whose capacities for nurturing affinities between disparate social, cultural, and political groups and for forging a trajectory towards moral, social, and political liberation challenge the disasters that currently befall this world.

Relentlessly destabilizing as *sui generis* and autochthonous mercenary pedagogy—i.e., spontaneous pedagogy wantonly designed to stimulate the curiosity of students, yet imposed in such a bourgeois manner so as to "save" those who live in situations of domestication only when they are reinitiated into the conditions of their own oppression—Freire's praxis of solidarity, that is, his critical pedagogy, speaks to a new way of being and becoming human. This "way of being and becoming" constitutes a quest for the historical self-realization of the oppressed by the oppressed themselves through the formation of collective agents of insurgency. Against the treason of modern reason, Freire aligns the role of the educator with that of the organic intellectual. It should come as no surprise, then, that against perspectives generated in the metropolitan epicenters of education designed to serve and protect the status quo, Freire's work has, even today, been selected for a special disapprobation by the lettered bourgeoisie and epigones of apolitical pedagogy as a literature to be roundly condemned, travestied, traduced, and relegated to the margins of the education debate. That Freire's work has been placed under prohibition, having been judged to be politically inflammatory and subversive and an inadmissible feature of academic criticism, is understandable given the current historical conjuncture. But it is not inevitable.

It is not the purpose of this chapter to address the often egregious misrepresentations of Freire's work by mainstream educators, or to simply situate Freire unproblematically within the context of First World efforts to ground liberation struggles in pedagogical practices. This chapter seeks merely to elaborate on one of the central themes of Freire's work, the role of the educator as an active agent of social change.

Critical Pedagogy Versus the Academy

While their political strategies vary considerably, critical educators of varying stripes (many of whom have been directly influenced by Freire's work) generally hold certain presuppositions in common which can be summarized as follows: pedagogies constitute a form of social and cultural criticism; all knowledge is fundamentally mediated by linguistic relations that inescapably are socially and historically constituted; individuals are synecdochically related to the wider society through traditions of mediation (family, friends, religion, formal schooling, popular culture, etc.); social facts can never be isolated from the domain of values or removed from forms of ideological production as inscription; the relationship between concept and object and signifier and signified is neither inherently stable nor transcendentally fixed and is often mediated by circuits of capitalist production, consumption, and social relations; language is central to the formation of subjectivity (conscious and unconscious awareness); certain groups in any society are unnecessarily and often unjustly privileged over others and while the reason for this privileging may vary widely, the oppression which characterizes contemporary societies is most forcefully secured when subordinates accept their social status as natural, necessary, inevitable, or bequeathed to them as an exercise of historical chance; oppression has many faces and focusing on only one at the expense of others (e.g., class oppression vs. racism) often elides or occults the interconnection among them; an unforeseen world of social relations awaits us and power and oppression cannot be understood simply in terms of an irrefutable calculus of meaning linked to cause and effect conditions; domination and oppression are implicated in the radical contingency of social development and our responses to it; and mainstream research practices are generally and unwittingly implicated in the reproduction of systems of class, race, and gender oppression (Kincheloe and McLaren, 1994; McLaren, 1992).

Freire's work certainly reflects this list of assumptions to different degrees and while his corpus of writing does not easily fall under the rubric of poststructuralism, his emphasis on the relationship among language, experience, power, and identity certainly give weight to certain poststructuralist assumptions. For instance, Freire's work stresses that language practices among individuals and groups do more than reflect reality; they effectively organize our social universe and reinforce what is considered to be the limits of the possible while constructing at the same time the faultlines of the practical. To a large extent, the sign systems and semiotic codes that we use are always already populated by prior interpretations since they have been necessarily conditioned by the material, historical, and social formations that help to give rise to them. They endorse and enforce particular social arrangements since they are situated in historically conditioned social practices in which the desires and motivations of certain groups have been culturally and ideologically inscribed, not to mention overdetermined. All sign systems are fundamentally arbitrary but certain systems have been accorded a privileged distinction over others, in ways that bear the imprint of race, class, and gender struggles (Gee, 1993). Sign systems not only are culture-bound and conventional but also are distributed socially, historically, and geopolitically (Berlin, 1993). For U.S. educators, this implicates our language use in Euro-American social practices that have been forged in the crucible of patriarchy and white supremacy (Giroux, 1993; Tierney, 1997).

Knowledge does not, according to the view sketched above, possess any inherent meaningfulness in and of itself but depends on the context in which such knowledge is produced and the purpose to which such knowledge is put. If there is no pre-ontological basis for meaning that is extralinguistically verifiable, no philosophical calculus that can assist us in making choices—then we can come to see language as a form of power that apprentices us to particular ways of seeing and engaging the self and others and this, in turn, has particular social consequences and political effects (McLaren and Leonard, 1993). Few educators have helped us to judge the political effects of language practices as much as Paulo Freire. And few educators have been as misused and misunderstood. Clearly, Freire does not see individuals and groups to be agentless beings invariably trapped in and immobilized by language effects. Rather, human beings are politically accountable for their language practices and as such, agency is considered immanent (McLaren and Lankshear, 1994; McLaren and Giroux, 1994). Freire's position reflects Gramsci's notion that the structural intentionality of human beings needs to be critically interrogated through a form of conscientization, or *conscientização* (this Portuguese word is defined by Freire as a deep or critical reading of commonsense reality).

The Educational Institution as (a) Moral Agent

When the surgical pick of Egas Moniz was poised to perform the first medical lobotomy (a procedure that, it may be recalled, won him the Nobel Prize and led reactionary advocates to consider lobotomies for individuals subversive of good citizenship practices) it was inconceivable to think that such an act of cerebral terrorism could be achieved at a cultural level more effectively and much less painfully through the powerful articulations of new and ever more insidious forms of capitalist hegemony. The emancipatory role of university and public intellectuals has been greatly diminished by this process, as well as the function of the organic intellectual. In fact, emancipatory praxis has been largely orphaned in our institutions of education as educators are either unable or refuse to name the political location of their own pedagogical praxis. Part of the problem is that postmodern traditions of mediation have become simulacra whose ideological dimensions cannot easily be identified with or organically linked to the most oppressive effects of capitalist social relations and material practices. The redoubled seduction of new information technologies not only rearticulates a submission to multinational financial strategies, but creates possibilities for a resignification of, resistance to, and popular participation in, the politics of everyday life. The fact that relationships between the specific and the general have become blurred by these new electronic forces of mediation has not only increased a reorganization and liberation of difference but has also posed a danger of further cultural fragmentation and dissolution limiting the struggle for strategic convergences among sites of intellectual production, the formation of new moral economies, and the expansion of new social movements. This disaggregation of public spheres and the massification of *mestizaje* identities makes it difficult to establish the solidarities necessary for developing liberating idioms of social transformation (Martín-Barbero, 1992; McLaren, 1995). Rey Chow poses an urgent question to U.S. intellectuals: How do intellectuals struggle against a hegemony "which already includes them and which can no longer be divided into the state and civil society in Gramsci's terms, nor be clearly demarcated into national and transnational spaces?" (1993: 16). Chow remarks that most oppositional university intellectual work derives from strategies which deal (after de Certeau's conceptualization of urban spatial practices) with those who wish to solidify a place or barricade a field of interest. What we need instead of strategies, argues Chow, are tactics to deal with calculated actions outside of specific sites. Strategic solidarities only repeat "what they seek to overthrow" (p. 17). In discussing de Certeau's distinction between strategies and tactics, Michael Shapiro notes that strategies belong to those who have legitimate positions within the social order and consequently are part of "a centralized surveillance network for controlling the population" (1992: 103). Tactics, on the other hand, "belong to those who do not occupy a legitimate space and depend instead on time, on whatever opportunities present themselves" (1992: 103). Tactics are associated with the performative repertoire—i.e., "the slipperiness of the sophistic stance"—of displaced, disenfranchised, and dominated people (Conquergood, 1992: 83). Tactics, in other words, are the "techniques of the sophist" in which the ethos of the formal meaning of sophistry is replaced by a resistant praxis of the contingent, the available, the possible (Conquergood, 1992: 82). In a world of scarce options, tactics can serve to camouflage resistance as a form of what Conquergood calls "improvizational savvy" (1992: 82). There are the actions of the class clown, the student who "goofs off," the teacher who seizes the space of a classroom lesson to engage in a dialogue with students about issues not on the formal curriculum. De Certeau describes tactical operations and maneuvers as follows:

> [A] tactic is a calculated action determined by the absence of a proper locus
> . . . The space of a tactic is the space of the other. Thus it must play on and
> with a terrain imposed on it and organized by the law of a foreign power. It
> does not have the means to keep to itself, at a distance, in a position of withdrawal, foresight, and self-collection: it is a maneuver "within the enemy's
> field of vision," . . . and within enemy territory. It does not, therefore, have
> the option of planning, general strategy . . . It operates in isolated actions,
> blow by blow. It takes advantage of opportunities and depends on them, being without any base where it could stockpile its winnings, build up its own
> position, and plan raids. . . . This nowhere gives a tactic mobility, to be sure,
> but a mobility that must accept the chance offerings of the moment, and
> seize on the wing the possibilities that offer themselves at any given mo-

ment. It must vigilantly make use of the cracks that particular conjunctions open in the surveillance of proprietary powers. It poaches in them. It creates surprises in them. . . . It is a guileful ruse. (cited in Conquergood, 1992: 82)

According to Conquergood, rationality itself is linked to the domain of strategy in that it derives its legitimacy (after de Certeau) in an established locus or place. Against the strategic imperatives of formal rationality founded on established rights and property, Conquergood posits what he calls "sophistic tactics" that "resist systematizing and totalizing discourses because they are dispersed and nomadic; they are difficult to administer because they cannot be pinned down." He further adds: "Artful dodgers and tacticians of resistance are branded disreputable by proprietary powers because they are always on the move and refuse to settle down" (1992: 83). It should be emphasized that the realm of resistance that can be tactical is not only classroom behaviors deemed counter-hegemonic but also the practice of theory, as Giroux has pointed out (1983; 1992).

Chow elaborates on the distinction between strategies and tactics as it relates to the politics of insurgent university educators:

We need to remember as intellectuals that the battles we fight are battles of words. Those who argue the oppositional standpoint are not *doing* anything different from their enemies and are most certainly not directly changing the downtrodden lives of those who seek their survival in metropolitan and non-metropolitan spaces alike. What academic intellectuals must confront is thus *not* their "victimization" by society at large (or their victimization-in-solidarity-with-the-oppressed), but the power, wealth, and privilege that ironically accumulate from their "oppositional" viewpoint, and the widening gap between the professed contents of their works and the upward mobility they gain from such words. (When Foucault said intellectuals need to struggle against becoming the object and instrument of power, he spoke precisely to this kind of situation.) The predicament we face in the West, where intellectual freedom shares a history with economic enterprise, is that "if a professor wishes to denounce aspects of big business . . . he will be wise to locate in a school whose trustees are big businessmen." Why should we believe in those who continue to speak a language of alterity-as-lack while their salaries and honoraria keep rising? How do we resist the turning-into-propriety of oppositional discourses, when the intention of such discourse has been that of displacing and disowning the proper? How do we prevent what begin as tactics—that which is "without any base where it could stockpile its wirmings" (de Certeau: 37)—from turning into a solidly fenced off field, in the military no less than in the academic sense? (1993: 17)

Chow reminds us that oppositional tactics within the university—often undertaken as the practice of Freirean "critical pedagogy"—can become dangerously domesticated precisely because they can be conscripted by leftist educators into the service of career advancements. Even employed with best of intentions, Freirean pedagogy can unwittingly locate itself as a voguish set of systematized strategies that carries with it the imprimatur of leftist high theory. Its adoption can be used for accruing academic property rights by those who wish to keep resistance a form of ludic play, a form of mimesis as distinct from praxis. To enact resistance as a tactical performative undertaking, a subversive maneuver designed to rupture and displace the unitary cohesiveness of the academy's master discourses and develop a pedagogy that operates outside of mainstream pedagogy's founding binarisms, would be considered too risky for educators who wish to enjoy the appearance of being radical without facing the hard decisions that could risk one's job security or possibilities for tenure. It is to a deeper understanding of the strategic and tactical relationships between the role of hegemony in the formation of public intellectuals and the function of the university itself in the context of wider social and political formations that Freire's work needs to be engaged. Freire's work also needs engagement with oppositional discourses dealing with higher education and the role of the intellectual as cultural critic.

What can be loosely described as postmodern social theory has been influential in, among other things, offering criticisms of material and economic causality and the Cartesian notion of subjectivity by placing an emphasis on reading social reality as a text, on language as a model of representation that helps "construct" social reality, on power as both a condition and effect of discourse, on world-construction as an interplay of signifying relations, and on unmasking Enlightenment conceptions of truth as the aesthetic effectiveness of the rhetoric of reading and writing practices. Freire's work has not addressed in any extended commentary current political debates surrounding the pedagogy and politics of postmodernism (McLaren and Leonard, 1993), but recent remarks situate these debates as ongoing "discoveries" that center around two possibilities: the denial of history and human agency or the recognition of history as a necessary human experience, one that is historically constituted (Freire, 1993a; 1993b). Freire writes:

> I would like to actively follow the discussions about whether the issue of post-modernity is an historical province in itself, a kind of *sui generis* meant in History as the starting point of a new History, almost without continuity with what went before or what is to come; without ideologies, utopias, dreams, social classes or struggles. It would be a "round time," "filled out," "smooth," without "edges," in which men and women would eventually discover that its main feature is neutrality. Without social classes, struggles or dreams to fight for, without the need for choice or,

therefore, for changes, without the game of conflicting ideologies, it would be an empire of neutrality. It would be a denial of history itself.

I would like to discover whether, on the contrary, postmodernity, like modernity, and traditionalism, on which presses a substantial number of connotations, implies a necessary continuity which characterizes History itself as a human experience whose form of being can filter from one moment in time to another. In this sense, each moment in time is characterized by the predominance and not by the exclusivity of its connotations.

For me, postmodernity today, like modernity yesterday, by conditioning men and women caught up in it, does not destroy nor did it destroy what we call their nature, which not being a priori of History, has been socially constructed exclusively through it. (1993a: 2)

Freire describes pedagogical practice within postmodernity as "one that humbly learns from differences and rejects arrogance" (p. 3). It is a practice that does not forcefully reject prior historical struggles, but rejects the arrogance and certainty that often accompanied them.

Writing from a critical postmodernist perspective, Sande Cohen (1993) has recently offered a forceful challenge to the timid and frequently duplicitous role which university intellectuals have assumed in relation to the sociality of capital and the "catastrophe of socialized expectations." Cohen's analysis has much to offer Freirean educators who wish to enter into conversation with postmodern social theory and who also wish to situate the challenge of critical pedagogy within university settings.

Following the persistent contentions of Baudrillard, Nietzsche, and others, Cohen maintains that objectivity can no longer hide or deny its subjectively based interests—a situation that has serious implications for the role of the intellectual in contemporary North American society. He writes:

> For intellectuals it is suggested that our texts and objects now fail to connect with everything *but our own simulacra, image, power, formation of exchange.* In doubting and negating everything, in affirming and consecrating everything, intellectuals remain prisoners of the futile role of the subject-in-consciousness and enforce the pretense that our efforts translate and represent for the truth of others, the reality of the world. (Italics in original, 1993: 154)

For Cohen, as for Freire, the dilemma of the intellectual lies in the failure to forcefully challenge the perils of capitalism. In response to this dilemma, Cohen mounts an articulate and vigorous attack on the U.S. professoriate. University discourse and practices are condemned as mobilizing the academicization and domestication of meaning through a modernist process of historicization—a process which, in effect, amounts to creating various self-serving theologies of the social that enable professors to speculate on the future in order to justify their social function as intellectuals. Resulting from this process are acute forms of antiskepticism leading in many instances to a debilitating cynicism. According to Cohen, universities and their academic gentry operate as a discursive assemblage directed at creating a regime of truth, a process that fails to undertake the important task of "inventing systems independent of the system of capital" (p. 3). In this instance, academic criticism is crippled by its inability to break from conventional categories such as "resemblance." Critical languages forged in the theoretical ovens of the bourgeois academy simply and regrettably pursue their own hegemony through the production of pretense and the desire for power. Further, in face of the cultural logic of late capitalism, "the category of the intellectual is disengaged from any possible antimodernist argument" (p. 68). This situation recenters "high status" knowledge within the liberal tradition of therapeutic discourse. According to Cohen, "Universities cannot speak to their own participation in the destruction of events without undoing their "need" and control structures" (p. 114).

Even Habermas' now popular appeal for a rational means of resolving differences and restoring democratic social life in the ideal speech situation is described by Cohen as "psychologically based moral economy" (p. 67) in which "intellectuals are empowered so long as they stay in the precut grooves of providing resocialization with concepts, theory, sophistication, the seductions, one might say, of bureaucratic integration" (p. 70). With this dilemma in mind, Cohen asserts:

> Why isn't capitalism—which makes mincemeat of real argumentation by its homogenization of signifiers, accomplished, for example, by the media's ordinary excessive displacement of analysis or the marginalization of unfamiliar cultural and social voices—rendered more critically? . . . Why is the economic mode so accepted in the first place as an unalterable form of social relation? Why is criticism so often an opposition that acts under the identity of a "loyal opposition"? (p. 70)

In order to escape the inevitability under capitalism of a modernist historicist recoding of knowledge, Cohen astutely adopts Lyotard's notion of "dispossession." Dispossession is recruited in this context in terms of "the dispossession of historicizing, narrating, reducing, demanding" (p. 72). More specifically, it refers to a form of "uncontrolled presentation (which is not reducible to presence)" (p. 73). It also points to the suspension of identification—including negative identification. Cohen also conscripts into the service of a critique of capitalism Hannah Arendt's concept of "active critique" of ends and goals "that never identif[ies] with time valuations which are, unavoidably, always already atrophied" (p. 113). We are advised here to "strangify"—a term he employs in tandem with an unyielding commitment to resubjectification—to making subjectivity different outside the acts of negation and opposition through the creation of insubordinate signifiers which loosen and "neutralize . . . the Platonic control on the power to select" (p. 118). To strangify is to engage in a non reduction of meaning that terrorizes all forms of equational logic, positive and negative (p. 119).

Cohen's project of strangification—a type of postmodern extension of Freire's term of conscientization—is directed at destabilizing and decentering the monumentalization of the already known and the militarization of existing sign systems established by the academic gentry and mandarins of high status knowledge whose participation is aimed at the legitimization of their own power. Along with smashing through the Western arcs of destiny—those supposedly unassailable narratives of individual freedom arching towards Disneyland, Aztecland, Inca Blinka, San Banadov, or Gangsterland—strangification unsettles foundational myths which anchor meaning in a sedentary web of contradictory appearances and pre-code the world in such a way that entrance to the world of "success" depends on the imprimatur of one's cultural capital and the potential for earning power.

A number of questions are raised by Cohen's analysis for those who are developing Freirean based pedagogical work. These questions include, among others:

- What importance do "postmodern theory" and "resistance post-modernism" have for the Brazilian sociopolitical context?
- The recent thesis on "the death of the subject" advanced by many post-structuralists (the individual is constituted by discourse or is simply a position in language, systems of signification, chains of signs) has called into question the feasibility of historical agency and political praxis. How can we think of agency outside of a tran-shistorical and prediscursive "I" and yet not fall into the cynical trap that suggests that individuals are simply the pawns of the interpretive communities in which they find themselves? If the subject has been aestheticized and reduced to simply a "desiring machine," how are we to address the concepts of morality and ethics and multidimensional forms of agency?
- How are we to react to those who proclaim the "death of History" thesis which decries the meta-narratives of the Enlightenment as misguided beliefs in the power of rational reflection? If we are to reject "grand theories" that essentialize others and speak for their needs from a perspective that refuses to critically interrogate its own ideological constitutiveness, then are we simply left with a micropolitics of local struggles? In other words, is it possible to build revolutionary global alliances in the postmodern era that do not

produce the same forms of technocratic capitalism that are part of the problem?

- If master narratives are colonizing practices that repress differences and the recognition of multiple identities, and if it is virtually impossible to represent the real outside the constraints of regimes of representation, how should we begin to rethink and practice liberation?
- While postmodern theorists have developed new understandings of desire as a means of criticizing the disabling effects of instrumental reason, how can we address pragmatically the project of human freedom?

Postmodern critiques of educational institutions such as those advanced by Cohen can be helpful to Freirean educators in placing social and educational critique within a wider contemporary problematic.

The Nocturnal Academy
and the Politics of Difference

Western intellectuals need to further understand that while affirming the experiences of subaltern groups is exceedingly important within a praxis of liberation, it is a highly questionable practice to render the "other" as transparent by inviting the other to speak for herself. Freire and other critics make this point very clear (Freire and Macedo, 1987; Freire, 1971; 1985). As Gaurav Desai (following Gayatri Spivak, Lata Mani, and Partha Chattergee) notes, the position of permitting the other to speak for herself is uncomfortably "complicitious with a Western epistemological tradition that takes the conditions of the possibility of subaltern counterinvention for granted without engaging in a critique of the effects of global capitalism on such counterinvention" (1993: 137). Since the oppressed speak for themselves within a particular sign structure, the language of critique adopted by the insurgent intellectual needs to be able to analyze the embeddedness of such a sign system in the larger episteme of colonialism and white supremacist, capitalist patriarchy. Insurgent intellectuals must apply the same critique to their own assumptions about the other as they do to the other's self-understanding. In fact, critical educators need to counterinvent a discourse that transcends existing epistemes (Desai, 1993). "We can," Linda Alcoff argues, "engage in a 'speaking to' the other that does not essentialize the oppressed and nonideologically constructed subjects." Summarizing Spivak, Alcoff points out that Western intellectuals must allow "for the possibility that the oppressed will produce a 'counter-sentence' that can then suggest a new historical narrative" (1991–92: 23). We need to question how events "position" Western intellectuals as authoritative and empowered speakers in ways that reinscribe the oppressed in discourses of colonization, patriarchy, racism, and conquest (Alcoff, 1991–92).

Jim Merod (1987) poses the challenge of the intellectual as follows:

> The critic's task is not only to question truth in its present guises. It is to find ways of putting fragments of knowledge, partial views, and separate disciplines in contact with questions about the use of expert labor so that the world we live in can be seen for what it is. (1987: 188)

The problem, as Merod sees it, is that there exists within the North American academy no political base for alliances among radical social theorists and the oppressed. He writes:

> The belief among liberal humanists that they have no "liberation strategy" to direct their steps is a vivid reminder of the humanities' class origin. Yet intellectuals always have something to fight for more important than their own professional position. North American intellectuals need to move beyond theory, tactics, and great dignified moral sentiments to support, in the most concrete ways possible, people harmed or endangered by the guiltless counter-revolutionary violence of state power . . . The major intellectual task today is to build a political community where ideas can be argued and sent into the world of news and information as a force with a collective voice, a voice that names cultural distortions and the unused possibilities of human intelligence. (1987: 191)

One important task of the critical educator is to translate cultural difference. This is certainly the challenge for Freirean educators. The act of translation is, in Bhabha's (1990) terms, "a borderline moment" (p. 314). As Walter Benjamin pointed out, all cultural languages are to a certain extent foreign to themselves and from the perspective of otherness it is possible to interrogate the contextual specificity of cultural systems (Bhabha, 1990). It is in this sense, then, that "it becomes possible to inscribe the specific locality of cultural systems—their incommensurable differences—and through that apprehension of difference, to perform the act of cultural translation" (p. 314).

All forms of cultural meaning are open to translation because all cultural meanings resist totalization and complete closure. In other words, cultural meanings are hybrid and cannot be contained within any discourse of authenticity or race, class, gender, essences. Bhabha describes the subject of cultural difference as follows:

> the subject of cultural difference is neither pluralistic nor relativistic. The frontiers of cultural differences are always belated or secondary in the sense that their hybridity is never simply a question of the admixture of

pregiven identities or essences. Hybridity is the perplexity of the living as it interrupts the representation of the fullness of life; it is an instance of itera-tion, in the minority discourse, of the time of the arbitrary sign—"the mi-nus in the origin"—through which all forms of cultural meaning are open to translation because their enunciation resists totalization. (1990, p. 314)

The subaltern voices of minority cultures constitute "those people who speak the encrypted discourse of the melancholic and the migrant" (Bhabha 1990: 315). The transfer of their meaning can never be total. The "desolate silences of the wandering people" (p. 316) illustrate the in-commensurability of translation which confronts the discourse of white supremacist and capitalist patriarchy with its own alterity.

As translators, critical educators must assume a transformative role by "dialogizing the other" rather than trying to "represent the other" (Hitchcock, 1993). The site of translation is always an arena of struggle. The translation of other cultures must resist the authoritative represen-tation of the other through a decentering process that challenges dia-logues which have become institutionalized through the semantic au-thority of state power. Neither the practice of signification nor translation occurs in an ideological void, and for this reason educators need to interrogate the sign systems that are used to produce readings of experience. As Joan Scott notes, "experience is a subject's history. Lan-guage is the site of history's enactment" (1992: 34). It is Freire's particular strength that he has developed a critical vernacular which can help to translate both the other's experience and his own experience of the other in such a way that ideological representations may be challenged. The challenge here is to rethink authoritative representations of the other in a critical language that does not simply reauthorize the impera-tives of "First World" translation practices. To do otherwise would open translation to a form of cultural imperialism. Experiences never speak for themselves, and certainly not those of the oppressed. Freire is careful to make sure his language of translation provides the oppressed with tools to analyze their own experiences while at the same time recogniz-ing that the translation process itself is never immune from inscription in ideological relations of power and privilege (Freire and Gadotti, 1995).

While Freire's dialogue does not centrally address the politics of race, his message can none the less be elaborated through an engagement with the work of Black insurgent intellectuals. Cornel West blames what he perceives as a decline in Black literate intellectual activity on the "rel-atively greater Black integration into postindustrial capitalist America with its bureaucratized, elite universities, dull middlebrow colleges, and decaying high schools, which have little concern for and confidence in

Black students as potential intellectuals" (hooks and West 1991: 137). He is highly critical of "aspects of the exclusionary and repressive effect of White academic institutions and humanistic scholarship" (p. 137) and, in particular, "the rampant xenophobia of bourgeois humanism predominant in the whole academy" (p. 142).

West sketches out four models for Black intellectual activity as a means of enabling critical forms of Black literate activity in the United States. The bourgeois humanist model is premised on Black intellectuals possessing sufficient legitimacy and placement within the "hierarchical ranking and the deep-seated racism shot through bourgeois humanistic scholarship" (p. 138). Such legitimation and placement must, however, "result in Black control over a portion of, or significant participation within, the larger White infrastructures for intellectual activity" (p. 140).

The Marxist revolutionary model, according to West, is "the least xenophobic White intellectual subculture available to Black intellectuals" (p. 140). However, West is also highly critical of the constraints Marxist discourse places on the creative life of Black intellectuals in terms of constructing a project of possibility and hope, including an analytical apparatus to engage short-term public policies. According to West,

> The Marxist model yields Black intellectual self-satisfaction which often inhibits growth; it also highlights social structural constraints with little practical direction regarding conjunctural opportunities. This self-satisfaction results in either dogmatic submission to and upward mobility with sectarian party or pre-party formations, or marginal placement in the bourgeois academy equipped with cantankerous Marxist rhetoric and sometimes insightful analysis utterly divorced from the integral dynamics, concrete realities, and progressive possibilities of the Black community. The preoccupation with social structural constraints tends to produce either preposterous chiliastic projections or paralyzing, pessimistic pronouncements. (p. 141)

It is important to point out amidst all of this criticism that West does recognize the enabling aspects of the Marxist revolutionary model in its promotion of critical consciousness and its criticisms of dominant research programs within the bourgeois academy.

The Foucaultian postmodern skeptic model invoked by West investigates the relationship among knowledge, power, discourse, politics, cognition, and social control. It offers a fundamental rethinking of the role of the intellectual within the contemporary postmodern condition. Foucault's "political economy of truth" is viewed by West as a critique of both bourgeois humanist and Marxist approaches through the role of Foucault's specific intellectual. The specific intellectual, according to West,

> shuns the labels of scientificity, civility, and prophecy, and instead delves into the specificity of the political, economic, and cultural matrices within which regimes of truth are produced, distributed, circulated, and con-

sumed. No longer should intellectuals deceive themselves by believing—as do humanist and Marxist intellectuals—that they are struggling "on behalf" of the truth; rather the problem is the struggle over the very status of truth and the vast institutional mechanism which accounts for this status. (p. 142)

West summarizes the Foucaultian model as an encouragement of "an intense and incessant interrogation of power-laden discourses" (p. 143). But the Foucaultian model is not a call to revolution. Rather, it's an invitation to revolt against the repressive effects of contemporary regimes of truth.

Selectively appropriating from these three models, West goes on to propose his own "insurgency model" which posits the Black intellectual as a critical, organic catalyst for social justice. His insurgency model for Black intellectual life recovers the emphasis on human will and heroic effort from the bourgeois model, highlights the emphasis on structural constraints, class formations, and radical democratic values from the Marxist model, and recuperates the worldly skepticism evidenced in the Foucaultian model's destabilization of regimes of truth. However, unlike the bourgeois model, the insurgency model privileges collective intellectual work and communal resistance and struggle. Contrary to the Marxist model, the insurgency model does not privilege the industrial working class as the chosen agent of history but rather attacks a variety of forms of social hierarchy and subordination, both vertical and horizontal. Further, the insurgency model places much more emphasis on social conflict and struggle than does the Foucaultian model. While Freire's critique of domesticating forms of pedagogy gives a specifically Latin American context for the development of the insurgent intellectual, West's own typology extends some central Freirean themes in order to deepen its engagement with issues of race.

Bell hooks describes an intellectual as "somebody who trades in ideas by transgressing discursive frontiers . . . who trades in ideas in their vital bearing on a wider political culture" (hooks and West 1991: 152). However, hooks argues that White supremacist capitalist patriarchy has denied Black women, especially, "the opportunity to pursue a life of the mind." This is a problem that is also firmly entrenched in the racist White university system that involves "persecution by professors, peers, and professional colleagues" (p. 157). Hooks rightly notes that "any discussion of intellectual work that does not underscore the conditions that make such work possible misrepresents the concrete circumstances that allow for intellectual production" (p. 158). She further elaborates:

Within a White supremacist capitalist, patriarchal social context like this culture, no Black woman can become an intellectual without decolonizing her mind. Individual Black women may become successful academics without undergoing this process and, indeed, maintaining a colonized mind may enable them to excel in the academy but it does not enhance the intellectual process. The insurgency model that Cornel West advocates, appropriately identifies both the process Black females must engage to become intellectuals and the critical standpoints we must assume to sustain and nurture that choice. (p. 160)

I have employed criticisms of the academy by West, hooks, and Cohen because concerns dealing with postmodern social conditions and theory and those of race and gender help to widen Freire's criticisms by situating his insights more fully within the context and concerns of North American liberation struggles, specifically as they address struggles of the poor, of women, and people of color (McLaren and Leonard, 1993; Freire, 1993a). Of course, there is room to broaden the context even further in relation to the struggles of indigenous peoples, of gays and lesbians, and other cultural workers within and outside of university settings. Freirean-based educators need to raise more questions related to race and gender so that these issues are given a more central focus in the struggle for social transformation. These include:

- In what ways have pedagogical practices been colonized by racialized discourses?
- What is the relationship between racial differentiation and subordination and dominant discourses about race and ethnicity? How are these relationships reproduced by white supremacist discursive regimes and communicative practices?
- While the struggle for racial and gender equality is deemed worthwhile, those who struggle on behalf of this worthy goal are often deemed deviant when they step outside of the legitimating norms of what is considered to be the "common culture." How are race and gender inequality reproduced within liberal humanist discourses?
- If there is no necessary racial teleology within the educational practices of most U.S. schools, how does the reproduction of racist discourses occur in most school sites?
- How does the hypervisibility of white cultures actually hide their obviousness in relations of domination and oppression?
- How does race constitute a boundary constraint on what is considered normal and appropriate behavior?
- In what ways are the conditions within the dominant culture for being treated justly and humanely predicated on utilitarian forms of rationality and the values inscribed and legitimated by bourgeois, working-class, and elite forms of white culture? How do these forms of rationality work within the episteme of a larger discourse of colonialism?

Despite these absent discourses, Freire's work remains vitally important in the current debates over the role of universities, public schools, and educational sites of all kinds throughout North America (Freire, 1985). Freire warns educators that the activity of reading the word in relation to the social world has been regrettably pragmatic rather than principled (Freire and Macedo, 1987). In other words, schooling (in relation to both universities and public schools) revolves around the necessity of differentially reproducing a citizenry distinguished by class, race, and gender injustices. The challenges of educators in both First and Third World contexts is to transform these reproductive processes. This idea needs to be nuanced.

Freirean pedagogy is set firmly against what Kristin Ross calls "the integral 'pedagogicizing' of society," by which she refers to the "general infantilization" of individuals or groups through the discourses and social practices of "the nineteenth-century European myth of progress" (1993: 669).

Ross conceives of critical pedagogy through what she refers to as the "antidisciplinary practice" of cultural studies. Drawing upon the revisionist theories of allegory of Walter Benjamin, Paul de Man, and others, Ross moves away from the essentialist conceptions of cultural identity informed by a symbolic (mimetic and synechdochical) model of experience and representation in which one part timelessly and ahistorically reflects the whole. According to the essentialist model, the plight of, say, white women in New York reflects the plight of black women in the southern United States. Rather than viewing this relationship as an unmediated one in which the plight of black women constitutes an authentic reflection of the plight of white women, Ross prefers to see this and similar relationships as allegorical rather than mimetic.

According to Ross:

> Allegory preserves the differences of each historically situated and embedded experience, all the while drawing a relationship between those experiences. In other words, one experience is read in terms of another but not necessarily in terms of establishing identity, not obliterating the qualities particular to each. (1993: 672)

E. San Juan, Jr., maintains that allegory as a formal device has specific advantages for shattering illusion:

> What happens in allegory is this: instead of inducing an easy reconciliation of antinomies, an existential leap into faith where all class antagonisms vanish and rebellious desire is pacified, allegory heightens the tension between signifier and signified, between object and subject, thereby foiling empathy and establishing the temporary distance required for generating critical judgment and, ultimately, cathartic action. (San Juan, Jr., 1988: 46)

Further, San Juan notes that allegory constitutes "a process of mis-aligning opposites." As such, it:

> . . . focuses on the crux of the contradictions and discharges a call, a polemical challenge. It images the transitional movement of difference from passive contemplation to active involvement, converting objects into process: the process of social production rupturing social relations. (San Juan, Jr., 1988:46)

Allegory, according to Terry Eagleton, is a "figurative mode which relates through difference, preserving the relative autonomy of a set of signifying units while suggesting an affinity with some other range of signifiers" (1990, p. 356). This challenges the Lukácsian idea of expressive totality and brings to mind Adorno's idea of constellation. For Adorno, the contradictory accomplice of the bourgeois Enlightenment—dominative reason—is challenged by totality. To engage totality from the perspective of a negative dialectics is to view totality allegorically, and in doing so defending totality against totalitarianism because the materialism of the aesthetic is never abandoned and, therefore, totality is never reduced to totalizing idealism. I stand with Eagleton when he notes that "those who indiscriminately demonize such concepts as unity, identity, consensus, regulation have forgotten that there are, after all, different modalities of these things, which are not equivalently repressive" (1990, p. 355).

Laura E. Donaldson remarks on the importance of allegorical vision in a feminist approach to the issues of homogeneity and universality. She does this by articulating allegory as a form of metanarrative that can negotiate "the contradiction between a radical politics of identity and a postmodern skepticism, an unqualified opposition and purely affirmative action, which threatens feminism from within" (1988–89: 20).

According to Donaldson, "Allegory not only exposes the ideological underpinnings of discourse, but also problematizes a symbolic metaphysics of presence, or in the case of a feminist standpoint, a radical politics of identity" (1988–89: 21). Whereas symbol is anti-paradoxical, excluding the logic of its two opposing units, allegory "implies a much more discontinuous relation between signifier and signified, since an extraneous principle rather than some natural identification determines how and when the connection becomes articulated" (21–22).

Donaldson's characterization of allegory in relation to feminism proves instructive:

> Allegory creates meaning metonymically by temporally displacing reference from one sign to the next; in other words, it's always mobile. Construction of meaning resists a representational truth or the attempt to find an invariant signified for the narrative which can then be placed before the reader for ac-

ceptance or rejection. Likewise, an allegorical feminism resists not only a representational view of women's truth but also the unified Cartesian subject which such a view presupposes. Allegory highlights the irrevocably relational nature of feminist identity and the negations upon which the assumption of a singular, fixed, and essential self is based. (1994: 22)

Citing James Clifford, Donaldson goes as far as asserting that all meaningful levels of a text, including theories and interpretation, are allegorical or are composed of multiple allegorical registers or "voices" (p. 22). No one register necessarily privileges the rest. Donaldson's comments echo Walter Benjamin's attack on the German Romantic theory of the symbol with its emphasis on the totalizing mystical instant in which the signifier fuses with the signified:

There is a great difference between a poet's seeking the particular from the general and his seeing the general in the particular. The former gives rise to allegory, where the particular serves only as an instance or example of the general; the latter, however, is the true nature of poetry; the expression of the particular without any thought of, or reference to, the general. Whoever grasps the particular in all its vitality also grasps the general, without being aware of it, or only becoming aware of it at a later stage. (Benjamin, cited in Taussig, 1992: 152)

Benjamin's concept of allegory does not permit the redemption of nature through transcendence since in allegory the signifier is held apart from its signified by "a jagged line of demarcation" which is both history and death (Taussig, 1992: 153). Ross conscripts similar insights about allegory into the service of a critical teaching about cultural identity. Since it is impossible to represent every cultural group in the curriculum, the task of critical pedagogy, in Ross' terms, is to construct cultural identity allegorically—for each group to see his or her cultural narrative in a broader and comparative relation to others and within a larger narrative of social transformation.

For students to recognize the historical and cultural specificity of their own lived experiences allegorically—i.e., in allegorical relation to other narratives—is especially urgent, since, as Ross puts it, we are living

at a time of growing global homogenization [in which] the non-West is conceived in two, equally reductive ways: one whereby differences are reified and one whereby differences are lost. In the first, the non-West is assigned the role for the repository for some more genuine or organic lived experience; minority cultures and nonwestern cultures in the West are increasingly made to provide something like an authenticity rush for blase or jaded Westerners, and this is too heavy a burden for anyone to bear. In the second, nonwestern experiences are recorded and judged according to how closely they converge on the same: a single public culture or global average, that is, how far each has progressed toward a putative goal of moderniza- tion. (1993: 673)

An emancipatory curriculum cannot present First and Third World cultures in the context of binary oppositions as relations of domination and resistance, since this move usually permits the First World perspec- tive to prevail as the privileged point of normative civilizations (Ross, 1993). While Freire's work calls attention to the danger of a reductive di- chotomization of First and Third World cultures, his interpreters often attempt simply to transplant Freire's perspective into First World con- texts as a fortuitous equivalence or natural counterpart to subaltern re- sistance without recoding Freire's arguments sufficiently in terms of First World contexts (Giroux, 1992; McLaren and Leonard, 1993; McLaren and Lankshear, 1994). This leads to an unwitting embrace of pedagogy as a Western "civilizing" practice.

As a teacher, Freire has provided the pedagogical conditions neces- sary to better understand how Enlightenment humanism and its specif- ically Eurocentric (and EuroAmerican) "voice of reason" has not always been insightful or even reasonable in exercising its transcontinental thinking in the service of truth and justice (Giroux, 1992). Freire's work helps us to further confront this issue as well as many others of concern to educators and cultural workers.

The perspectives of Freire can help deepen the debate over the role of the university in contemporary North American culture and, by exten- sion, can also help to situate the struggle of Latin American educators within the concerns of postmodern and insurgent criticisms of the academy as exemplified by the perspectives of West, hooks, and Cohen.

In a world of global capitalism we need counterhegemonic global al- liances through cultural and political contact in the form of critical dia- logue. Samir Amin (1989) notes that we collectively face a problem that "resides in the objective necessity for a reform of the world system; fail- ing this, the only way out is through the worst barbarity, the genocide of entire peoples or a worldwide conflagration" (p. 114).

In attempting to develop a project premised on the construction of an emancipatory cultural imaginary that is directed at transforming the conditions that create the victims of capitalist expansion, educators need to go beyond simply severing their arterial connections to the forces of production and consumption that defraud them through the massification of their subjectivities and that kill poor people who cannot afford food or heating oil in the winter. They need to create new al- liances through a politics of difference. William G. Tierney (1997) offers educators the challenge of making alliances with gay and lesbian constituencies as part of a larger struggle at the level of everyday life. Unless educators are able to forge such alliances with gay and lesbian organizations, worker movements, and the struggles of indigenous peoples, present and future generations face the prospect of becoming extensions of multinational corporations within the larger apparatus of capitalist expansion and in the service of unequal accumulation and further underdevelopment in the peripheral and semi-peripheral countries of Latin America and Eastern Europe. In short, what is needed is a politics of radical hope. Hope needs to be conjugated with some aspect of the carnal, tangible world of historical and material relations in order to be made a referent point for a critically transformative praxis. While anti-racist, anti-sexist, and anti-homophobic struggles are urgent and important in their own right, I am suggesting that these new social movements have the common goal of transforming the exploitative social relations of global capitalism.

We are reminded by Freire and his colleagues not to engage in controversies about difference, but rather to be encouraged to dialogue about difference. It is in this sense that the university is invited to become truly plural and dialogical, a place where students are not only required to read texts but to understand contexts. A place where educators are required to learn to talk about student experiences and then form this talk into a philosophy of learning and a praxis of transformation.

I have recently witnessed in Brazil an experiment using Freire's work in conjunction with contributions by critical educators in Europe and the United States at a high school consisting of 1,000 students who live in an industrial zone in Porto Alegre. The project is currently supported by the Sindicato des Trabalhadores nas Indústrias Metalúrgicas, Mecânicas e Material Elétrico de Porto Alegre and directed by Nize Maria Campos Pellanda. Here, the curriculum has been forged out of dialogues among teachers, researchers, and scholars from many different countries in both First and Third Worlds. Both elementary and high school students are encouraged to make active alliances with social movements and link their classroom pedagogies directly to social issues facing the larger community. While there exists a great deal of political opposition to this school for workers from both reactionary and neoliberal educators, administrators, and politicians, the experiment itself is a testament to the Freirean vision of transcultural alliances and geo-political realignment.

Freirean pedagogy argues that pedagogical sites, whether they are universities, public schools, museums, art galleries, factories, or other spaces, must have a vision that is not content with adapting individuals to a world of oppressive social relations but is dedicated to being maladaptive, to transforming the very conditions that promote oppression and exploitation. This means more than simply reconfiguring or collectively refashioning subjectivities outside of the compulsive ethics and consumerist ethos of flexible specialization or the homogenizing calculus of capitalist expansion. It means creating new forms of sociality, new idioms of transgression, and new instances of popular mobilization that can connect the institutional memory of the academy to the tendential forces of historical struggle and the dreams of liberation that one day might be possible to guide them. This is a mission that is not simply Freirean, but eminently human.

Rather than grounding his pedagogy in a doctrinal absolutism, Freire's attention is always fixed on both the specific and generalized other. Categories of identity, when confronted by Freire's practice of conscientization, are vacated of their pretended access to certainty and truth (Giroux, 1993; McLaren and Lankshear, 1994). What has endeared Freire to several generations of critical educators, both in terms of a respect for his political vision and for the way he conducts his own life, is the manner in which he has situated his work within an ethics of compassion, love, and solidarity.

To disentangle hope from the vagaries of everyday life, to disconnect human capacity from the structures of domination and then to reconnect them to a project where power works as a form of affirmation and a practice of freedom is, these days, to invite cynical critics to view Freire's work as a nostalgic interlude in a world whose modernist dream of revolutionary alterity has been superseded by the massifying logic of capitalist accumulation and alienation. Yet Freire's work cannot be so easily dismissed as an anachronistic project that has failed to notice history's wake-up call from recent postmodernist critiques. Many, but not all, of these critiques have relegated human agency to the dustbin of history, along with modernist projects of emancipation including those, like Freire's, that continue to be informed by socialist and humanistic ideals. To argue in this climate of the simulacrum, as does Freire, that freedom can be both true and real is to instantly arouse skepticism and in some quarters, to provoke derision.

As educators who take Freire's message to heart, we need not only to create oppositional Chicano/a, African-American, and Asian ethnicities but, indeed, to reinvent the very notion of ethnicity. This is because current approaches to pluralism in the schools often masquerade as democratic education. Further, we need to address not only the discursive constructions of race but also economic exploitation and the manner in which such forms of ethnicity are structurally imbricated and intertwined in the tapestry of capital. In this way, educators can participate in analyzing our cultural and social present and in decolonizing the Euro-American mind, and, moreover, in organizing affectively our responses to and encounters with the world. We need to remember that the forms of pleasure we produce and the economies of affective investment we create as educators and cultural workers will have political consequences by which history will remember us. Are we going to invest in society's weakest and most vulnerable members? Are we prepared to take on the responsibility of making history?

The answer to this question may well depend on the extent to which we see the possible historical present described by Subcomandante Marcos as pertinent not merely to Mexico, but to the entire world:

> Para construir un mundo feliz: Cuando la angustia llegue a su pecho, siga las siguientes instrucciones para cambiar al mundo. Primero, constrúyase un cielo más concavo, píntese de verde o café, colores terrestres y hermosos; salpíquese de nubes a discreción, cúelguese cuidadosamente una luna llena de occidente, digamos a tres cuartas partes sobre el horizonte respectivo donde oriente inicia lentamente el ascenso de un sol brillante y poderoso, traiga a hombres y mujeres, ábrales el paso con cariño y ellos empezaran a andar por si sólos. Contemple con amor el mar. De estancia en el séptimo día.
>
> Segunda parte: Reuna los silencios necesarios, fórjelos de sol, mar y lluvia y polvo y noche; con paciencia vayase dando uno de sus extremos; elija un traje marrón y un pañuelo rojo, espere al amanecer y con la lluvia por irse marche a la gran ciudad. Al verlo, los tiranos huiran atrerrorizados, atropellandose unos a otros, pero no se detenga. La lucha apenas inicia.[3]

Subcomandante Marcos
Aguascalientes de la Selva Lacandona
Chiapas, Mexico

> To construct a happier world: When anguish reaches your heart, adhere to the following directions for changing the world. First, create a more concave sky; paint it with earthy and beautiful colors, green or brown; splatter it with clouds accordingly; carefully hang a moon full of the West, about three quarters over the respective horizon from which the East slowly begins the rising of a brilliant and powerful sun; bring men and women, open a path for them with affection and they will begin to walk on their own. Contemplate the ocean with love. Be at rest on the seventh day.
>
> Part two: unite the necessary silences, forge them with the sun, ocean, and rain and dust and night; with patience begin assuming one of your extremes, pick out a dark suit and red handkerchief, wait for the dawn and with the parting rain march toward the great city. Upon seeing you, the tyrants will flee, terrorized and running over each other. But don't stop. The struggle will have just begun. (Translation Carlos Tejeda and Claudia E. Ramirez)

Subcomandante Marcos
Aguascalientes de la Selva Lacandona
Chiapas, Mexico

Subcomandante Marcos of the Zapatistas, Chiapas, Mexico

For both the oppressed and nonoppressed alike, Freire's life and work have served as a life-affirming bridge from private despair to collective hopefulness to self and social transformation. Just as U.S. foreign policy towards Latin America over the last two decades has been directed at defeating Guevarist-inspired struggle on behalf of the suffering poor, U.S. educational policy has consisted essentially of defeating the threat of Freirean-inspired pedagogical vision within its own borders. Freire's army of educators, far larger than Che's Bolivian *foco* of fifty guerrillas, is facing a late capitalist crisis of struggle. Captured in a tiny schoolhouse in La Higuera and executed, Che is still alive in spirit even as his image continues to be mass-marketed and exploited by the forces of capital. The spirit of Freire's pedagogy, while still cultivated from schoolhouses like those of La Higuera, to university seminar rooms and electronic journals on the internet, has yet to inspire a revitalization of public schooling, as the mass appeal of public education has been dwindling under capital's seductive sign of privatization. Undaunted, Freire continues to provide a language of demystification and reenchantment in our flightpath of self-making, one that has no endpoint but nevertheless has a critical direction. The political optic that guides Freire's work is fashioned not so much from dialectics (with its emphasis on collectivity and scientific objectivity vs. false consciousness), as it is from dialogue (with its emphasis on reciprocal engagement, subjectivity, and performance/community), and in this light he is closer to Lévinas, Buber, and Bakhtin than he is to Marx. In so far as he addresses individuals as more than the capricious outcomes of historical accident, or exceeding the abstract boundaries of metaphysical design, Freire's work presupposes a subject of history and a culture of redemption. In this sense he is close to Marx.

At a time in U.S. culture in which history has been effectively expelled from the formation of meaning and hope has been quarantined in the frenetic expansion of capital into regions of public and private life hitherto unimaginable and unthinkable, Freire's pedagogy of liberation is one we dismiss at our peril.

Notes

1. For an analysis of this process in the context of schooling, see McLaren (1994a, 1994b, 1995); McLaren and Lankshear (1994); Giroux and McLaren (1989, 1994).

2. See Charles Acland (1994).

3. *La Jornada*, September 21, 1994, 14.

References

Acland, Charles. (1994). *Youth, Murder, Spectacle: The Cultural Politics of "Youth in Crisis."* Boulder, CO: Westview Press.

Adorno, Theodor. (1967). *Prisms.* Cambridge: MIT Press.

Alcoff, Linda. (1991–92). The problem of speaking for others. *Cultural Critique*, no. 20, 5–32.

Amin, Samir. (1989). *Eurocentrism.* New York: Monthly Review Press.

Attali, Jacques. (1991). *Millennium.* New York: Random House.

Berlin, Jim. (1993). Literacy, pedagogy, and English studies: Postmodern connections. In Colin Lankshear and Peter McLaren (Eds.), *Critical Literacy: Politics, Praxis, and the Postmodern* (pp. 247–270). Albany: State University of New York Press.

Bhabha, Homi K. (1990). *Nation and Narration.* London and New York: Routledge.

Brosio, Richard, A. (1993). "Capitalism's Emerging World Order: The Continuing Need for Theory and Brave Action by Citizen-Educators." *Educational Theory* 43(4), 467–482.

Chow, Rey. (1993). *Writing Diaspora: Tactics of Intervention in Contemporary Cultural Studies.* Bloomington and Indianapolis: Indiana University Press.

Cohen, Sande. (1993). *Academia and the Luster of Capital.* Minneapolis: University of Minnesota Press.

Conquergood, Dwight. (1992). Ethnography, rhetoric, and performance. *Quarterly Journal of Speech* 78, 80–123.

de Certeau, Michel. (1984). *The Practice of Everyday Life.* Trans. Steven Rendall. Berkeley: University of California Press.

Desai, Gaurau. (1993). The invention of invention. *Cultural Critique* 24, 119–142.

Donaldson, Laura E. (1988–89). (Ex)changing (wo)man: Towards a materialist feminist semiotics. *Cultural Critique* 11, 5–23.

Eagleton, Terry. (1990). *The Ideology of the Aesthetic.* London: Basil Blackwell.

Freire, Paulo. (1971). *Pedagogy of the Oppressed.* New York: Seabury Press.

Freire, Paulo. (1985). *The Politics of Liberation: Culture, Power, and Liberation.* South Hadley, MA: Bergin and Garvey.

Freire, Paulo. (1993a). *A Note From Paulo Freire.* Communication and Development in a Postmodern Era: Re-Evaluating the Freirean Legacy. International Conference Programme. University Sains Malaysia, December 6–9, Penang, Malaysia.

Freire, Paulo. (1993b). Foreword. In Peter McLaren and Peter Leonard (Eds.), *Paulo Freire: A Critical Encounter* (pp. ix–xii). London and New York: Routledge..

Freire, Paulo. (1994). Paulo Freire and higher education. Miguel Escobar, Alfredo Fernández, and Gilberto Guevara-Niebla (Eds.) with Paulo Freire. Albany: State University of New York Press.

Freire, Paulo, and Gadotti, Moacir. (1995). We can re-invent the world. In Peter McLaren and Giarelli, Jim (Eds.), *Critical Theory and Educational Research* (pp. 257–270). Albany: State University of New York Press.

Freire, Paulo, and Macedo, Donaldo. (1987). *Literacy: Reading the Word and the World.* South Hadley, MA: Bergin and Garvey.

Gee, Jim. (1993). Postmodernism and literacies. In Colin Lankshear and Peter McLaren (Eds.), *Critical Literacy: Politics, Praxis and the Postmodern* (pp. 271–296). Albany: State University of New York Press.

Giroux, Henry. (1992). Paulo Freire and politics of postcolonialism. *Journal of Advanced Composition* 12(1), 15–26.

Giroux, Henry. (1993). *Border Crossings.* New York: Routledge.

Giroux, Henry, and McLaren, Peter. (Eds.). (1989). *Critical Pedagogy, the State, and Cultural Struggle.* Albany: State University of New York Press.

Giroux, Henry, and McLaren, Peter. (Eds.). (1994). *Between Borders.* London and New York: Routledge.

Hitchcock, Peter. (1993). *Dialogics of the Oppressed.* Minneapolis: University of Minnesota Press.

hooks, bell, and West, Cornel. (1991). *Breaking Bread: Insurgent Black Intellectual Life.* Boston: South End Press.

Kincheloe, Joe, and McLaren, Peter. (1994). Rethinking critical theory and qualitative research. In Norm K. Denzin and Yvonna S. Lincoln (Eds.), *Handbook of Qualitative Research* (pp. 138–157). Newbury Park, CA: Sage.

Lefebvre, H. (1975). *Metaphilosophie.* Frankfort: Suhrkamp.

Martín-Barbero, Jesus. (1992). *Communication, Culture, and Hegemony: From Media to Mediation*. London: Sage.

McLaren, Peter. (1992). Collisions with otherness: Multiculturalism, the politics of difference, and the enthographer as nomad. *American Journal of Semiotics* 2(2–3), 121–148.

McLaren, Peter. (1994a). *Life in Schools*. White Plains, NY: Longman.

McLaren, Peter. (1994b). *Schooling as a Ritual Performance*. London and New York: Routledge.

McLaren, Peter. (1995). *Critical Pedagogy and Predatory Culture: Oppositional Politics in a Postmodern Era*. London and New York: Routledge.

McLaren, Peter, and Giroux, Henry. (1994). Forward. In Moacir Gadotti (Ed.), *Reading Paulo Freire: His Life and Work* (pp. iii–xvii). Albany: State University of New York Press. .

McLaren, Peter, and Lankshear, Colin. (Eds.). (1994). *Politics of Liberation: Paths from Freire*. London and New York: Routledge.

McLaren, Peter, and Leonard, Peter. (Eds.). (1993). *Paulo Freire: A Critical Encounter*. London and New York: Routledge.

Merod, Jim. (1987). *The Political Responsibility of the Critic*. Ithaca and London: Cornell University Press.

Miyoshi, Masao. (1993). A borderless world? From colonialism to transnationalism and the decline of the nation-state. *Critical Inquiry* 19, 726–751.

Parry, Benita. (1993). A critique mishandled. *Social Text* 35, 121–133.

Ross, Andrew. (1989). *No Respect: Intellectuals and Popular Culture*. New York and London: Routledge.

Ross, Kristin. (1993). The world literature and cultural studies program. *Critical Inquiry* 19, 666–676.

San Juan, Jr., E. (1988). *Ruptures, Schisms, Interventions: Cultural Revolution in the Third World*. Manila, Phillipines: De La Salle University Press.

Scott, Joan W. (1992). Experience. In Judith Butler and Joan W. Scott (Eds.), *Feminists Theorize the Political* (pp. 22–40). New York and London: Routledge.

Shapiro, Michael J. (1992). *Reading the Postmodern Polity: Political Theory as Textual Practice*. Minneapolis: University of Minnesota Press.

Taussig, Michael. (1992). *The Nervous System*. New York: Routledge.

Tierney, William G. (1997). *Academic Outlaws: Queer Theory and Cultural Studies in the Academy*. Thousand Oaks, CA, and London: Sage.

The Ethnographer as Postmodern Flâneur: Critical Reflexivity and Posthybridity as Narrative Engagement

I knew that when the great guiding spirit cleaves humanity into two antagonistic halves, I will be with the people. And I know it because I see it imprinted on the night that I, the eclectic dissector of doctrines and psychoanalyst of dogmas, howling like a man possessed, will assail the barricades and trenches, will stain my weapon with blood, and, consumed with rage, will slaughter any enemy I lay hands on. And then, as if an immense weariness were consuming my recent exhilaration, I see myself being sacrificed to the authentic revolution, the great leveler of individual will, pronouncing the exemplary mea culpa. *I feel my nostrils dilate, savoring the acrid smell of gunpowder and blood, of the enemy's death; I brace my body, ready for combat, and prepare myself to be a sacred precinct within which the bestial howl of the victorious proletariat can resound with new vigor and new hope.*

—Che Guevara, *The Motorcycle Diaries*

This is the paradox never to be resolved: the endemic in determination renders man free to choose, yet this freedom is invariably deployed in frenzied efforts to foreclose the choice.

—Zygmunt Bauman, "Searching for a Centre that Holds"

The central theme of this collection of reflections is that both the world of academic science and that of everyday life need the agency required of the self-reflexive *flâneur*. This chapter—originally developed as a type of discursive montage—was provoked by reflecting upon my own location as *flâneur* in both academic settings and those of the mundane world of popular culture. It developed out of the social trajectory of my own formation as an ethnographer and the social historical conditions of possibility that enable me to exist within the structured spaces, prestige hierarchies, and struggles of academia yet provoke me *flagrante bello* to remain, for the most part, outside of such spaces. Yet being "outside" the academy while remaining "officially" within it carries with it certain risks surrounding the *rapports de force* within university life, most notably the risk of being ambushed by the world, being subjectivized by it as one seeks to escape the crippling banality and sterility of formal institutions of higher learning. A theme that repeats itself throughout this chapter is that the professional *flâneur* as an outsider within is trapped between an identification with the bloom and buzz of the popular and a perverse loyalty to the strident strictures of academic science yet frequently fails to understand how she is positioned simultaneously in both social spaces.

I take as my primary object of investigation the situatedness of the *flâneur/flâneuse*—the primordial ethnographer—within postmodern, postorganized, late capitalist culture, since for me the figure of the *flâneur/flâneuse* embodies an attempt in urban settings to live within the blurred and vertiginous strategies of representation and the shifting discourses of capitalism's marketing strategies and mechanisms and merge with them. This merging is strategic and should not be confused with fusion (this will be made clearer in the final section of the chapter), since the *flâneur/flâneuse* still tries (albeit often in vain) to retain some form of detachment by setting "a pace that is out of step with the rapid circulations of the modern metropolis" (Tester 1994, 15). The *flâneur/flâneuse* seeks out the mystery of daily life, unaware that such seeking can surreptitiously fuse with the very logic of commodity, which fascinates, thrills, and repulses with equal force.

More specifically, I seek to problematize the reflective gaze of the ethnographer and the reading of ethnographies. In doing so, I describe the formation of the reader and writer of ethnography who lives the dual role of *flâneur/flâneuse* and critical theorist, as incompatible as these roles might appear at first glance. I wish to shed some light on the dilemma faced by the urban ethnographer, who lives in the in-between spaces of the city, cannot escape his or her memories, and in his or her creatively charged strolling always already occupies the existential geography of his or her own desire and fear as one who lives in the thrall of metropolitan existence and the postmodern hybridity of cosmopolitan public spaces. The diary excerpts that I include represent spontaneous, unreflective, and random thoughts, which are meant to exist in tension with the theoretical formulations of the central text. They are moments when I recognize the need to interrogate the discourses of self/other that locate me as gringocentric, as informed by gueroconsciousness. While seeking asylum in the crowd (Benjamin 1983) in what Morawski (1994, 189) calls "the homogenized heterogeneity of the surrounding world," the *flâneur/flâneuse* is the prototype of the urban ethnographer. How the ethnographer's location in space by way of speed technology (e.g., a computer terminal, flights to many different places around the globe), moral technology (a commitment to a revolutionary praxis of liberation), and the textual and discursive economy of academics work together to impinge upon his or her *flâneurism* will be touched upon but not systematically developed. In this regard, my journal entries are to be considered antitexts in which private memories shape formal thought through both necessity and disposition and in ways that outrun my conscious intention. Such antitextual reflections betray a necessary partiality. They become events that rupture the continuity of my theoretical understanding as well as its formal logic. Yet at the same time, the multidimensionality of *flâneurism* is heightened through an intersection of discursive and nondiscursive practices.

Saturday, August 6, 1995, West Hollywood

I think only of the open road and yearn to get a bike and join my compas. *One of my coauthors and coeditors once died momentarily in a motorcycle accident. Since his "death" we have written a number of articles and coedited several books. He was pronounced as having been dead for several minutes; today he can't recall if he had any visions of angels and continues to ride his Triumph. I have always wanted a Norton 500, which is what Che rode across Latin America. The thought of his Poderosa II inspires me. Yet I am haunted by the feeling that my spirit has already died with Che's. A trip to Havana in 1987 in search of his memory only left me frustrated, ready to abandon academia altogether. They say Che's remains are buried under an airport runway. If his sandals are discovered with his remains, maybe they will be put up for auction by Lloyd's of London. Maybe they will discover if his hands were severed. Juan Peron's were sliced off with an electric saw.*

My position as author will reflect the figures of ethnographers as *flâneurs/flâneuses*, the image of urban spectators who dwell in prohibitive spaces both inside and outside of academia, losing themselves in their incognito observations, indulging in the thrill of public spaces; whose identity, personal and professional, depends upon acts of *flânerie*; who are the mirror image of postmodern, late capitalist culture; and who are emptied of all modern practices of the self in order to make way for the creation of new postmodern subjectivities. This perspective is meant to be suggestive and heuristic rather than definitive and is a means of unmooring ethnography from some of its debilitating modernist discourses and of demoting the epistemological certainty that surrounds them.

Of course, the figure of the *flâneur* is most often associated with the writings of Baudelaire, Zola, Balzac, Benjamin, Dumas, Kracauer, and Sartre—a transitory, solitary bohemian figure who strolls the streets and boulevards of the city in the thrall of violent urban dislocations (usually Paris but also London and Berlin); who seeks incognito the meaning of modernity; who searches for the eternal in the fleeting and transitory and discovers a unity between the transient and the timeless; and who discovers both the particular in the universal and the universal in the particular—what David Frisby (1994, 98) refers to as "the ever-same in the new; antiquity in modernity; representation of the profane in the mythical, the past in the present." What I wish to emphasize—thematically at least—is the idea that as ethnographic readers and writers of texts, and as the authors and subjects of the texts of our own lives, we experience *flânerie* as being at the root of all the intellectual and political work that we do. According to Elizabeth Wilson, the *flâneur* replaced the bohemian during the decline of bohemia during France's Second Empire. In this case, the *flâneur* "appears as the ultimate ironic, detached observer, skimming across the surface of the city and tasting all its pleasures with curiosity and interest" (1992, 97).

Rob Shields notes, "The *flâneur*, like the prostitute, risks being swallowed up by the goods in the stores and becoming little more than a commodity or a mannequin: 'the sandwich man' whose identity is hidden by the large advertising sign carried front and back" (1994, 75).

Monday, August 7, 1995, Westwood, Los Angeles

I am trying to reflect on my feelings about the Gypsy Cafe. Before moving to West Hollywood, I came here almost every evening to write. My apartment was so small, I became claustrophobic. A large number of U.C.L.A. students frequent the Gypsy, mostly the undergraduate crowd. They annoyingly chatter to their friends and pretentiously smoke their American Spirit cigarettes. Right now someone is reading an advertisement for phone sex with female body builders and wrestlers. I am unable to feel serious about what I do in such an atmosphere. My work suffers, but this is the only cafe in Westwood that I find tolerable. Here I become the flâneur *peering at the world from the margins "like the ragpicker assembling the refuse, like the detective seeking to bring insignificant details and seemingly fortuitous events into meaning constellation" (Frisby 1994, 99). Everything I do seems headed for the dustbin of history. I think of my* compañeros y compañeras *in Mexico, Argentina, Brazil, and wonder if their revolutionary praxis is purer, more real. How can anyone take anything seriously in this city, in this world of fluff and tinsel, of murder, hopelessness, poverty, and ostentatious wealth—all thrust in your face (which you are constantly urged to have "lifted" in Beverly Hills).*

Whereas historically the *flâneur*—the nineteenth-century stroller of the turbulent streets of the industrial city who rubbed shoulders with the bohemians, dandies, courtesans, workers, grisettes, soldiers, drunkards, and ragpickers—confronted "the space-time dislocation and disorientation due to the expanding scale of social relations" (Shields 1994, 77) and lived a life of "space-time psychosis" in a futile search for individuality and agency, the late-twentieth-century *flâneur* of the postmodern present confronts a world where nature has been almost eclipsed by the commodity form. Shields rightly notes that "the *flâneur's* problems are as timely for us at the close of the twentieth century as they were for the Parisian dandy of the nineteenth century" (1994, 77). The success of mass production of "the look" through media advertising need not be rehearsed here. Suffice it to say that here in the West we are constantly seduced by the tantalizingly empty commodities and their fatal strategies that have penetrated our structures of thinking and feeling, acquiring their own logic.

Commenting upon Benjamin's depiction of the *flâneur*, Eagleton describes the *flâneur* as a "drifting relic of a decaying petty bourgeoisie" who is something of an allegorist (1981, 25). "Strolling self-composedly through the city, loitering without intent, languid yet secretly vigilant," the *flâneur* becomes an expression of the contradictory nature of the commodity form as "both *flâneur* and the commodity tart themselves up in dandyish dress" (25–26). According to Eagleton,

> The *flâneur* at once spiritually pre-dates commodity production—he strays through the bazaars but prices nothing—and is himself the prototypical commodity, not least because his relationship to the masses is one of simultaneous complicity and contempt. In this, indeed, the *flâneur* resembles the allegorist, for both dip randomly into the ruck of objects to single out for consecration certain ones that they know to be in themselves arbitrary and ephemeral. (26)

Tuesday, August 8, 1995, East Los Angeles

East LA is busy as usual. I'm thinking of all the pinche gringos cabrones *who voted for Proposition 187. I'm imagining Ron Prince, initiator of the proposition, deported from the United States or locked up in the county jail. Vale cacahuate. Too bad it's just a fantasy. But it is hard to swallow that 23 percent of Latinos, 36 percent of Democrats, and 54 percent of first-generation immigrants also voted for this insidious measure. The answer to this lies in the secret of capitalism's success. "Andale, ya ves," I can hear Marx whispering from the grave. My eye catches a group of what the locals call "cha-cha goddesses" with penciled eyebrows, matte burgundy lips, and brown lip liner, whom I'm told are probably on their way to the Eastside clubs like Baby Doe's or Florentine Gardens in Hollywood. I find my reaction to be uncomfortably conditioned by the media and public discourse about East LA and Latinas as the exotic Other, as the object of male desire. Here is where I am trapped by the very discourse of sexism I struggle against. I'm thinking about what it takes to be a citizen in the white metaculture known as Gringolandia. For this Canuck gabacho from El Norte del Norte (Canada), thrown into the identity politics of academic struggles over the possibility of critical agency in a postmodern culture, I'm depressed by such a focus on cultural politics at the level of the superstructure. I'm not interested in shopping retro in the secondhand stores of Venice Beach or Boyle Heights as a way of subverting the high-fashion doyens of the metropole who serve up bulimia and anorexia as de rigeur taste. The issue for me is to question my professorial role as an adjunct of the state, as a legitimator of patriarchal capitalist culture and sovereign epistemological languages, of research models and the imperialist values inscribed in them. I want to pluck out these guero eyes and cut out this gringo tongue. I want to see the world through an imagination purged of whiteness. I worry about the essay that's going to come out of these field notes—about the* flâneur/flâneuse. *I worry about not only the textual politics of deconstruction but also the politics of resource allocation and political economy. I want to move beyond helping students adjust to Gringolandia. I want to help them maladjust to* gabacho *injustice. I can see the extraordinary expanse of my own Anglocentrism, sentimentalizing the effects of capitalism, derealizing it, turning it into the empire of the gaze. This was supposed to be the afternoon that I would start to read* In the Realm of the Diamond Queen, *but the park bench I'm sitting on is burning up in the hot LA sun.*

What is important to emphasize is that the figure of the *flâneur,* "the detective of street life" (Shields 1994, 61) who is "caught between creativity and commodification" (35), who carefully and scrupulously observes the sights and sounds of metropolitan life, thereby calling the world's bluff of civilized existence, and who engages in a "discernment of the subtle pleasures of urban life"—a type of "pedestrian connoisseurship and consumption of the urban environment" (61)—is not a monadic subject or detached, autonomous voyeur of the world of asphalt and brick but a situated observer, located in material relations of power and privilege. Ethnographers as *flâneurs* cannot escape their positionality as both subjects and objects of the gaze. They are not transcendentally removed from the messy web of social relations that shapes both themselves as observers and those whom they choose to observe. They do not live in some *post-histoire* moral universe where value judgments cease to exist.

The *flâneur* or dandy whose aim is to be aimless, to shun any idée fixe, to master the intellectual poker face, must negotiate the everyday scene of postmodern hybridity. He must bring some semblance of meaning to intercultural social relations within the frenetic narratives and signs that are available without the gaze of the *flâneur* assimilating the other. At the micropolitical level of hegemonic social relations, the *flâneur* is an agent of the empire. *Flânerie*, notes Shields, is "an attempt to appropriate and reinvigorate the position of spectator to transform the display of empire into a spectacle which (it is hoped) can be 'mastered'" (1994, 75). He makes the following important observation:

The *flâneur* reimagines the world and rebuilds a cognitive mapping of newly expanded socio-economic relations. Once again we find ourselves faced with the chiasmus of the imaginary *flâneur* (in the sense of being a literary figure) as an active "imaginer." Benjamin draws a close link between *flânerie*, imagination and dreaming. This process takes place first via a reconstruction of the situation from collecting the evidence or "traces" of social relations in commodities. However, a more ambiguous process of consumption and self-implication is also involved. An interpretive attempt to grasp the totality of social relations through a *verstehen*-like experiencing of the "aura" of the sense of commodity consumption in the arcades requires the *flâneur* to become part of the process of commodity exchange as a "participant observer." (1994, 75)

To what extent does the city, bathed in all of its commercialism and philistinism, take possession of the *flâneur*; to what extent does the condition of postmodernity force the *flâneur* to turn more and more inward yet become more and more ethically disabled in terms of acquiring an ability to effect change, to apprise himself of responsibility? Priscilla Parkhurst Ferguson astutely observes that political and social transformation and the incertitude and confusion brought on by "a changed and changing population" make it difficult, if not impossible, for *flâneurs* "to narrate the connections among the several parts [of the city]" (1994, 39). They are obliged to advance "the cult of *nouveauté* or ritual of fashion" as the bacillus through which history becomes homogenized (Eagleton 1981, 28). Postmodern *flâneurs* and *flâneuses*, or ethnographers of everyday urban life, find little to establish coherent narratives that can fuse the warring contingencies of daily existence under late capitalism. They are obliged through their willing participation in semiotic guerrilla warfare to uncover the deep narratives that remain buried within schemes of representation occurring in contemporary urban spaces. They are motivated to understand how such schemes of representation are linked to regimes of discourse and patterns of social relations and regulations not only locally but also globally through the development and proliferation of new technologies.

In other words, postmodern *flâneurs/flâneuses* negotiate spatial and temporal narratives in private, public, and hybridized spheres and wrestle with the tension between the contingent and the universal, between presence and absence, between utopias and heterotopias, between temporal disjunctions and historical trajectories, and between implosions and explosions of subjectivity.

Thursday, August 10, 1995, East Berlin

Sitting at the next table to us are these pathetic Euro-kids eating their flan desserts and speaking in German and French interchangeably and with pro-

nounced bourgeois gestures. Just like the kids I've read about in European newspapers. Possibly children of parents working at the European Commission in Brussels or of fonctionnaires in West Berlin. I wonder how their education—in their respective lycée or gymnasium or comprehensive school— might have shaped their view of East Germany. How different were their high schools from the barrio high schools of Los Angeles Unified, which many of my doctoral students attended. I am repulsed by the wealthy classes and find it hard to observe them. Flânerie *fails me.*

Ethnographic *flâneurs* are prohibited from intersubjective exchange, yet they often learn something from their failed attempts. Shields remarks: "As a consumer of sights and goods, the *flâneur* is a vicarious conqueror, self-confirmed in his mastery of the empire of their gaze while losing his own self in the commodified network of popular imperialism" (Shields 1994, 78).

David Frisby notes in the work of Benjamin that the *flâneur* as a strolling sightseer, as a conceptual detective, suggests a methodology. *Flânerie*, in this sense, refers to both consuming and producing texts detachedly and actively. *Flânerie* consists, therefore, of

> activities of observation (including listening), reading (of metropolitan life and of texts) and producing texts. *Flânerie*, in other words, can be associated with a form of *looking*, observing (of people, social types, social contexts and constellations); a form of *reading the city* and its population (its spatial images, its architecture, its human configurations); and a form of *reading written texts* (in Benjamin's case, both of the city and the nineteenth century—*as* texts and of texts *on* the city, even texts as urban labyrinths). The *flâneur*, and the activity of *flânerie*, is also associated in Benjamin's work not merely with observation and reading but also with *production*—the production of distinctive kinds of texts. The *flâneur* may therefore not merely be an observer or even a decipherer, the *flâneur* can also be a producer. . . . Thus, the *flâneur* as producer of texts should be explored. (1994, 82–83)

It is important to consider that postmodern urban *flâneurs* and *flâneuses*, often enmeshed in a world of enthroned meaninglessness, are also producers of ethnographic texts. It is virtually impossible to produce such texts impartially, in isolation, uncontaminated by the giddy buzz and blur of discursive formations and practices, since the act of reading itself is ideological. In fact, such texts are often contingent on the terms according to which the European observer of the streets was invented. David Frisby underscores the concept of the *flâneur* as the producer of narrative texts when he writes: "The activity of the *flâneur* is not exhausted in strolling, observing or reading the signifiers of the modern metropolis. Benjamin's own activity in producing the hitherto most illuminating account of the *flâneur* involved the *reading* of texts *on* metropolitan modernity and the production of texts on that modernity" (96).

Friday, August 11, 1995, East Berlin, Former Gestapo Headquarters

I've never seen so many photographs of Himmler in one place. Himmler personified evil. During the death marches of the Jewish slave laborers near the end of World War II, Himmler ordered that the remaining Jews be kept alive. He is reported to have remarked to a Jewish representative: "Perhaps it's time for us Germans and you Jews to bury the hatchet." Because of the playful fiction of flânerie, *I can leave the scene I am observing by creating a border, the crossing of which will take me away from the site of my observation and the role of observer. It's all a play—and to play "is to rehearse eternity." Only inside the play of the assignment, to engage in and write about ethnography as* flânerie, *do I commit myself to academic convention, do I confine the freedom of my choice to a framework or narrative not of my making but inflicted on me by other players. But the scene itself is a player, and a formidable one because it is mostly made up of memory—not my memory but those of torturers and their victims. If this event is textual play, it is a hideous discursive adventure. My* flânerie *brings me into a space where I am dialogized by the screams that were heard fifty years ago. The screams of Kristallnacht, the crimes of the Ordnungspolizei, the Einsatzgruppen, the SS, Göring, Goebbels, the Gestapo. Returning to me are thoughts of my father, Lawrence Omand McLaren, who fought the Nazis in Europe as a soldier in the Royal Canadian Engineers. Later that evening in a hotel conference room, the screams of the innocent echo in my lecture and choke my words into tiny pebbles that seem to roll off the podium.*

According to Bauman, the goal of the *flâneur* is "to rehearse contingency of meaning" (1994, 142). It is to rehearse the unrehearsable. The *flâneuse* is in tacit agreement with herself to live the fiction of her emptiness as the empty fullness of the real. What is known in the qualitative literature as grounded theory is built on *flânerie*; it is the hope for openness to the world, an openness untainted by prejudice, to enter a state of receptive innocence. The *flâneur*, notes Bauman, seeks the aim of his wanderings, the reason for his gaze. He seeks new narratives while purging himself of those that have already arrived, even those that inform his desire to free himself from them. But the gaze always already has narrative intentionally, a motivated way of seeing, even as the *flâneur's* gaze seeks to escape the fixity of time. Bauman describes the *flâneur* as on vacation from reality, as reproducing the "contingency of life instead of confining it" (1994, 141). As a stranger in the crowd, the *flâneur* is able to control the strangeness of the scene by choosing to ignore it.

The difficulty of enticing students to pay greater attention to their *flânerie* has to do with postmodern life as *flâneurisme*, with the fact that our exterior lives have become managed by larger narratives linked to production and consumption; we are forced to play at *flâneurisme* in a world in which fiction has made reality disappear. We are living in the panoptic fortresses of our cities (LA seems worse than Paris or Berlin), where identities are *always already* structured in dominance in the form of capitalist dependency. Bauman (1994, 154) describes this as

> the body drill of modern places of confinement and centralized surveillance turned into post-modern—thoroughly individualized and freely exercised—passions for jogging and dieting. The sexual drill of modern moral guardians turned into post-modern frantic search for the advice of sexual experts and counsellors of partnership. The modern assignment of social identities-tied-to-the-class turned into post-modern individual assembly and disassembly and reassembly of market-supplied lifestyle-tied identity kits. The modern medicalization and psychiatrization of social problems rebounded in post-modern horror of disease and toxic substances that cause it by entering the body or touching the skin. Central supply, individual consumption. Dependence that conditions freedom and depends on it for it reproduction; freedom that reinforces and rejuvenates dependence and depends on it for its exercise.

If, as Bauman notes, "the post-modern *flâneur* cannot but see the world (as far as he can see it) as the site of past or potential nomadic expeditions" (1994, 155) and if the *flâneur*, whose nomadic desire is now manufactured by rented dreams on videotape and who constitutes the entire world as a consumer expedition, allows us to live more comfortably, harbored in our alienation, then we need to question those forms of subjectivity that structure us as *interpreters*, as *ethnographers* who have been raised as *flâneur/flâneuse* poets amid the city streets of the postmodern necropolis and under the guardianship of the postmodern state. If we wish a *flânerie* to dethrone consumer hegemony and to adopt a *critical flânerie*, are we seeking a contradiction in terms? Can we create a *flânerie* capable of resisting the swindle of civilization?

What motivates the *flâneur/flâneuse* is not some primal narrative linked to desire but rather what Jean Baudrillard calls "the vertigo of seduction" (1990, 139). To be seduced is to be lifted out of oneself and into the "play of the world." The world is composed of sovereign, fatal eruptions. The play of the world tears us from our narrative of instinctual belonging, from those narratives born of a libidinal economy, from our Oedipal history, from our fantasies and repressions. Seduction takes us to the realm of appearance and away from the realm of meaning and interpretation. It is antinarrative. It takes us to the realm of pure objects, to the world of kind and cruel illusions, to the antitheater of destiny. Theory, like ceremony, notes Baudrillard, is the initiator of violence, since it acts in order to discriminate, in order to connect according to the rules. Critical postmodern *flâneurs* create violence when they defend us from the seduction of the world, when they wrench us back to the world of metaphor and meaning through the violence of theory-building, when they assign to the world the vocation of a symptom, and when they assign to appearances the reign of hidden motives.

According to Lash and Urry (1994), the spacialization and semiotization of contemporary political economies opens up new possibilities for critical self-reflexivity and social relations at the level of everyday life, in both cognitive and aesthetic-expressive dimensions. The authors are referring to forms of self-reflexivity that are both constitutive of and constituted by changes in social structures and personal biographical narratives brought about by late capitalism. High modernity has now superseded the discourses of objectivity of earlier modernity with more personalized, subjective temporalities in the form of new, self-created narratives. The advanced differentiation of social relations and institutions of modernity has given way to a high modernity of hyperdifferentiation into internally referential or autopoetic systems of "pure relationship" (Lash and Urry 1994). Viewed from this perspective, a larger role is given to agency as the abstract systems that serve as sources of reflexivity change from political institutions to cultural, media, and education institutions. Lash and Urry develop the important concept of *aesthetic reflexivity* based on the work of Charles Taylor, Alasdair MacIntyre, and Michael Waltzer. Lash and Urry claim that the Cartesian and Enlightenment tradition that dealt with "disengaged reason" primarily stressed cognition, whereas the romantic-aesthetic high-modernist tradition stressed aesthetic knowledge. They further argue that the latter tradition dealt primarily with symbol and the former with allegory. Romantic expressionism developed by Goethe, Hegel, and Schiller saw symbol presuming a natural order comprising the unity of the sensual and spiritual and a compatibility between aesthetic life and morality. The tradition of allegory founded in Baudelaire and Nietzsche rejected the unity of the sensual and spiritual, and aesthetic life was seen as incompatible with moral life. In this case, symbol is grounded in the assumption of a unity of form and content outside of the conceptual order of language, whereas allegory separates form and content, privileging the signifier and denying a separate order of meaning. Allegory's shift away from transcendence and toward the immediacy of *local* contexts ruptures the notion of expressive unity and views the subject as decentered. Allegory speaks to a reflexivity built on the notion of cultural hybridity. Critical hermeneutics best fits as a means of exploring such hybridity. We will visit briefly the concept of cultural hybridity as it relates to the construction of identity in the section that follows.

Sunday August 13, 1995, East Berlin

Checkpoint Charlie; Gestapo Headquarters; the site of the train station that transported Jews out of Berlin to the camps; walls everywhere riddled with bullet holes from World War II battles; photo exhibits of Nazi execution squads. I wanted to urinate on Hitler's bunker site but there was too much construction going on everywhere and I was unable to locate the site. I can't relax in this city. Police vans are everywhere in anticipation of violence surrounding the Kurdish hunger strikers. An East Berlin artists' colony in an old abandoned building; young people with shaved heads, black boots, and nose rings; the Reichstag unwrapped. A flânerie *haunted by history's silences.*

The question of identity is a nagging one for our postindustrial, postmodern *flâneur/flâneuse*. It is a nagging issue because of the disappearance of the unitary, self-directed subject and the stress on the decentered subject that has been encouraged to celebrate its *"mestizaje,"* or border-crossing, characteristics (McLaren 1995). For hybridity or border-crossing dimensions of identity formation may be structural (pluralization of the available modes of organization both locally and globally) and could include, for instance, urbanization as the fusion of precapitalist and capitalist modes of production in border zones of, say, Latin America and the United States; hybridity may also be cultural in terms of the production of multiple identities and the decentering of the social subject (Pieterse 1995). Hybridity also refers to the reflexiveness of *global consciousness.* As Pieterse notes,

> How do we come to terms with phenomena such as Thai boxing by Moroccan girls in Amsterdam, Asian rap in London, Irish bagels, Chinese tacos and Mardi Gras Indians in the United States, or "Mexican schoolgirls dressed in Greek togas dancing in the style of Isadora"? How do we interpret Peter Brook directing the Mahabharata, or Ariane Mânouchkine staging a Shakespeare play in Japanese Kabuki style for a Paris audience in the Théâtre Soleil? (1995, 53)

How do we make sense of this hybridization, what Pieterse claims is "foregrounding the *mestizo* factor," and creolization that "highlights what has been hidden and valorizes boundary crossing" (1995, 54)? And what about the neoimperialistic undercurrents of global intercultural exchange? Is it enough to say that we all are better social agents because of the multiple forms of cultural contact we experience in postindustrial urban contexts? While *mestizaje* identity as articulated by McLaren, Anzaldúa, and others refers to a *counternarrative* that builds community within the margins of culture, it also has an assimilationist inflection in Latin America (referring to a gradual "whitening" of the population and culture and the reproduction of elite European ideologies; see Pieterse 1995, 54). According to Valle and Torres (1995), Mexico's ruling Partido

Revolucionario Institucional "invokes the term to maintain the hegemony of a one-party state" (148). Further, Valle and Torres note that "where in Mexico, the term has been co-opted to legitimize and integrate the nation's *mestizo* middle class and peripheral regional cultures, here in the United States its lived experience occurs beyond official sanction. Valle and Torres argue that on this side of the border, *mestizaje* refers to a refusal to prefer one national culture at the expense of others. It is inclusive and can have transgressive features that are adaptive and strategic. The border crosser "willfully blurs political, racial, or cultural borders in order to better adapt to the world as it is actually constructed" (148–149). It is both transnational and postnational. As an adaptive strategy, it can be threatening even amidst the decline of the imperial West. Valle and Torres note that "the border crosser *que se amestiza* in the act of transgression, inevitably undermines the discourses of the nation-state while, paradoxically, contributing to the same state's economic well-being by providing cheap surplus labor" (149).

While viewing identity as *mestizaje* ushers in important ways of unsettling the isolationist narratives of nationalism, racism, cultural chauvinism, and religious triumphalism, it also opposes the challenge of some new forms of sociality based on cooperation, imagination, translocal cultural expressions, and new forms of competition (Valle and Torres 1995, 64). Consequently, Pieterse remarks that when discussing hybridity we need always to pay attention to the *terms* of the mixture and the conditions surrounding the mixture and cultural mélange. This mandates for the critically reflexive *flâneur/flâneuse* an understanding of the means by which hegemony is both reproduced and refigured in the process of hybridization. It also emphasizes the close attention that must be paid to similarities and transcultural historical affinities as well as to differences. The idea of translocal cultures and the politics of hybridity deals with more than difference as mixture but also, as Pieterse notes, with the process of similarities across differences (see also Kanpol and McLaren 1995). It also has important implications for new forms of narrative hybridity in terms of biotechnology and information technologies such as the notion of cyborg identity (see McLaren 1995). The central question is: How productive is it to work with the notion of hybrid cultures/identities if all cultures result from mixtures (Pieterse 1995)? One way that it appears productive resides in the means by which hybridity is able to counter forms of essentialism (Pieterse 1995).

Valle and Torres emphasize that the "aggressive disregard for boundaries and unexpected inclusions" of *mestizaje* identity must be understood within the context of global transformation, including the unequal development resulting from the emerging conditions of postindustrial society. *Mestizaje* consciousness cannot ignore the neocolonial present and its own deformation in the cauldron of virtual capitalism. Syncretism, hybridity, *creolite, mestizaje, mestissage,* crossover, global ecumene, global localism, and local globalization need to be understood with respect to postcolonial diasporic movements of peoples and the global circulation of mass-mediated commodities. This point is underscored by Shohat and Stam (1994), who write that "hybridity is an unending, unfinalizable process which preceded colonialism and will continue after it. Hybridity is dynamic, mobile, less an achieved synthesis or prescribed formula than an unstable constellation of discourses" (42).

Postcolonial hybrid identities, with their multilayered displacements and diasporic histories, constitute problematic forms of agency. According to Shohat and Stam (1994),

> A celebration of syncretism and hybridity per se, if not articulated with questions of historical hegemonies, risks sanctifying the *fait accompli* of colonial violence. For oppressed people, even artistic syncretism is not a game but a sublimated form of historical pain, which is why Jimi Hendrix played the "Star Spangled Banner" in a dissonant mode, and why even a politically conservative performer like Ray Charles renders "America the Beautiful" as a moan and a cry. As a descriptive catch-all term, "hybridity" fails to discriminate between the diverse modalities of hybridity: colonial imposition, obligatory assimilation, political cooptation, cultural mimicry, and so forth. Elites have always made cooptive top-down raids on subaltern cultures, while the dominated have always "signified" and parodied as well as emulated elite practice. Hybridity, in other words, is power-laden and asymmetrical. Whereas historically assimilation by the "native" into a European culture was celebrated as part of the civilizing mission, assimilation in the opposite direction was derided as "going native," a reversion to savagery. Hybridity is also cooptable. In Latin America, national identity has often been officially articulated as hybrid and syncretic, through hypocritically integrationist ideologies that have glossed over subtle racial hegemonies. (43)

George Lipsitz argues that the notion of hybridity—articulated by Gloria Anzaldúa and others as *mestizaje* sensibility—has often been misunderstood as meaning that one can simply construct whatever identity one pleases. Lipsitz maintains, rightly in my view, that "some postmodern critics have wrongly understood Anzaldúa and other intellectuals from aggrieved racial communities to be saying that we can choose any identities we want. But the *mestizaje* consciousness articulated by Anzaldúa depends upon situated knowledge, on her identity as a woman, a worker, a Chicana, and (in Anzaldúa's case) a lesbian. Her concept entails appreciation of the things that people learn through struggle. Members of embattled communities have to 'theorize' about identity everyday; they have to calculate how they are viewed by others and how they want to view themselves" (1994, 142).

The limits to and possibilities surrounding hybridity as the basis of identity can be found in the carnival. As Helen Gilbert notes, "Carnival rejoices in the hybridization of forms and languages . . . the bricolage, the fragmentation, the trickery, the collapsing of boundaries which occurs when spaces designated as stage and auditorium become interchangeable" (1994, 110). The problem is that without a political agenda that includes social criticism in the service of social justice, hybridity becomes another means of reinscribing empire and the controlling silences of domination.

According to the critical *flâneur,* identity is not so much formed through hybridization as through a form of syncretism. In this regard, Marcos Becquer and Jose Gatti point out that the term hybrid "may . . . still presuppose the 'pure' origin of elements—that is, their fixed, essential identities—prior to their hybridization" (1991, 66). The idea of hybrid identity, these authors claim, fits within a logic of contradiction rather than a logic of antagonism and thus tends to unwittingly privilege current hierarchical forms of subjectivity linked to the normative concept of ethnic purity. Syncretism exceeds the autotelic logic of contradiction and synthesis that is bound up with most current usages of hybridity. In addition, syncretism "points to the tactical articulation of different elements" (69) contingent upon relations of power and historical specificity. With the concept of syncretism there doesn't exist a presumed "originary fixity" or "necessary belongingness," as identities are mutually modified in their encounter with each other. During this process differences are not displaced or dissolved. Syncretism suggests a form of tactical solidarity in facing common challenges while not forsaking differences. It foregrounds the political rather than the essentialized concepts of articulation and identity. It further emphasizes a heterogeneity of distinct communities that have differing relations with each other. According the Becquer and Gatti, "Syncretism designates articulation as a politicized and discontinuous mode of becoming. It entails the 'formal' coexistence of components whose precarious (i.e., partial as opposed to impartial) identities are mutually modified in their encounter, yet whose distinguishing differences, as such, are not dissolved or elided in these modifications, but strategically reconstituted in an ongoing war of position (1991, 69).

In the case of hybridity, we partake of a closed system in which opposites clash and are resolved in the (re)production of a higher unity external to them, a unity guaranteed only by the "pure" differentiation of the elements presumed to exist in the first place. In contrast, syncretism "signals, not the pre-ordained telos of a redemptive higher unity contained within a diachronic self-unfolding, but the historicized interchange between elements based on the complex play of differences and affinities in a collective will to hegemonize" (Becquer and Gatti 1991, 70). Syncretism is defined in terms of antagonistic relations rather than contradictory relations. It is defined by Becquer and Gatti against the way it has been described in most anthropological accounts, as a process in which the colonized disguise their gods in the symbols of the colonizer, as in Santéria, for example. This common depiction of syncretism reinforces the binary opposition between the colonizer and the colonized. According to Becquer and Gatti, syncretism refuses to reify differences and therefore denies the binary opposition of "self" and "other." In this way Becquer and Gatti are able to repoliticize syncretism by arguing that it points to the double movement of alliance and compromise. Syncretic identity is able to critique and reconstruct difference as counterhegemonic practice rather than as simply serving as a space of identity where antagonisms are erased in the continuous multiplication of differences.

For the postmodern *flâneur/flâneuse*, identity must take into account the recognition of one's site of enunciation, and this often means abandoning the ventriloquistic illusions of speaking from where one is not and directing ethnographers to examine their own local terrains of identity formation. Equally important is preventing local knowledges and standpoints from becoming conscripted into the service of the universal everywhere (i.e., the space of the white Anglo Protestant heterosexual male). Kamala Visweswaran (after Rey Chow) underscores the importance of the coalitional subject, that is, of using subject positions and discursive positioning as a means of forging alliances with other subjects. This is, of course, an important means of dismantling the unified, autonomous, self-determining subject of modernity. It is also important to remember, notes Visweswaran, that subject positions often arise from a series of displacements—especially in the case of women of color. Visweswaran is here speaking about multiple-voiced subjectivity that is "lived in the resistance to competing notions for one's allegiance or self-identification" (1994, 91–92). Of course, how the mobile constellation of race, class, gender, caste, and nation come to be articulated in relation to each other poses many questions, since relations of power are so various and multiple.

The question that must be raised at this point is: How do we articulate new syncretic identities in the United States that meet the conditions of dignity and freedom? How do we include in the universal those groups placed below its threshold—African Americans, Latino/as, gays, and lesbians. In this regard, William Connolly calls for a "participation in the ambiguous politics of enactment" (1995, 185). For Connolly, inclusion in a universal right paradoxically creates a barrier to further attempts at pluralization because it leads to closure in the structure of universals.

Each pluralizing move toward justice migrates from an abject other. The politics of enactment is a dialectical movement that works best retrospectively—because it exposes absences in the practice of justice. When, for instance, you invoke the universal, you must also invoke the injuries of those practices not considered to be part of the universal. We can never reach the point of justice without absence. There will always be a missing fullness. When democracy fails to embody ruptures and antagonisms, when it ceases to be restless, it will no longer be democracy; it will have transmuted into social relations more hospitable to what we prefer to call facism. According to Connolly, difference always exceeds universal justice. Justice, therefore, is always a form of constitutive uncertainty. We need, as Connolly puts it, a maintenance of dissonant interdependence between the practice of justice and the ethos of critical responsiveness. When a new group shifts the operational constellation of identities and difference, the practice of justice becomes fundamentally important. Justice and critical responsiveness must bind together in what Connolly refers to as "a relation of dissonant interdependence." However, the ethos of critical responsiveness is more fundamental and therefore exceeds the codes of justice nourished by it, since it does not rely on the universal ground invoked by conventional theorists of justice. The ethos of critical responsiveness means coming to terms with the relational and contingent aspects of one's identity and responding to the injuries that occur when universal justice is put into practice. It means, too, acknowledging the reciprocal contestability of competing discourses of justice.

Also important in the discussion of hybridity and syncretism in the making of the postmodern *flâneur/flâneuse* is to acknowledge M. M. Bakhtin's notion of dialogized hybridity. Bakhtin wrote that "only a dialogic participatory orientation takes another person's discourse seriously. . . . Only through such an inner dialogic orientation can my discourse find itself in intimate contact with someone else's discourse, and yet at the same time not fuse with it, not swallow it up, not dissolve in itself the other's power to mean" (cited in Schultz 1990, 142). This sentiment on the part of Bakhtin echoes the critical responsiveness spoken by Connolly and takes up the position that the categories used to explain one's meaning should not digest that meaning and make it one's own in the sense of dissolving such meaning or repressing such meaning or fusing such meaning with one's own expressed ideology. In this sense, we could perhaps say that the *flâneur/flâneuse* "strove with extraordinary dedication and artistry to take as little from the world as possible, and to restore what he did take away as best he could" (Schultz 1990, 143). It is true that when considering our individual voices in relation to the voices of others, there exists an inevitable gap between interlocutors precisely because no two speakers fully understand what the other means. Yet we still can form an agreement with the perspectives of others—and this enables cultures to exist as assemblages of heteroglot elements that form what Bahktin calls an "open unity" (cited in Schultz 1990). Agreement is not the same thing as a fusion of perspectives, since agreement is always dialogic, which means that it does not result in a monologic fusion of voices into an overarching impersonal truth. The concept of hybridity must take into account the shifting of fixed boundaries, and this is difficult if not impossible when engaging in abstract or rational forms of dialogue. Dialogized hybridity has more in common with the carnival in which boundaries are interrogated, challenged, and overcome, yet new and different boundaries come into being. Hybridity in the sense that I am using it, after Bakhtin, suggests the development of a hybrid multilingual and multicultural consciousness in order to maintain a surplus of vision, a liberating perspective. This has little, if anything, to do with establishing a uniform or unitary cohesiveness of views but rather "a dialogic *concordance* of unmerged twos or multiples" (Bakhtin, cited in Schultz 1990, 147).

A more measured and sustained exploration of dialogized hybridity/syncretism would entail the further development of a theory of dialogue through an engagement with the works of Lévinas, Buber, and Freire, a task that is precluded by the space allotted here. Suffice it to say that dialogized hybridity/syncretism with respect to consciousness refers to a *critical consciousness*, a consciousness that rejects both the giddy whirl of mindless relativism and the inscrutable force of biological determinism or epistemological monomania. As Schultz warns, such hybridity/syncretism renounces all monologic premises:

> To resist in this way the temptation to epistemological monomania should make the critic, and the ethnographer, more sensitive to the ground of diversity and dialogue out of which social and linguistic change arises. Linguistic and cultural freedom is discerned in the way people reaccent and mix the generic forms they inherit from the past or borrow from contemporaries. We never begin with a clean slate, but this does not mean that we cannot attain, with effort, a significant degree of expressive liberty. (1994, 141)

Monday, August 14, 1995, East Berlin

We met Wolfgang Haug at Brecht's former house, now a restaurant. During dinner, my back rested on the wall of a cemetery. The graves of Brecht and Engels were nearby. Perhaps the good conversation—if not the pungent aroma of the sauerkraut—aroused their spirits. I'm not sure why I have spent so many days visiting cafés visited by famous figures in history. Perhaps to be closer to a time that was prior to its own simulacra, a real time, a time that was felt to be—dare I say it?—original. Is it possible to engage in flânerie *to-day—or just a parody of it. Can criticism, and social analysis, even exist in hyperreality? Has authenticity ever existed?*

A theme emphasized throughout this chapter is that *flânerie* consti-tutes the precondition of sociological reflection (Tester 1994, 18) and that the current conditions of the postmodern popular (not to mention the popularity of postmodernity) necessitate that an effort be made at criti-cal reflexivity. Sadly, it is all too often the case today that ethnographic agency either has been unable to recognize itself outside of its preconsti-tuted and precarious unity in language or else it has lapsed into a narcis-sistic infatuation with uncovering the subjectivity of the *ethnographer-flâneur/flâneuse* herself. This concluding section argues that in order to transform itself into an emancipatory political practice, ethnography as postmodern *flânerie* needs to be conjugated with the contingency of his-torical struggle and in terms of establishing a posthybrid dialogism.

Like his counterpart in the nineteenth century, the *flâneur* is "a man of pleasure," a man "who takes visual possession of the city," and a man who is the embodiment of the "male gaze" (Wilson 1992, 98). Public space is still largely masculine, organized largely for the convenience and recreation of men. Within postmodern urban spaces, the sexual economy of the postmodern *flâneur* still privileges the male's freedom to look, to evaluate, and to possess (Wilson 1992). The *flâneuse* of the nineteenth century (primarily a writer or a journalist) did not have the same opportunities as men to wander the streets. The postmodern *flâneuse* has considerably more opportunity to stroll than her earlier counterpart but cannot match the opportunities that patriarchal capi-talism provides the male.

Anthony Giddens (1991) has written that the self-constitution of iden-tity is a "reflexively organized endeavor" and that relations of race, class, and gender need to be understood in light of providing differential ac-cess to forms of self-actualization and empowerment. Postmodern soci-ety offers disillusionment and hope in reanimating the possibilities for narrative identities that will enable new forms of critical reflexivity. In a postmodern political economy, time and space become emptied out and more abstract, since space is constructed not primarily to live in but to move through (Lash and Urry 1994). This disembedding and increas-ing abstraction of time and space that have spread into international market economies privileges utility and functionalism at the expense of affectively charged symbols. We are witnessing postmodern sign value replacing modernist use value and exchange value, and deterritorializ-ing almost completely the object of meaning. Time is reduced to a series of "disconnected and contingent events, as exemplified in the rock video and the advent of the 'three-minute culture'" (16). Identity is easily mutated through video narratives and operates not through affectively charged symbols such as equality of opportunity and socialism but rather through postmodern "spectacular events of violence and cultural flamboyance" (16). Our culture is one of zero tolerance, not simply for drugs that cross the border but for human border-crossers known as immigrants. It is an era of the politics of purity. I have rehearsed this argument in detail elsewhere (most notably in McLaren 1995), and my aim here is to briefly explore not only the disabling aspects of postmodern cultures but also some enabling aspects.

According to Lash and Urry (1994), the spatialization and semiotization of contemporary (disorganized or postorganized) political economies opens up new possibilities for critical self-reflexivity and social relations at the level of everyday life, both in cognitive and aesthetic-expressive dimensions. They are referring to novel forms of self-reflexivity that enable—for instance, in the case of the postmodern *flâneur/ flâneuse*—different ways of organizing subjectivity and cultural identity in light of the changes in political institutions and social formations brought about by economic restructuring at a global level. Here, the postmodern *flâneur/flâneuse* as political agent can be traced to the nineteenth-century Réfractaires. The question uncoils: Can we use new ways of organizing subjectivity to create a self-reflexive social agent capable of dismantling capitalist exploitation and domination?

Wednesday, August 16, 1995, Paris

Again, the dead live during this visit. The Cimetière du Montparnasse became a day of meditating at the graves of Baudelaire—the father of the flâneur—*Jean-Paul Sartre, Simone De Beauvoir. The conversation that I had with Baudelaire's ghost should have been taped. I could have sold it to* Hard Copy. *The day before we paid our respects at the graves of Truffaut and Nijinsky, in Montmartre. We tried for almost an hour to find Man Ray but he eluded us. And the day before that we had discovered the graves of Proust, Schindler, Simon Signoret, Yves Montand, Edith Piaf, Oscar Wilde, Chopin, Kardac, and yes, Jim Morrison at the Cimetière du Père Lachaise. Kardac's teachings are popular in Brazil, I've noticed. Today we visited the tombs of Rousseau and Voltaire at the Panthéon. Perhaps the greatest kinship we have with others is the gnostic kinship of the grave. We will all be brothers and sisters there. I read today that the ailing former French president, Mitterrand, has just purchased his cemetery plot. Nowhere near Sartre's and Beauvoir's. I am not surprised.*

The question can now be raised: If the postmodern *flâneur/flâneuse* as ethnographic agent has assumed a narrative identity built upon cultural hybridity in a world undergoing a process of structural hybridity on a global basis, then in what sense does this call for a new kind of reflexivity with respect to both global and local contexts and concerns? What would such a self-reflexivity look like as a form of dialogized ethnographic *flânerie*? To answer such questions we will need to visit some of the recent perspectives of Pierre Bourdieu.

Thursday, August 17, 1995, Paris

Luckily I chose the Dali Museum over the Arc de Triomphe for Thursday's excursion, saving us the minor inconvenience of being killed by a terrorist bomb that exploded today. We went to the bomb site and I found a piece of metal that was perhaps part of the bomb. Since the bomb was in an empty trash can and trash cans are everywhere in Paris, it made for nervous flânerie. Fear motivates your faculties of observation. Furtive glances take on new meaning. After listening to the French news reports, I should be taking notice of who might be Algerian. I should become uncomfortable around Arab men in dark glasses and chin stubble. Where do I find some political insight into the situation in Algeria? Is my French—learned in Canadian grade school and now mostly forgotten—sufficient for such a conversation, even if I were to find a participant? Is my anxiety sufficient to pursue a conversation? The demonization of the Muslim by the West tries to grip me as I struggle to decolonize my mind. How has the culture of imperialism been written on me, in me, through me?

A crucial question that emerges in relation to the development of the postmodern *flâneur/flâneuse* (the prototype of the critical ethnographer) has to do with the question of reflexivity as sociological praxis. For instance, in their engagement with the oppressed and in their connection to certain populist exhaltations of popular culture, do postmodern *flâneurs* simply reproduce the dominated in their subordination and the dominant in their relations of superordination, as they confuse acts of resistance with a playful inversion of social hierarchies—acts that actually reconfirm such hierarchies at the most basic level? If we follow our discussion of the *flâneur/flâneuse* as ethnographic agent, as a sociologist *par excellence*, what does it mean to take part in self-reflexive praxis? During the late 1980s and early 1990s, the practice of self-reflexivity has become de rigeur in the salons of postmodern anthropology. Yet I would argue, along with Bourdieu, that the fashionable forms of ethnographic apostasy practiced among the avant-garde bourgeoisie that have developed out of postmodern interpretive skepticism, textual reflexiveness, and (neo-formalist) hermeneutic cultural interpretation based on *différance* or out of (an often frivolous) infatuation with the unconscious of the researcher (as in the confessional diaries popularized by postmodern ethnographers) need to be reconsidered in light of their lack of potential for sociological transformation. According to Bourdieu, critical reflexivity directs itself to the epistemological unconscious of sociological practice—to the "unthought categories of thought" in relation to the organizational and cognitive structure of the discipline. Further, it gestures toward the study of the very act of construction of the object—that is, the work of the objectivation of the objectivating subject (Wacquant, cited in Bourdieu and Wacquant 1992, 41). This means distinguishing between anthropological practice informed by abstract logic and that informed by practical logic. Wacquant states it thus:

> Sociological reflexivity instantly raises hackles because it represents a frontal attack on the sacred sense of individuality that is so dear to all of us Westerners, and particularly on the charismatic self conception of intellectuals who like to think of themselves as undetermined, "free-floating," and endowed with a form of symbolic grace. For Bourdieu, reflexivity is precisely what enables us to escape such delusions by uncovering the social at the heart of the individual, the impersonal beneath the intimate, the universal buried deep within the most particular. (Bourdieu and Wacquant 1992, 44)

Mainstream sociology, for the most part, is impertinent to this form of sociological reflexivity. Bourdieu is able to uncoil a series of concerns that have been compressed by the weight of everyday sociological routine. What might seem among sociologists as a narcissistic concern with the personal narrative of the ethnographer (e.g., biographical narrative, personal intellectual history) can be transformed, in Bourdieu's view, into a form of epistemic reflexivity. I sign my agreement with Wacquant when he writes: "Far from encouraging narcissism and solipsism, epistemic reflexivity invites intellectuals to recognize and to work to neutralize the specific determinisms to which their innermost thoughts are subjected and it informs a conception of the craft of research designed to strengthen its epistemological moorings." (Bourdieu and Wacquant 1992, 46).

Epistemic reflexivity as articulated by Bourdieu fashions itself as an approach that is able to "safeguard the *institutional bases for rational thought*" (Wacquant, italics in original, in Bourdieu and Wacquant 1992, 48), grounding rationality in history and producing a self-reflexive rational subject. Finally, epistemic reflexivity attempts to overcome the nihilistic relativism of deconstruction (e.g., Derrida) and the scientistic absolutism of modernist rationalism (e.g., Habermas). According to Wacquant, historical rationalism enables Bourdieu to reconcile deconstruction with universality and reason with relativity by anchoring sociological practice in the historically constructed structures of the scientific field. In doing so, Bourdieu affirms the possibility of scientific truth yet argues against the transcendentalist illusion of transhistoric structures of consciousness or language. He affirms the contingency of social categories and their political embeddedness. Yet he still believes that in some cases, universally valid truths still hold, and this is evident in his examination of the historical conditions of possibility for the deconstructive enterprise itself. In Bourdieu's view, the final goal of epistemic reflexivity is to "denaturalize and defatalize the social world; that is, to destroy the myths that cloak the exercise of power and the perpetuation of domination" (Wacquant in Bourdieu and Wacquant, 50).

The postmodern *flâneur/flâneuse* rejects the strong claim of relativism—that beliefs held within different cultures are completely incommensurable—since if we accept this to be the case, we would not even possess the background of consensus necessary to recognize cultural difference. The problem resides with the epistemic privilege given to the West, in which history enjoys ethnic privilege: the superiority of European people and culture (Chatterjee 1986). Consequently, the postmodern *flâneur/flâneuse* must question the moral and political consequences of representing social life within post-Enlightenment theories of progress. This calls for a certain type of epistemic reflexivity that I characterize as postmodern Marxist reflexivity.

Kamala Visweswaran (1994) makes a distinction between deconstructive ethnography and reflexive ethnography that I find particularly instructive. According to Visweswaran, reflexive ethnography, like normative ethnography, rests on the "declarative mode" of imparting knowledge to a reader whose identity is anchored in a shared discourse. Deconstructive ethnography, in contrast, enacts the interrogative mode through constant deferral or a refusal to explain or interpret. Within deconstructive ethnography, the identity of the reader with a unified subject of enunciation is discouraged. Whereas reflexive ethnography argues that the ethnographer is not separate from the object of investigation, the ethnographer is still viewed as a unified subject of knowledge that can make hermeneutic efforts to establish identification between the observer and the observed. Deconstructive ethnography, in contrast, often disrupts such identification in favor of articulating a fractured, destabilized, multiply-positioned subjectivity. Whereas reflexive anthropology questions its authority, deconstructive anthropology forfeits its authority. Both forms of anthropological practice are useful in developing a critical sociological self-reflexivity. In fact, both forms of ethnographic critique have been used to uncover the deep strata of Western cultures of schooling and expose the predicates that make possible certain species of Eurocentrism (McLaren 1993).

Friday, August 18, 1995, Paris

There's a bench not far from the Louvre, and it seems like a good time to get started on In the Realm of Diamond Queen. *But I can't help feeling discom-*

fort at the thought of how all Parisian museums make me think of last month's visit to the Getty Museum after an uncommonly lousy fish dinner in Malibu. I feel vulgarized, as though LA is forcing me to stain the purified traces of History's most aesthetic moments. Is it possible to enjoy historical Paris once you've been to the Getty Museum?

Self-reflexivity as a political project requires a certain degree of essentialist strategy (not to confuse my use of "essentialism" here with that generally criticized in the politics-of-identity debates). I identify my own *flânerie* as essentialist—as that of a Marxist social theorist, cultural critic, and critical ethnographic theorist—if by the term "essentialist" I am able to critically reenvision my conception of ethnographic agency while living a posthybrid identity (posthybridity here refers to hybrid consciousness inflected toward a postnational critical reflexivity). For instance, I consider my own understanding of what constitutes the political identity of a subject in relation to ethnographic practice to be different from a non-Marxist reading of the subject. I am an essentialist in the sense that I approach the narrativity of ethnographic *flânerie* and agency in specific ways: through the historically diverse traditions of Marxist theory and their political, critical, and textual practices; through the social and cultural specificity of Marxist forms of address; and, most important, through attempting to live in the world as a Marxist.

Further, I take as axiomatic that all experiences of the *flâneur/flâneuse* be historicized and treated as gendered and racialized practices. From a Marxist standpoint, the critical ethnographer as *flâneur/flâneuse* must seek to do more than defetishize, displace, and unsettle oppressive reading and writing practices by challenging their frameworks and presuppositions in terms of their links to patriarchal practices and capitalist social relations. Rather, the critically self-reflexive *flâneur/flâneuse* needs to transform the very social relations and cultural and institutional practices out of which oppressive reading and writing practices (ideologies) develop. The critically self-reflexive *flâneur/flâneuse* is not a subject position that is easily assumed, since it is an emergent *clustering* of positions, and as such is untotalizable; it is not grounded in a fixed and intractable notion of difference but in a different way of provisionally "fixing" acts of reading and writing the world so that they both free the object of analysis from the tyranny of fixed, unassailable categories and revision subjectivity itself as a permanently unclosed, always partial, narrative engagement with text and context. To become a critically self-reflexive *flâneur/flâneuse* requires a narrative engagement whose conditions of possibility are always understood to be *mediated*, for instance, by relations of class, gender, sexuality, and ethnicity and whose effects are always acknowledged to be multiple and played out in numerous and often contradictory ways. This mandates a social theory that is attentive to both a political economy and a cultural politics. Consider Michael Keith's recent remarks in his discussion of the sociology of the street: "The spaces of the street are, in other words and a familiar language, contradictory. And a language of contradiction usefully returns us to the agenda of political economy, not in search of Hegelian resolution but for bearings. Paul Gilroy has recently argued forcefully that 'the problem with the cultural left' is that they have never been cultural enough. It is worth echoing this with the comment that cultural politics without political economy will be equally rudderless" (1995, 309).

What would some of the guiding conceptions of the postmodern Marxist *flâneur/flâneuse* look like? Recently, Jack Amariglio and David Ruccio (1994) have articulated some characteristics of what they describe as "postmodern Marxism" that I believe are worth summarizing as a means of locating the *flâneur/flâneuse* in an emergent tradition of self-reflexivity that combines Marxian imperatives with new postmodern insights. According to Amariglio and Ruccio, postmodern Marxian assumptions include, among others, the following: Needs are not exogenous and do not exist prior to and independent of the social context in which such needs are expressed; all patterns of capitalist consumption involve differentiation within and across social groups; needs are only partly determined by markets or planning and are also determined by subjectiveness informed by race, class, ethnic, and gender relations; disorder, decentering, and uncertainty constitute key aspects of Marxian economic discourse, replacing the modernist Marxian emphasis on economic laws of motion; the concepts of historical conjuncture and contingency as well as that of overdetermination (à la Althusser) help to explain economic value as something that depends on a concatenation of economic and noneconomic forces; economic processes are not essences of laws that causally determine their effects; there exists "no inexorable or preordained trajectory for the capitalist economy" (28); and in addition to eliminating the preordained historical subject, postmodern Marxism rejects any teleological historical process and asserts that there is "no necessary end to any process of change and/or transition" (28). Further, postmodern Marxists assert that no special class has been granted a privileged status in constructing the plot of history, that the subject is always open, and that forms of subjectivity—despite being overdetermined—never coalesce or become unified. Knowledge that may be categorized as Marxist eschews "the premises and logical consequences of classical—empiricist and rationalist—epistemology" (30).

Friday, September 29, 1995, Halle, Eastern Germany

Ever since they closed down the chemical plant here in Halle, unemployment has been at a record high. My presentations to the educators are over, and now I've hit the mean streets of Halle with my comrade, Mike Cole, a work-ing-class Marxist professor from Brighton, England. Mike had recently taken me to task in an article he cowrote for the British Journal of Sociology of Ed-ucation *(Cole and Hill, 1995). He thinks I've given up my Marxist roots. He's wrong on that score. We drank beer in the pubs, and he kept on questioning my Marxist credentials. I don't know what I have to do short of tattooing a hammer and sickle on my forehead to get him to shift the topic. My posi-tion—that you can be a Marxist and still incorporate certain ideas from poststructuralism—doesn't sit well with him. We disagreed but remained comrades. We asked dozens of pub crawlers what they thought of the new united Germany in comparison to the former East Germany. Nearly every-body wanted the old GDR back, since at the very least they had steady jobs in those days. While people were now permitted to travel outside of Germany, who could afford to do it? And according to the residents of Halle with whom we spoke, the West Germans almost seemed to wish that the wall would go back up. We ended up jumping in a cab with a bunch of blokes at a pub, thinking we were going to another seedy pub, and found ourselves at a brothel. The beer was good, and Mike and I decided to interview some of the prostitutes about working conditions in the new eastern Germany. It was get-ting late, and the* vatos locos *who came into the bar at about 4 A.M. looked pretty mean and angry in their short cropped hair and black boots. A serious drinker, Mike was two freeway exits past plastered when he began to make some comments to the young men with the steel-toed boots. Since we both are foulmouthed louts, I encouraged Mike to leave with me before things be-came too tense. As we got up to leave, Mike slipped on a patch of water on the cement floor and went crashing through a table, splitting open his head. The brothel keeper and bartender, a man no more than three-and-a-half-feet tall, helped me drag Mike—whose head was pulsing tall arcs of blood—to a taxi. The cab driver refused to take Mike in his car because of the blood arch-ing (rather impressively, I thought) from between Mike's eyes. I rushed into the brothel (it looked as if there was a party in progress designed by Hierony-mus Bosch) and, with no towels available, got some sanitary napkins from two women and used them to stem the bleeding; another cab driver found my efforts acceptable and I poured Mike into the backseat, where I kept ap-plying pressure to his head. The next day Mike took the train to Prague. I tried to read* In the Realm of the Diamond Queen *again but just couldn't concen-trate. The cold wind and dampness were too depressing.*

If all knowledge is discursive and if all events are overdetermined, then can we ever arrive at the truth of an idea? As postmodern Marxist *flâneurs/flâneuses* of urban spaces and places, is the best that we can do merely to accept the incommensurability of discourses and reject the search for some "interdiscursive form" that can help us adjudicate among the wild plurality of discourses that we find in cosmopolitan settings? Must we accept the fact that all truths are contingent and that we can judge based only upon the social effects of such truths? To the extent that the reading practices of the postmodern Marxist *flâneur/flâneuse* are embedded in webs and networks of interrelated social practices, can we hope for critical discourses that can create alternative ways of world-making, shaping history as they are shaped by history? In response to such questions, I am arguing for a *theoria* of praxis, that is, purposeful practice and action guided by critical reflection and a commitment to revolutionary praxis. What is important to emphasize is that the critical rationality that guides our praxis as critical ethnographers of contemporary social texts and that assists us in engaging the narratives of those who have been marginalized and excluded must reject the historical logic in which their exclusion and marginality is inevitable. This is certainly in keeping with Bourdieu's emphasis on epistemic reflexivity and commitment to a rational, scientific approach to truth rather than to revealing a transcendental or transhistorical structure of consciousness. It is in this light that the *flâneuse* of contemporary cosmopolitan spaces and places can avoid fusing with the object of the gaze and resist the commodification of both her senses and her commonsense.

Friday, December 29, 1995, East Los Angeles

Here in Baby Doe's in East LA, I catch myself thinking about the role of the church. It appears as if the Catholic Church has been looking out for us mortals in these current times. Those of us who live in necropolis LA are especially appreciative of the church's efforts to give us saints. Maybe the church—like the German government—is worried about the growing influence enjoyed by the scientologists (Tom Cruise, John Travolta, and Sonny Bono have distinguished themselves among the ranks). We now have Clare of Assisi, designated our patron saint of television, and Matthew, our patron saint of bankers. But it is our secular, unofficial saints that carry us through in our most difficult moments in the sweatshop of our souls—saints like Jesús Malverde of Mexico, who protects the drug dealers, and Saint Simon of Guatemala, who watches out for the vatos locos de atiro, *and Tijuana's Juan Soldado, saint of border-crossers. Earlier I stopped by a* herbería *on Cesar Chavez Avenue to buy figures of Saint Simon and Jesús Malverde. I like the way the saints are indigenized and syncretized to produce particular inflections of Santéria. I've been told that here in East LA criminals pray to Jesús Malverde for special protection from the LAPD. I think this* vato loco *saint could easily be the patron of all the* gabachos *in Pete Wilson's government and should be given a special spot on the altar in Newt Gingrich's office shrine. How else can you explain why Newt is still pontificating on Capital Hill and making* Time *magazine's Man of the Year instead of resting behind bars where he belongs? Suddenly the strobe lights in Baby Doe's join the car lights outside in a dance on the window across from the table where I am sitting. Through the window I notice that the highways are filled with streams of cars, and my mind follows them off the ramps and into the streets, where they disappear into the night sky.*

Sunday, January 7, 1996, West Hollywood

Diana Ross looks so good. So does RuPaul. So do the West Hollywood Cheer-leaders and so do the Dykes on Bikes. I'm watching them make a video just a few minutes away from my place, near the clubs on Santa Monica Avenue. Something about the whole scene is weird and wonderful. The evening is in high gear. Tonight I'm going to start In the Realm of the Diamond Queen.

Friday, January 26, 1996, Juárez, Mexico

Another border town. As I look through my guero *eyes, the bridge from Pasiente is crowded with lean-looking cars and Wheel of Fortune dreams. My Mexicano colleague remarks that the* pollero *on the side of the road with the Dallas Cowboys hat is trying to figure a new angle on getting a family past the guards and into El Paso. The drug dogs sniff around our jeep. There's a long wait into the other zone.*

El Paso, with its hundreds of cardboard and cinderblock colonias *(illegal subdivisions), its raw sewage pouring into the Rio Grande, smiles across the border at Juárez, whose sewage canals flow through the valley. Industrial parks and the presence of Fortune 500 companies—GM, Ford, Packard Electric, Zenith, Chrysler, Honeywell—give the illusion of success at the borderlands. But don't expect U.S. companies who run the* maquiladoras *to concern themselves with issues like health and the environment. Profit always takes precedence over cholera. Disinvestment in urban infrastructure and refusal of basic city maintenance is evident everywhere. The wealthy suburban elite are lining their pockets.*

I love to work the border. To walk past the bars, the restaurants, vatos on their cellular phones, the policía *pulling a* movida chueca, *the parking generals in 1950s New York cab driver hats, the near brushes with vatos locos who are* buscando putazos, *the next-day* cruda, *and eating* menudo *at Sanborns in the morning. As I look around I see the invisible hands of Euro-American colonization; I see the USA sneezing and this town getting pneumonia. I see the results of gringo economic injustice. It will take more than dialing Super Barrio's cellular hot line to rid the city of its problems. From this place you can look north and stare right into the sphincter of Gringolandia. Met with some professors from Mexico City and shared some ideas about qualitative research. Fell asleep in a bar, dreaming of Cabbagetown, Toronto, and the smell of fish and poultry at Kensington Market. When I awoke, I saw a dog in the back alley and wondered if it could lick my conscience clean. Maybe tonight I'll start to read* In the Realm of the Diamond Queen. *Or maybe I'll just walk the streets instead.*

Saturday, March 23, 1996, Omaha, Nebraska

The audience faces us in the Rose Theater, Omaha, Nebraska. With Freire to my far left and Boal to my immediate left, it is a moment of anticipation, since neither Paulo, Augusto, nor I were told what the format of this part of our con-

*ference would be. Billed in the flyer as "Freire, Boal, and McLaren on Stage To-
gether for the First Time in History," it sounded like typical gringo-hype to me
and unwittingly framed as a spectacle what should have been advertised as a
dialogue. I seemed to take the brunt of the criticism on the issue on how gender
is dealt with in critical pedagogy. I told the audience that I wanted to expand
the issue of gender to include ethnoracial identity and that I must take responsibility for my location as a white male, not just as a deracialized male. And I
must work toward the abolition of whiteness. Strangely, a group of white
women responded that my whiteness had absolutely nothing to do with my
maleness and I was just avoiding the question of my maleness. And thus went,
for me, one of many climactic moments of the Pedagogy of the Oppressed Conference. After the panel, I met dozens of participants who were glad the issue of
race had finally come up, since it had been noticeably absent, so they argued,
in many of the sessions they had attended thus far.*

Thursday, May 9, 1996, Florianopolis, Brazil

*Each time I give a speech here I realize how partial my knowledge is com-
pared to the students or the workers. Today during my visit with Father Wilson, I was reminded of the terrible beauty among the people in the favela. I
think about the massacre at favela Vigario Geral in Rio three years ago when
General Nilton Cerqueira's security initiatives were in full swing and when a
police death squad murdered twenty-one people. Father Wilson looks the
same, perhaps thinner. He made me a wonderful fish stew. The tires of his car
had recently been slashed, the windows broken. The note on the broken
windshield read: "You see what we have done to your car. We can do this to
you." Father Wilson is not popular with the favela's drug dealers. During my
talk at the university, I wondered how culpable North American educators
were in depicting marginal outsiders of Latin America as people devoid of
history. What is the role of the university educator? Words are revolutionary
tools when they critique systems of thought and not merely other words. It is
true that words do not take to the streets, but when used to criticize and transcend structures of domination they can serve as vehicles of liberating praxis.*

Friday, May 10, 1996, Rio de Janeiro

*The steps of Candelaria Cathedral are quiet. There are no flowers, candles, or
monuments to the street children massacred by the police in 1993 for the
crime of being poor and destitute. I was careful not to disturb the Macumba
offerings on the street corners of Copacabana near my hotel. There was an
enormous chandelier dominating the room where I lectured. In the evening I
bought some plaster figures of some Orixás at a shop that keeps local Um-
banda practitioners well supplied. I thought about the child who survived
the Candelaria massacre. He was wounded in an ambush after testifying
against the police. Rumors have it that he went into hiding in Switzerland. I
talked to some educators about "racismo cordial," or subtle ways that Brazil-
ians practice racism. There is a not-so-subtle example of racism in the story*

(l-r) Paulo Freire, Peter McLaren, and Augusto Boal in the Rose Theater, Omaha, Nebraska, March 23, 1996. Photo courtesy of Marta P. Baltodano.

circulating about Luciano Soares Ribeiro, who was hit by a BMW sedan. The car owner did not help him because he thought Luciano—a young black boy—must have stolen the bicycle. When Luciano was finally transported to a hospital, the doctor would not help him because it was believed that Luciano was too poor to pay for his medical treatment. When Luciano died awaiting treatment, a receipt for his newly purchased bicycle was found in his pocket. How can we locate, map, and challenge racism in its nationalist, transnationalist, and postnationalist incarnations?

Monday, May 13, 1996, Rio de Janeiro

Closing Comments

Dear brother and sister educators. We are living at a time of intense upheaval. The trajectory of international capital that begins in the cunning boardrooms of national conglomerates and ends in the suffering faces of the inhabitants of places such as Rocinha appears to be unassailable and invincible. And yet I believe that the fragile vibrations of hope that I see in the eyes of the dispossessed will one day bring forward victory's gaze. I say this knowing full well that the conditions of emergence of victory are shifting perilously and that unions and strikes and revolutions are fast being reinvented as historical fictions. Yet I say to you that in our shackled voices we will yet find new ways to struggle. If we remain silent we shall surely perish, and if we rise up as a collective spirit to challenge injustice we shall perish still. Yet it is better to perish alongside one's compañeros y compañeras *than to perish standing alone in cynical solidarity and mutated longing with the new barons of postindustrialism, who offer nothing to the people but empty dreams and fleeting intimations of plenitude. So, brothers and sisters, let us rise up to meet our destiny, our arms locked together and our fists raised defiantly. If the contours of such an invocation seem rendered in nostalgia, then I stand willingly accused. I would rather the nostalgia of modernist hope than the false fulfillment of contemporary society.*

Tuesday, May 14, 1996, Rio de Janeiro

I was removed from the rest of the line at the airport terminal and taken to a private room to be searched by airport security. I thought it might be a strip search, but they just checked under my clothes and emptied my pockets. A minor indignity when compared to the daily lives of the people in the favelas. During the flight to São Paulo I wondered about many things. What kinds of coordination among the left will be necessary to put an end to the deceit of capital? Is this thought perhaps even a ruse of capital itself?

Friday, June 7, 1996, South Central Los Angeles

The acoustics under the freeway made the gunshot blast deafening. Carlos, my student, grimaced with a sharp pain in his left ear as he slammed on the brakes. Juan, another of my students and a former marine, quickly located the smoke through his window on the passenger side and told Carlos to hit the gas pedal. I was crouched in the backseat. With the smell of gunpowder in the air, we peeled out of there. South Central can occasionally be unkind to motorists. We were driving back to East LA after a failed attempt to get a ticket for the De La Hoya versus Chavez fight for the electrician who does some work for Carlos. At Carlos's house we switched from the car to Carlos's van and took about ten of Carlos's relatives and friends with us to the fight. I spent the evening cheering with a Mexican flag in one hand. It was a great evening until we got back to the van and noticed that half of the bumper had been peeled back from the body. On the way back to East LA I wondered what the city might have been like in better times, for instance, when the lowriders used to cruise Whittier Boulevard on Saturday nights in their chrome-lined, chop-topped ramflas resplendent with suicide doors, microflake paint jobs, hydraulic lifts, and with titanium plates under their frames. In those days car clubs like the Imperials, Sons of Soul, and the Dukes would form caravans along the streets with "Angel Baby" by Rosie and the Originals wafting from the speakers of their '57 Chevys. Should I be romanticizing a past that wasn't mine to experience? I know I'm in trouble when that happens. How has the Anglocentric dream factory of Hollywood shaped the direction of my desiring? How is my own formation within gabacho myths of self/other fa-

Peter McLaren, delivering speech in honor of Che Guevara, Rosario, Argentina.

talizing and naturalizing forms of Otherness? Back at Carlos's house we feast on tacos and listen to the diehard Chavez fans whine.

Tuesday, June 11, 1996, West Hollywood

I noticed a copy of the Los Angeles Times *carried a front-page photograph of Boris Yeltsin doing a Russian version of the "jerk" on a stage with two females in miniskirts during a rock concert in Rostov. Less prominently positioned on the page was a story about the firebombings of southern African American churches. If these had been churches populated by whites, the National Guard would have been called out months ago. Tomorrow I leave for Argentina, having been invited to give a series of talks to coincide with Che's birthday. Maybe I'll find his spirit there, maybe in the cold Argentine winter air or maybe in the smile of a stranger or perhaps in the reflections of a struggling student trying to find her soul.*

Monday, June 17, 1996, Rosario, Argentina

After my speech in honor of El Che, delivered on his birthday, I left the hotel to find the building where El Che was born. I ended up in McDonald's, spending six pesos on a fucking cuarto de libra con queso, papás medianas y gaseosa mediana. *A* matté *meeting with the HIJOS has been organized for this evening, and I've been invited to speak about the politics of memory. As I was preparing notes for the meeting, I noticed a glint in the eye of a young woman sitting at a nearby table, eyes that I swore were hundreds of years old. I was prompted to think: Maybe there is a mystical line of succession for revolutionaries as there is for Tibetan lamas. I began looking for a possible reincarnation of El Che. Come to think of it, there was something terribly mysterious about the teenager at the checkout counter. I wonder . . .*

Tuesday, September 24, 1996, Nikko, Japan

The baboons on this hillside, a few miles from the Toshogu Shrine, have decided to attack my shoulderbag and empty it of its edible contents, almost sending my copy of In the Realm of the Diamond Queen *down a steep ravine. Jenny's hair was the target of a few furious swipes from baboons leaping high in the air. Jenny pulled back in time, but a startled Japanese woman was not so fortunate, as her hair soon became a human trapeze. I thought about the famous wood carving that we saw on the stable at Toshogu an hour earlier—the "see no evil, hear no evil, and speak no evil" monkeys—and found the situation mildly ironic.*

Wednesday, September 25, 1996, Tokyo

The residents of this postmodern megalopolis seem to outdo the Angelenos in their self-conscious addiction to fashion and presentation of the self that reflects confidence and self-satisfaction without smugness and a gentle narcissism. Pornographic comics are widely read by men of all ages on the subways and by taxi drivers on their breaks near the Imperial Palace. The comics depict men having sex with young girls in school uniforms who are often depicted in bondage. This appears to reflect the ethos of the enjo kosai—*compensated dates—a euphemism for older men paying schoolgirls for sexual favors. There is no law against sexual relations between men and girls under eighteen in Tokyo. However, prostitution is illegal. The* enjo kosai *is found scandalous by many Japanese, and activist groups are mobilizing to stop the practice. Prices for consumer goods are outrageously high. Here, capital is king. I met some Japanese education scholars who are searching for better ways to teach non-Japanese residents Japanese, and also their native languages and/or dialects. It is a privilege to know this group of educators. My talk at the United Nations University was on the topic of the abolition of whiteness. At the end of my presentation, a listener asked if I felt that the Japanese "aspired to whiteness." Not to white skin, she was quick to assure me, but to an affluent, Western, lifestyle. Back in my hotel I read a confession in the* Japanese Times *by a former WWII officer in the Imperial Japanese Army who was expressing deep remorse about the colonialist exploitation of the Chinese by the Japanese military and his participation in the shooting, beheading, and torturing of Chinese villagers. Self-reflexivity of this kind is everywhere evident among the educators that I spoke with. I wonder how many U.S. military officers could publicly ex-*

press their remorse for their own imperialistic acts of aggression in which they participated on behalf of the U.S. government.

Thursday, September 26, 1996, Tokyo

Here in the Shibuya distict, Aaliyah is playing on a giant TV screen. The subway reminds me of a culture of exhaustion. People are nodding off everywhere I look. The corporations are sucking every last yen out of the workers. They are working long hours and putting in extra time just to keep their jobs, and the quality of life is on the decline as material prosperity rises. In the subway car, all the men wear stylish suits. I've never seen so many suits crammed together in one place outside of a Brooks Brothers sale. The subways are neat and clean and run on time. There are clean public toilets everywhere. People are helpful to strangers to the city.

Friday, September 27, Kamakura

The only time during this trip to Japan that I saw an individual lose his or her temper occurred today, oddly enough (for me) at the Kencho-Ji Temple, a Zen monastery. Kencho-Ji is the most important of the five Zen temples of Kamakura and is the oldest Zen training monastery in Japan. Jenny had removed her shoes and gone into the hojo (Dragon King Hall) to meditate, and I decided to wait for her outside. Kneeling beside her was an Italian tourist who had not left his shoes far enough from the door of the hojo. I watched a Zen monk walk by, grab the tourist's shoes, and hurl them down the temple steps. He entered the hojo and screamed at the tourist, who quickly exited the temple. The tourist made a bad situation worse by climbing up the stairs with his shoes in hand and defiantly placing them at the same site from which the monk had hurled them down the stairs. Suddenly the monk started to shove the tourist by the shoulders, almost sending him down the hojo steps. A shoving match began—it was nasty—and finally the tourist left, shouting something at the monk that wasn't very hard to translate. What was the explanation? A lesson in Zen discipline? Zen xenophobia? A bad day for the monk? Miscues or a racialized misunderstanding on the part of the tourist? All of the above? I will have to discuss this incident with my Japanese colleagues.

Saturday, September 28, 1996, Tokyo

Conrad Rook's Chappaqua is playing at the Tokyo International Film Festival and I've always wanted to see it since enjoying his Siddartha in 1973. Rooks was an alcoholic at fourteen and a junkie for most of his life, yet his passion for experimental film brought him in collaboration with Aldous Huxley, Man Ray, photographer Robert Frank, Ravi Shankar, and Philip Glass. Chappaqua offers viewers an outstanding lineup of talent: Jean-Louis Barrault, William Burroughs, Allen Ginsberg, Ornette Coleman, Swami Satchidanada, the Fugs, and Rooks himself. The film was never given national release in the United States (any wonder?) even after winning the Silver Lion at the Venice Film Fes-

tival in 1966. I've been trying to see the film for years, and it looks as if I will have to keep trying, since it opens a few days after we leave.

I did manage to finish Anna Lownhaupt Tsing's *In the Realm of the Diamond Queen* and also Tanya M. Luhrmann's *The Good Parsi*. Both books make some important points that need to be considered in any critical ethnography. They pose the question: Can the asymmetry between the ethnographer and participants be used productively to achieve a morally desirable good? This question is especially urgent given that, as Tanya Luhrmann points out, exploitation is the basis of anthropology as a profession. Anthropology must continue "to look for difference within the complexity of global, urban-impacted culture rather than looking from outside at the isolated, illiterate other and his bullock cart" (1996, 235). Critical ethnography must help participants or field subjects understand how they are heard by the ethnographer. In discussing Michael M.J. Fischer's conception of "experiential tesselation," Luhrmann emphasizes the importance of understanding the perception of others through patterns established in the ethnographer's own past. Here the ethnographer and field subject move beyond the Manichean embrace of us-against-them relations and become implicated in the subjectivity of each other. Here as well, the narrator is not a single voice but a complex interweave of textuality within the multi-stranded time and psychocultural space of history. Luhrmann notes: "Only if anthropology can reposition itself effectively, as an interpreter of a changed and radically reconstituted collection of global polities in which the act of interpretation is not an exploitation but a tool for responsible and effective cross-cultural understanding, can the discipline flourish into the next century" (239). Similarly, Tsing calls for an anthropology "of intersecting global imaginations" (1993, 289). This involves more than an us-versus-them contest and can be sought after by a critical analysis of "joined, divergent, and asymmetrical personal and institutional histories of both anthropologist and informant" (297).

The very spontaneous act of describing, such as in my random and relatively uncritical diary entries, needs to be interrogated for its "linguistic market" and the ways in which "unthought categories of thought"—normative assumptions—carry common sense. I have been arguing throughout these pages that critical ethnographers need to view social agents as reflexive subjects that operate in contexts that involve both opportunities and constraints with respect to the potential transformation of social structures. Social contexts for action become, in this view, strategic sites for negotiating and calculating the structural-conjectural complexities of social life. Furthermore, agents are viewed as possessing the capacity to strategically calculate actions within relational complexes of social constraints and possibilities and within specific time-space horizons of action (Jessop 1996). In *La Misère du Monde*, Bourdieu argues that the ethnographer should elicit answers only to questions that come from the respondents or participants. Otherwise the respondents' answers will suffer from the "imposition effect" of the ethnographer's own categories. In this sense Bourdieu invokes an injunction to avoid not only linguistic domination but also "the ultra-subjectivism of ethnomethodology and the scientific over-simplification of positivism" (Fowler 1996, 13). He throws down the sociological gauntlet in arguing that the objectifier and his gaze must be objectified by the participants themselves. Fowler writes:

> Bourdieu argues that the reflexive sociologist must be consistently aware of the impact of the social structure on the interview itself, particularly in terms of the linguistic market it sets up. He suggests at this point that a double sociodicty is necessary, that is to say, the explication of worldview according to the subject's social position must be applied to the researcher as well. Paradoxically, the smaller the social distance between the investigator and the respondent, the greater the social unease of the former. For in objectifying the other, she is forced to objectify herself. (1996, 13)

Sunday, April 6, 1997, West Hollywood

Allen Ginsberg died yesterday. In a Toronto restaurant in the late 1960's, Ginsberg warned me that I was taking too much LSD. Maybe I should have taken his advice. Now, thirty years later, I wonder what happened to those "angelheaded hipsters" of my past, and if I am still one of them. I long to bleach away my whiteness in the hot L.A. sun, I drift into dizzy reverie reading "A Methedrine Vision in Hollywood," searching for an angry fix of hope.

Is it possible that a scrap of memory, a figural trace, or a fading afterimage can reinvent itself as the perverse totality of theory? Ethnographers would do well to remain suspicious of their professional loyalties inasmuch as their academic identifications foreclose a stepping out of those systematic dimensions that preclude them from analyzing the broader narratives of imperialism and from sharing the collective responsibility to understand the multiple spaces that map us tactically and strategically as agents of social, cultural, and economic change. Critical ethnographers recognize the arrogance of speaking for others, and also the presumptuousness that feeds the notion that men and women can speak for themselves. Knowledge is never transparent to the speaking subject, so we can never be sure who is really served by our words, or whom we nourish and fortify with our criticisms. We begin speaking for ourselves only when we step outside of ourselves—only by becoming other. It is in recognizing ourselves in the suffering of others that we become ourselves.

Notes

Thanks to Lauren Langman for his insights on the *flâneur*.

References

Amariglio, Jack, and Ruccio, David F. (1994). "Postmodernism, Marxism, and the Critique of Modern Economic Thought." *Rethinking Marxism* 7(3), 7–35.

Baudrillard, Jean. (1990). *Fatal Strategies.* New York: Semiotext(e).

Bauman, Zygmunt. (1994). "Desert Spectacular." In Keith Tester, ed., *The Flâneur* (138–157). London and New York: Routledge.

Bauman, Zygmunt. (1995). "Searching for a Centre That Holds." In Mike Feather-stone, Scott Lash, and Roland Robertson, eds., *Global Modernities* (140–154). London: Sage.

Becquer, Marcos, and Gatti, Jose. (1991). "Elements of Vogue." *Third Text* 16/17, 65–81.

Benjamin, Walter. (1983). *Charles Baudelaire: A Lyric Poet in the Era of High Capitalism.* Trans. H. Zohn. London: Verso.

Bourdieu, Pierre. (1988). *Homo Academicus.* Cambridge: Polity Press; Stanford: Stanford University Press.

Bourdieu, Pierre. (1993). *La Misère du Monde.* Paris: Seuil.

Bourdieu, Pierre, and Wacquant, Loïc J.D. (1992). *An Invitation to Reflexive Sociology.* Chicago: University of Chicago Press.

Chattergee, Partha. (1986). *Nationalist Thought and the Colonial World.* Minneapolis: University of Minnesota Press.

Cole, Mike, and Hill, Dave. (1995). "Games of Despair and Rhetorics of Resistance: Postmodernism, Education, and Reaction." *British Journal of Sociology of Education* 16(2), 165–182.

Connolly, William E. (1995). *The Ethos of Pluralization.* Minneapolis: University of Minnesota Press.

Eagleton, Terry. (1981). *Walter Benjamin: Or Towards a Revolutionary Criticism.* London and New York: Verso.

Ferguson, Priscilla Parkhurst. (1994). "The Flâneur on and off the Streets of Paris." In Keith Tester, ed., *The Flâneur* (22–42). London and New York: Routledge.

Fowler, Bridget. (1996). "An Introduction to Pierre Bourdieu's 'Understanding.'" *Theory, Culture and Society* 13(2), 1–16.

Frisby, David. (1994). "The Flâneur in Social Theory." In Keith Tester, ed., *The Flâneur* (81–110). London and New York: Routledge.

Giddens, Anthony. (1991). *Modernity and Self-Identity.* Cambridge: Polity Press.

Gilbert, Helen. (1994). "De-scribing Orality: Performance and the Recuperation of Voice." In Chris Tiffin and Alan Lawson, eds., *De-Scribing Empire: Postcolonialism and Textuality* (98–111). London and New York: Routledge.

Guevara, Che. (1995). *The Motorcycle Diaries: A Journey Around South America.* Ann Wright, trans. London and New York: Verso.

Jessop, Bob. (1996). "Interpretive Sociology and the Dialectric of Structure and Agency." *Theory, Culture and Society* 13(1), 119–128.

Kanpol, Barry, and McLaren, Peter. (1995). *Critical Multiculturalism.* Westport, CT: Greenwood Press.

Keith, M. (1995). "Shouts of the Street: Identity and the Spaces of Authenticity." *Social Identities* 1(2), 297–315.

Kincheloe, Joe. (1993). *Toward a Critical Politics of Teacher Thinking.* Westport, CT: Bergin and Garvey.

Lash, Scott, and Urry, John. (1994). *Economies of Signs and Space.* London: Sage.

Lipsitz, George. (1994). "The Bands of Tomorrow Are Here Today: The Proud, Progressive, and Postmodern Sounds of Las Tres and Goddess 13." In Steven Loza, ed., *Musical Aesthetics and Multiculturalism in Los Angeles* (139–147), vol. 10 of *Selected Reports in Ethnomusicology.* Los Angeles: Department of Ethnomusicology and Systematic Musicology, University of California.

Loewen, James W. (1995). *Lies My Teacher Told Me: Everything Your American History Textbook Got Wrong.* New York: Touchstone.

Luhrmann, Tanya M. (1996). *The Good Parsi: The Fate of a Colonial Elite in a Postcolonial Society.* Cambridge and London: Harvard University Press.

McLaren, Peter. (1993). *Schooling as a Ritual Performance: Towards a Political Economy of Educational Symbols and Gestures.* London and New York: Routledge.

McLaren, Peter. (1995). *Critical Pedagogy and Predatory Culture: Oppositional Politics in a Postmodern Era.* London and New York: Routledge.

Morawski, Stefan. (1994). "The Hopeless Game of Flânerie." In Keith Tester, ed., *The Flâneur* (181–197). London and New York: Routledge.

Pieterse, Jan Nederveen. (1995). "Globalization as Hybridization." In Mike Featherstone, Scott Lash, and Roland Robertson, eds., *Global Modernities* (45–68). London: Sage.

Schultz, Emily A. (1990). *Dialogue at the Margins: Whorf, Bakhtin and Linguistic Relativity.* Madison: University of Wisconsin Press.

Shields, Rob. (1994). "Fancy Footwork: Walter Benjamin's Notes on *Flânerie.*" In Keith Tester, ed., *The Flâneur* (61–80). London and New York: Routledge.

Shohat, Ella, and Stam, Robert. (1994). *Unthinking Eurocentrism: Multiculturalism and the Media.* New York and London: Routledge.

Tester, Keith. (1994). "Introduction." In Keith Tester, ed., *The Flâneur* (1–21). New York: Routledge.

Tsing, Anna Lownhaupt. (1993). *In the Realm of the Diamond Queen.* Princeton: Princeton University Press.

Valle, Victor, and Torres, Rudolfo D. (1995). "The Idea of *Mestizaje* and the 'Race' Problematic: Racialized Media Discourse in a Post-Fordist Landscape." In Antonia Darder, ed., *Culture and Difference: Critical Perspectives on the Bicultural Experience in the United States* (139–153). Westport, CT: Bergin and Garvey.

Visweswaran, Kamala. (1994). *Fictions of Feminist Ethnography.* Minneapolis: University of Minnesota Press.

Wilson, Elizabeth. (1992). "The Invisible Flâneur." *New Left Review* 191, 90–11.

Jean Baudrillard's Chamber of Horrors: From Marxism to Terrorist Pedagogy

Peter McLaren and Zeus Leonardo

I just can't breathe in this world of petitioning intellectuals. . . . I no longer take a position as intellectual. My work now is to make things appear or disappear.
—**Jean Baudrillard,** *Baudrillard Live*

History is a strong myth, perhaps, along with the unconscious, the last great myth.
—**Jean Baudrillard,** *Simulacra and Simulation*

He made his appearance on the stage sporting a silver jacket with se-quined lapels, blue shirt, and glasses that looked too large for his face and that dominated his short frame. The crowd grew larger as the per-former read his works with a heavy French accent. He was accompanied by the Chance Band. He needed no introduction, for this was the fa-mous French intellectual who dared to tell us to "oublier Foucault." This was America's favorite Parisian littérateur and cultural critic: the icono-clastic Jean Baudrillard. Pleased at having won $100 at the slots on his first night at the event, he was captivatingly gloomy and suicidal. The event was called "Chance" and was sponsored by the Art Center College of Design in Pasadena. It also featured chaos theorists, beat poets, a *bu-toh* dance troupe from Los Angeles, rock bands, performance artists, gamblers, stockbrokers, and new age enthusiasts. Baudrillard was in his element: the professor as lounge lizard, reading pataphysical texts in-stead of singing "Feelings." Why not? If Marshall McLuhan can do a cameo appearance in Woody Allen's *Annie Hall,* why can't Jean Bau-drillard dress like a card shark and do a gig in a Nevada casino?

The work of Jean Baudrillard is vital in understanding the cultures of late capitalism, the parodic, terroristic, and pestilential world of "ecstatic" nihilism that Georges Bataille (1985) captures in the metaphor of the Solar Anus and Arthur Kroker (1986) describes as "excremental culture." Jean Baudrillard is the Grand Expositor of the social as corpse, transfiguring through his apocalyptic prose the social into an effigy of a rotting cadaver, its stench and putrescence made all the more beautiful in the ecstasy of its decay. For over two decades Baudrillard's work has transfixed and perplexed several generations of scholars with its heuristic power, its bourgeois indignation, and its chilling eulogistic pronouncements about the fate of the postmodern urbanopolis and the vestigial remains of all that is dead. His work represents a sublime connoisseurship of decay. Part catechism, part slight-of-thought, his work is a mixture of academic pyrotechnics, blistering social criticism, and a circus act on the order of a linguistic Cirque de Soleil. Educators who work in the criticalist tradition need to challenge current collective arrangements of cultural enunciation that crystallize the subject like a gallstone lodged in the bladder of the social, rendering critical agency hopelessly trapped in metacodes and dominant conventions; and Baudrillard can help them do it. Baudrillard's contention that capitalism is part of a larger rationalization process associated with a new type of proliferation of signs, a new type of dissemination of values, and a new type of radical semiurgy associated with cybernetic and semiotic systems presents a formidable task to educators working with students who often act as if modern values have been declared dead under the current conditions of hyperreality. We believe that Baudrillard's work, although crucially flawed, offers important lessons for educators teaching at a time when the capitalist state is able to overcode machineries of domination and exploitation by molecularizing and particulating the masses while at the same time seducing them to its pulsing flows of fascist desire.

Baudrillard's cultural critique of Western society is a significant contribution to critical theory yet one that remains shrouded in relative obscurity. Educated as a sociologist and profoundly influenced by the ideas of his teacher, Henri Lefebvre, and the work of Roland Barthes, Baudrillard has moved in his heuristic and catalyzing project from a Marxist to a post-Marxist (and at times politically reactionary) analysis of everyday life. In assaying the crisis of meaning that overtook many French thinkers such as Foucault and Lyotard, Baudrillard formulated a sophisticated method of analysis, the controlling themes of which were modulated by central Marxist assumptions, producing an unexpected locus of inertia in the individual subject.

While Baudrillard's ideas have engaged such critical thinkers as Mike Gane, Arthur Kroker, Mark Poster, and Douglas Kellner, they remain, for the most part, enigmatic for many readers. This is due, in part, to his conceptual iconoclasm and idiosyncratic writing style, which is most evident in his later works. Apotheosizing the end of agency in the era of the simulacra, Baudrillard represents the "postmodern scene itself" and has reached guru status in some circles as the theoretician of postmodernism par excellence. The *Canadian Journal of Social Theory/Revue Canadienne de Théorie Politique et Sociale* is largely dedicated to Baudrillard's ideas and works. However, Gane notes Baudrillard's absence from the following important collections (1991a, 46): Joan Miller's encyclopedia, *French Structuralism* (1981); John Thompson's *Studies in the Theory of Ideology* (1984); J. Merquior's *From Prague to Paris* (1986); Peter Dews's *Logics of Disintegration* (1987); V. Descombes's *Modern French Philosophy* (1979); and A. P. Griffith's *Contemporary French Philosophy* (1988). Some critics among the left view Baudrillard as moving the left beyond Marxist critique, while other left intellectuals criticize Baudrillard for rejecting Marxism tout court in his later works. Clearly, Baudrillard's impact has been felt throughout the academy.

Baudrillard is described by Kroker as "the unwitting sorcerer of the Marxian legacy," (1986, 121) whose "great refusals of the referential categories of history, society and normalizing power, accurately indicate a fundamental rupture in the objective constitution of advanced capitalism" (1986, 187). While we might want to disagree about Baudrillard's credentials as a Marxian theorist, there is little doubt that he is one of the most important theorists of "bad infinity," of the Fascist character of social life, of the semiotics of the sign, and of the hieroglyphics of cynical power. Baudrillard has brazenly ascended into the world of postmodern theorizing through acts of semiotic outlawry, through outrageous claims and brazen theoretical formulations. He has become the philosopher of the fractal stage of value; "the Darth Vader of postmodernism" and contemporary "prophet of doom" (Cook 1994, 150); Kid Symbol strutting through viral culture; a pataphysician of cyberspace and practitioner of rhetorical science who delights in offending readers with excrementitous social diagnosis from his clinic of metavulgarity; an exponent of theoretical violence whose pen serves as a magical *bâton-à-physique,* lighting up cyberspace like a Roman candle; a linguistic acrobat who dangles from his feet on the catwalk above the stage. With tongue wagging he taunts the ringmasters of the academy.

Baudrillard's eclectic approach to cultural analysis makes a sweep of all the major theoretical frameworks. Marxism, psychoanalysis, feminism, semiotics, structuralism, poststructuralism, modernism, and postmodernism are just some of his "hostages." Baudrillard traces various concepts throughout his vast corpus of writing, the most important being the fate of the object in society.

In this chapter, we map some central aspects of Baudrillard's engagement with Marxism in his vainglorious search for a radical theory of contemporary cultural studies. From Baudrillard's structural Marxism (as shown in works like *The System of Objects*) to an epistemological break with political economy (e.g., *Mirror of Production*), and finally to his announcement of the death of Marxist categories (e.g., *Fatal Strategies*), we will assess Baudrillard's revolutionary praxis. Moreover, we will provide a textual analysis of some of Baudrillard's works and appraise his ideas as they contribute to radicalizing social theory as well as point to their limitations. Critical commentaries by Kellner and Gane will also help synthesize Baudrillard's engagement with as well as disengagement from Marxian critique.

Baudrillard's first book, *The System of Objects,* was published in 1968. It is here that Baudrillard first embarks on his study of the object system. Arguing that one of Marx's limitations was his neglectful nonengagement with the politics of consumption, Baudrillard attempts to interpret the meanings that people construct through their consumption of objects. Analyzing the evolution of material production, Baudrillard finds that the object's relation with the subject constitutes a considerable part of daily consumptive practices. Purchasing the latest market object becomes a new mode of self-fulfillment. For instance, Baudrillard writes, "In the United States 90 percent of the population experience no other desire than to possess what others possess. From year to year, consumer choices are focused *en masse* on the latest model which is uniformly the best" (1988a, 11; italics in original). Social relations among individuals are no longer forged at the level of interpersonal relationships but instead are expressed directly through the objects that they own. That is, objects signify subject relations through their differential status. Social relations become object relations.

At the structural level, purchasing the market object is less about consuming the commodity than reproducing the existing social order. Baudrillard explains: "Let us not be fooled: objects are *categories of objects* which quite tyrannically induce *categories of persons*. They undertake the policing of social meanings, and the significations they engender are controlled. Their proliferation, simultaneously arbitrary and coherent, is the best vehicle for a social order, equally arbitrary and coherent, to materialize itself effectively under the sign of affluence" (1988a, 16–17; italics in original). Systems of objects are, according to Baudrillard, systems of social distinctions and their regulation. Subjects traverse the universe of purchasing choices available to them in order to achieve differentiation from others through coded differences and associative chains that encourage a hallucinatory identification with reality. This is accomplished through a mass production of objects as serialized commodities. The traditional relationship between an idiosyncratic object and its owner is ruptured. Mass reproduction of the same object alters the owner's relation to the material possession, now seen as something to be manipulated.

According to Baudrillard, social difference is achieved at the level of the object as sign. Baudrillard clarifies: *"In order to become the object of consumption, the object must become sign . . .* It is in this way that it becomes 'personalized,' and enters in the series, etc.: it is never consumed in its materiality, but in its difference" (1988a, 22; italics in original). The sign code stratifies consumers by assigning prestige and value hierarchies to objects through their difference from other object forms in the series, creating what Baudrillard calls "ambiance." Objects themselves pose as alibis for the daily consumption of human relations. People do not consume the objects that they purchase, they consume signs. Nike's Air Jordans are purchased less for the shoes' utility than for what they signify: that you can be like Mike. Baudrillard exclaims: "The code is totalitarian; no one escapes it" (1988a, 19). Early in his writing career, Baudrillard developed concepts that would reverberate throughout his prolific academic career. Concepts like the sign, code, and object were preoccupations that would continue from this point into the future present and present future. In addition, Baudrillard's relationship with structural Marxism became clear. At this stage in his writing, Baudrillard began to underplay more traditional Marxist categories (e.g., human labor) in order to emphasize the process of consumption, or social labor.

In *Consumer Society* (1988b), Baudrillard continues his critique of the object and of consumption. The object form assumes even more significance in its relation to consumers: "We are living the period of the objects: that is, we live by their rhythm, according to their incessant cycles. Today, it is we who are observing their birth, fulfillment, and death; whereas in all previous civilizations, it was the object, instrument, and perennial monument that survived the generations of men" (1988b, 29). Here, people are viewed as surviving their objects, pointing to the increasing functionality of objects such that they no longer possess the same aura with which previous societies had endowed them. Object ownership exists only in an instrumental relationship to the owner. The sentimentality and history associated with some objects become less pertinent, since an almost perfect replica of the object can be (re)produced. Baudrillard's fetishism of the object begins to reveal itself. For Baudrillard, the object possesses an "aura," a certain vitality that is unmistakably suggestive of human sociality. In comparison, human characteristics devolve. People become functionaries of consumer society as they are motivated to purchase more and more objects in order to feel integrally connected to the social milieu.

Following a system of objects is a system of constructed and conditioned needs and a dependency on consumption to fulfill those needs.

Baudrillard challenges the concept of human needs that are based on natural rights theory or the concept of species-being. Baudrillard's concept of need is not as straightforward as rational choice economists would have us believe. Needs arise out of specific modes of production and social organization. Baudrillard reminds us: "Needs are not so much directed at objects, but at values. And the satisfaction of needs primarily expresses an *adherence to these values*. The fundamental, unconscious, and automatic choice of the consumer is to accept the life-style of a particular society (no longer therefore a real choice: the theory of the autonomy and sovereignty of the consumer is thus refuted)" (1988b, 37; italics in original). Baudrillard accomplishes a symptomatic reading of consumption at the level of hegemony. Consumers buy into the code of consumption rather than the object itself and are subjectively formed within a value system rather than a culture of consumers. However, Baudrillard's model appears too unyielding, lacking the space for the consumer's relative autonomy and sovereignty. Describing the will to consume as an "automatic choice," Baudrillard fails to explain how choices centered around the act of consumption are mediated by individual consumers and groups (e.g., boycotts). Whereas values are to a large degree internal to an individual, subjects engage the formation of consciousness in various ways; for some it is a critical engagement and for some it is a passive one. Being a consumer does not necessarily mean uniformity or conformity. In fact, we prefer a later response to John Kenneth Galbraith: "We are aware of how consumers resist such a precise injunction, and of how they play with 'needs' on a keyboard of objects. We know that advertising is not omnipotent and at times produces opposite reactions; and, we know that in reference to a single 'need,' objects can be substituted for one another" (1988b, 41–42). In this passage Baudrillard appears to recognize consumer resistance and relative power.

In consumer society, consumers are motivated increasingly to make more and more decisions when purchasing objects. Baudrillard notes, after Galbraith, that this freedom to choose is imposed on the consumer by the code as a form of duty (1988b, 39). Baudrillard explains:

Few objects today are offered *alone*, without a context of objects to speak for them. And the relation of the consumer to the object has consequently changed: the object is no longer referred to in relation to a specific utility, but as a collection of objects in their total meaning. Washing machine, refrigerator, dishwasher, have different meanings when grouped together than each one has alone, as a piece of equipment (*ustensile*). The display window, the advertisement, the manufacturer, and the *brand name* here play an essential role in imposing a coherent and collective vision, like an almost inseparable totality. Like a chain that connects not ordinary objects but *signifieds*, each object can signify the other in a more complex super-object, and lead the consumer to a series of more complex choices. (1988b, 31; italics in original)

It is in this sense that objects can be regarded as possessing their own sociality. Like consumers, objects belong in "imagined communities" (Anderson 1991) sedimented at the level of consumer imagination and creatively motivated. Baudrillard continues:

> The arrangement directs the purchasing impulse towards *networks* of objects in order to seduce it and elicit, in accordance with its own logic, a maximal investment, reaching the limits of economic potential. Clothing, appliances, and toiletries thus constitute object *paths*, which establish inertial constraints on the consumer who will proceed *logically* from one object to the next. The consumer will be caught up in a *calculus* of objects, which is quite different from the frenzy of purchasing and possession which arises form the simple profusion of commodities. (1988b, 31; italics in original)

In a sense, we may consider objects as conspiring with one another within a system of signifiers. It is this totality of objects in a perpetual play of difference that now constitutes the functional compatibility of individuals and objects.

Consumption choices often "position" the consumer into buying "ensembles" from the same brand so as to maintain compatibility. In some cases, functional compatibility predetermines future purchases: Only the same company supplies the required item that will complete the ensemble. Other tactics may be built-in obsolescence or false, merely cosmetic, improvements. Consumer needs are atomized, disciplined, and specified to the most minute detail. At this level of decisionmaking, choices are structured like a flowchart where every subsequent decision is already anticipated by the code of consumption. More important, Baudrillard's critique implies a change in social relations. Just as objects become unambiguous in their functional compatibility, subject relations become overwhelmingly functional. That is, people with similar object possessions may limit their interactions to those with people who own similar objects. In this manner, objects dictate the horizon of relations among people. A change in object relations mirrors a corresponding effect in subject relations.

Baudrillard's singular contribution to Marxist discourse is the ingenious way he links the code of consumption to the capitalist mode of production. Consumption and production are intricately linked, with consumption linked to discourse and production linked to ideology. Consumption extends the productive forces to invade spheres of life previously thought to be outside of human labor. The code of consumption encroaches on social life at the level of the quotidian. Though the concepts of consumption and production can be discerned as separate processes, they result in a singular ideological effect when considered together: capitalist domination. Baudrillard writes: "It can all be explained only if we acknowledge that needs and consumption are in fact an *organized extension of productive forces. . . .* The truth about consumption is that it is *a function of production*" (1988b, 43–46; italics in original). Consumption represents the social cognate of production and could also be considered as defining a social logic that organizes and controls everyday life. To mimic Steven Best's phrase (1994), Baudrillard's model reflects the consumption of reality and the reality of consumption.

According to Baudrillard, signifiers are not used, as Marxists claim, to manipulate the masses into consuming objects they do not want. The objects of consumption are the signifiers themselves, signifiers structured into a code. The revolution is *not* about resisting and transforming the social relations of production but about unsettling the code through the creation of new forms of symbolic exchange and systems of signs. Commodities are not only material objects; they are also social signifiers. Signs may not be material, but they permit themselves to be conscripted through advanced capitalist media technologies in the service of manipulation and profit.

Despite the theoretical complexity evident in much of Baudrillard's writing, some problems arise in Baudrillard's model of consumption as a social activity. Baudrillard totalizes alienation to the point where consumers fail to discern that which is human and that which is commodity. The Marxist problematic of revolution becomes less of a possibility in a world where alienation is just a fact of everyday life, where the need to consume is virtually indistinguishable from the need for liberation. Baudrillard's work thus lacks the critical element of subjective agency or critical self-reflexivity in his theory of consumption (Kellner 1989, 18–19). Social classes are seen as classes-in-themselves and not classes-for-themselves. Baudrillard highlights few, if any, forms of resistance to consumption. Instead, the portrait we receive is one of an alienated imaginary. Yet does not the very fact that Baudrillard is writing a critique of consumer society point to possibilities of subverting the code even when using a commodified method, for example, writing a book to be sold?

Baudrillard advances a methodological trope dipped in a radical skepticism which argues that demystification as a counterdiscourse is actually a recuperative logic, a limit condition in which the critique itself serves as an accomplice of the object of criticism (Pefanis 1991, 70). Criticism of positive and negative versions of a discourse does not displace the centrality of the object of critique or a critical distance from that object. The process of demystification is itself a structural component of an entire hegemonic system of thought. According to Baudrillard's logic, even his own writing cannot be critical (Pefanis 1991, 71).

In a 1981 publication, *For a Critique of the Political Economy of the Sign*, Baudrillard casts his floating eye on the problematic of the object in capitalism. Using semiotic Marxist critique that is indebted to the project of Lukács, Baudrillard does an impressive job of introducing a new category to the Marxist notions of use and exchange value: sign value. He argues in a singularly impressive fashion that as consumerism evolves, complexifies, and becomes more abstract, objects begin to signify value as sign form rather than their enjoyment (use) or worth in the marketplace (exchange). Baudrillard explains: "They [objects] no longer 'designate' the world, but rather the being and social rank of their possessor. . . . It is certain that objects are the carriers of indexed social significations, of a social and cultural hierarchy . . . it is certain that they constitute a code" (1981, 32–37). Thus, it becomes more obvious that consumption represents a systematization of class differentiation and social classification. Objects in the home, for example, designate "*social membership*" and their manipulation as the "social tactic of individuals" (1981, 35–36; italics in original).

Usurping the foundations of Ferdinand de Saussure's linguistic semiotics, Baudrillard strips the signifier (linguistic term) from the signified (intended meaning) and the referent (object) as a means of exposing consumption structured at the level of language. Baudrillard unpacks the culture of consumption as an activity in which individuals consume objects for their symbolic value. Objects signify their value through a linguistic structure rather than a practical one. It is here that consumers participate in a "conspicuous consumption" or inconspicuous consumption (underconsumption) of goods for their labels and brands, thereby displaying their prestation (Baudrillard 1981, 30).[1] In an introduction to Roland Barthes' ideas about the object in society, Mike Gane summarizes:

> The problem of understanding the significance of objects is thus one of establishing function, of meaning; or, in other words, there is in the object a struggle between function and a meaning which "renders it intransitive, assigns it a place in what might be called a tableau vivant of the human image-repertoire." And then there is a third element, a restoration of the sign to function, into the "spectacle of function" just as it is possible that a sign be transformed into an "unreal function" (e.g., a raincoat that could not function as such). (1991a, 36)

Barthes and Gane introduce the nonfunctionality of signs that are nevertheless meaningful or objects that operate at the level of sign value bereft of use value. In a similar vein, Best summarizes Marx and Debord's thoughts on the object. He writes,

Marx spoke of the degradation of *being into having*, where creative praxis is reduced to the mere possession of an object, rather than its imaginative transformation, and where emotions are reduced to greed. Debord speaks of a further reduction, the transformation of *having into appearing*, where the material object gives way to its representation as sign and draws "its immediate prestige and ultimate function" as image. The production of objects *simpliciter* gives way to "a growing multitude of image-objects" whose immediate reality is their symbolic function as image. Within this abstract system it is the *appearance* of the commodity that is more decisive [than] its actual "use-value." (1994, 48; italics in original)

In the current "time of the sign," image value confounds and camouflages use and exchange value. Appearance is said to supersede substance. The increasing separation of the social from the agent promulgated by late capitalism inflects the meaning of (as well as infects) social relations by promoting an ethics of distinction. This is accomplished through the abstract function of the sign and its displacement of the concrete. Symbolism usurps the reality principle and inaugurates the principle of abstraction.

Signaling one's social status by means of distinction is evident in consumer manipulation of object signs and their redundancy. In order to reiterate her status differentiation from other people, a consumer might emphasize, for instance, the placement of the television in a room, the furniture around it, and the protective accessories that shroud it (Best 1994, 54–56). As the object system dominates social life, objects become more central to human space. In this example, the television structures the human interactions revolving around it, thereby creating an ambience that extends subjectivity vis-à-vis the object. Later, the remote control becomes an extension of the human hand. Objects of consumption circulate like capital for the purpose of social distinction, much like the way language is structured around the social prestige of its signs (Kellner 1989, 21). What results is the simultaneous production of the commodity as sign and the sign as commodity (Baudrillard 1981, 147). Domination no longer resides primarily in the control of the means of production. Rather, domination can be attributed more to the control of the means of consumption. Moreover, this is accomplished at the level of the mode of signification (previously mode of production) in everyday life. In a similar fashion, Wolfgang Haug's (1971) concept of commodity aesthetics captures some of the insights about the commodity that Baudrillard tries to convey: Sensuality and aesthetics are employed in the act of consumption in order to stimulate desire and to reproduce the socioeconomic order that produces consumer culture.

A central concern of Baudrillard's work is the extension of Marx's concept of "commodity fetishism." According to Baudrillard, within the current capitalist mode of production, a diversified consumer system serves as an alibi for the productive forces that define capitalism's organizational structure: exploitation of labor and human depotentiation. Kellner explains: "Commodity fetishism thus projects values onto objects that are socially produced, mystifies them and fails to recognize their social-material underpinnings, just as in pre-capitalist societies individuals fetishized natural objects like trees or the moon as divine or supernatural, failing to see that they were simply products of nature" (1989, 22). Thus, commodity fetishism provides a diversion for the ideological production of things and their concomitant social relations. By endowing commodities with mystical powers, individuals or groups mystify the process of labor extraction in capitalism. But Baudrillard finds Marx's original formulation of commodity fetishism problematic:

> All of this presupposes the existence, somewhere, of a non-alienated consciousness of an object in some "true," objective state: its use value? . . . By referring all the problems of "fetishism" back to superstructural mechanisms of false consciousness, Marxism eliminates any real chance it has of analyzing the *actual process of ideological labor.* By refusing to analyze the structures and the mode of ideological production inherent in its own logic, Marxism is condemned (behind the facade of "dialectical" discourse in terms of class struggle) to expanding the reproduction of ideology, and thus of the capitalist system itself. (1981, 89–90; italics in original)

Baudrillard advises:

> The term "fetishism" almost has a life of its own. Instead of functioning as a metalanguage for the magical thinking of others, it turns against those who use it, and surreptitiously exposes their own magical thinking. . . . We would have to abandon the fetishist metaphor of the worship of the golden calf . . . and develop instead an articulation that avoids any projection of magical or transcendental animism, and thus the rationalist position of positing a false consciousness and a transcendental subject. (1981, 90)

Baudrillard turns the concept of fetishism against itself and some of its uncritical proponents. He suggests that Marxism's unquestioning acceptance of the concept of labor fetishizes it as a nonideological process and prevents Marxists from reflecting on their own analysis and revealing it, too, to be ideological work. In this way Marxism is complicit in reproducing commodities at the level of ideology and discourse: theory as labor.

Baudrillard has managed to distinguish four different logics, those of practical operations (utility; use value); equivalence (the market; exchange value); ambivalence (the gift; symbolic exchange); and difference (status; sign value). He uses these logics to make the claim that irreducible primary needs do not govern human behavior but have been replaced by lifestyle and values. Within Baudrillard's fourth order of differences, "the fractal" serves as a metaphorical extension of Benoit Mandelbrot's geometry of fractals. This fourth order, which Baudrillard refers to as the period "after the orgy," is vaguely posthistorical. It further consists of a hyperrealization of former utopias whose value has been completely fractalized and that now occupies the site of the irradiation of all value, the complete absence of reference and the absolute and total victory of metonymy.

In his more poststructuralist critique of the subject as the disintegrated knower, Baudrillard claims that all consciousness (the object included) is alienated in a capitalist mode of production. Achieving subjecthood in capitalism is meaningless for Baudrillard if subjects do not question the "actual process of ideological labor." We eventually see Baudrillard's growing disenchantment with Marxism transforming itself into a posture of condemnation; Marxism is irrevocably trapped in the snares of its own productive logic. By the end of *For a Critique of the Political Economy of the Sign*, Baudrillard is shown seeking an alternative to production in symbolic exchange, a concept he takes up more fully in following books. There is also a glimmer of what will become throughout his career a prolific engagement with issues involving the media and theories of communication.

For Baudrillard, what produces the real is a sign effect, or the effect of many signs in collision. Referents, therefore, serve merely as alibis and do not exist as real states. Referents are simulations that partake of the mutations of the law of value. The transformation of the commodity into the sign is, for Baudrillard, "the secret destiny of capital in the twentieth century" (Kroker and Cook 1986, 121). In fact, Baudrillard claims that the roots of nihilism exist within acts of consumption. This is clear in his disclosure that "the theory of the sign was the *morphology* of the double-metamorphosis of capital, and thus the structural genesis of the 'magic' and 'alchemy' of the fetishism of the commodity" (Kroker and Cook 1986, 121; italics in original).

Baudrillard's blustery rewriting of Marxian theories of production and the politics of exchange revolutionizes and propels Marxist analysis into the realm of the social semiotic. The insight is as provocative as it is unsettling: Value at the level of the sign is constructing agency through the production of subjectivity. Nevertheless, some limitations in Baudrillard's model have been pointed out by several key authors. While generally accepting the thesis of the "political economy of the sign," Mark Gottdiener criticizes Baudrillard's semiurgical model (proliferation of signs) for underplaying the persistence of use and exchange value. In short, Gottdiener argues that sign value is the latest child of capitalism in the conditions of postmodernity (1994, 37). In addition, the model Baudrillard puts forth underplays the possibility of consumption as a mode of self-valorization. Baudrillard sees consumption as an instrument of capitalist domination that obscures the way consumers purchase goods for their enjoyment and utility. Further, Michel de Certeau considers the phenomenon of people "borrowing" (euphemism for stealing) items from work as a form of resistance to the code of consumption (Kellner 1989, 28). This is not mainly a question of morality but one of coping with the exploitation of human labor. Some workers even intervene between sales and the market by stealing products from work and selling them to buyers for a fraction of their market price, thereby subverting an otherwise "smooth" system, or the capitalist imaginary that Baudrillard describes. Furthermore, use value still has great implications for certain people who only buy "what they need, not what they want." Although Baudrillard's semiotic thesis would proclaim that this merely designates their social difference, buying only what you need suggests to us the persistence of utility and necessity. And finally, poor people who cannot "keep up with the Joneses" sometimes practice the cultural politics of wearing hand-me-downs. To avoid consumption, some people keep their old clothes and knickknacks and hand down these items to family members and friends as a way to save them money.

John Fiske offers another interpretation of consumption as a productive activity. According to Fiske, consumption serves as an outlet for the need to create some meaning out of everyday life and is never merely an obligatory act in the service of the dominant ideology. Though these acts alone are not sufficiently radical, they nevertheless are progressive, oppositional, and rarely unconscious (Cook 1994, 155). Tania Modleski considers Fiske's position (which resonates with some of the positions held by some members of the Frankfurt School) woefully flawed because the capitalist logic that suggests that everyone can take part in consumption, that meaning-making through consumption is anticipated by the culture industry, is really just an ideological mystification produced by the culture industry itself (Cook 1994, 157). Modleski undermines the idea that subjects can seize and appropriate the cracks and fractures in "the cultural logic of late capitalism" (Jameson 1993). Fiske's positivity recognizes the shimmers of agency that offer hope for social transformation in the face of anomie. Nevertheless, Modleski brings us full circle to Baudrillard's problematic. To what extent does making the code more tolerable actually transform social life? Does everyday resistance serve only to postpone cultural revolution and to reproduce the dominant systems of intelligibility and social relations of power and privilege? Bradley Macdonald (1995) has made a similar observation with respect to the situationists' use of *détournement*. While the situationists argued that *détournement* reworked the spectacle so as to escape the prison house of the spectacle itself, disarticulating a part of the hegemonic process as a move toward the creation of "free spaces" for the development of new needs and desires, Macdonald argues that "the spectacle has been able to use *détournement*-like techniques to reinforce itself" (1995, 107; italics in original).

The Mirror of Production (1975) continues Baudrillard's engagement with Marxism. More important, it signals his point of departure from Marxist political economy and its economistic, workeristic, and classical conceptions. Baudrillard charges that rather than displacing production, Marx actually replaces one mode of production with another. Marx, therefore, limits the radical direction of his own critique by naturalizing the concept of production. In effect he simply "mirrors" capitalism with socialism. Just as Marx prophesied the demise of capitalism, Baudrillard predicts that production itself must be "burst asunder." The problem, in this case, is not the mode of production but rather the code of production. Baudrillard's eerie description begins like this:

> A specter haunts the revolutionary imagination: the phantom of production. Everywhere it sustains an unbridled romanticism of productivity. The critical theory of the *mode* of production does not touch the *principle* of production. All the concepts it articulates describe only the dialectical and historical genealogy of the *contents* of production, leaving production as a *form* intact. (Baudrillard 1975, 17; italics in original)

Baudrillard's revealing analysis left many social theorists openmouthed because he uncoiled such a seemingly simple and accepted notion, one that had become second nature and common sense to most Marxists. Ideologically encrypted in Marxian discourse, production now appears naked and vulnerable. Previously assumed to be a crucial element that separated humans from animals, productivity, as defined in the Marxian lexicon, is now assailed as an oversimplification blushing like a child caught after years of telling stories: "It is the concept of production, then, which is submitted to a radical critique" (Baudrillard 1975,23).

In perhaps his most didactic prose, Baudrillard painstakingly scrutinizes what he perceives as concepts embedded in the ideology of production. The first of these concepts is the law of value. Baudrillard observes, "Failing to conceive of a mode of social wealth other than that founded on labor and production, Marxism no longer furnishes in the long run a real alternative to capitalism. Assuming the generic schema of production and needs involves an incredible simplification of social exchange by the law of value" (1975, 29). By reducing social life and relations to a calculus of value, Marxism fails to subvert the notion that humans do not have to be constituted through the determinacy of the law of value. Instead, people can enjoy the ambiguity of symbolic exchange that destroys value as its opposite other.

Another important Marxian concept that comes under fierce interrogation is that of work or labor. Baudrillard argues that by reducing human fulfillment to labor, Marx forgoes the idea that people may find their potential in other nonproductive endeavors, like communication, a position that echoes other critics of Marx such as Jürgen Habermas (Kellner 1989, 41; see also Poster 1994). Baudrillard advances the idea that in his well-known idealization of the work ethic, Marx makes the error of differentiating between alienated labor and authentic labor. In fact, Baudrillard asserts: "*In this Marxism assists the cunning of capital. It convinces men that they are alienated by the sale of their labor power, thus censoring the much more radical hypothesis that they might be alienated as labor power, as the 'inalienable' power of creating value by their labor*" (1975, 31; italics in original). Baudrillard asserts that labor is a term specifically born under the sign of production. As such, all labor power, whether in a capitalist or socialist economy, is always already alienated. He writes: "With German workers the old Protestant ethic of work celebrated, in a secular form, its resurrection. Marxism would be that between a religion of the masses and a philosophical theory—not a great deal of difference" (1975, 36). Baudrillard suggests that with production as the doctrine, the opiate of labor can ensure that the proletariat keeps the cogs of political economy turning. Even nonwork is easily co-opted by the code of production as the negation of work, its "repressive desublimation," serving as its mirror. The revolutionary subject no longer resides in the worker but in those out-of-work wretched of the earth who are even more alienated than workers themselves. In short, people want work. The radical impetus is to come from elsewhere: in students, people of color, and women (Baudrillard 1975, 134). To Baudrillard, labor is no longer axiomatic; its finality has been challenged.

At this point, Baudrillard's target is Marx's apparent overreliance on work. Despite its trenchant analysis of labor, Baudrillard's critique does not explain why certain forms of work appear more alienating than others. For example, workers who are accorded more autonomy on the job usually do not react so negatively to their labor. It is not uncommon that these particular workers take their work home with them. If necessary, they work during their off days (usually weekends) without pay or pecuniary benefits. In contrast, workers with less control over their jobs and who are alienated from human interaction often resist working without pay. In addition, there is a radical separation between workdays and nonworkdays, where nonworkdays become totally associated with leisure or relaxation. In other words, work stops outside of the workplace. There may even be a strong aversion to any mention of work or its associations. The progression we are suggesting here is that the more alienating the job, the greater its separation from the autonomy of non-work time. With more control of the labor process, work and everyday life become more congruent. As it is, most workers lacking control over their labor look forward to retirement.

Due to the currently authoritarian, teacher-centered curriculum, many students in U.S. schools resist the very notion of work. They detest classwork, group work, library work, and homework. In Jean Anyon's 1980 study of five elementary schools she finds that students trained for the "capitalist class" practice more self-reliance, are given assignments that challenge creativity, and are in classes that are more intellectually stimulating. Their counterparts, students trained for the "working class," practice more procedural drills, are taught to focus on mechanics of learning ("getting it right"), and, as a result, struggle against having to do "work." She suggests that not only does "schooling in capitalist America" (Bowles and Gintis 1976) prepare students for different relationships with work, differential amounts of control over student work reflect a similar curve of fulfillment regarding the work itself. Paulo Freire reminds us that "work that is not free ceases to be a fulfilling pursuit and becomes an effective means of dehumanization" (1994, 126). Baudrillard does not account for this gradation of difference among vocations and the element of alienation.

Nor does Baudrillard sufficiently address the distinction between labor and work. While Marx sees the primacy of labor as the means to humanize nature and naturalize humanity, Hannah Arendt marks a distinction between labor and work (Aronowitz and DiFazio 1994). Work is a reified activity that has an objective existence independent of the needs of the producer or consumer. While both labor and consumption function to reproduce labor power and are necessary human activities, work, on the contrary, extends beyond the reproductive function of labor and consumption and consists of the fusion of thought and deed; work is a political activity that potentially constitutes freedom. Today, work relations have been destroyed by regimes of production and consumption, and work regrettably has collapsed into labor. Baudrillard's thesis converges on Arendt's idea that workers are now subordinated to their machines. Political relations once associated with work are now commodities bought and sold in the marketplace (Aronowitz and DiFazio 1994). An analysis of deterritorialized capital reproduction under the sign of Jeremy Bentham's panopticon has led Aronowitz and DiFazio to the importance of human agency in a postwork (reduction of working hours) society accompanied by new social movements. Baudrillard is less optimistic about the role of human agency in the pursuit of freedom in a world where the agent no longer exists.

In a reflexive move, Baudrillard charges that Marx's anthropology is caught in its own Western epistemological snares. In fact, this accounts for the terrorism that Marxist ethnographers impose on non-Western subjects. According to Baudrillard, there exist no modes and relations of production, no scarcity, and no surplus in primitive societies. These are all categories associated with political economy. The uncritical employment and universalization of these concepts by Marxist anthropologists lead to forms of imperialist violence directed at symbolic societies. Baudrillard singles out for criticism Godelier's work on kinship societies, especially his submission to the principles of production. Baudrillard's disgust is evident:

> There are no producers; there are no "means of production" and no objective labor, controlled or not. There are no needs and no satisfactions that orient them: this is the old illusion of subsistence economy! . . . Subsistence plus surplus: only the presupposition of production permits this quantitative reduction to additional functions *neither of which* makes sense in primitive exchange. . . . These acrobatics of the reduction of factors and the remixing "in the dominant" is only conceptual violence. We now know that it is even more destructive than missionaries or venereal disease. (1975, 74–77; italics in original)

Baudrillard criticizes the anthropology of Godelier and Marx, maintaining they lack awareness of the epistemological premises of their work. In other words, historical materialism is historical. According to Baudrillard, primitive societies espouse no productive concepts and only "produce" to the point of reciprocal or symbolic exchange, a thesis Baudrillard is opposing to production. Surplus is limited because it institutes uneven power relations by breaking the equilibrious bond of reciprocity. We see here some evidence of the general trend of critically assaulting the Western worldview, a trend that was becoming prevalent at the time *The Mirror of Production* was written. Baudrillard indicts: "The limits of this culture 'critique' are clear: its reflection on itself leads only to the universalization of its own principles" (1975, 89). It reflects a certain "*ethnocentrism of the code*" (107; italics in original). Just as oppressors themselves are not free when oppressing another, a society mistaken about itself is likewise in bondage.

For Baudrillard, symbolic exchange becomes most important as a point of departure from the deadweight of political economy. The problem of domination is not merely an objectification of the dominated but an exchange that always involves a violation of reciprocity. The gift requires a countergift in order to cancel it and preserve equilibrium. Likewise, production is not only a process of producing something but one of destroying something else (Baudrillard 1975, 95–99). Production entails destruction, purity is always stained, cleansing always gives birth to a new virus.

Baudrillard critically appropriates his ideas about the gift from Marcel Mauss, later to be systematized by Georges Bataille in a theory of symbolic exchange. In a study of Polynesian and Melanesian primitive societies, Mauss writes:

> Many ideas and principles are to be noted in systems of this type. The most important of these spiritual mechanisms is clearly the one which obliges us to make a return gift for a gift received. . . . To refuse to give is . . . the equivalent of a declaration of war. . . . No one was free to refuse a present offered to him. Each man and woman tried to outdo the others in generosity. There was a sort of amiable rivalry as to who could give away the greatest number of most valuable presents. . . . The objects are never completely separated from the men who exchange them. . . . Failure to give or receive, like failure to make return gifts, means a loss of dignity. (1967, 5–40)

Furthermore, these gifts are considered by the people as "animate things" and include the power and the spirits of their giver. Later, Bataille appropriates some of the key ideas of Mauss and creates what he calls a "general (or solar) economy" (as opposed to political) modeled after the sun and its unwavering gift of energy. Bataille bases his economy on "visions of excess," on the idea that humans are inclined to waste, expend, and destroy—a model honoring the potlatch that Mauss constructs after witnessing symbolic changes in the Polynesian and Melanesian islands (Kellner 1989,42).

Bataille's interpretation of the potlatch made a profound impression on Baudrillard, since it signaled for Baudrillard a deep level of reciprocal relations that went beyond the structuralist conception of economic determinism. He links this deep order of reciprocal symbolic exchange to archaic and primitive notions and practices, eventually embracing a symbolic Freud and radicalizing his notion of the death drive, which he turns against the whole interpretive machinery of psychoanalysis (Pefanis 1991). Baudrillard discovers an antieconomic principle of exchange in Bataille's concept of the order of death and its signifying chain: excess, ambivalence, gift, sacrifice, and paroxysm (Pefanis 1991, 113).

As Baudrillard picks up more speed in his critique of Marxist doctrine, he becomes more dismissive of its potential as radical alterity. His ideas assume a more apocalyptic tone as he portentously announces the end of certain Marxist categories such as labor, value, and productivity. In what could be considered a pataphysical move, Baudrillard abandons Marxism in search of noncasual epiphenomena and hysterical power. He considers the masses to have blocked the economy by setting sign value against use value in a hypersimulation of sign value amounting to a pathological manipulation of the differential relations of the sign system (Genosko 1994, 10). Kellner considers this "broadside attack and dismissal of Marxism *tout court* unfair and unwarranted" (1989, 53). In a meticulous reading of Baudrillard, Kellner observes that Baudrillard's attempt to eliminate competing theories assumes a mode of writing complicitous with the imperatives of a capitalist mode of intelligibility. Baudrillard's pronouncement of the end of political economy does not seem to have sufficient empirical backing. Capital's ability to reproduce itself, circulate, and create new spaces on a global scale contradicts the thesis that capital is on its last leg. In fact, its nucleation throughout the globe has increased through dramatic post-Fordist shifts in late capitalist production and consumption. The gap between the rich and poor in the United States is widening significantly and can be attributed in part to the relation of individuals to the means of production: in late capitalism, finance capital.

Maurice Zeitlin (1989, 145–147) argues that the U.S. capitalist class continues to maintain its financial domination over the country. He reports that as of 1983, the richest 0.5 percent of all U.S. families, or the "super rich," own 15.3 percent of the net value of all real estate (and 35.6 percent of the commercial real estate), 46.5 percent of the value of all corporate stock, and 77.0 percent of the value of the trust assets owned by all families. The second half of the richest 1 percent, or the "very rich," own another 4.2 percent of all real estate (and 6.5 percent of the commercial real estate), 13.5 percent of the corporate stock, and 5.0 percent of the trust assets. This means that the richest 1 percent of families own over two-fifths of the net wealth of all families in the United States. With respect to unearned income (property income, dividends, capital gains, interest, rent, etc.), or what we will call "nonwork," people in 1979 with an adjusted gross income (AGI) of $20,000–$25,000 earned about 90 cents of every dollar, whereas those with an AGI of over $1 million earned only 14 cents for every dollar they made. This suggests that control of the means of production is not an obsolete notion. Capital is still king. And since America's top 1 percent live in affluent neighborhoods, their high property taxes ensure that their children will attend schools with the most funds and resources, not to mention the cultural network with which they will associate and the cultural capital they will accumulate. Zeitlin's findings—as well as the writings of Noam Chomsky and others—suggest that work or how we construct pecuniary worth through labor remains as viable today as it has been in the past as a site of struggle for emancipation and social justice. In addition, Zeitlin contributes to the deconstruction of the myth that poor people are shiftless and lazy. Baudrillard's wholesale rejection of Marxism substantively weakens what is an otherwise often scintillating problematization of Marxist accounts of production.

In Baudrillard's search for an alternative radical position to Marxism, his turn to symbolic exchange produces *Simulations* (1983a) and "Symbolic Exchange and Death" (1988c). In a creative move, Baudrillard outlines a genealogy of three orders of the simulacrum, no doubt influenced by Michel Foucault's *Order of Things* (Kellner 1989, 78) and the writings of Marshal McLuhan. Baudrillard parallels the evolution of the simulacra with that of the law of value. He writes:

- *Counterfeit* is the dominant scheme of the "classical" period, from the Renaissance to the industrial revolution.
- *Production* is the dominant scheme of the industrial era.
- *Simulation* is the reigning scheme of the current phase that is controlled by the code.

   The first order play of simulacrum is based on the natural law of value, that of the second order on the commercial law of value, and that of the third order on the structural law of value. (1983a, 83; italics in original)

Before the counterfeit era, the obliged signifier always referred to its destined signified. The sign remained unambiguous in a caste, or "cruel," society. No peasant could walk around in clothing properly designated for aristocrats. Fashion was nonexistent or heavily restricted. However, during the Renaissance the counterfeit product emancipated the obliged sign. A person could transcend class status to a limited degree by assuming signs of another class. People accomplished this through a "natural" logic of appearance grounded by the real. During the industrial revolution, mass production further emancipated the sign by producing an almost unlimited amount of copies of an original. The "series" was born under the law of equivalence. An object's existence became indebted to its very reproducibility. Labor power itself followed this same logic of producing the equivalent amount of social labor for the series (Baudrillard 1983a, 84–86).

In the current historical conjuncture, which Baudrillard refers to as the era of "simulation," the demarcation between the copy and its original implodes. In fact, "the very definition of the real becomes: *that of which it is possible to give an equivalent production*. . . . At the limit of this process of reproducibility, the real is not only what can be reproduced, but *that which is always already reproduced*. The hyperreal" (Baudrillard 1983a, 146–147; italics in original). The code has not only been realized in its full terror, it has been hyperrealized. Like the DNA double helix, reproduction is doubly simulated to perfection. Value is accomplished at the structural play of the code as an ideal combinatory model. In Baudrillard's growing affinity for the "weak theory" of Nietzsche, he cites the German nihilist: "Down with all hypotheses that have allowed the belief in a true world" (Baudrillard 1983a, 115). All subjective attempts to capture the real and its companion, the truth, have dissolved into the simulation of the real and the truth. We are left with only the detritus of reality.

In another apocalyptical announcement, Baudrillard declares:

> This is the end of labor, the end of production, and the end of political economy.
>
> This is the end of the signifier-signified dialectic that permitted the accumulation of knowledge and meaning, the linear syntagm of cumulative discourse. Simultaneously, this is the end of the use of use value–exchange value dialectic, that which made social accumulation and production possible; the end of the linear dimension of discourse and commodities; the end of the classical era of the sign; and the end of the era of production. (1988c, 127–128)

Effects outrun their causes in the age of the death of linearity and history, an epoch where the model enables the map to generate the territory (Baudrillard 1983a, 2). In the age of simulation, the reality principle no longer exists— thus the end of the real and its rugged and hirsute companion, Marxism. The code is complete and engulfs any resistance to it. The alternative is that which is reversible, the indeterminate.

The reproduction of objects is primary in Baudrillard's thesis. The origin of things is not an original but a code—a formulae—so that now complete reversibility is possible and even death ceases to be real. It is now the era of complete relativity, of floating signifiers unable to cling to anything real and of the inauguration of simulacra. Everything is undecidable, as the code thrillingly neutralizes all values. "Signs are ablaze" (Genosko 1994) and terrorize social life. Labor becomes a sign among signs. Labor's product no longer maintains any correlation with the actual work that goes into producing it. Rather, the type of labor a person does distinguishes her from other laborers as pure sign. There are no means of production, since there are no ends of production (Baudrillard 1988c, 133). The sign-object is a fusion of both economic exchange and symbolic exchange in which sign exchange is based on the semiological system's differential values—the code. The code affixes individuals on a register of status. The sign-object signifies a reified relationship between individuals and the index of social status based on a commutable code (Pefanis 1991). According to Baudrillard, we have moved beyond the political economy of Marx, the disciplinary strategies of Foucault, and Debord's society of the spectacle. We are now experiencing a world where the medium of the message has been transfigured into the aperture of the real. The real and the real-seeming are the same:

> We are witnessing the end of perspectival and panoptic space (which remains a moral hypothesis bound up with all the classical analyses on the "objective" essence of power) and thus the *very abolition of the spectacular*.

Television, for example, in the case of the Louds, is no longer a spectacular medium. We are no longer in the society of the spectacle, of which the situationists spoke, or in the specific kinds of alienation and repression that it implied. The medium itself is no longer identifiable as such, and the confusion of the medium and the message (McLuhan) is the first great formula of this new era. There is no longer a medium in the literal sense: it is now intangible, diffused and diffracted in the real, and one can no longer even say that the medium is altered by it. (Baudrillard 1994, 30; italics in original)

In schools, grades do not designate any direct correlation with skill or intellect, but remain, like labor, signs or, better yet, simulations of status. Like labor, grades lie dead in the belly of the code. They remain forever ablaze; even their labyrinthine travels through the digestive system and their evacuation from the anus of the socius do little to dim their glimmering and resplendent fecalicity. In a similar manner death becomes transfigured into a sublime orgasm, a semiotic bravura. In Baudrillard's universe of satellitized subjectivity, agency has been imploded along with the social. Kroker and Cook note:

With Baudrillard, political theory begins with a refusal of the privileged position of the *historical subject*, and with an immediate negation of the question of historical emancipation itself. Baudrillard's is not the *sociological* perspective of disciplinary power in a normalizing society (Foucault) nor the *hermeneutical* interpretation of science and technology as "glassy, background ideology" (Habermas). In his theorisation there is no purely perspectival space of the "panoptic" (*Oublier Foucault*) nor free zone of "universal pragmatics." Baudrillard's political analysis represents a radical departure from both the sociology of knowledge and theorisations of power/norm because his thought explores the brutal processes of dehistoricisation and desocialisation which structure the new communicative order of a signifying culture. (1986, 185; italics in original)

Baudrillard's model offers some light on school tests and exams. He writes, "The entire system of communication has passed from that of a syntactically complex language structure to a binary sign system of question/answer—of perpetual *test*. Now tests and referenda are, we know, perfect forms of simulation: the answer is called forth by the question, it is design-ated in advance" (1983a, 116–117; italics in original). Thus, school testing communicates very little outside of the code's circuit of general terrorism. The educational system applies tests if only to simulate that students have learned something real, that something valuable and meaningful has been communicated to them. In actuality, however, tests only testify to the death of facts; nothing, therefore, needs to be communicated as such. As criticalists have observed, tests serve only to point out the general failure of the whole educational system to provide students with a meaningful educational experience. Testing is more of an instrument to simulate control, a control that is empty because power is now dead (Freire 1994; Giroux 1993; McLaren 1995).

At this point in his engagement with poststructuralism, Baudrillard turns his cultural critique toward a dizzying perspective where aleatory forces dominate over "social" (this is dead, too) life. We couldn't help feeling slightly inebriated as we read Baudrillard's books from this period. Perhaps it would help to read them in conjunction with a viewing of Oliver Stone's movie about Jim Morrison's 1960s group, the Doors, our having felt "stoned" after watching it. Both texts in different ways explore the possibilities of semiotic overload and excess. At this point, we wish to indulge in several brief commentaries. One, Baudrillard's semiological idealism seems to lead him to a certain form of sign fetishism (Kellner 1989, 62, 100). Second, he uncritically underplays the role of manipulation in the media by suggesting that we are somehow beyond the "society of spectacle" and that the masses want only spectacle (Best 1994). As such, Baudrillard's model lacks the "power" to deconstruct political interests and their sources. Baudrillard leaves control of social processes in the hands of a mystified and disembodied nonentity. By leaving out the actors and architects of policies and control of political discourse, Baudrillard cannot hold particular groups of people accountable for their actions. Meanwhile, Ronald Reagan, Pete Wilson, and Newt Gingrich have a field day. On this point, we prefer Edward Herman and Noam Chomsky's manipulation theory, wherein they expose the media's corporate filters and analyze how the media "manufactures consent" (1993). If we use a framework that takes into consideration social relations and agents and their interests, school "dropouts" may be more accurately perceived as "push outs" (Fine 1991).

Third, although the masses' silence, as Baudrillard explains in *In the Shadow of the Silent Majorities* (1983b), may be read as their vengeful refusal to participate in or vote on the positions being offered, it can be interpreted as the general alienation of a mass of people from the political (due) process in the interest of the few. And such motivated neglect, of which the masses are certainly and unavoidably complicitous, has real consequences: lack of control over decisions that affect the direction of people's lives. This is not to suggest a homogeneous oppressive class (the elite) and a monolithic oppressed class (the masses). Issues of race, class, gender, and culture interlock the indices of privilege and disenfranchisement. Last, Baudrillard leaves little in the way of a productive ground from which to develop agential solidarity and a praxis of social transformation. In a vertiginous world where people are hyperindividuated, Baudrillard articulates little hope for political projects outside of the limited tactical advantage of hyperconformity. At most, we can look forward to the perpetual spiral of simulations. Meanwhile, suffering and pain continue. Marx's concept of use value may have been idealistic, but Baudrillard's reterritorialization of the term as "an ideological guarantee of exchange value," as "abstract social labor" and as the inscription of utility at the heart of the object (Pefanis 1991, 74), is theoretical hyperbole at its most brazen and political paranoia at its most obscene. We are less concerned about false needs and consumer engineering than we are with people acquiring a roof over their heads and three square meals a day. Reality can be transformed in Baudrillard's universe to the "aleatory mutations of the indeterminacy principle" (Pefanis 1991, 80), but those who are constituted by the regime of signs still suffer from their effects even if such effects have no truth referent in reality.

The metaphysical turn in Baudrillard's writing is clearly the dominant trope that he will maintain from here on. Not as didactic as his previous works, this period's production concentrates more on defacing conventional discourse. Baudrillard relies more heavily on the poetics of language and an elliptical writing style and less on systematic or rigorous analysis. Having announced the death of multiple key concepts (labor is no longer axiomatic, in political economy the real has been absorbed into the hyperreal, the social has lost its specificity, etc.), Baudrillard continues his search for a transgressive theory of cyberculture.

In another book from this period, Baudrillard's victims are psychoanalysis and feminism. In *Seduction* (1979), Baudrillard destabilizes the sign through reversibility and unsettles the concept of opposition as the basis of meaning. Seduction is introduced as a practice "based on the attraction of the void—presence which hides absence" (Tseelon 1994, 126). For instance, seduction "substitutes an *appearance* of democracy for *absence* of real social change"; it exists "where *an attempt for meaning* . . . masks *a meaning void*" (126). In *Seduction*, Baudrillard charges that psychoanalysis is the psychological cognate of production. Obsessed with the production of latent meanings in sexual discourse, psychoanalysis follows its sibling with a political economy of the body. According to Baudrillard, Freudian psychoanalysis has assumed too much influence, its libidinal economy gaining finality status. And its descendants in Luce Irigaray and others have made destiny out of anatomy. As a theory of appearances, seduction challenges the anatomical depth of psychoanalysis (Baudrillard 1979, 9). Emphasizing passion and gaming, seduction ruptures Freud's value-driven desire, "the body as the material infrastructure of desire" (34). One does not have far to look to find "energy" advanced as a mode of production of the unconscious and "pleasure" as either a saving or surplus (Gane 1991a, 116). The circulation of desire is a mimesis of the circulation of capital.

Baudrillard claims that Freud's story is only that, a story. Baudrillard posits the opposite story, that women have been dominant this whole time. Sexual repression, fear of castration, and penis envy have all been instituted by men to control women's power, their reversibility. Ironically, men have created their own solution to this problematic through sexual liberation and the male as the harbinger of this revolution. But Baudrillard maintains that women were never oppressed or alienated. This is a male story (Baudrillard 1979, 15–20). Sexuality is masculinity's narrative, seduction femininity's game. However, femininity must not be confused with the correspondence in sexuality between the feminine and a particular sex. Rather, Baudrillard uses "feminine" to signify the "transversal" form of sex, an indeterminate sex (Gane 1991a, 149). Baudrillard admits that women "being closer to this other, hidden mirror (with which they shroud their image and body) are also closer to the effects of seduction. Men, by contrast, have depth, but no secrets; hence their power and fragility" (1979, 68). Offering seduction as the (destructive) alternative to production, Baudrillard announces yet another set of deaths: meaning, sexuality, and hence, sexism. Feminist theory's problem all along has been its overemphasis on sexual oppression. With the death of the sexual, sexism also will perish.

As a play and challenge to the artifice, seduction welcomes the sexual objectification of women. Baudrillard explains:

> Our entire morality condemns the construction of the female as a sex object by the facial and bodily arts. . . . In opposition to all these pious discourses, we must again praise the sex object; for it bears, in the sophistication of appearances, something of a challenge to the naive order of the world and sex; and it, and it alone, escapes the realm of production (though one might like to believe it subjected to the latter) and returns to that of seduction. . . . The feminine was always the effigy of this ritual, and there is a frightful confusion in wanting to de-sanctify it as a cult *object* in order to turn it into a *subject* of production, or in wanting to rescue it from artifice in order to return it to its own "natural" desires. (1979, 92; italics in original)

In opposition to most feminist theories, Baudrillard suggests that the discourse on women's subjecthood be debunked as another male attempt to institute power over women. With power being everywhere, this only signals that it is nowhere. That is, in response to Foucault, power's ubiquity is its own death (Baudrillard 1987). Only objects are seductive through their play on literalness and surface; subjects are productive in their irreversible metaphoricity and depth. Objects consume in an extreme sense (consummation), whereas subjects create surplus we call meaning (Gane 1991a, 118).

Once again, Baudrillard advances his search for the pure object. The objectification of women's bodies as sex objects implicates, among other things, pornographic activity. Gane clarifies: "It is not sexuality on display in pornography, as many think; it is the absorption of reality into hyper-reality. This accounts for so-called voyeurism; it is precisely the break-down of the sexual scene and the eruption of the obscene. The sexual appears so close to the subject that it confounds itself. It is the end of illusion and the end of imagination" (1991a, 152). To Baudrillard, pornography is sex that is more than sex: hypersex. There is no need to imagine anything; it is all there for you to see, right down to the pores on the skin. It is the "more visible than the visible—this is the obscene" (Baudrillard 1990a, 55). Pornography is seductive, has nothing to do with desire, and should be objectified. Psychoanalysis started the Big Bang that instituted sexuality. It has since imploded, or reversed itself into the Big Squeeze. Sexuality has collapsed under its own gravity, unable to supply the "energy" it needed to survive. Seduction is the void that remains because, as Anthony Wilden might suggest, it is "a dissent of a higher logical type than that to which it is opposed" (Baudrillard 1988c, 122).

Like symbolic exchange, seduction is a form of gift. One seduces in order to be seduced. One is seduced and is obliged to seduce in return. Seduction is the willingness to perpetuate the game and its stakes to maximal intensity. The pervert is the one who tries to fix the game and stabilize it under a law in order to render it predictable and irreversible. Seduction works by rules and ruses that remain unspoken (Baudrillard 1979, 127). Baudrillard clarifies that games are not centered on contingency but on obligations and seduction (1979, 143). Though seduction is the absence of predictability, it maintains a patterned randomness (1979, 138), much like Mandelbrot's "chaos theory." The only people oppressed and repressed are those who fail to be seduced.

Baudrillard's attempt to seduce readers into finding a radical departure in his theory of appearances brings into question the whole construction of sexuality, male hegemonic control over female bodies, and the structures of psychoanalysis as a sufficient framework for feminist theory. Following the exclusivity of his metaphysics in explaining material relations, Baudrillard makes the mistake of assuming that social life will change because we create different stories about men and women. Educators will supposedly find it possible to liberate the educational system, its workers, and its students simply by talking differently about gender relations. Certainly some important changes may result from changing the myths that we tell one another about ourselves. But Freire's reminder that revolutions do not occur just because we create them in our own minds (1994) may help ameliorate Baudrillard's otherwise provocative yet antiproductive formulation. A radical theory must have its praxiological dimension or theory degrades into mere verbalism or an abreaction to the circuit of production. In turn, praxis must be directed at objective changes, or material relations. Without this crucial pairing, stories may become the opiate of the masses. And this ultimately is what is missing in Baudrillard's theory. Seduction offers little, if no, heuristics for action.

Despite its claims to transcend sexuality and sexism, seduction maintains a sexist line of reasoning. Its themes of appearance, objectification of women's bodies, and women as seductresses mystify gender oppression. Baudrillard chooses to eschew the materiality of sexism by creating an elaborate scheme that circumvents his own complicity as a man who participates in sexist relations. For example, take one of Baudrillard's analyses of a story. In the film and novel *The Collector*, the female character resists her captor for many days, after which time she finally decides to "seduce" him. In response, the "protagonist" shuns her and then undresses her and takes pornographic pictures. She becomes ill, falls into a coma, dies, and he places her pictures in his butterfly scrapbook. He buries her in the backyard and the cycle is foreshadowed by his search for a new victim. Baudrillard's analysis goes as such:

> A need to be loved, but an inability to be seduced. When, finally, the woman is seduced (it is enough that she wants to seduce him) he cannot accept his victory: he prefers to see it as a sexual malediction and punishes her. It is not a question of impotence (it is never a question of impotence). He prefers the possessive spell cast by a collection of dead objects—the dead sex object being as beautiful as a butterfly with florescent wings—to the seduction of a living being who would demand his love in return. (1979, 122–123)

First, the focus of Baudrillard's analysis is not the female character's oppression: the forceful kidnap, the psychological torment culminating in her death and its objectification. Baudrillard's emphasis is on the protagonist's failure to seduce as if he were the one who has suffered in the exchange. Baudrillard does not problematize the obvious violence that the protagonist perpetrates on the victim and that Baudrillard simulates by neglecting the reality principle.

Indeed, in another piece, "The Obscenario," Baudrillard explains an event involving a feminist, a man inflicted with polio, and himself. During a lecture on seduction, the woman challenges what she considers Baudrillard's sexist discourse. During the exchange, the woman slips the handicapped man's cigarette in and out of his mouth so that he can smoke. Baudrillard names this event as a sign that the woman is raping him through this "poor [unassuming] wreck." Her revenge was sweet and there was nothing Baudrillard could do about it (Kellner 1989, 183; Gane 1991a, 61). Whether the woman was intending to "seduce" Baudrillard, we cannot tell. What we receive is Baudrillard's imaginary. Does the woman's action literally mean what it signifies for Baudrillard? It would be ludicrous to assume that Baudrillard's actions and description of the event have no structural meaning. Baudrillard's irresponsible use of "rape" slingshots the reading back to the structures of domination. He strips rape of its violence and power. In spite of Baudrillard's desperate attempts to transcend sexuality, he re-presents the event as a sexual/ sexist practice.

The Collector is reminiscent of the fable "Beauty and the Beast," where the female representative, Beauty, falls in love with her oppressor, the Beast, or the representative of maleness. In light of Baudrillard's analysis of *The Collector*, he would have us believe that as long as seduction is exchanged or returned, women should ignore violence directed toward them or practiced upon them. That is, women are drawn to men who mistreat them as long as they are being seduced by the mistreatment: the male's imaginary. Finally, Baudrillard offers this explanation for the female character's decision to seduce the protagonist and its outcome: "Perhaps the price paid by beauty and seduction is to be confined and put to death, because they are too dangerous, and because one will never be able to render her what she has given. One can then only reward her with her death" (1979, 123). Murder as reward? According to Baudrillard, women do not want to be respected or given sovereignty; they want to be seduced. Our current condition does not call for the cliché of love; it yearns for love that is more than love, love to the nth power: seduction. Baudrillard asserts that love is "hot," whereas seduction is "cool." Baudrillard's apparent romanticism is confounded by his Nietzschean aristocracy. In fact, the female character's decision to seduce can be explained another way.

In her analysis of *Story of O*, Jessica Benjamin describes O's quest for subjectivity (1988). In the story, O's masters give her specific instructions to fulfill their will and sexual desires. Using Bataille's Hegelian dialectics of erotic violation, Benjamin explains O's submission as a vicarious attempt to gain subjectivity through her masters' recognition of her as an object (albeit an alienated subjectivity). In turn, the masters' privilege is sustained by O's recognition of her masters' subjective power over her. This points out the problem of submission as well as domination. Benjamin recognizes O's quest for subjective agency inscribed by the discourse of gender domination. Though her analysis does not devote enough attention to the masters' actual violence, Benjamin's analysis of women's participation in their own oppression successfully articulates aspects of unconscious motivation. By focusing on this second element, Benjamin highlights the moments of agency and potential resistance in the complicitous act of women's submission to men.

Consider, too, Baudrillard's explanations of racism. Admittedly, there is a conceptual brilliance in Baudrillard's articulation of violent otherness. He writes: "Racism does not exist so long as the other remains Other, so long as the Stranger remains foreign. It comes into existence when the other becomes merely different—that is to say, dangerously similar. This is the moment when the inclination to keep the other at a distance comes into being" (1993, 129).

Baudrillard notes that racism is an obsession with becoming "other." It is a "temptation at the heart of every structural system: the temptation to fetishize difference" (1993, 129). Racism in this view becomes "variations in the order of signs." According to Baudrillard, the Spanish massacred the Native Americans because they failed to understand difference. When Native Americans allowed themselves to be part of a negotiable otherness, they began to practice "self-immolation" and "allowed themselves to die." We disagree with Baudrillard that racism is mere "abreaction to the psychodrama of difference" and that it is an issue that is mainly cosigned to the empire of signs. We do not agree that the Native Americans' "strange collusion in their own extermination represented their only way of keeping the secret of otherness" (1993, 133). We do agree with Baudrillard that the European claim to universality located within the humanist virtues of modernity is an underlying feature of racism and that the European colonizers concealed their contempt for and disgust at the other under the guise of altruism. But to claim that the Native Americans' cruel human sacrifices and alleged religious fanaticism made the Spaniards ashamed of the emptiness of their own Christian faith (and their secular faith in gold and commerce) and provoked them to exterminate the native inhabitants is, we argue, ludicrous in light of the arguably greater fanaticism and brutality historically detailed in the history of Spanish colonial Catholicism.

We are profoundly disturbed at Baudrillard's suggestion for confronting the racism that has been created on a global basis by universal structural differentiation: to be more racist than racist. Genosko summarizes Baudrillard's position thus:

> The primitive societies of the future can only escape extermination if their alterity is essential, radical and singular. This is the utopia which may exist after structural differentiation has been destroyed. Even so, those who carry out such exterminations are also condemned, according to Baudrillard, in the long term by their own systems of extermination. Baudrillard's effort here is to push racism to its extreme in order to destroy it. In order to accomplish this critical task, it is necessary to be more racist than racist (the standard Baudrillardian formula of more x than x remains the same), but without knowledge of the consequences or at least the willingness to turn a "blind eye" to them. In the short term, the effects will be disastrous. In the structural game of differences, all differences are close and nothing is truly exotic; there is neither an Absolute Other nor an incomparable non-structural Difference. These are the dirty secrets of *exotisme*: anti-feminism, anti-egalitarianism, hyperracism and anti-colonialism, but the last only by default. (1994, 135; italics in original)

We are not prepared to play off the short-term effects of the "cure" of "hyperracism" against the long-term effects of structural "racism," since in this case, we believe "*la cura es peor que la enfermedad*" (the cure is worse than the disease). Hyperracism follows the same logic as Baudrillard's hyperconformity as a mode of resistance: If you send back to racists their own logic, racism will somehow implode and be defeated. We do not endorse Baudrillard's theoretical predisposition to blame the indigenous oppressed for their subjugation and extermination by European oppressors.

Baudrillard's metaphysics reaches its latest apogee in his book *Fatal Strategies* (1990a). Claiming once again that a radical strategy is one that is "ex-centric," Baudrillard looks to dismantle the revolutionary theory based on the subject with one that is based on the banality of the object. It should be made clear from the outset what Baudrillard means by this. Mimicking Alfred Jarry's pataphysics, Baudrillard clarifies: "When I speak of the object and its fatal strategies I speak of people and their inhuman strategies" (Gane 1991a, 174). Rejecting what he considers the "banal" modernist theory of the determinable subject, Baudrillard inaugurates the revenge of the object, or that which is more banal than banal: fatal. The object strikes back! In a giddy universe of empty forms, Baudrillard outlines his fatal strategy: "The world is not dialectical—it is sworn to extremes, not to equilibrium, sworn to radical antagonism, not to reconciliation or synthesis. This is also the principle of Evil, as expressed in the 'evil genie' of the object, in the ecstatic form of the pure object and in its strategy, victorious over that of the subject" (1990a, 7).

Baudrillard's break from Marxism is completed in his announcement of the subject's death. In fact, Baudrillard contends that the object (Marx's commodity) may have always been the dominant matrix (dominatrix?). Like the black hole's event horizon, the subject has passed across the threshold from where she cannot return. This is the event horizon and the horizon of the event, the "pure event" (1990a, 17). Today's objective logic swallows everything, even the enlightened subject and reproduces it as discharge, as excrement, as pure loss. At this point in Baudrillard's extremism, it is surprising that he does not use the theoretical particle, tachyon. According to theoretical science, tachyon is a particle that exceeds the speed of light. Therefore, tachyons reach their destination (e.g., people) even before it registers them. We feel only the spatial effects of tachyons.

According to Baudrillard, we live in cancerous times, but there is nothing about this situation to deplore. Revolution from without has failed, and according to Baudrillard, our hope lies in involution. The masses are like a cancerous cell that engulfs its host cell, the social. Baudrillard writes: "In traditional pathology, somatic or psychosomatic, the body reacts to external aggressions—physical, social, psychological: exoteric reaction. With cancer it's a matter of an esoteric reaction: the body rebels against its own internal organization, undoes its own structural equilibrium" (1990a, 30). Appropriating Gilles Deleuze's insightful turn of phrase, Baudrillard maintains that the (social) body is reacting against its own organs ("the body without organs").

During virulent periods, the pedagogical model is that of the terrorist. To Baudrillard, a self-proclaimed "theoretical terrorist," terrorism represents one of the ultimate indeterminate acts. He writes:

> We are all hostages, and we are all terrorists. This circuit has replaced that other one of masters and slaves, the dominating and the dominated, the exploiters and the exploited. Gone is the constellation of the slave and the proletarian: from now on it is the hostage and the terrorist. Gone is the constellation of alienation; from now on it is that of terror. It is worse than the one it replaces, but at least it liberates us from liberal nostalgia and the ruses of history. It is the era of the transpolitical that is beginning. (1990a, 39)

Baudrillard implies that, like the terrorist, students should take their teachers as hostages and vice versa, for it is better to take people hostage than be taken hostage (1990a, 40). Terrorists should be appreciated for their random acts of violence, their purposeless goals, and their extremism, a truly fatal strategy patterned after the pure object. There is no meaning whatsoever in schooling, but there is everything to challenge.

Kellner's criticism of this stage in Baudrillard's writing is clear and to the point. Kellner writes:

> Was his [Baudrillard's] word processor (if he has one) taking over his thought processes? Or was his television set controlling his imagination? . . . Desiring sovereignty, he projects sovereignty onto objects. Desiring revenge, he projects revenge onto objects. Supremely ironic, Baudrillard projects objective irony onto objects. Desiring to become a destiny and fatality himself—recall Nietzsche for the psychological roots of this peculiar lust—he ascribes destiny and fatality to objects, and conjures up a fatal universe. Increasingly indifferent to the fate of society and his fellow human beings, Baudrillard ascribes indifference to that supreme object of objects, the masses. Himself impatient, he ascribes impatience to the masses and to the object world. Losing critical energy and growing apathetic himself, he ascribes apathy and inertia to the universe. Imploding into entropy, Baudrillard attributes implosion and entropy to the experience of (post)modernity. (1989, 167, 180)

What can one add to such a critique? If we are to salvage anything from Baudrillard's latest ruminations, it is this. In order to avoid the ludicrous implications of his theory of the object and his insistence that all metaphors are dead metaphors, we may read figuratively his theory of the object's revenge as the strategy of those who have been historically objectified: workers, people of color, women, gay women and men, and other marginalized groups. To revolutionize social life, we may reconstitute meaning from the perspective of those who have been objectified.

Baudrillard's pronouncement of the death of the subject becomes the death of the subject *as we have known him*: the banal bourgeois Western male. Knowing this may help us in the task of rethinking the subject as a social agent of transformation.

We agree with Kellner and Best (in press) that the object is not triumphant over the subject in our present culture of the simulacra. Rather, our present social organization is best conceptualized as an intensification of capitalist modernity rather than a wholly new Order of the Hyperreal. Kellner and Best are correct in arguing that Baudrillard's society of generalized economy is an extension of what Kellner has termed "technocapitalism" (1989). Baudrillard is least convincing when he articulates a social order outside of political economy or the social relations of production. Kellner and Best write: "The productive use of Baudrillard therefore need not entail the need to renounce political economy and the whole modern lexicon; we acknowledge the conceptual advances of Baudrillard's theorizations of media and semiotics, while rejecting their extreme phrasing, their linkage to an apocalyptic concept of rupture, and their pessimistic and quietistic political conclusions" (in press).

It is at this point that we applaud the attempt by Guy Debord and the situationists to move from the sphere of culture to the arena of everyday life when fashioning strategies of *détournment* in the service of social and political justice. According to Macdonald,

> The Situationist notion of cultural politics, unlike some contemporary postmodern arguments for textual politics, clearly understands the limitations that a purely cultural strategy encounters. The point is not to *see politics as a text* or cultural work (and by that very fact, assume that textual play is political play), but to *make politics a textual site* for the creation of freedom and play. This latter emphasis recognizes that while there are important connections between cultural struggles and political practices, agency in one sphere must ultimately be translated into the terms of the other if there is to be a realization of that cultural potentiality. (1995, 107; italics in original)

Debord's concept of agency is closer to that of Paulo Freire (1994) and suggests a consciously articulable form of praxis grounded in critical self-reflexivity. And while such a praxiological activity begins as micropolitical discourse and cultural arrangements, it links such struggle to the arena of macropolitical structures.

Insofar as critical pedagogy must be concerned with relationships of power and privilege, including those that specifically structure the relationships of race, class, and gender, it appears that an ethical ideal of social justice is needed, of which little adequate account can be found in

Baudrillard's work. In addition, an account is needed of the conditions under which a praxis of liberation might be constructed. Consider the absolute cynicism from which Baudrillard articulates his idea of the social, and you will better understand his idea of the dilemma critical educators face:

> As for the social, one could say that its obscenity has fully ripened today, like that of the cadaver of which one cannot rid oneself, or more precisely which enters that accursed stage of putrescence. It is at this point, before withering and assuming the beauty of death, that the body passes through a truly obscene stage and must at all cost be conjured and exorcised, since it no longer represents anything, no longer has any name, and its unspeakable contamination invades everything. (1990b, 187)

For Baudrillard, the social is the realm of the obscene; it flows into everything; it assists in the decomposition of the real and the violent submergence of the symbolic into the real. For Baudrillard, there is nothing redeemable about the social, nothing that is worth saving: "Beyond, or short of this terrorist and hyperreal sociality, of this omnipresent blackmail of communication, is there a good substance of the social, an ideality of social intercourse which can and must be liberated? The answer is clearly no: the balance or harmony of a certain social contract has disappeared on the horizon of history, and we are doomed to this diaphanous obscenity of change" (1990b, 190–191).

Baudrillard's call for hyperconformity is highly problematic for cultural workers interested in creating a revolutionary praxis. For Baudrillard, it is possible to resist the terror of simulation and to escape its hideous truth only through one's maximum absorption into the regime of simulation itself. The semiological structure is overwhelmingly impervious to subversion in Baudrillard's account. There is little attention given to how signs are resisted and transformed. The regime of signs is seemingly invincible. Unlike Baudrillard, we do not believe signs to have a life of their own but to be connected as much to class struggle as they are to the totalitarian-bureaucratic machineries of state power. We believe that signs must be defamiliarized, decentered, and unsettled but that social relations must also be transformed as part of the struggle over the construction of social subjectivities and the struggle toward socialism. We believe that critical pedagogies are not fully constituted and fully delineated domains of struggle but that they possess the potential to overthrow the bourgeois state.

We are sympathetic to Felix Guattari's concept of a micropolitics of desire, a form of political struggle that begins from the plurality of partial struggles, a struggle that attempts neither to represent the masses nor to interpret their struggles. It is a micropolitics of desire that does not locate its authority in a transcendent object; nor is its sole object of antagonism the bourgeois state. Rather, as Guattari (1995) notes, it centers itself "on a multiplicity of objectives, within the immediate reach of the most diverse social groupings" (230). Centrally ordered movements releasing the serialized masses into the streets are not part of Guattari's revolutionary project. Rather, "the connection of a multiplicity of molecular desires . . . would catalyze challenges on a large scale" (230–321).

Such a project does not work from an "ideal *unity* which *represents and mediates multiple* interests" (Guattari 1995, 231; italics in original). It works instead from a "*univocal multiplicity* of desires whose process secretes its own systems of tracking and regulation" (231; italics in original). There is no unique objective, no totalizing unity. Rather than a grouping of the masses according to standardized objectives, there exists the univocality of the masses' desire. We need to recognize that modern fascist democracies depend upon the historical transversity of the machines of desire. A micropolitics of desire sets itself against the totalitarian chemistry of fascism through micropolitical anti-fascist struggle. This is the urgent struggle educators must undertake now and in the years to come. Baudrillard can give us some of the theoretical tools for launching such a struggle, but it is up to us to forge these tools into weapons of war in the fight against capitalist machineries of domination.

Notes

1. Charles Levin (translator) notes that prestation "indicates a feeling of obligation to an irrational code of social behavior" (Baudrillard 1981, 30).

References

Anderson, Benedict. (1991). *Imagined Communities: Reflections on the Origin and Spread of Nationalism*. London: Verso.

Anyon, J. (1980). "School Class and the Hidden Curriculum of Work." *Journal of Education* 162, 25–48.

Aronowitz, S., and DiFazio, W. (1994). *The Jobless Future: Sci-Tech and the Dogma of Work*. Minneapolis and London. University of Minnesota Press.

Bataille, Georges. (1985). *Visions of Excess: Selected Writings, 1927–1939*. Trans. Allan Stoekl et al. Minneapolis: University of Minnesota Press.

Baudrillard, J. (1975). *The Mirror of Production*. Trans. Mark Poster. St. Louis: Telos Press.

Baudrillard, J. (1979). *Seduction*. Trans. Brian Singer. New York: St. Martin's Press.

Baudrillard, J. (1981). *For a Critique of the Political Economy of the Sign*. Trans. Charles Levin. St. Louis: Telos Press.

Baudrillard, J. (1983a). *Simulations*. Trans. Paul Foss et al. New York: Semiotext(e).

Baudrillard, J. (1983b). *In the Shadow of the Silent Majorities.* Trans. Paul Foss et al. New York: Semiotext(e).

Baudrillard, J. (1987). *Forget Foucault.* Trans. Nicole Dufresne. New York: Semiotext(e).

Baudrillard, J. (1988a). "The System of Objects." In Mark Poster, ed., *Jean Baudrillard: Selected Writings.* Stanford: Stanford University Press.

Baudrillard, J. (1988b). "Consumer Society." In Mark Poster, ed., *Jean Baudrillard: Selected Writings.* Stanford: Stanford University Press.

Baudrillard, J. (1988c). "Symbolic Exchange and Death." In Mark Poster, ed., *Jean Baudrillard: Selected Writings.* Stanford: Stanford University Press.

Baudrillard, J. (1990a). *Fatal Strategies.* Trans. Philip Beitchman et al. New York: Semiotext(e).

Baudrillard, J. (1990b). *Revenge of the Crystal: Selected Writings on the Modern Object and Its Destiny.* Trans. Paul Foss et al. London and Concord: Pluto Press.

Baudrillard, J. (1993). *The Transparency of Evil Essays on Extreme Phenomena.* Trans. James Benedict. London and New York: Verso.

Baudrillard, J. (1994). *Simulacra and Simulation.* Trans. Sheila Faria Glaser. Ann Arbor: University of Michigan Press.

Benjamin, J. (1988). *The Bonds of Love: Psychoanalysis, Feminism and the Problem of Domination.* New York: Pantheon Books.

Best, S. (1994). "The Commodification of Reality and the Reality of Commodification: Baudrillard, Debord, and Postmodern Theory." In Doug Kellner, ed., *Baudrillard: A Critical Reader* (41–67). Stanford: Stanford University Press.

Bowles, S., and Gintis, H. (1976). *Schooling in Capitalist America.* New York: Basic Books.

Cook, D. (1994). "Symbolic Exchange in Hyperreality." In Doug Kellner, ed., *Baudrillard: A Critical Reader* (150–167). Stanford: Stanford University Press..

Debord, G. (1983). *The Society of the Spectacle.* Detroit: Red and Black.

Fine, M. (1991). *Framing Dropouts.* New York: State University of New York Press.

Freire, P. (1994). *Pedagogy of the Oppressed.* New York: Continuum.

Gane, M. (1991a). *Baudrillard: Critical and Fatal Theory.* London: Routledge.

Gane, M. (1991b). *Baudrillard's Bestiary: Baudrillard and Culture.* London: Routledge.

Gane, M., ed. (1993). *Baudrillard Live: Selected Interviews.* London and New York. Routledge.

Genosko, G. (1994). *Baudrillard and Signs: Signification Ablaze.* London and New York: Routledge.

Giroux, H. (1993). *Border Crossings.* New York and London: Routledge.

Gottdiener, M. (1994). "The System of Objects and the Commodification of Everyday Life: The Early Baudrillard." In Doug Kellner, ed., *Baudrillard: A Critical Reader* (24–40). Stanford: Stanford University Press.

Guattari, F. (1995). *Chaosophy.* Trans. Suzanne Fletcher et al. New York: Semiotext(e).

Haug, W. (1971). *Critique of Commodity Aesthetics: Appearance, Sexuality, and Advertising in Capitalist Society.* Trans. R. Bock. Minneapolis: University of Minnesota Press.

Herman, E., and Chomsky, N. (1993). *Manufacturing Consent*. New York: Pantheon Books.

Jameson, F. (1993). "Postmodernism and the Consumer Society." In E. Ann Kaplan, ed., *Postmodernism and Its Discontents* (13–29). London and New York: Verso.

Kellner, D. (1989). *Jean Baudrillard*. Stanford: Stanford University Press.

Kellner, D. (1994). "Introduction: Jean Baudrillard in the Fin-de-Millennium." In Doug Kellner, ed., *Baudrillard: A Critical Reader* (1–23). Stanford: Stanford University Press.

Kellner, D., and Best, S. (in press). *The Postmodern Imagination*.

Kroker, A., and Cook, D. (1986). *The Postmodern Scene: Excremental Culture and Hyper-Aesthetics*. New York: St. Martin's Press.

Macdonald, B. (1995) "From the Spectacle to Unitary Urbanism: Reassessing Situationist Theory." *Rethinking Marxism* 8(2), 89–111.

Mauss, M. (1967). *The Gift*. New York: W. W. Norton.

McLaren, P. (1995). *Critical Pedagogy and Predatory Culture: Oppositional Politics in a Postmodern Era*. New York and London: Routledge.

Pefanis, J. (1991). *Heterology and the Postmodern: Bataille, Baudrillard and Lyotard*. Durham and London: Duke University Press.

Poster, M. (1994). "Critical Theory and Technoculture: Habermas and Baudrillard." In Doug Kellner, ed., *Baudrillard: A Critical Reader* (68–88). Stanford: Stanford University Press.

Tseelon, E. (1994). "Fashion and Signification in Baudrillard." In Doug Kellner, ed., *Baudrillard: A Critical Reader* (119–132). Stanford: Stanford University Press.

Zeitlin, M. (1989). *The Large Corporation and Contemporary Classes*. New Brunswick, NJ: Rutgers University Press.

5 Gangsta Pedagogy and Ghettocentricity: The Hip-Hop Nation as Counterpublic Sphere

Race is the modality in which class is lived.
—**Eric Lott (1994)**[1]

I was beautiful; after all, my skin was as rich and as dark as wet, brown mud, a complexion that any and every pale white girl would pray for. . . . My butt sat high in the air and my hips obviously gave birth to Creation.
—**Sister Souljah (1995)**[2]

Black athletes . . . white agents
Black preacher . . . white Jesus
Black entertainers . . . white lawyers
Black Monday . . . white Christmas
—**Chuck D, "White Heaven . . . Black Hell"**

It's your world
(and yours and yours and yours)
and what you see,
it was not meant for me.
It's your world,
but you don't have to be lonely
'cause in your world,
you are truly Free!
—**Gill Scott-Heron (1976)**

When Harvard scholar Henry Louis Gates Jr. defended the imagery and lyrics of 2 Live Crew at their highly publicized 1990 trial, claiming that the group's album, *As Nasty as They Wanna Be,* was not obscene on the grounds that the lyrics and imagery were derived from the venerable

African American tradition of "signifying" and "playing the dozens," no doubt many critics were thinking that the controversy over rap would probably go the way of the debates over rock 'n' roll in the 1950s: it would generally "fade away." At the time of the trial it was difficult to imagine not only the public furor over rap music—gangsta rap in particular—but also the extent to which Washington would develop its anti-rap campaign, signaling a "moral panic" destined to become one of the lightning rods in the 1996 presidential campaign and a flash-point in the current debate over race relations. As former Secretary of Education and Drug Czar William J. Bennett joins forces with C. DeLores Tucker, the conservative activist with the National Political Caucus of Black Women, to publicly denounce gangsta rap as a seductive, immoral force, presidential candidates, Bob Dole, Phil Gramm, and Pat Buchanan have decided not only to join in the condemnation of Time Warner (which up to the time of this writing owns interests in a number of rap record labels) but also to launch a frontal assault on Hollywood's entertainment industry and all those liberals who were likely to defend affirmative action, government assistance programs for non-documented workers, or gay-rights initiatives.

Despite the fact that the Geto Boys' lead rapper, Bushwick Bill, recently thanked Dole for $300,000 worth of publicity,[3] the attacks have had a considerable negative effect on the rap industry, prompting Time Warner to fire record executive Doug Morris and to be reportedly (as of this writing) negotiating its way out of a $100 million share in Interscope Records, distributor of Snoop Doggy Dogg, Dr. Dre, and Tupac Shakur.[4]

Gangsta rappers follow a long line of musicians denounced by the moral custodians of U.S. culture as prime instigators of juvenile delinquency—a list that includes, among others, Frank Sinatra, Elvis, the Beatles, the Sex Pistols, Metallica, and Prince. Members of my generation, puzzling over the 2 Live Crew trial or reflecting on the earlier public debates surrounding the subliminal messages purportedly inserted into songs by Judas Priest and Ozzy Osborne, are perhaps reminded of earlier controversies that accompanied the Rolling Stones' hit "Satisfaction," or the two-and-a-half-year analysis by J. Edgar Hoover's G-men of the Kingsmen's 1963 hit, "Louie, Louie."[5] The investigation by FBI sound technicians and cryptographers of this pop chant (which merely recounts a lovesick sailor's return to his Jamaican sweetheart) seems ironic now, given the fact that the teen anthem has since appeared as the backdrop of numerous films, charity telethons, and wine cooler ads.[6] The debate over gangsta rap has captured the public imagination at a time when the nation is vigorously reevaluating public policies surrounding affirmative action and urban reform. This has given gangsta rap an urgency and public visibility far greater than earlier debates over rock 'n' roll and morality. Sister Souljah had been criticized by President Clinton and others for inciting violence against white people when in fact she had told a journalist only that she could understand why some black people might want to kill white people: "In the mind of a gang member, why not kill white people? In other words, if you've been neglected by the social and economic order of America, and you've become casual about killing, you would have no hesitancy about killing somebody white."[7] In providing a sociological insight she was roundly condemned—unfairly—as a hate-mongerer. Rapper Chuck D. maintains that rappers themselves don't necessarily feel violent towards whites. Rappers are contemporary urban messengers from God: "It's not me, or Ice Cube, or Sister Souljah's feelings—we're just the messengers, and how you gonna kill the messenger? The best thing about rap is it's a last-minute warning, the final call . . . a last plea for help on the countdown to Armageddon."[8] Chuck D sees rap as the 'hood's equivalent of CNN.

As I complete some final editing to this essay, which takes the form of an interrogative excursion into the subject of gangsta rap, the *Los Angeles Times* reports that rap singer Dasean Cooper (J-Dee), a member of Da Lench Mob, was recently sentenced to 29 years to life for the 1993 murder of his girlfriend's male roommate at a party in Inglewood.[9] Terry (T-Bone) Gray, another member of Da Lench Mob, has also been charged with murdering one individual—and wounding another—at a Los Angeles bowling alley. Da Lench Mob's 1992 single, "Who You Gonna Shoots Wit Dat," was cited in the Cooper case by the prosecuting attorney in an attempt to paint murders by rap artists as "life imitating art." Criminal charges have recently been filed against Snoop Doggy Dogg (who is awaiting trial for allegedly driving the getaway car during a murder) and Tupac Amaru Shakur, San Francisco Bay Area rapper and former member of the Digital Underground (arrested for sexually assaulting a 19-year-old woman whom he and his friends had held captive in a hotel room). The widow of slain Texas police officer Bill Davidson has sued Tupac for allegedly inciting a 19-year-old car thief, Ronald Ray Howard, to murder Davidson with a nine millimeter pistol. After listening to the mantra-like lyrics of Shakur's song "Crooked Ass Nigga," from his album *2Pacalypse Now*, which describes a drug dealer on a rampage with a nine millimeter pistol and contains a reference to "droppin' the cop," Howard claims that he "snapped" and shot Davidson as a result of being instructed by the lyrics. Dan Quayle cashed in on the media attention by visiting Davidson's grieving daughter and announcing that Tupac's music 'has no place in our society." These events have induced the breach birth of the gangsta rap media elite and have added to hip-hop's hype as hard-edged urban drama muscled onto a compact disc. (As this book goes into production, Tupac lies dead of gunshot wounds that he received in Las Vegas after attending the Mike Tyson–Bruce Seldon boxing match. He was shot while driving in a car with Death Row Records co-founder and president, Marion "Suge" Knight. Although he bragged defiantly about the tough life in the 'hood, and had "Thug Life" and an AK-47 assault weapon tattooed across his abdomen, his Grammy-nominated 1995 hit single, "Dear Mama," was a tender ballad written for his mother. Tupac's mother, Afeni Shakur, was a member of the Black Panther Party and was pregnant with Tupac while she was serving time in a New York prison for allegedly plotting to blow up department stores and police stations. He sang: "Even as a crack fiend always was a black queen." The name Tupac Amaru comes from a sixteenth-century Incan chief whose name means "shining serpent." Tupac Amaru was the last Incan leader to be defeated by the Spanish. He was executed in 1572. The Tupac Amaru Revolutionary Movement led by Nestor Cerpa Cartolini is currently holding hundreds of international diplomats hostage in the Japanese embassy in Lima, Peru. Tupac's posthumous "The Don Killuminati: The 7 Day Theory" is expected to replace the Beatles' "Anthology 3" as the nation's best-selling album.

Eazy-E's recent death from AIDS (Eazy-E was a former member of NWA, a financial contributor to the Republican party and the head of Ruthless Records, the first significant rapper-owned record label) has left the hip-hop nation stunned. Early this April, the Los Angeles Police Department joined with FBI agents in Operation Sunrise, sweeping through a 30-block area of South Central LA, arresting gang members of the Eight-Tray Gangster Crips, a gang that came into public prominence during the 1992 uprising with its involvement in the attack on truck driver Reginald O. Denny and other motorists at the intersection of Florence and Normandie. East LA Chicanos are still recovering from the news of the slaying of Selena, superstar of Tejano music and heroine of Molinatown's Chicano barrio in Corpus Christi. Among gangsta rappers, the mood of the city felt all too familiar.

By late October, when jury selection in the murder trial of Snoop Doggy Dogg, his bodyguard, and his friend began in Los Angeles, defense attorneys (including Johnnie L. Cochran Jr.) were preparing to "play the LAPD card" in their attack on police evidence tampering. In the post-Simpson era, the lawyers representing Snoop Doggy Dogg (a.k.a. Calvin Broadus, former member of the Long Beach Insane Crips) and his associates stand a good chance of landing further blows to the credibility and integrity of the police. A few months earlier Snoop Doggy Dogg was praised by President Bill Clinton and Ice-T for writing a letter to 60 gang sets in Los Angeles and honoring their efforts to "keep the peace." As Snoop Doggy Dogg's words of thanks were sounded at a celebration at the International House of Blues in West Los Angeles, sets from the Imperial Courts, Jordan Downs, and Nickerson Gardens housing projects in Watts sat down with the Fruit Town Pirus of Compton and sets from Long Beach, the Pueblo Bishops 5 Duce Mid-City Gangsters, the 5 Duce BCG, the Santana Block Crips, the V-13s and Shoreline Crips of Venice, and the Parkside Manor Circle City Pirus of Los Angeles. When, at this afternoon gala, a Crip, a Blood, and a Latino gang member cut a cake in unison, gangsta rappers had symbolically joined forces with Bill Clinton's four-member Color Guard, present at the ceremonies as a sign of "respect."

For someone who grew up listening to Robert Johnson's Delta Blues, who used to frequent the Colonial Tavern on Toronto's Yonge Street to hear musician friends jam with Muddy Waters, who idolized Lightning Hopkins, and who wanted to play the blues harp like Little Walter, rap music was not a natural transition for me. Ska, rock-steady, and reggae helped to broaden my musical sensibilities, but, even so, rap was a taste that was difficult to acquire at first. In recent years I have grown to greatly appreciate gangsta rap as an oppositional political practice, but despite its possibilities for articulating an oppositional performative politics, gangsta rap remains, in some senses, a problematic cultural practice.

In this article I am generally referring to *gangsta rap* and do not wish to conflate this term with those of *rap* or *hip-hop*. When I speak generally about rap music as a form of black cultural address, without specifically calling it gangsta rap, I am emphasizing rap music's situatedness within hip-hop culture, its criticism of the dominant white culture's racial and economic discrimination, and the contradictory urban expressions of African American economic and racial marginality. Here I share Tricia Rose's perspective that rap "is a black idiom that prioritizes black culture and that articulates the problem of black urban life."[10] I am referring to rap artists as cultural workers engaged to a large extent in "the everyday struggles of working-class blacks and the urban poor."[11] Jeffrey Louis Decker refers to such cultural workers as "hip hop nationalists" who function in the manner suggested by Gramsci's description of organic intellectuals.[12]

With what some rap critics might call its numbing psychorealism; its fixing of "in-your-face" rhymes to social meltdown and bass rhythms to urban disaster; its commodification of black rage through high-volume and low-frequency sound; its production of sexualizing fugues for an imploding Generation X; its ability to provoke a white hellification of black youth with "attitude"; its seventh sons in blue or red bandanas and ten-dollar gold tooth caps "droppin science" and warning their homeboys against "tell-lie-vision," the "lie-bury," and public school "head-decay-tion"; its dance culture of the Handglide, Flow, Headspin, King Tut, Windmill, Tick, Float, Wave, and freestyle; its production of affective economies of white panic around a generalized fear of a black planet; its sneering, tongue-flicking contempt of public space; its visceral intensity and corporal immediacy; its snarling, subterranean resistance; its eschatological showdown of "us" against "them"; its "edutainers" down with the brothas in the street; its misogynist braggadocio; its pimp-inspired subjectivity; its urban war zone counternarratives; its home-brewed polymerized anarchism; its virulent autobiographical hype; its Five Percenters flashing their ciphers, 7s, and crescent moon and star within a large sun, praising "Father Allah"; its irreverent first-person narratives powered by gats and urban souljahs high on malt liquor; its rhythmic macho boastfests by brothas in Carhartt jackets; and its dissentious themes and high-pitched contempt for the white petit bourgeoisie and the yuppie heirs of the over-class who can afford to sidestep the frenetic dizziness of reality, gangsta rap has occasioned much public debate over the last few years. Gangsta rap is merely the latest incarnation of the rap music industry in general.

Tricia Rose notes that rap music was "discovered" by the music indus-try, the print media, the fashion industry, and the film industry during the five years after music entrepreneur Sylvia Robinson released "Rap-per's Delight" in 1979. Rose further declares that rap music needs to be situated within Afro-diasporic traditions and cultural formations of the English- and Spanish-speaking Caribbean and in the context of specific historical musical junctions such as urban blues, be-bop, and rock 'n' roll. Further, rap needs to be considered in light of such factors as the creation of the postindustrial city and the larger social movement of hip-hop. For instance, rap music can be traced to, among other cultural and social elements, the hip-hop nationalism of the 1960s, such as the Black Panthers, Malcolm X, gender politics; New York City's political context of the 1970s; postindustrial shifts in economic conditions, including ac-cess to housing, the formation of new communication networks; blax-ploitation films such as Melvin Van Peebles's *Sweet Sweetback's Baadasss Song;* deindustrialization; the relocation of people of color from different parts of New York City into the South Bronx; city planning and projects such as the Title I Clearance program; the system of crews or posses as means for alternative youth identities: disco music and the cross-fertilization among rapping, break dancing, and graffiti writing.[14]

In the 1980s we started to see rap music emerging in other urban ghet-tos in major cities such as Houston's fifth ward, Miami's Overtown, Boston's Roxbury, and South Central, Watts, and Compton, in Los Angeles. The Los Angeles rappers have spawned a specific rap style that, Rose notes, must be seen in the context of narratives specific to poor, young, black, male subjects in Los Angeles. Rose writes that Los Angeles rappers "defined the gangsta rap style."[15] and "spawned other regionally specific hardcore rappers such as New Jersey's Naughty by Nature, Bronx-based Tim Dog, Onyx, and Redman, and a new group of female gangsta rappers, such as Boss (two black women from Detroit), New York–based Puerto Ri-can rapper Hurricane Gloria, and Nikki D."[16] When examining the roots of rap, or rap's inflection into gangsta rap genres, we need to examine the conjunctural specificity of many factors, including those listed above.

White and black listeners alike are drawn to this surly form of urban apostasy, fashionable deviancy, and stylized outlawry, whose message and transgressive status dig pretty close to the eschatological roots of holy war. Gangsta rap has been accused by some middle-class whites as well as some black professionals of fomenting the anger, racial hatred, and lawlessness that led to the LA uprising of 1992. Of course, in tandem with such dispatches from the bourgeoisie was a studied ignorance about the irreversible structural unemployment faced by many blacks in the inner city, the dismantling of social services, and the progressive hardening of racial lines.

The LA media have not been known for their celebration of rap as a musical genre since the heyday of its Compton rappers: MC Ren, Dr. Dre, Yella, Ice Cube, and Eazy-E (who left groups such as The CIA and World Class Wreckin Cru in order to work collaboratively as NWA—Niggas With Attitude—from 1987 to 1992). Instead, the media have preferred to demonize and hellify the genre that these young Angelenos from Watts, Compton, and South Central—"the nihilistic school of Los Angeles–centered gangsta rappers"—helped to create.[17] Following their more politicized hard-core and hard-beat counterparts in New York (such as Run-DMC and KRS-1) on the East Coast (such as Notorious B.I.G.), in the footsteps of New York's Grandmaster Flash and the Furious Five, and fellow Angelenos Gil Scott-Heron, the Watts Prophets, and the Last Poets (a group of black nationalist lyricists), LA rap artists provided the space for the development of a new form of social criticism. This form of social criticism was apotheosized in Ice Cube's *The Predator,* which offered a potent commentary on the LA uprising of 1992. The cultural power and promise of rap resided in its powerful dramatization of white racism. In "We Had to Tear This Motherfucker Up" Ice Cube (a.k.a. O'Shea Jackson) sentences former LAPD officers Stacey Koon, Laurence Powell, and Timothy Wind to death for the beating of Rodney King.

Like their New York counterpart, Afrika Bambaataa, former member of the Black Spades street gang and founder of the hip-hop community, Zulu Nation (made up of African American, Puerto Rican, Afro-Caribbean, and Euro-American youths and based on the Zulu military system), LA rappers Ice-T, Tone Loc, Ice Cube, and Eazy-E were also former gangbangers. Many of these rappers were products of the economic and cultural upheavals that had assaulted and displaced numerous multiethnic urban communities; their futures were bound up in the dimming job market by inner-city trade vocational schooling. For instance, hip-hop originator DJ Kool Herc (whose original rap style was influenced by prison "toasting") attended Alfred E. Smith auto mechanic trade school; Grandmaster Flash studied electronic repair work at Samuel Gompers vocational high school; and Salt 'n' Pepa both worked as telemarketing representatives at Sears and were intent at one time on nursing school.[18] These working-class black youths were able to escape the uncertain futures constructed for them in an era of deindustrialization. They are some of the lucky few to succeed as part of a financially lucrative musical phenomenon. However, it is a phenomenon often accused of fomenting racial panics and urban youth criminality. Just ask Charlton Heston and Oliver North.

Emerging in the 1970s from the epicenters of hip-hop culture—the blue-collar housing units of America's postindustrial cities—rap music developed among relocated black and Puerto Rican male youths of the South Bronx who celebrated break dancing, graffiti, B-Boy, and wild style fashions.[19] Puerto Rican rap has incorporated inflections from salsa, variations of which are drawn from *Santéria* rhythms, as is the case of the music of Tito Puente (himself a priest of *Santéria).*

Some of the major strands of hip-hop culture (in which rap, style, and politics become mutually informing inflections) can be traced from the jive talkers of the be-bop era to the reggae-based sounds of Jamaican DJ Kool Herc in the West Bronx in 1973 and Jah Rico in north London around 1976. Hip-hop youth in the Bronx and London sympathized with the economic and social struggles of young people in Jamaica and Soweto, wore dreadlocks ("Funki Dreds") with shaved back and sides created by Jazzy B and Aitch for the Soul II Soul crew, or combined the Philly Cut or skiffle with shaved diagonal lines, bleaching, or perms.[20] Shifts in clothes displayed a taxonomy of funky sartorial motifs, from Teenybopper to Home Boy to hard-rocker to Afrocentric; and from Hustler to Superfly to Daisy Age to Cosmic (via Rifat Ozbek). With styles eventually shifting to athletic and leisure wear, Home Boys and Fly Girls started sporting sweatshirts, cropped shorts, "pin-tucked" baggy jeans, baseball caps, chunky gold chains, Dukie Ropes, and leather pendants.[21] Then came the "hoodies" and the "triple fat" goose down jackets.

Influenced by the music of Curtis Mayfield, the funk of James Brown, be-bop, and rhythmic jazz, rap is an impressive amalgam of complex musical formations. Some ethnomusicologists consider such formations to be extensions of African expressive forms such as "playing the dozens" and "signifying" as well as the praise songs of the African storyteller, or *griot.*[22] In saying this, however, I am reminded of Tricia Rose's important admonition that hip-hop not be reduced to its African musical origins as oral traditions.[23] Hip-hop needs to be understood, argues Rose, as a "secondary orality" bound up in an electronically mediated reality that is conjuncturally embedded in relations of power and politics. Rose further notes that "rap musicians are not the only musicians to push on the limits of high-tech inventions. Yet, the decisions they have made and the directions their creative impulses have taken echo Afro-diasporic musical priorities. Rap production resonates with Black cultural priorities in the age of digital reproduction."[24]

Tricia Rose's discussion of mass-produced repetition undercuts perspectives by Adorno, Attali, and Jameson by arguing that repetition in rap is not always connected to the commodity system of late capitalism in the same way as other musical forms. She argues that repetition in mass-cultural formations can also serve as a form of collective resistance.[25]

The operational or performative logics of gangsta rap vary but what is constant is what Lawrence Grossberg calls "affective agency"—its ability to articulate "mattering maps" in which agency is defined as brushing up against the prison of everyday life.[26] Michael Dyson describes the emergence of rap within a context that emphasizes its situatedness as a cultural form of resistance. According to Dyson,

> Rap music grew from its origins in New York's inner city over a decade ago as a musical outlet to creative cultural energies and to contest the invisibility of the ghetto in mainstream American society. Rap remythologized New York's status as the spiritual center of black America, boldly asserting appropriation and splicing (not originality) as the artistic strategies by which the styles and sensibilities of black ghetto youth would gain popular influence. Rap developed as a relatively independent expression of black male artistic rebellion against the black bourgeois *Weltanschauung,* tapping instead into the cultural virtues and vices of the so-called underclass, romanticizing the ghetto as the fecund root of cultural identity and authenticity, the Rorschach of legitimate masculinity and racial unity.[27]

Tricia Rose describes hip-hop culture, from which rap and eventually gangsta rap evolved, in a more global context:

> Hip hop is an Afro-diasporic cultural form which attempts to negotiate the experiences of marginalization, brutally truncated opportunity and oppression within the cultural imperatives of African-American and Caribbean history, identity and community. It is the tension between the cultural fractures produced by postindustrial oppression and the binding ties of Black cultural expressivity that sets the critical frame for the development of hip hop.[28]

Rap's beginnings as highly politicized and powerfully eclectic music can be seen in such songs as "Rapper's Delight" by the Sugarhill Gang in 1979, Brother D's (Daryl Asmaa Nubyah) "We Gonna Make the Black Nation Rise," recorded in 1980, and Afrika Bambaataa and Soul Sonic Force's 1982 recording of "Planet Rock." According to Dick Hebdige, Bambaataa "has been known to cut from salsa to Beethoven's Fifth Symphony to Yellow Magic Orchestra to calypso through Kraftwerk via video game sound effects and the theme from *The Munsters* television series back to his base in James Brown."[29] Bambaataa—who ran a sound system at the Bronx River Community Center—would also mix the theme from the *Pink Panther* with bits and pieces of songs from the Monkees, the Beatles, and the Rolling Stones.[30]

Poison Clan, AMG, Hi-C, Nu Niggaz on the Block, Compton Cartel, 2nd II None, Mob Style, and Compton's Most Wanted did not emerge in a social vacuum. When former LAPD Chief of Police Darryl Gates proclaimed that "we may be finding that in some Blacks when [the chokehold] is applied the veins or arteries do not open up as fast as they do on normal people," he was reflecting the sentiments of the white dominant culture of law enforcement in Los Angeles.[31] Not only was he demonizing African Americans as biologically subnormal, he was adding to the criminalization of black youth in general, corralling connotations of black masculinity into the operative lexicon of unimpeachable white common sense. The LAPD term describing "African Americans in the vicinity" as "Gorillas in the Mist" provoked Da Lench Mob to title their album *Guerrillas in tha Midst.* Some cultural critics were beginning to view rap artists as agents of revolutionary consciousness. When Operation HAMMER sent Chief Gates and his minions into the streets of South Central to pick up "suspicious looking" black youth, harass them, and build up the data base of the LAPD's task force, gangsta rappers were portraying the practice of law enforcement as a form of racial and class warfare.

After the release of NWA's 1988 debut album, *Straight Outta Compton,* white audiences were treated to urban nightmares of white throats being slit in midscream. NWA's hit crossover recording, "Efil4zaggin"—"niggaz 4 life" spelled backward—was the first hardcore rap collection to reach number one on the pop charts. Then "Cop Killer" hit the airwaves, with Ice-T's hard, pounding, and pimpified lyrics smashing through listeners' ribs like a brass-knuckled fist, tagging a "don't fuck with me" on their hearts with an aerosol can of his digitized blood. The media went ballistic in condemnation of this new transgressive musical form known as "gangsta rap," which was even propelling white audiences into adopting black inflection and "ghetto" identification. Ice-T became buoyant after President Clinton publicly criticized "Cop Killer" and sixty congressmen signed a letter condemning the song: "Very few people have their names said by the president, especially in anger. It makes me feel good, like I haven't been just standing on a street corner yelling with nobody listening all the time. . . . It lets you know how small this country is."[32]

Ice Cube's 1990 hit "Endangered Species," from the album *Amerikkka's Most Wanted,* captures the attitude that many gangsta rap lyrics reflect with respect to law enforcement agencies:

Every cop killer ignored
They just send another nigger to the morgue
A point scored.
They could give a fuck about us
They'd rather find us with guns and white powder
Now kill ten of one to get the job correct.
To serve, protect and break a nigga's neck.

This was heavy stuff in a society too preoccupied with consolidating its hegemony through frontal assaults on the welfare state and labor coalitions to concern itself with a bunch of "lowlifes" singing about their crime-ridden hoods. Latino rap didn't really become popular until 1990, during a groundswell of public panic surrounding the growing Latino population in the United States and amidst the reactionary tactics of the English Only Movement. Mellow Man Ace went gold with *Mentirosa*, and Kid Frost's (a.k.a. Arturo Molina) Chicanismo-inspired debut album, *Hispanic Causing Panic*, became the rap anthem of La Raza.[33] Chicano rapper ALT (a.k.a. Al Trivette) fuses insights of barrio life in El Monte and Rosemead into African American rap in albums *ALT* and *Stone Cold World.*

The amazing thing about the disjunctive barrage of ghetto moments known as rap was that it sold, turning inner-city homeys such as Mixmaster Spade into deities in gold chains, hawking their rap wares on the very mean streets that they rapped about. Since those early days, gangsta rap has even gone platinum with Dre's *The Chronic* and Snoop's *Doggystyle.*

In the eyes of many ghetto youth, society is going under and gangsta rappers and hepcats from the barrios are the new prophets, sounding their nationalist warnings over a Roland TR 808 drum synthesizer as the world about them swirls into the urban vortex, like DeNiro's ex-convict character in *Cape Fear,* whose savaged and tattooed body writhes while his soul speaks in tongues as both sink beneath the foaming waters.

Death Row Records, run by Andre (Dr. Dre) Young and Marion "Suge" Knight, is the nation's most profitable producer of gangsta rap, grossing a total of $90 million from tape, CD, and merchandise sales in 1993 and 1994.[34] Affiliated with media giant Time Warner, this Westwood-based firm boasts a corporate logo of a hooded man in an electric chair. Death Row Records has not escaped the controversies surrounding its stars' involvement in criminal violence. At a party for its out-of-town retailers and promoters held hours after Snoop Doggy Dogg (Calvin Broadus) took top honors at the Soul Train Music Awards, a fan was brutally stomped to death. Young is currently serving a five-month term in Pasadena City jail for parole violation. (In 1992 he was convicted of breaking another rap producer's jaw and hitting a New Orleans police officer in a hotel brawl.) A year earlier he was convicted of slamming a TV talk-show host into a wall at a Hollywood club. Knight was also convicted of assault with a deadly weapon. According to Dre, "America loves violence. America is obsessed with murder. I think murder sells a lot more than sex. They say sex sells. I think murder sells."[35] However, Death Row Records publicly denounces gang violence, and the firm has donated $500,000 to a South Central antigang program.

Russell Simmons, CEO of Def Jam Recordings (the largest African American–owned company in the record business) defends rap as a way to reach kids in Beverly Hills:

> And the most important thing is this. It's very, very important that there be communication between kids that would generally not talk to each other. Your kids may not be bad, but it's pretty sure they know some who are. Your kids are surrounded by those kids. So maybe some kid in Beverly Hills listens to rap and gets a better idea of what some kids in Crenshaw are thinking. And as that kid in Beverly Hills grows up and goes to college, maybe he'll keep a little bit of that in his consciousness, and maybe even grow up to do something about it.[36]

Simmons's justification for rap and gangsta rap as the contemporary hope for shaping the consciousness of rich white kids in Beverly Hills certainly overestimates rap's potential for political resistance and social transformation through the mobilization of Generation X. Yet, it vastly underestimates the power of capitalist hegemony to produce, promote, and protect the vested interests of dominant culture in Western society, and what it takes to construct counterhegemonic social practices.

Shortly after the 1992 LA Intifada, pop singer Michelle Shocked and freelance writer Bart Bull mounted a powerful (if not profoundly misguided) denunciation of gangsta rap in an issue of *Billboard.* Claiming it to be a contemporary recoding of a turn-of-the-century white racist stereotype, a racist revival of the minstrel tradition as embodied in the nineteenth-century "coon song," they proclaimed that the "chicken-thieving, razor-toting 'coon' of the 1890s is the drug-dealing, Uzi-toting 'nigga' of today."[37] Ice Cube is criticized by Shocked and Bull as a "greed artist" who, through albums such as *The Predator,* is profiting from the conditions that produce the underclass through his production of a "Zip Coon Toon Town" version of Los Angeles, "a coon song fantasyland." This perspective is echoed by New York essayist and music critic Stanley Crouch, who calls gangsta rap "the selling of coon images" and who compares record executives who produce gangsta rap to "high tech slave traders."[38] Crouch condemns gangsta rap for portraying black people as wild savages and as badges of black authenticity, as the "real" voices from the hood. Taking issue with Crouch's position, the Geto Boys' lead rapper, Bushwick Bill (whose physical status as a one-eyed midget has not been lost on rap's media critics) describes rap as an "opera to people in the ghetto."[39] Rock critic Dave Marsh argues that the attack on rap is directed at new access to the mainstream media by America's underclass. He condemns the anti-rap campaign by William Bennett and C. DeLores Tucker as 90s-style McCarthyism. Former *Wall Street Journal* writer and critic Martha Bayles blames the offensive lyrics in much of today's music not on African American music but on the avant garde European art school thinking that she calls "perverse modernism."[40]

In Mexico border towns like Tijuana, *narcocorrido* ballads (historically derived from the narrative style of Nahuatl epic poetry and Andalusian romantic verse from the 16th century) tell stories of drug dealers who prevail in the face of the authorities. Narcocorrido balladeers have provoked the wrath of anti-drug spokespeople such as Marta Rocha de Diaz, president of Housewives of Playas de Tijuana. The public debate is similar to that surrounding gangsta rap. Los Tucanes sing narcocorridos about smugglers who take heroin, cocaine, and marijuana across the border into the U.S. The popularity of Los Tucanes and Los Tigres del Norte has provoked critics to condemn narcocorridos for mimicking U.S.-style gangsta rap.

David Troop's *Rap Attack: African Jive to New York Hip Hop,* Houston Baker's *Black Studies: Rap and the Academy,* and Tricia Rose's brilliant *Black Noise: Rap Music and Black Culture in Contemporary America*[41] are just a few of the burgeoning scholarly commentaries on rap that offer a much more congenial account of rap's potential for developing forms of counterhegemonic resistance than the account of gangsta rap that is offered by Shocked and Bull. For these critics, it is important to understand how and why the terms governing the popular responses to rap have come into being and how they have, to a large extent, become naturalized. Accordingly, these writers maintain the need to see hip-hop in a much broader context: as a global cultural practice that is articulated through the tropes and sensibilities of the African diaspora and the history of Afro-America, and that creates a "diasporic interchange" and "diasporic intimacy" among struggling black peoples the world over who are fighting racism and capitalist exploitation.[42] As Nick De Genova emphasizes, "rather than as an expression of social pathology, gangster rap's imaginative empowerment of a nihilistic and ruthless way of life can be better understood as a potentially oppositional consciousness—albeit born of desperation, or even despair."[43] Common subjective understandings of alienation among oppressed groups are articulated through rap; as a cultural force it is integral in providing black urban youth with both an expression of race and with codes of solidarity. As De Genova puts it, "gangsta rap can be found to transcend the mere reflection of urban mayhem and enter into musical debate with these realities, without sink-ing into didacticism or flattening their complexity."[44] Rap needs to be understood not so much for its musical poaching through "sampling" as for the way that it is premised on what Tricia Rose calls "transformations and hybrids"—developing "a style that nobody can deal with." She writes that

> transformations and hybrids reflect the initial spirit of rap and hip hop as an experimental and collective space where contemporary issues and ancestral forces are worked through simultaneously. Hybrids in rap's subject matter, not unlike its use of musical collage and the influx of new, regional and ethnic styles, have not yet displaced the three points of stylistic continuity to which I referred earlier: approaches to flow, ruptures in line and layering can still be found in the vast majority of rap's lyrical and music construction. The same is true of the critiques of the postindustrial urban America context and the cultural and social conditions which it has produced. Today, the South Bronx and South Central Los Angeles are poorer and more economically marginalized than they were ten years ago.[45]

Strutting apocalyptically across the urban landscape, today's gangsta rappers have, for some listeners, become the new black superheroes invested with dangerous, ambiguous, uncontrolled, and uncontrollable powers, the force of nature bound up with self-conscious and grandiose marginality. You don't fuck with these brothers and sisters and live to tell about it. Shocked and Bull's dismissive appraisal of gangsta rap as a message primarily mediated by whites eager to be titillated by the thrilling despair within aggrieved black urban communities in the form of "bad nigga" narratives and hyperbolic masculinism underscores their view that the production and performativity of rap is directly at the expense of the structurally subordinated black subject. But is gangsta rap really "an exaggerated defiance feigned for commercial purposes," signifying steroids for sculpting rage, or perhaps a "mock nihilism that parallels the ambiguous accommodationism displayed in subversive forms of minstrelsy"[46] or, to borrow a phrase that Charles Pierce used in another context, a "phony menace that is little more than Tomming with your hat turned backward"?[47]

Some gangsta songs, for instance, promote a stereotypical (re)framing that depicts the gangsta rapper as both sociopath and criminal. Stereotypes are recast and refigured so that the negative connotations (of laziness, violence, etc.) become positive attributes of strength, of power, and of resistance to white domination. While the mock nihilism in gangsta rap "is an inherently resistive element," it has also "been a key element in its commercial exploitation."[48] While Angela Davis has decried the sexism of rap, she comments, somewhat reluctantly, on the power evoked by the image of the black man—as gun-toting revolutionary—that is offered up to the public by gangsta rap: "Many of the rappers call upon a market-mediated historical memory of the black movement of the sixties and seventies. The image of an armed Black man is considered the 'essence' of revolutionary commitment today. As dismayed as I may feel about this simplistic, phallocentric image, I remember my own responses to romanticized images of brothers (and sometimes sisters) with guns."[49]

Bell hooks argues that much of the sexism and misogyny that riddles rap songs is based on an assertive patriarchal paradigm of competitive masculinity and its emphasis on physical prowess. Decker presents Sister Souljah's role as a member of Public Enemy between 1990 and 1992 as deflecting gender-based criticism away from Public Enemy and constructing "an alibi for the stereotypical hypermasculinity of black men"[50] through her exclusive emphasis on racial politics and her allegiance to a hip-hop nationalism that tends to objectify the black woman as a sign of "Mother Africa."[51] However, black female rappers have done much to present affirming images of black women outside the binary couplet of good girl/bad girl that dominates the patriarchal culture of gangsta rap. For instance, Queen Latifah (Dana Owens) has challenged racist white America's view of black women as "welfare queens" and unwed mothers as well as challenged the view of some black nationalists that women accept roles subordinate to men. For Latifah, women are not the "bitches" signified by some male rap artists. According to Steven Gregory,[52] the welfare mother (defended by Queen Latifah and other female rappers)

> is a privileged site, where the brutalities of racism, patriarchy, and post-Fordist economic restructuring are mystified and, indeed, eroticized as the reproductive pathologies of black poverty. It is precisely this displacement of a politics of real bodies for a biopolitics of patriarchal desire that renders the iconography of the welfare mother and the inner city serviceable to a wide spectrum of cultural and political projects, ranging from the misogynist beats of gangsta rappers, to the more sober, but no less phallocentric, politics of welfare reform. What these projects share, whether as an appeal for a more "paternalistic" state authority . . . the aggressive policing of "group home turnstiles" or the selective re-tooling of black masculinity à la *Boyz 'N the Hood,* is the conviction that patriarchy is the bedrock of nation-building.[53]

Queen Latifah refuses the role given to the black woman within hip-hop nationalism—that of Isis—which merely symbolizes the imperialist glories of Egypt and the African empire. Latifah's Afrocentric expression is remarkable, not only because it is devoid of the concomitant sexism of nationalism but because it challenges the masculine logic of nation as well.[54]

Rose believes that it is hypocritical of black middle-class critics of rap lyrics not to launch the same level of moral criticism at black urban poverty as well as sexism and racism. She asserts that

> the problem is: one, that technology brings these vernacular practices, the practices most vulnerable to middle-class outrage, into spaces where they

might never have been heard twenty-five years ago; and two, rappers are vulnerable, highly visible cultural workers, which leaves them open to increased sanctions. But sexism, at the level of the toast and the boast, is only a subset of structurally sanctioned sexism. In that way, all manner of cultural practices and discourses that do not challenge the structures upon which these ideas are based wind up confirming them. Why, then, is the concern over rap lyrics so incredibly intense, particularly from Black middle-class guardians? Why not the same level of moral outrage over the life options that Black folks face in this country? It seems to me we need a censorship committee against poverty, sexism, and racism.[55]

Few cultural formations exist within popular culture that are stronger and more potent politically than gangsta rap. According to Kristal Brent Zook, "To say that rap is no more than a sad by-product of oppression is to take an explanatory, defensive stance when, in actuality, rap is a fundamental component of what may be the strongest political and cultural offensive gesture among African Americans today."[56] Rap is a powerful offensive medium in the way that it raises havoc with white middle-class complicity in and complacency with institutionalized racism; its dialogic pulsions disarticulate white supremacist governing narratives; it ruptures consensual images of blacks whom middle-class whites wish would "know their place." As De Genova argues,

> for its white listeners, gangster rap truly reconstitutes "the tyranny of the real"—both by musically and lyrically reconfiguring the real tyranny of the ghetto-space of death and destruction, and by reconfirming, *through* these phantasms of the "other," the sanitized comfort (and privilege) that comes with the tyrannical tedium of suburban, middle-class reality. It is here that we can discern a shared "culture of terror," a musical conjunction of the terror lived in Black ghettoes, and the enchanting terror *dreamed* in white suburbia.[57]

Rap unmakes feelings of security and safety in middle-class homes and neighborhoods. It indexes areas of concrete rage and generalized despair that are normally hidden from the official view of American democracy. De Genova powerfully captures this reality when he argues that gangster rap evokes

> a bilateral "culture of terror" in a dislocated "space of death": hegemonic (racist) fantasies about stereotypical "Blackness" and the self-destructive ("savage") violence of the urban ghetto-space, are conjoined with the nihilistic, lawless (oppositional) terror-heroism of proud, unapologetic self-styled "niggers"—Niggas With Attitude, Geto Boys, Compton's Most Wanted, et al.—who fulfill the prophesy and the promise of systemic violence and orchestrated destruction. Thus, gangster rap serves up white America's most cherished gun-slinging mythologies (heroic American

dreams) in the form of its worst and blackest nightmares, while it empowers Black imaginations to negate the existential terror of ghetto life (and death) by sheer force of the will.[58]

Following Kobena Mercer, George Lipsitz notes that rap is not a radical form in itself but has to be understood as a function of culture. He remarks that "culture functions as a social force to the degree that it gets instantiated in social life and connected to the political aspirations and activities of groups. It is here that hip hop holds its greatest significance and its greatest challenge to interpreters."[59]

Bell hooks lucidly illustrates that the context out of which rap has emerged is intertwined with the public stories of black male lives and the history of the pain suffered by black men in a racist society. She is worth quoting at length:

> Rap music provides a public voice for young black men who are usually silenced and overlooked. It emerged in the streets—outside the confines of a domesticity shaped and informed by poverty, outside enclosed spaces where . . . [black bodies] . . . had to be contained and controlled. . . . The public story of black male lives narrated by rap speaks directly to and against white racist domination, but only indirectly hints at the enormity of black male pain. Constructing the black male body as site of pleasure and power, rap and the dances associated with it suggest vibrancy, intensity, and an unsurpassed joy in living. It may very well be that living on the edge, so close to the possibility of being "exterminated" (which is how many young black males feel) heightens one's ability to risk and make one's pleasure more intense. It is this charge, generated by the tension between pleasure and danger, death and desire, that Foucault evokes when he speaks of that *complete total pleasure* that is related to death. Though Foucault is speaking as an individual, his words resonate in a culture affected by anhedonia—the inability to feel pleasure. In the United States, where our senses are daily assaulted and bombarded to such an extent that an emotional numbness sets in, it may take being "on the edge" for individuals to feel intensely. Hence the overall tendency in the culture is to see young black men as both dangerous and desirable.[60]

The most politically astute rappers take the racist and sexist stereotypes of black males and recontextualize them so that within popular culture, criminalized and hypersexualized black youths now become fearless rebels "standing up" heroically to the white man's exploitation. This fusion of heroism and criminality, of pleasure and pain, occurs without denying the endemic effects of institutionalized racism, patriarchal structures, heterosexist relations, and class exploitation. De Genova captures this point when he notes that "gangster rap exposes the multivalence and equivocation of racial essentialism: it evokes all of the conflicted meanings and opposed values which congeal simultaneously around a shared set of socially charged signifiers that comprise a single racial nomenclature."[61] Matthew Grant argues that gangsta rap results from the relationship between the criminalized underclass and the overclass reaching a point "where they can mutually benefit from the destabilization of the middle-class majority."[62] According to Grant, what makes gangsta rap so attractive to the middle-class white consumer is not its attempt to develop a revolutionary consciousness among its listeners, but rather the actively transgressive character of its assaults on middle-class taboos against violence. Gangsta rap provides white consumers who yearn to be part of the hip-hop nation with shocking images in which "the norms of bourgeois liberality are violated in an orgy of paradoxically subaltern elitism."[63] Through the politics of voyeurism, white youth can become the menacing urban *baaadman.*

Far from being a dispiriting successor to rhythm and blues, gangsta rap occupies a formidable yet not unproblematic space of resistance to racial oppression. A more productive account of gangsta rap, Grant argues, would examine its "celebration of insanity based as a singularly gendered obsession"—what he calls "the insane investment of the real."[64] Grant writes that

> the fantasy of losing it, of stepping over the limit of reason and civility, of surrendering oneself to the intoxication and ecstasy of violence uninhibited by the strictures of reason, is an important component of male subjectivity (which herein seems to cross boundaries established by class or skin color). Madness, among men, is something that must be endured or overcome (unless one is completely overwhelmed and obliterated by it). The flip side of this adventurist relation to the insane is the wholesale projection of insanity onto women as one legitimation of their exclusion from certain segments of the social order.[65]

Maintaining that the criticism leveled at rappers—that they wildly sensationalize urban life—is wrongly dependent upon holding rappers to the same ineluctable standards that inform the genre of social realism. Grant offers a spirited defense of gangsta rap, noting that the

> insanity that speaks through the voice of rap music is not simply a brand of psychic exoticism: it is the mental state produced by the process of racist oppression to which these bodies are subjected. The radical decentering of the subject, either through the use of drugs or through the use of semiautomatic weapons (and what could be more decentering than "a hole in your fuckin' head"?), which finds its expression in rap, a decentering celebrated by poststructuralists and postmodernists everywhere, results from an intensely decentering material configuration of the real. The insane distor-

tions of gangsta rap actually make their representations realistic. It's just a psychorealism thing.[66]

Representation, as Grant points out, is not just about adducing an accurate or realistic depiction of an event from many possible interpretations. It also speaks to forms of political advocacy that, in the case of gangsta rap, deal primarily with the Kafkaesque and carceral universe of the black urban male. (There are also "hard core" female rappers such as Manhole, a Latina from LA, and Boss, a classically trained African American musician who did not grow up in the hood but raps about it as if she did.)

Echoing the music of Dr. Dre and Snoop Doggy Dogg, Grant remarks that prison has become the educational alternative for black men: "the generalized form of social space for the underclass." Moreover, he argues that "hard core" gangsta rap constitutes a political program that he describes as an urban guerrilla movement. As a social force, however, gangsta rap overwhelmingly fails in its attempt to organize effectively, since, according to Grant, it has at its disposal only an "anarchofascist politics of drug dealership and gang-bangerism."[67] After all, NWA's drug dealing was decidedly "precapitalist" and, Grant maintains, no match for "the internationally organized capitalist bloc with its huge armies, advanced armaments, and high-tech domestic security systems."[68] Despite its failure to bring forth the hegemonic articulations that would make Gramsci proud, gangsta rap does present what I would call a contingent or provisional utopian longing—a trace, within a tapestry of violent imagery, of what is needed to bring about social justice. Grant puts it this way: "Gangsta rap, in spite of its contradictions, in spite of what is retrograde in it (like its often vicious sexism and homophobia), at least contains elements that give us a glimpse of what a radically oppositional culture could look like."[69] De Genova echoes a similar sentiment when he remarks that "rap music flourishes in the contradictory interstices of hegemonic appropriation and a fairly self-conscious and articulate politics of oppositional maneuvering."[70]

I locate gangsta rap as an "oppositional practice" in the sense that Michel de Certeau uses the term. While de Certeau is referring to the actions of the Amerindians, I believe his ideas are applicable to many contemporary groups—e.g., African Americans—who find themselves exploited and oppressed. According to de Certeau,

> even when they were subjected, indeed even when they accepted, their subjection . . . often used the laws, practices, and representations that were imposed on them by force or by fascination to ends other than those of their conquerors; they made something else out of them; they subverted them from within—not by rejecting them or by transforming them (though that occurred as well), but by many different ways of using them in the service of rules, customs, or convictions foreign to the colonization which they

could not escape. They metaphorized the dominant order; they made it function in another register.[71]

For instance, Shocked and Bull's criticism of rap overlooks rap's oppositional possibilities. It overlooks the fact that, among other things, gangsta rap has conflated the image of the "real nigga" and the "bad nigger" of black urban folklore. However, this distinction is admittedly unclear at times and, as Tommy Lott himself notes, the mass media's politicizing of the "bad nigger" idiom has led to a "troublesome conflation" of the "heroic badman" of folklore and the "bad nigga" of rap.[72]

The politics of resistance in gangsta rap needs to be located within the globalization of capital, the international circuit of debt and consumption, the deindustrialization, deskilling, and de-unionization of work in the expanding service sector. For instance, while it points to the structural instability of capitalist America and the production of urban rage, and while it wages political war against the white sentinels of the status quo, it remains ideologically aligned with capitalist interests, glorifying crass materialism and celebrating conspicuous consumption. As such, rap as a form of resistance can be conflictually located along a series of semantic axes; it varies, in other words, from song to song, from artist to artist, and from listener to listener, depending upon the performative moments that are meant to be signified. In other words, gangsta rap does not constitute a master trope of urban criticism, an ur-text of cultural resistance but is read differently by different groups. Oppressed minorities are more likely to resonate with rap for its political critique, while middle-class white groups are more likely to be drawn to rap for its aestheticization of transgression. De Genova makes an important point when he claims that "what emerges in gangster rap, like the figure of Bigger Thomas, is 'a snarl of many realities.' Gangster rap would seem to provide a very different kind of 'therapy' for those who live its nihilism, than the shock treatment it provides for those who live in mortal terror of it."[73] Tommy Lott notes, for instance, that "with the commercializing of gangsta rap we can no longer speak in a totalizing manner of rap music. Instead, this designation must be reserved for specific rap tunes."[74]

I believe that it is instructive to locate rap as a challenge to the bourgeois political and racialized structures which discursively articulate what counts as the quintessential American experience. Elsewhere I have argued that the cultural logic of late capitalism has reinscribed the moral order within the United States around the practice of consumption and the secular redemption of acquiring wealth.[75] The structural unconscious of American popular culture (the term *structural* is meant to draw attention to the fact that the social structure is folded into individual and collective forms of subjectivity which operate through the language of myth) has been occupied by the figure of the serial killer as the last frontiersperson, the last autonomous subject, the last "true" American who can act.

America—Europe's other—has often been considered the promised land.[76] But when all the old myths based on America as the promised land are demythologized, when the Protestant millenarianist project to recreate Zion in the streets of Los Angeles end in the Intifada of 1992, then the quintessential apocalyptic moment becomes the act of random murder. America is exporting this myth through film (*Love and a .45, Natural Born Killers, Pulp Fiction),* music, and other cultural formations.

The gangsta rapper serves in this context to remind white audiences that Utopia is lost, that the end of history has arrived (but not in the way Francis Fukuyama predicted), that the logic of white Utopia is premised upon white supremacy and exploitative social relations, and that whites have mistakenly pledged their loyalty to the Beast. Gangsta rap reveals the white millenarianist project of democracy to be grounded upon a will to sameness, a desire to drive out people of color from the mythic frontier of the promised land. In this sense, gangsta rap transforms the "brothas" into avenging angels who call upon whites to redeem themselves or face the wrath of God—a God who will send forth not locusts or floods but angry black urban dwellers taking to the streets.

Just as the black subject has always operated as a metaphor for chaos and instability, the Los Angeles uprising of 1992 literalized this metaphor as one of physical terror. In a world where history has already been purchased by the wealthy, the losers have no choice but to steal some of history back again. The agents of leadership will not be the good Rodney Kings on television but the "bad niggaz" in the streets.

Before we can answer the question of whether hip-hop culture itself is preventing gangsta rap from evolving into a social movement, we need to gain a deeper understanding of the semantic orbit surrounding the politics of difference in gangsta rap. Do we accept, for instance, the resistive elements of gangsta rap only in the context of the production of aesthetic pleasure, rather than the promotion of a political agenda only because acts of resistance can be defused as well as diffused into a politics of the sublime? Has the commercialization of gangsta rap imploded into the political such that these two characteristics are indistinguishable? Does the conflation of gangsta rap's commodification and political project effectively cancel both rather than dialectically reinitiate a productive political tension around a project of social justice and a praxis of liberation? Does rap's repackaging of oppositional codes along aesthetic lines merely reduce gangsta rap to a more marketable form of cultural capital that can be traded within existing capitalist frameworks of power and privilege? Can the same questions be raised about hip-hop movies such as *Krush Groove, A Thin Line Between Love and Hate, Set It Off,* and *Booty Call*?

De Genova argues that gangsta rap does escape the nihilistic aestheticism of which it has been accused by linking such aestheticism with the politics of the street:

> Gangster rap, even more than other types of hip hop, raises the free-for-all aesthetic far above and beyond the music's formal level: gangster rap celebrates a free-for-all in the streets. Here it becomes possible to imagine the transcendence of a merely aesthetic nihilism which can be contained by commodification to imagine an articulation of this highly public nihilist aesthetic with the street, the place where the sideshow can become the main event.[77]

The street or neighborhood, it should be pointed out, becomes a liminal site: "The symbol of 'the ghetto' in gangster rap becomes its fire-brand of 'authenticity.' The ghetto comes to be valorized not only as a 'space of death' (and destruction) but also as a space of survival and transcendence; not merely a 'heart of darkness,' it is also the heart of 'Blackness.'"[78]

Gangsta rap is concerned with the articulation of experiences of oppression that find their essential character among disenfranchised urban black and Latino populations. Rap helps to communicate symbols and meanings and articulates intersubjectively the lived experience of social actors. The ontological status of the gangsta rapper resides in the function of the commodity of blackness, but a certain quality of blackness that is identified through the expressive codes of the rapper is the "inner turmoil" of the oppressed black subject of history. Here, blackness (or Latino-ness) marks out a heritage of pain and suffering and points to the willingness and ability of oppressed groups to fight against injustice "by any means necessary." Gangsta rap songs are able to demonstrate how popular white constructions of black men and women ultimately seek to instantiate control over people of color in order to contain them culturally as well as physically. Rap exposes the hidden and hardened fissures and faultlines of democratic social life, revealing the underpinnings of social justice to be little more than a convenient cultural fiction.

Much of the hard-core political gangsta rap provides a type of hallucinatory snapshot of everyday life on America's mean streets—a video canvas of Fortress USA—which evinces fearful images of black rage and destruction, images that typically endure in gangsta rap videos but unfortunately do little to transform the social and material relations which produce them. Violence in gangsta rap has become an Adamic ritual that creates a world of order through disorder that performatively constitutes both the gangsta himself or herself and the object of their violence. In other words, the founding language of the gangsta is violence. It is within this rationality that the image of the gangsta circulates like a political sign within an imagined community of oppressed and resisting subjects. Invading the space of other gang bangers or that of dominant groups in binary-coded struggles (black vs. white, male vs. female, cops vs. black community) helps to stabilize the subjectivity of the gangsta rapper and to contingently anchor identity through a negative interjection of the Other, a negation of whatever threatens it: bitches, rival gangs, the police, etc. The paramount hegemonic voice that gangsta rappers struggle against—and this is true for its eastern Caribbean and east London counterparts—is law and order. Gangsta rappers challenge the hegemonic modes of thought that are embedded in formal conventions—educational, legal, sexual, and others.

It is important to understand that while gangsta rap suffers from problems of misogyny and nihilism and while the capitalist culture industry amplifies the aesthetic dimension of rap at the expense of its political pronouncements, rap also produces important forms of nationalistic thought that work to nurture forms of coalition building and community. For instance, Zook notes that

> both the form and content of rap express black autonomy, self-determination, and cultural pride. But what is perhaps most fascinating is not only the way that rap confirms a sense of imagined, metaphorical community, but rather, the fact that this fantasy of "home" is simultaneously constructed materially through the very modes of production, marketing, and the critical discourses which surround it. In other words, just as [Benedict] Anderson argues that literary forms such as the newspaper and the novel made European nationalisms possible, I would say that the forms of television, music videos, film, literary works, and the networks involved in producing these forms are also nurturing a heightened sense of racial collectivity, group solidarity, and even political responsibility—all of which are important elements of nationalist thought.[79]

Gangsta rappers assume a contradictory attitude to black nationalism. On the one hand, they identify with the liberation struggles in Africa, yet on the other hand, they are wary of focusing too much attention on Africa and Afro-centrism for fear of deflecting concern from the serious problems in America's inner cities. According to Robin D.G. Kelley, rappers "contend that the nationalists' focus on Africa—both past and present—obscures the daily battles poor Black folk have to wage in contemporary America."[80]

While it does little to offer a project of transformation, gangsta rap manages, by bursting through the representational space of whiteness and by advancing political solidarity in the form of an imagined community of struggle, to depict what Grant describes as the "proprietary position that whites occupied during the days of slavery (and *mutatis mutandis* still enjoy today)."[81] Whites who are most threatened by gangsta rap's aggressive and adversarial masculinity attempt to consolidate their opposition in a white woman/black beast symbolic order mythologized in white supremacist discourses which have lately been discursively reinforced by prominent politicians such as Newt Gingrich, Jesse Helms, Pat Buchanan, and Pete Wilson. It is possible, too, that white consumers of gangsta rap are drawn to a self-consciously exaggerated display of sexuality, much the same way that rhythm and blues artists captured white audiences in the fifties. As Medovoi notes,

> Of course, sexuality had long been a principal theme of rhythm and blues, but the youthful white audience now took an interest in exaggerating and redirecting its sexual themes symbolically across the race line. Chapple and Garofalo quote R&B artist John Otis recalling: "We found that we moved the white audiences more by caricaturing the music, you know, overdoing the shit—falling on your back with the saxophone, kicking your legs up. And if we did too much of that for a black audience they'd tell us—'Enough of that shit—play some music!'"[82]

While hard-core rap artists such as Snoop Doggy Dogg, Da Lench Mob, Ice Cube, Eazy-E, Niggas with Attitude, and Naughty by Nature unquestionably create politically motivated music, the politics can often be traced to a black nationalist focus. A key issue emerges here. It has to do with the fact that the aesthetic power of the music creates a pleasure among listeners which may even be against the values of the progressive listeners. Tommy Lott reports on a similar issue when he notes that the rap group Public Enemy (which often expresses black nationalist imperatives) is the favorite rap group in some racist white communities such as South Boston.

The controversial rap single "Fuck Rodney King" by former Geto Boy Willie D., makes the powerful claim that during the LA uprising of 1992, "Rodney King so willingly took the moral low ground and turned himself into an establishment ad for social harmony" through his plaintive plea, "Can we all get along?"[83]

> *Fuck Rodney King, and his ass.*
> *When I see the mother fucker I'm a blast*
> *Boom in his head, boom boom in his back*
> *Just like that*
> *Cause I'm tired of the [ ] niggers*
> *Sayin increase the peace*
> *And let the violence cease*
> *When the Black man built this country*
> *But can't get his for the prejudiced honkey . . .*
> *But when it's time for the revolution*
> *I'm a click click click, fuck this rap shit*

> *Cause money ain't shit but grief*
> *If ya ain't got no peace*
> *Gotta come on with it*
> *Get down for my little Willies*
> *So they can come up strong and live long*
> *And not be scared to get it on!*[84]

Rather than identifying the song as an example of black nihilism—the image typically conjured by the lyrics—Lott suggests that it constitutes an incisive political critique. In Lott's view, Willie D.'s song "demands the autonomy and agency wards of the state lack."[85] Willie D.'s rap demands the type of political change that would make the violence he calls for unnecessary.

Tommy Lott's analysis of the term *nigga* is instructive. He claims, rightly in my view, that gangsta rap has creatively reworked and recoded in a socially transgressive and politically retaliatory manner the social meaning of the term in ways that distinguish it from the taboo term used by white racists and from the often self-hating inflections of the term expressed by black professionals.[86] Not only is the racist meaning of the term *nigga* recoded by the gangsta rappers but its ambiguity now shifts, depending on the contexts of its enunciation and reception. When gangsta rappers revise the spelling of the racist version of the word *nigger* to the vernacular *nigga* they are using it as a defiant idiom of a resistive mode of African American cultural expression which distinguishes it from the way that, for instance, white racists in Alabama might employ the term. Further, Lott notes that the vernacular *nigga* permits a form of class consciousness among the black urban "underclass" or lumpen proletariat in the sense that it distinguishes black urban working-class youth from those middle-class black professionals who feel denigrated whenever the term is used. According to Robin D.G. Kelley,

Nigga speaks to a collective identity shaped by class consciousness, the character of inner-city space, police repression, poverty, and the constant threat of intraracial violence. . . . In other words, Nigga is not merely *another* word for black. Products of the postindustrial ghetto, the characters in gangsta rap constantly remind listeners that they are still second-class citizens—"Niggaz"—whose collective experiences suggest that nothing has changed *for them* as opposed to the black middle class. In fact, Nigga is frequently employed to distinguish urban black working class males from the black bourgeoisie and African Americans in positions of institutional authority. Their point is simple: the experiences of young black men in the inner city are not universal to all black people, and, in fact, they recognize that some African Americans play a role in perpetuating their oppression. To be a "real nigga" is to be a product of the ghetto. By linking identity to the "hood" instead of simply skin color, gangsta rappers implicitly acknowl-edge the limitations of racial politics, including black middle-class re-formism as well as black nationalism.[87]

Within the sociohistorical conjuncture of current US urban centers, the gangsta has become a sign of immanence, an alteration of signification between *nigger* and *nigga* relayed to infinity. Through its cultural fusions, intercultural encounters, and expressive articulations, we are invited by gangsta rap to visit spaces we have never lived physically, nor would ever wish to—spaces that function significantly in the manufacturing of iden-tity. George Lipsitz remarks that "music not only shapes and reflects dom-inant and subordinate social and cultural relations, but . . . music making and other forms of popular culture serve as a specific site for the creation of collective identity."[88] Rap artists continue to move within Henri Lefebvre's "theatrical or dramatized space" by creating a new legacy of in-surgency and struggle, one that menaces the prestige hierarchies of white supremacy, that constructs critical aperçus about human dignity and suf-fering, and that sets itself in opposition to melioristic reform and on the side of revolutionary transformation. As such, it serves as a "social force."[89] Yet I wish to underscore that it cannot be celebrated as a form of oppositional consciousness by uncritically attributing political con-sciousness to rap artists merely because of their social location as urban "underdog" musicians. Nor can we, as Lipsitz maintains, after Kobena Mercer, argue that music is in itself politically transgressive. Rather, music becomes a "social force" only "to the degree that it gets instantiated in so-cial life and activities of groups."[90] The political inflections of music need to be understood in terms of their cultural, historical, and geopolitical specificity. Lipsitz further argues that the expansion of transnational capi-tal does not, prima facie, sound the death knell of political resistance but rather that "the reach and scope of transnational capital" can make in-digenous musical forms more powerful as forms of resistance.

Gangsta rap is essentially a diasporic cultural politics and positions it-self as such against cultural displacement and capitalist exploitation. For this reason we can't unproblematically articulate white rappers ("wiggers" or "white niggers") into the rap resistance movement. Cul-tural borrowings by white rappers are not necessarily problematic but can be seen as troublesome when consideration is given to the way gangsta rap is cognitively mapped by white rappers: the cultural circuits along which such borrowings travel and how these borrowings become fused to dominant Euro-American "universal" meanings, knowledge claims, and social conventions addressed to "the other." Imitation *of* the other doesn't necessarily mean identification *with* the other, yet at the same time it doesn't necessarily exclude such an identification. The

Beastie Boys and House of Pain are examples of white rappers with some crossover appeal to black audiences. However, Lipsitz warns that "powerful institutions attach prestige hierarchies to artistic expressions in such a way as to funnel reward and critical attention to Euro-American appropriators, and because ethnocentric presumptions about the universality of Western notions of art obscure the cultural and political contexts that give meaning to many artifacts from traditional cultures that are celebrated as pure form in the West."[91] While there is, to be sure, a depoliticizing aspect to commodification, this contradiction is also a primary condition of gangsta rap's political enablement. Following bell hooks, Grant underscores the fact that because consumers could ignore the political message or information disseminated throughout the music that it also implies the contrary: consumers could pay attention to precisely that element.[92] Gangsta rap creatively exploits the contradictions brought on by commodification to construct a guerrilla warfare of the airwaves—a war waged through what I have called elsewhere the media's "perpetual pedagogy."[93] Grant speaks to this issue when he writes that

> we could thus conceive of a diffuse war of resistance and liberation being waged against the forces of white supremacy with rap music serving as its communication system. . . . Rap music, as the objectified representative of the gangsta, invades the white world and steals white kids. . . . Ice-T also understands his intervention, his invasion, pedagogically. He teaches white kids about racism and power. In addition, he maintains that this music supplies the white youth with an alternative vocabulary in which to articulate their rebellion against the parental authority structure.[94]

At its best, gangsta rap urges the creation of cooperatives of resistance, zones of freedom, where strategies and tactics of liberation can emerge, where the opposite of local struggles does not collapse into some abstract universalized call for emancipation in the form of a master narrative that brings premature closure to the meaning of freedom, where the opposite of local struggles brings to mind not the master trope of the universal but rather the concept of reciprocal relations at the level of the social. This alternative points to the idea of peoples' collective struggle to advance a project of hope lived in the subjunctive mode of "as if" yet grounded in the concreteness of everyday life. It is within the dialectical relationship between local and more broad, collective struggles that gangsta rap accelerates the anger and rage that is the very condition of its existence. Unlike more mainstream musical forms such as heavy metal or rock, which tend to displace issues dealing with relations of power between black and white populations onto quarantined spaces and which often elide conflicting and contradictory relations premised upon racialized and differential relations of power and privilege, gangsta rap troubles the certainty and unsettles the complacency of existing power arrangements between blacks and whites. I would argue that the multicultural nihilistic hedonism that Newt Gingrich's authoritarian populist millenarianism hates with such a frenzied passion is really one of the few sources of oppositional popular discourses remaining in a nation morally flattened by the weight of the New Right's rhetorical cant that demonizes, hellifies, and zombifies African Americans, Latinos, the poor, and the disenfranchised.

Yet in saying this there is evidence that gangsta rap is running its course within the circuits of capitalist commodification. In a recent issue of *The Los Angeles Reader,* Steve Appleford[95] writes that "another album cover with a gun thrust in your face is as shocking and dangerous now as Madonna without clothes."[96] He cites MC Ren as saying that "we wanted to put Compton on the map, so we rapped about what went on in Compton. . . . But now it's like everybody's talking the same shit, people talking about shit we did years ago, you understand? You've got to advance, man. . . . Everybody right now is just stuck."[97] Ren remarks that "you got all these fools coming out now, they think all you got to do is just cuss, talk about weed, low ridin', shit like that, and you can get a record deal, you know what I'm saying? Rap is fucked up, man. It started a few years ago when somebody realized this shit is making money."[98]

According to Appleford, Ice-T now rejects the gangsta label, preferring to describe his music as "reality rap." When gangsta rap restricts itself to the politics of the ghetto, white viewers see it as a threat that is constrained to certain areas of life that they can avoid at the everyday level. When you have easy access to the "black threat" for entertainment purposes, it becomes more familiar and therefore less intimidating. On the other hand, ghettocentricity is a constant reminder to white viewers that they themselves are white. Whiteness—that absent presence that outlines the cultural capital required for favored citizenship status—becomes, in this instance, less invisible to whites themselves. The less invisible that whiteness becomes, the less it serves as a tacit marker against which otherness is defined.

There have been some recent alternative movements within rap, such as G-funk and rap/be-bop fusion. For instance, R&B artists such as Me'Shell Ndegéocello are experimenting with aspects of hip-hop and soul. Recently in the *LA Weekly,* Donnell Alexander[99] surveyed some alternative rap, arguing that while hard core gangsta rap (Big Mike, MC Eiht, Jeru, Treach) is now mainstream, alternative rap groups such as Digable Planets, Spearhead, Justin Warfield, the Broun Fellinis, and Michael "Basehead" Ivey haven't been able to develop much of a following outside of white college students. And there is the question of the powerful forces of commodification from the marketplace. Is rap's restricted code of black solidarity against oppression being elaborated for financial gain by the white-dominated culture industry? Is it being diffused into an aesthetic style that can be danced to or played because of its growing availability as a cultural code?[100] Is it being depotentiated because it is being wrenched away from the cultural contexts that made it meaningful?

The politics of commodification and appropriation that have been confronting gangsta rap artists in the face of the hypermobility of capital is reminiscent of the phenomena occurring with salsa and *rockero* in the context of Puerto Rico. For instance, Javier Santiago-Lucerna[101] discusses how artists like Ruben Blades and Willie Colon, whose earlier musical productions resonated with a progressive politics, have been absorbed into the politics of the marketplace. According to Santiago-Lucerna, salsa music and the cultural *comarrona* have been transformed into spaces constituted with the cynical sign of consumer culture. In fact, the music being produced in the local rock scene and among local punk bands is currently far more hard-edged politically than salsa, *nueva trova,* and *musica campesina,* as the bands Whisker Biscuit, Kampo Viej, Descojon Urbano, La Experiencia de Tonito Cabanillas, and Sin Remedio can attest. For instance, in "Urban Fuckup," Descojon-Urbano sings:

> *Oye es que me da gusto*
> *Cada vez que cogen a un politico corrupto*
> *Que cabroneria, que barbaridad*
> *el pobre se jode y el rico tiene mas*
>
> *[It gives me so much pleasure*
> *every time they catch a corrupted politician*
> *What shit, what an atrocity*
> *the poor are fucked, while the rich have more]*[102]

The issue of political domestication and product commodification is on the surface somewhat different in the case of gangsta rap because oppositional political rap is now mainstream. Therefore, it is hard to see what other kinds of music might soon replace rap's hard-edge political critique. Perhaps forms of rap will develop that are not coded in the image of the hypersexualized gang banger and that begin to address issues of economic exploitation, misogyny, and homophobia.

Critics of gangsta rap need to take seriously Rosemary Hennessy's[103] suggestion that "in postmodern consumer culture the commodity is a central means by which desire is organized."[104] In other words, listeners of gangsta rap affectively invest in the music and video productions. The music produces certain structures of feeling, particular economies of affectivity. But the logic of the commodity conceals certain invisible social relations that need to be considered. The commodity, argues Hennessy, after Marx, is not material in the physical sense alone but rather in the sense that "it is socially produced through human labor and the extraction of surplus value in exchange."[105] Commodity fetishism refers to the "illusion that value resides in objects rather than in the social relations between individuals and objects."[106] In other words, commodity fetishism "entails the misrecognition of a structural effect as an immediate property of one of its elements, as if this property belonged to it outside of its relation to other elements."[107]

Gangsta rap as a commercial product needs to be understood not simply in terms of the way it transgressively signifies social life but in terms of the exploitation of human labor and the way in which the social relations of production and consumption organize everyday human life: in short, in terms of its commodity fetishism. De Genova notes that

> commodified rap music was able to proliferate through the virtual pillage of an ever-expanding universe of already-existing commodified music—instantiating the semblance of something like a parodic auto-cannibalization of the commodity form. The very essence of hip-hop music, as a musical genre which begins with the unabashed appropriation of pre-recorded, mass-produced, commodified music, demonstrates that "public culture" is inevitably and unassailably "public-access culture"—a free-for-all.[108]

Gangsta rap's relation to the corporate marketplace, its potential for expropriation, and its reproduction of ideologies historically necessary to commodity exchange—such as patriarchal ones—is an important issue that needs to be addressed. In other words, gangsta rap needs to be viewed not merely as an ideological formation, cultural signifier, or performative spectacle, but also as the product of historical and social relations. Gangsta rap needs to be seen not only in discursive terms but rather in terms of the materiality of discourse. By materiality of discourse I refer to "the ways culture constructs subjectivities, reproduces power relations, and foments resistance" insofar as these relations and practices are "shaped by social totalities like capitalism, patriarchy, and imperialism as they manifest differently across social formations and within specific historical conjunctures."[109] This is not to say, however, that gangsta rap at the level of the oppositional spectacle is not an important popular counterdiscourse.

Thomas Cushman's important work on understanding the diffusion of revolutionary musical codes raises some important questions about rap (which, unfortunately, exceed the scope of this essay). These questions demand an analysis of the social evolution of gangsta rap as a musical style as it is situated within the world capitalist system. This suggests examining gangsta rap as a restricted code (condensed, context-specific cluster of symbols and meanings) that articulates the existential experience of subordinate groups of African Americans and Puerto Ricans and their everyday dissent. It also means tracing rap's diffusion into an elaborated code (context-free, universal) across time and space into new social contexts and analyzing how its original, organic, revolutionary expression as a means of addressing race and class exploitation has been diffused.[110] For instance, what is to prevent gangsta rap from becoming, in Cushman's terms, a casualty of "a highly developed, world-wide culture industry that operates precisely by scanning the world environment for disturbances, selectively amplifying and altering certain aspects of those disturbances and re-presenting them to large audiences who receive them as entertainment commodities"?[111]

Gangsta rap creates identity through a racial system of intelligibility that produces binary distinctions between blacks and whites, an us-against-them discursive matrix. As a performative signification anchored in the context of the urban ghetto, it constitutes part of the regulatory practices of the dominant culture while at the same time resisting and critiquing this culture.

Diane Fuss, following Frantz Fanon, argues that under conditions of colonialism, blacks are "forced to occupy, in a white racial phantasm, the static ontological space of the timeless 'primitive.'"[112] In this "imaginary relation of fractured specularity," blacks are denied by the white Imperial Subject, the alterity or otherness necessary to achieve subjectivity. Interpellated and fixed into a static objecthood, blacks become neither an "I" nor a "not-I," becoming instead a degraded and devalorized signifier, a fragmented object, a form of pure exteriority.

The transcendental signifier "white," according to Fuss, is never a "not-black," but rather operates from its own self-proclaimed transparency, as a marker that floats imperially over the category of race, operating "as its own Other" and independent from the sign "black" for its symbolic constitution. In terms of the colonial-imperial register of self-other relations, which, as Fuss notes, operates in psychoanalysis and existentialism on the Hegelian principle of negation and incorporation in which the other is assimilated into the self—the white subject can be white without any relation to the black subject because the sign "white" exempts itself from a dialogical logic of negativity. But the black subject must be black in relation to the white subject.

For instance, whereas white rap singer Vanilla Ice was once referred to as "the Elvis of rap," the black singer Al B. Sure was referred to as "the Black Elvis." Lionett cites remarks made by Patricia Williams, who points out the parodic nature of these labels: "Elvis, the white black man of a generation ago, reborn in a black man imitating Elvis." Lionett adds that Elvis is "reborn in Vanilla Ice, a white man imitating the black rapper imitating Elvis: a dizzying thought." The point here is that in the depiction of each rap artist, the major point of reference is white culture.[113]

Imperialist acts of assimilation and incorporation are located at the level of the unconscious. The gangsta is simultaneously a mimicry of subversion and subjugation. Drawing on Homi Bhabha's notion that colonial mimicry possesses the possibility of resisting and subverting dominant systems of representation (through the possibility of mimicry slipping into mockery) as well as subtending them, I want to argue that when it ironizes the role of the incorporated black subject, gangsta rap (at least in its video incarnations) undermines the image of the impotent black subject, de-transcendentalizing it and rendering it unstable.[114] However, when the gangsta rapper undertakes a "parodic hyperbolization" (to borrow Fuss's term) of the subjugated black man—in the figure of the gangsta with a gun—but does not connect it to a larger political project of liberation, this may rupture the image of the subjugated black subject but fail to unsettle the exploitative relations connected to white supremacist patriarchal capitalism. By not connecting its subversion to a larger politics of possibility, gangsta rap runs the risk of ironizing its own act of subversion and parodying its own performance of dissent in such an I-don't-give-a-fuck fashion that, rather than erode dominant social relations of exploitation and subjugation, it may actually reinforce them.

The social realism that accompanies much of the gangsta rap of Ice Cube, Ice-T, and others is situated within a larger political agenda and sets the context for portraying the role of the rapper (qua oppositional cultural forms) as a "truth sayer" and noble revolutionary subject fighting the injustices of the white-controlled mega-state. It also builds the ground for a more sustained critique of racist and capitalist social relations.

But in some of the rap videos of, say, Sir Mix-A-Lot or 2 Live Crew, unrealistic portrayals occur of the dissenting black male subject, depicting him as living in ostentatious luxury, surrounded by black and white women massaging their breasts on his car window ("put 'em on the glass") or swaying their G-stringed buttocks in his welcoming face. In this instance, there is a tendency to recuperate a reversionary politics, because the lifestyle of the black hepcat dissenter appears to be exaggerated to the point of parody. Such a parodic representation of the successful black consumer (where women are presented as thong-clad commodities to be plucked from swimming pools) tends to defray and to occlude a larger politics of liberation outside of commodity culture. In this case, the landscape of rap is defoliated in terms of race, class, and gender issues, while dissent is defused into issues of who has the most "babes who got back." In another sense, however, it's also possible to look at 2 Live Crew's videos in a different light. It's possible to overlook the sexism and the hyperbolizing of the black male-as-womanizer by focusing on the consumer trappings of the black rapper—swimming pools, fancy cars, beautiful houses, and available sex. Acquiring these "trappings" becomes a form of resistance because they are not available to the average white or black subject. The problem here is rap's apparent legitimation of capitalist social relations of consumption. Do rappers— including gangsta rappers—just want to make the pleasures of patriarchal capitalism available to all black males?

Can gangsta rap move beyond Benjamin's shock effects, its decontextualization as an effect of its mechanical reproducibility, beyond the space of its own commercial structures, beyond its ideological prohibitions, its structures of expectation, its demarcations of despair—all of which create a locus of signifying phantasms and perverse forms of the "other," which, in turn, collaborate with neoliberal approaches to politics that ultimately wrest away rap's oppositional potency? To create a praxis of both opposition and possibility, gangsta rap needs to undertake the construction of new identities that are refractory to commodification. It must continue to perturb society, to shape culture on a deeper level. Hip-hop culture must provide spaces of resistance and transgression, without succumbing to political incoherence. Only in this way will it be able to prevent its revolutionary potential from being articulated to the terms of the official culture of consumption that defuses adversarial codes into the cultural logic of the aesthetic.

Despite the always-present threat of commodification, gangsta rap still poses a serious challenge to the formation of new identities of resistance and social transformation. The new identities surrounding various articulations of gangsta rap hold both unforeseen promises and potential dangers. As Lipsitz remarks, "to think of identities as interchangeable or infinitely open does violence to the historical and social constraints imposed on us by structures of exploitation and privilege. But to posit innate and immobile identities for ourselves and others confuses history with nature, and denies the possibility of change."[115]

The challenge that confronts gangsta rap in particular and hip-hop culture in general is the extent to which it contributes to the de-familiarization of the Western sovereign subject, the Euro-American imperial subject, and the extent to which it can become self-conscious of the relations of power and privilege that create the context for and overdetermine its cultural exchanges. This means, as I have argued above, linking a politics of semiotic subversion to a critique of the material social relations of exploitation that have been largely responsible for the problems faced by people of color in the United States.

Manning Marable speaks to a new articulation of the concept of blackness that is defined not in racial or ethnic/cultural terms but as a political category that speaks to new forms of political mobilization:

> We must find new room in our identity as people of color to include all other oppressed national minorities—Chicanos, Peurto Ricans, Asian/Pacific Americans, and other people of African descent. We must find the common ground we share with oppressed people who are not national minorities—working-class people, the physically challenged, the homeless, the unemployed, and those Americans who suffer discrimination because they are lesbian or gay. I believe that a new multicultural America is possible, that a renaissance of Black militancy will occur in concert with new levels of activism from the constituencies mentioned above. But it is possible only if we have the courage to challenge and to overturn our own historical assumptions about race, power, and ourselves. Only then will we find the new directions necessary to challenge the system, to "fight the power," with an approach toward political culture that can truly liberate all of us.[116]

In its most politically enabling formations, gangsta rap is able to create a space of resistance in which black identity is not dependent upon whiteness to complete it. It escapes colonial mimesis through a series of cultural relays that keeps identity fluid and shifting. The particular liberatory values that are affirmed in gangsta rap need, however, to co-reside with other resonant values rooted in the contingency and radical historicity of oppressed groups throughout the globe. For white folks this means not simply a *tolerance of* difference but rather a critical *engagement with* difference on a global scale.

The recent death of Tupac Shakur provides a bitter lesson about the best and worst of gangsta rap. Tupac's reputation as one of the most hard-core of the gangsta rappers and his obsession with living the "authenticity" of the streets as a "real nigga" eventually rebounded against him as he brought together his own brand of what Mike Dyson calls "thuggery and thanatopsis."[117] Dyson remarks that "the Real Niggas are trapped by their own contradictory couplings of authenticity and violence. Tupac's death is the most recent, and perhaps most painful, evidence of that truth."[118] Dyson further notes that Tupac's own project constituted "a sad retreat from a much more complex, compelling vision of black life that gangsta rap and hard-core hip-hop, at its best, helped outline."[119] In his art of "celeterrogation" (what Dyson calls "the deft combination of celebration and interrogation") Tupac embodied the best and the worst of gangsta rap. Dyson eloquently comments:

by joining verbal vigor to rage—about material misery and racial hostility, about the avalanche of unheard suffering that suffocates black lives before they wake, walk or will their own survival—hard core rappers proved that theirs was a redemptive vulgarity. At their best, they showed that the real vulgarity was the absurd way too many black folk perish on the vine of fruitless promises of neighborhood restoration, of racial rehabilitation. The hard core hip-hopper proved that the real vulgarity was the vicious anonymity and punishing silence of poor black life, with which they broke faith every time they seized a mike to bring poetry to pain. . . . But, in the end, despite all his considerable gifts, Tupac helped pioneer a more dangerous, even more destructive, trend in hard-core hip-hop that, ironically, draws from the oral energy of the orthodox black culture from which he sought thuggish refuge. Tupac yearned to live the life he rapped about in his songs. That golden ideal was the motive behind gospel passions in black culture to close the gap between preaching and practice, between what one said and what one did.[120]

As long as African Americans and other historically marginalized social groups are perceived by whites to be artificial constructions—in effect, artificial white people—who exist largely to be economically exploited or else reinvented and rewarded by whites in the sphere of leisure culture for their own entertainment, then it is unlikely that democracy will ever be achievable. As long as the rules by which society functions continue to be defined by the white majority, and the interpretation of such rules continues to be controlled by a dominant capitalist elite, then the concept of equality is nothing but a hollow term. As long as the liberal pluralistic society in which we all participate is controlled a priori by our failure to address the problem of material exploitation, then gangsta rap will operate out of necessity as a serious critique of U.S. cultural life. As long as the politically unifying cultural understanding that pluralists posit as the framework for democratic social life continues to read narratives such as gangsta rap as necessarily threatening to social harmony, then success in our society will always be racially determined.

Equal access to shared symbols of nationhood do not spell democracy for any group when such symbols are discouraged from being interrogated, reanimated, and transformed. More importantly, equal access to the material necessities of human survival and dignity must be made a fundamental prerequisite for democracy. Anything less than this makes a mockery of the ideal of social justice. In this context, the "brothas" and "sistahs" of gangsta rap are demanding that democracy live up to its promises. They challenge—by any means necessary—democracy to rearticulate its mission in view of the current urban nightmare in which the melting pot itself has melted in a postpluralist firestorm. How must we rethink identity when the container can no longer contain, when the ladle dissolves in the mixture, when the signifier ceases to signify?

If British sociologists Scott Lash and John Urry are correct in asserting that "we are not so much thrown into communities, but decide which communities—from youth subcultures to new social movements—we shall throw ourselves into," then what sort of aesthetic (hermeneutic) reflexivity is required in the case of gangsta rap?[121] What is at issue when the ideographic mode of gangsta-ing is counterposed to conduct regulated by the abstract norm-governed social structure of the state? Is this a question of what Lash and Urry call "race-baiting neo tribes" or the beginning of "new communitarian social movements"? What happens when the wild zones of information flows and networks of the so-called underclass enter into a marriage with the new informational bourgeoisie?

In an era in which the subject is located as ambivalent and grounded in lost referents and instabilities within signifying chains, gangsta rap draws needed attention to the importance, not only of dis-identifying with the cultural obvious but also of recognizing that the difference rendered most invisible in the production of postmodern cultural representations is the difference between rich and poor. We are viscerally reminded by gangsta rappers that cultural identities and practices remain tied to capital's drive to accumulate profits through the appropriation of labor that relies historically on forms of racism, patriarchy, and imperialism.[122]

Epilogue

The casket carrying the body of Notorious B.I.G. (Christopher Wallace, a.k.a. Biggie Smalls) rests in a hearse winding its way past 226 St. James Place in the rapper's old Brooklyn neighborhood toward the Frank E. Campbell Funeral Chapel in Manhattan's Upper East Side. Two black Cadillacs filled with flowers—the letters B.I.G. are spelled out in brilliant red carnations—are spotted driving through Bedford-Stuyvesant. At the open casket service, fans stricken with grief catch a glimpse of Junior M.A.F.I.A., Flavor Flav, Dr. Dre, Spinderella, and Sister Souljah. For the postmodern theorist, there is a whole lot of signifying going on. For the people lined up outside the funeral home—who don't have the consolation of the sociology seminar room—the issue is not one of semiotics but of survival. It is not an event that calls for interpretation. It is an event that calls for a commitment to struggle.

Notes

Special thanks to Carlos Tejeda. Ash Vasudeva, Warren Crinchlow, Makeba Jones, Karl Bruce Knapper, Michelle Knight, Mike Seltzer, and Nicole Baker for their helpful suggestions.

1. Eric Lott, "Cornel West in the Hour of Chaos: Culture and Politics in *Race Matters.*" *Social Text* 12, no. 3 (1994): pp. 39–50.

2. Sister Souljah, *No Disrespect* (New York: Random House, 1994).

3. Jesse Katz, "Rap Furor: New Evil or Old Story," *Los Angeles Times*, Aug. 5, 1995, pp. 1, 18, 19; Steve Proffitt, "Russell Simmons: Defending the Art of Communication Known as Rap," *Los Angeles Times*, Aug. 27, 1995, p. M3.

4. Time Warner Inc. has formally abandoned its $115 million stake in Interscope Records, blaming the split on contractual provisions that prevented the company from monitoring the content of Interscope's gangsta rappers such as Dr. Dre and Snoop Doggy Dogg. Bob Dole claimed responsibility for this development claiming he "shamed" Time Warner into dropping their gangsta rappers ("Time Warner to Abandon Gangsta Rap," *Los Angeles Times*, Sept. 28, 1995, pp. 1, 13).

5. Katz. Richard Berry's original hit in 1955, "Louie Louie," was Afro-Calypsonian yet was influenced by the Rhythm Rockers, a Chicano-Filipino band from Orange County, California. Band members had introduced Berry to René Touset's "Loca cha cha," which provided Berry with the model for "Louie Louie." See George Lipsitz, "The Bands of Tomorrow Are Here Today: The Proud, Progressive and Postmodern Sounds of Las Tres and Goddess 13," in Steven Loza, ed., *Musical Aesthetics and Multiculturalism* (Los Angeles: University of California, Department of Ethnomusicology and Systematic Musicology, 1994), pp. 139–147. "Louie Louie" has been recorded by more than 300 artists, for example, Ike and Tina Turner, the Kinks, the Beach Boys, Tom Petty and the Heartbreakers, Frank Zappa, Iggy Pop, and even the Rice University Marching Owl Band. A resident of South Central Los Angeles, Berry contributed vocals to the Robins' "Riot in Cell Block No. 9" and Etta James's "Roll with Me Henry (the Wallflower)."

6. Ibid.

7. Cited in Douglas Rushkoff, *Media Virus* (New York: Ballantine Books, 1996), p. 163.

8. Ibid.

9. John L. Mitchell, "Third Trial Ruled out in Slaying by Officer," *Los Angeles Times*, Feb. 4, 1995, pp. B1, B8. See also Rosalind Muhammad, "LA Gangs Honored in Keeping the Peace," *Final Call* 14, no. 21, Aug. 16, 1995, pp. 4, 10.

10. Tricia Rose, *Black Noise: Rap Music and Black Culture in Contemporary America* (London: Wesleyan University Press, 1994), p. 4.

11. Jeffrey Louis Decker, "The State of Rap: The Time and Place of Hip Hop Nationalism," in *Microphone Friends: Youth Music, Youth Culture*, ed. Andrew Ross and Tricia Rose (New York: Routledge, 1994), p. 101.

12. Katz. Richard Berry's original hit in 1955, "Louie Louie," was Afro-Calypsonian yet was influenced by the Rhythm Rockers, a Chicano-Filipino band from Orange County, California. Band members had introduced Berry to Rene Touset's "Loca cha cha," which provided Berry with the model for "Louie Louie." See George Lipsitz, "The Bands of Tomorrow Are Here Today: The Proud, Progressive and Postmodern Sounds of Las Tres and Goddess 13," in Steven Loza, ed., *Musical Aesthetics and Multiculturalism*.

14. Ibid.

15. Ibid., p. 59.

16. Ibid.

17. Tommy Lott, "Black Vernacular Representation and Cultural Malpractice," in *Multiculturalism: A Critical Reader*, ed. David Theo Goldberg (Cambridge: Basil Blackwell, 1994), p. 246.

18. Tricia Rose, "A Style Nobody Can Deal With: Politics, Style, and the Postindustrial City in Hip Hop," in Ross and Rose, *Microphone Friends,* pp. 71–88.

19. George Lipsitz, *Dangerous Crossroads: Popular Music, Postmodernism, and the Poetics of Place* (London: Verso, 1994).

20. Carol Tulloch, "Rebel Without a Pause: Black Street Style and Black Designers," in *Chic Thrills: A Fashion Reader,* ed. Juliet Ash and Elizabeth Wilson (Berkeley: University of California Press, 1993), pp. 84–98.

21. Ibid.

22. Kristal Brent Zook, "Reconstruction of Nationalist Thought in Black Music and Culture," in *Rockin' the Boat: Mass Music, and Mass Movement,* ed. Rebee Garofalo (Boston: South End Press, 1992), p. 257.

"Playing the dozens" and "signifying" are variations of African American linguistic practices or traditions which can be characterized as ritualized verbal contests or wars of words. The "dozens" are confrontations of wit, intellect, and repartee played out in lingual games of one-upmanship that are distinguished by lexical originality and creativity, mental dexterity, and verbal innovation and agility in the effective deployment of clever and sarcastic insults or put-downs. A continuation of a rich African diasporic oral tradition that has been distilled through the lens of the African American experience, playing the dozens and signifying are the ultimate expression of brains over brawn—spoken word showdowns that have transformed and elevated a marginalized community's collective humor, anger, joy, and pain in the face of adversity into a game of survival, a ritualized form of entertainment, and a highly valued and respected socio-cultural art form. See James Percelay, Monteria Ivey, and Stephan Dweck, eds., *SNAPS* (New York: Quill/William Morrow, 1994), pp. 8–9, 16–23, 27–35, 161–167.

23. Rose, *Black Noise.*

24. Tricia Rose, "Give Me a (Break) Beat! Sampling and Repetition in Rap Production," in *Culture on the Brink: Ideologies of Technology,* ed. Gretchen Bender and Timothy Druckrey (Seattle, WA: Bay Press, 1994), p. 251.

25. Rose, *Black Noise,* p. 4.

26. Lawrence Grossberg, "Is Anybody Listening? Does Anybody Care? On 'The State of Rock,'" in Ross and Rose, *Microphone Friends,* pp. 41–58.

27. Michael Dyson, "The Politics of Black Masculinity and the Ghetto in Black Film," in *The Subversive Imagination: Artists, Society, and Social Responsibility,* ed. Carol Becker (London: Routledge, 1994), pp. 159–160.

28. Rose, "A Style Nobody Can Deal With," p. 71.

29. Dick Hebdige, *Cut 'n' Mix* (London: Comedia, 1987).

30. Ibid.

31. Robin D.G. Kelley, *Race Rebels: Culture, Politics, and the Black Working Class* (New York: Free Press, 1994), p. 184.

32. Cited in Rushkoff, p. 164.

33. Juan Flores, "Puerto Rican and Proud, Boyee! Rap, Roots, and Amnesia," in Ross and Rose, *Microphone Friends.*

34. Jack Cheevers, Chuck Philips, and Frank B. Williams, "Violence Tops the Charts," *Los Angeles Times,* Apr. 3, 1995, pp. 1–18.

35. Ibid., p. 18. Young and Knight have since broken up their partnership. With a record eight criminal convictions (mostly for assault and weapons charges), Marion "Suge" Knight is currently serving time in a Chino prison while awaiting

a Superior Court hearing. In 1995 he entered no-contest pleas to two accounts of assault that involved the beating of two rappers in a Hollywood recording studio. Under a plea bargain he was given a suspended nine-year prison term and five years probation. Since it was discovered that Knight had cut a record deal with the original prosecutor's 18-year-old daughter and had lived in the prosecutor's Malibu Colony house through the summer of 1996, the prosecutor was dropped from the case. At the MGM Hotel in Los Vegas, just hours before Tupac Shakur was fatally wounded in a car driven by Knight, a surveillance videotape showed Knight and several Death Row employees attacking a Crips gang member. This led to the revoking of Knight's parole. Death Row Records is currently under investigation by the Federal Bureau of Investigation, the Internal Revenue Service, the Bureau of Alcohol, Tobacco and Firearms and the Drug Enforcement Administration for funding crimes by the Mob Piru set of the Bloods street gang, for allegedly engaging in business deals with "drug kingpins" Michael Harris and Ricardo Crockett, and for dealing with entrepreneurs linked to organized crime factions that included New York Mafia figures Joseph Colombo Jr. and Alphonse "the Whale" Mellolla. (Chuck Philips and Alan Abrahamson, "U.S. Probes Death Row Record Label's Money Trail," *Los Angeles Times*, December 29, 1996, pp. A1, A34, A35).

36. Proffitt, p. M3.

37. Matthew T. Grant, "Of Ganstas and Guerrillas: Distance Lends Enchantment," *Appendx 2* (1994): p. 44.

38. Katz, p. 18

39. Ibid.

40. Ibid.

41. David Troop, *Rap Attack: African Jive to New York Hip Hop* (London: Pluto Press, 1984); Houston Baker, *Black Studies: Rap and the Academy* (Chicago: University of Chicago Press, 1993); Rose, *Black Noise.*

42. Lipsitz.

43. Nick De Genova, "Gangster Rap and Nihilism in Black America: Some Questions of Life and Death," *Social Text* 13, no. 2 (1995): p. 113.

44. De Genova, p. 114.

45. Rose, "A Style Nobody Can Deal With," p. 83.

46. Tommy Lott, "Black Vernacular Representation and Cultural Malpractice," p. 247.

47. Charles P. Pierce, "Sunshine Is Back!" *Los Angeles Times Magazine*, Apr. 23, 1995, pp. 12–15, 35, 36.

48. Tommy Lott, p. 246.

49. Angela Davis, "Discussion," in *Black Popular Culture*, ed. Gina Dent (Seattle, WA: Bay Press, 1992), p. 327.

50. Decker, p. 109.

51. Ibid., p. 110.

52. Steven Gregory, "Race and Racism: A Symposium," *Social Text* 13, no. 1 (1995): pp. 16–21.

53. Gregory, p. 20.

54. Decker, p. 116.

55. Tricia Rose, "Black Texts/Black Contexts," in Dent, *Black Popular Culture*, p. 226.

56. Zook, p. 256.

57. De Genova, p. 111.

58. Ibid., p. 107.

59. Lipsitz, p. 38.

60. bell hooks, *Black Looks: Race and Representation* (Boston: South End Press, 1992), pp. 35–36; emphasis in original.

61. De Genova, p. 107.

62. Grant, p. 45.

63. Ibid. See also the important work of Stephen Haymes, *Race, Culture, and the City: A Pedagogy for Black Urban Struggle* (Albany: State University of New York Press, 1995).

64. Grant, p. 47.

65. Ibid.

66. Ibid.

67. Ibid., p. 51.

68. Ibid.

69. Ibid.

70. De Genova, p. 105.

71. Michel de Certeau, *The Practice of Everyday Life* (Berkeley: University of California Press, 1984), pp. 31–32.

72. Tommy Lott, p. 249.

73. De Genova, p. 116.

74. Tommy Lott, p. 246.

75. Peter McLaren, *Critical Pedagogy and Predatory Culture* (London: Routledge, 1995).

76. Jon Stratton, "The Beast of the Apocalypse: The Post-Colonial Experience of the United States," *New Formations* 21 (winter 1993): pp. 35–63.

77. De Genova, p. 106.

78. Ibid., p. 119.

79. Zook, p. 263.

80. Kelley, p. 212.

81. Grant, p. 52.

82. Leerom Medovoi, "Mapping the Rebel Image: Postmodernism and the Masculinist Politics of Rock in the U.S.A.," *Cultural Critique* 20 (winter 1991–92): p. 165.

83. Eric Lott, see note #1, p. 41.

84. Ibid., pp. 41, 43.

85. Ibid., p. 42.

86. Tommy Lott, p. 246.

87. Kelley, p. 210; emphasis in original. Kelley also points out that the term *nigger* made a "comeback" at the height of the Black Power movement of the 1960s when a distinction was made between *nigger* and *negro*—the latter signified a sellout or a brainwashed black person.

88. Lipsitz, p. 127.

89. Ibid., p. 89.

90. Ibid., p. 90.

91. Ibid., p. 58.

92. Grant, p. 40.

93. McLaren.

94. Grant, p. 41.

95. Steve Appleford, "The Rise and Fall of Gangsta Rap," *Los Angeles Reader,* Mar. 3, 1995, pp. 8–11, 56.

96. Ibid., p. 9.

97. Ibid.

98. Ibid., p. 11.

99. Donnell Alexander, "Closed Border: The Hip-Hop Nation Deports Alternative Rap. Michael Ivey's B.Y.O.B.," *LA Weekly* 17, no. 17, Mar. 24–30, 1995, pp. 39–40.

100. Thomas Cushman, "Rich Rastas and Communist Rockers: A Comparative Study of the Origin, Diffusion, and Delusion of Revolutionary Musical Codes," *Journal of Popular Culture* 25, no. 3 (1991): pp. 17–61.

101. Javier Santiago-Lucerna, "Nothing's Sacred, Everything's Profane: Rock Isleno and the Politics of National Identity in Puerto Rico" (paper presented at York University, Toronto, Mar. 1995), 16–17.

102. Ibid.

103. Rosemary Hennessy, "Queer Visibility in Commodity Culture," *Cultural Critique* 29 (winter 1994–95): pp. 31–76.

104. Ibid., p. 52.

105. Ibid., p. 53.

106. Ibid.

107. Ibid.

108. De Genova, pp. 105–106.

109. Hennessy, p. 33.

110. Cushman, pp. 17–61.

111. Ibid., p. 48. According to Christian Parenti, prisoners are being exploited as cheap labor and their wages are used to pay for their incarceration. He notes that "the California Department of Corrections is also trying to find a niche in Japan's jeans market with its new line of 'Gangsta Blues.' Thus, the much deplored hip-hop culture of African-American and Latino youths—which has embraced the look of denim workclothes—is being imitated, glorified, and sold back to the public by the very criminal justice system that claims to wage war on Gangsta culture" (Parenti, *New Statement and Society,* Nov. 3, 1995, pp. 20–21).

112. Diane Fuss, "Interior Colonies: Frantz Fanon and the Politics of Identification," *Diacritics* 24, nos. 2–3, (summer–fall 1994): p. 21.

113. Françoise Lionett, *Postcolonial Representations: Women, Literature, Identity* (Ithaca, NY: Cornell University Press, 1995), p. 10.

114. Homi Bhabha, "Of Mimicry and Man: The Ambivalence of Colonial Discourse," *October* 28 (1984): pp. 125–133.

115. Lipsitz, p. 62.

116. Manning Marable, "Race, Identity, and Political Culture," in Dent, *Black Popular Culture,* p. 302.

117. Michael Eric Dyson, (1996). "Tupac: Living the Life He Rapped about in Song." *Los Angeles Times,* Sunday October 22, p. 3.

118. Dyson, p. 3.

119. Dyson, p. 3.

120. Dyson, p. 3.

121. Scott Lash and John Urry. *Economies of Signs and Space* (London: Sage, 1992), p. 316.

122. Teresa Ebert, "The Surplus of Enjoyment in the Post-al Real," *Rethinking Marxism* 7, no. 3 (1994): pp. 137–142.

6 Global Politics and Local Antagonisms: Research and Practice as Dissent and Possibility

Peter McLaren and Kris Gutierrez

In this chapter we attempt to revisit the general criteria that distinguish educational ethnography, curriculum, and pedagogy as a critical enterprise. Over the past several decades especially, the notion of "critical" has managed to attract a number of different meanings when used in conjunction with literacy, pedagogy, multicultural education, and educational research in general. Following what we perceive to be the domestication and recent parti pris of the term, the elastic adjective "critical" has become synonymous with problem-solving skills, with conscripting certain cognitive reasoning abilities in the service of resolving practical problems, as in the case of "critical thinking." Too often lost in this reduction of the term "critical" to an ensemble of discrete cognitive skills and quantifiable units of analysis are the ethical and political dimensions of educational research. It is these dimensions that we strongly believe the term "critical" should invoke and around which the purpose and practice of pedagogy should be built. Consequently, the term "critical" as we are using it to describe research and pedagogical practices connotes a remove from the way the term has been interpolated by normative psychologically based problem-solving approaches. We are criticizing the term as it is presently used to fetishize knowledge yet disparage its location in arenas of ideological and material contestation. This chapter sketches an ethical approach to educational research and practice centered largely around the recent work of sociologist Zygmunt Bauman on the topic of postmodern ethics.

It has rather strikingly come to our attention that many of our students and some of our colleagues remain confused about exactly what the term "critical" is supposed to designate when it is used, for instance, in conjunction with ethnography, pedagogy, and multicultural education. In attempting to sketch a provisional response to this and related questions that are frequently posed to us in our classes and in our research sites, we wish to stress one primary concern: The materialist and nondiscursive dimensions of social life have become cavalierly dismissed in a research climate that seems to have become infatuated with the primacy of textual exegesis (as in the practice of postmodern ethnography or curriculum studies). In so doing, we wish to rethink qualitative classroom research and pedagogical practice from a more materialist, global perspective. We wish to emphasize that our attempt is exploratory rather than definitive and does not attempt to articulate a unified critical methodology or system. Since our commentary is suggestive rather than prescriptive, it does not propose to exemplify a totalizing model of critical practice by interlinking contingent facts into a formal system.

While the development of a pragmatic theory of language (which includes, among other instances, the appropriation of sociolinguistics and speech-act theory) has opened up interesting and valuable avenues in educational ethnography for the exploration of discourse as cultural critique and political action and has occasioned promising lines of development for the study of the construction of subjectivity, we believe that the nondiscursive lines of capitalist flows have been all but ignored. Following Wittgenstein's observation that rational argumentation can take place only within a language game, we are suggesting that the politics of identity and difference that characterize contemporary educational research—debates over essentialism, social construction, the politics of cultural studies, the politics of deconstruction, and so on—are essentially *internal* to the politics that characterize contemporary global politics and lack historical and geopolitical specificity (Zaretsky 1995). Addressing changes in the terms of the debates over politics and identity in the 1970s and 1980s, Eli Zaretsky argues:

> At that juncture, "the linguistic turn"—the idea that language shapes and does not merely represent reality—led to the stress on ambiguity and indeterminacy. Advocates of "difference" urged a politics aimed less at establishing viable identities than at destabilizing identity claims, a politics that eschewed such terms as groups and rights in favour of such terms as places, spaces, alterity and subject positions, a politics aimed to operate on the margins of the society and the interstices of the culture rather than at society's supposed centre. (1995, 256)

We believe that this emphasis on the linguistic turn in educational analysis has deflected too much attention away from an analysis of both local and global economic and cultural shifts. We also maintain that the present conditions in our schools are as much a part of moral indifference as they are a result of the current economic flows within late capitalism. While we challenge the perspective that does not reveal the relativism or situatedness of morality, we do not fall victim to the beliefs and practices that would make everyday life hopeless. As Bauman notes, "The horrors of inner cities, mean streets, once thriving and now dying communities orphaned by business ventures which used to keep them alive, but now—for the soundest and most rational of reasons—moved to greener pastures, are not victims of exploitation, but of abandonment resulting from *moral indifference*" (1995,264).

In making such a claim, we argue that we are presently witnessing a new global commodity culture as well as a moral economy where wants and needs are increasingly organized by capital as capitalism establishes equivalencies between individuals and things that allows, in effect, everything to be *paso a paso* substituted for everything. Equivalencies are established between bodies and goods in an open market. Morality is organized around a *procedural bureaucratic logic* linked to the maximization of profits over individual rights and social justice.

What is especially significant about these new predatory times in which the United States continues its protracted dependency on capitalist expansion is that U.S. citizens have become trapped by the ecocidal desire to endlessly consume. We take seriously the Deleuzoguattarian philosophy of desiring production and the notion that the capitalist axiomatic is fundamentally different from a social code. Whereas a social code "establishes indirect, limited relationships between entities based on qualitative, non-economic difference," an axiomatic "establishes direct relationships between entities based on abstract qualities" (Bogue 1989, 101). Ronald Bogue describes this concept as follows:

> Put simply, the capitalist machine takes an abstract flow of labour (deterritorialized workers) and an abstract flow of capital (deterritorialized money) and conjoins the two flows in various relations (the set of abstract rules for the conjunction of the flows comprising an axiomatic). The particular qualities of human subjects in any concrete situation result from a specific conjunction of the abstract flows. The *socius* does not need to mark people, simply abstract qualities. . . . Worker and capitalist (and all variations thereof) are functions of capital, mere points of the become-concrete of abstract qualities. (1989, 101)

Bogue notes, following Deleuze and Guattari, that "the capitalist sign . . . means nothing, but simply functions within the economic process as a medium for transcoding and coordinating various components of the circuit of production, exchange, distribution, and consumption" (1989, 102). We are also sympathetic to Deleuze and Guattari's notion of libidinalized production, which challenges the traditional Marxist distinction among production, distribution, and exchange and problematizes the distinction between use value and exchange value. According to Deleuze and Guattari, everything is production, and the production of needs or lack is a function of the market economy choreographed by the dominant class. Because we believe educational ethnography ignores the impact of more densely globalized corporate circuits of production and consumption, we wish in this chapter to emphasize the prevalence of the capitalist axiomatic and highlight the following: the globalization of culture and communication structures, the world system as characterized by determination and flux, the increase of immigrants and refugees, the development of a service class with a taste for fashionable consumer services, decentralized and disorganized capitalist flows, the deepening of social and spacial inequalities, the decline in the number of hierarchically organized national classes, and the supplanting of goods by services as the driving force of internationalization (Lash and Urry 1994; Zaretsky 1995; McLaren 1995).

At a time of postnational politics (Rosenau 1990), we find ourselves in the midst of two interactive worlds with overlapping memberships: a state-centric world and a multicentric world of actors such as transnational corporations, ethnic groups, and church organizations (Pieterse 1995). According to Bauman (1995), and following Hobsbawm, the current proliferation of separatist nation-states and the "fissiparousness of nationalisms" are evidence not of the triumph of the nation-state but rather of the collapse of the nation-state as the main carrier of sovereign identities. Today's world economy is run by extraterritorial economic elites "who favor state organizations that *cannot* effectively impose conditions under which the economy is run, let alone impose restraints on the way in which those who run the economy would like it to be run; the economy is effectively transnational" (Bauman 1995, 251). In fact, what facilitates the free movement of capital and commodities more than anything else is the splintering of political sovereignty. The global flow of merchandise and capital depends on a fragmentation—or reparochialization—of sovereign territories. We are arguing for the development of a framework (at this stage no more than an abstract typology of the problem) for better understanding the ways in which the micropolitics of the urban classroom are, in fact, the local instantiations of the sociopolitical and economic consequences of a rapidly expanding global marketplace. For instance, to what extent are local communities merely transit stations for the circulation of commodities administered by transnational executives in the worldwide distribution of capital? What role does capital play in identity-assembling processes?

We suggest that recent local antagonisms evident both in the larger social community and in the educational arena are inextricably linked to the politics of neoliberalism driven by an expanding global capitalism. For example, recent political assaults on affirmative action, multiculturalism, and undocumented immigrants are tied to a larger cultural and political logic linked to the model of *homo economicus* and the politics of neoliberalism and, thus, are necessarily connected to the cultural practices of the community, that is, schooling. The movement toward economic rationalism and new global strategies of capital accumulation has joined the assault on what is left of the welfare state (superannuation, guaranteed minimum wages, health and education sectors, etc.), rationalizing the role of schools as supply mechanisms—as a necessary subsector of the economy in the struggle for ascendancy in the global marketplace (McLaren 1995). Consequently, our desires as citizens are exceedingly vulnerable to the ideological assaults of the country's antigovernment priesthood—*par le droit du plus fort*—which oversees institutions of private power that serve profit and corporate advantage. In the backdrop of these larger-scale assaults, our ongoing studies of urban education vividly illustrate how the educational arena and, in particular, the urban classroom have become the terrain upon which economic, cognitive, aesthetic, and moral spaces are being regulated and contested. As the boundaries of economic power shift, their attendant moral boundaries become more rigid. We witness this in the ways in which the urban classrooms become more restricted and exclusive spaces as the students' lives and experiences broaden to cover a much larger sociocultural terrain.

In such a context, we maintain that educational research should increase its focus on issues related to race, gender, and socioeconomic status and, with more determinate effort, on the shifting ground of capitalist exploitation and the cultural production of workers in terms of both the increasing globalization of capital and the international circuit of debt and consumption, the reskilling of workers in heavy industry, the deskilling and deunionization of work in the expanding service sector, and finally in terms of what Aronowitz and DiFazio (1994) have recently referred to as the "jobless future." The process of the deskilling of workers begins in schools. Such relationships have been underexplored by educational researchers.

Often trapped within truncated research agendas, educational researchers throughout the United States remain, for the most part, tied to a logic of empiricism that ignores larger vectors of power and their intersection with broader social and cultural relations, global forces of production and consumption, and revitalized agencies of hegemonic rule. From this perspective, we argue that micro- and macroanalyses establish an important context for challenging current educational reforms and related educational research that suggest that critical ethnography and pedagogy can become the vehicles for connecting the local and the global in school sites and for pushing the boundaries of educational and social reform. Similarly, critical literacy and biliteracy can become the tools for mediating this transformation.

Endless acts of consumption provoked by the *danse macabre* of capitalism organizes subjectivity in specific ways around the general maxim: I purchase, therefore I am. That this is a maxim that holds ominous consequences for citizenship and global politics cannot be gainsaid. The schools and other institutions within the dominant public spheres have not only created discourses that legitimate existing systems of intelligibility tied to the cultural logic of late capitalism (McLaren 1995) but have also constructed an economy of affective investment that channels feelings of anxiety, disappointment, despair, and unrest due to relations of exploitation and systems of domination pervading the logic of individualism. Such a logic creates a social alibi whereby the subject of capital is encrypted into the social milieu in a way that hides his or her genealogy, eclipsing concerns about justice, equality, and reciprocity by taking social issues and analysis and hyperpersonalizing them. Bell hooks caustically frames this issue in the following way: "We don't need politics. We don't need struggle. All we need is desire. It is desire that becomes the place of connection. This is a very postmodern vision of desire, as the new place of transgression that eliminates the need for radical politics" (1995, 44).

In affirming the compatibility of individualism, capitalism, and the cultural logic of consumption, the United States has made its democracy untenable. At a time when capitalism has transformed all social relations to commodity relations of universal equivalence, and reduced all production to the equivalence form, the United States desperately needs the *idea* of democracy to be retained as a necessary, "well founded" illusion. Zygmunt Bauman (1995) argues: "Moral devastation, not moral progress is the consequence of waiting for the 'deregulated' markets to 'bring out the best in people'; in Mulgan's words, 'selfishness and greed, and corruption in government and business, came to be the hallmarks of the neoconservative era'" (264).

Whether we are examining the production of identity from the *durée* of daily-time, the *Dasein* of life-time, or the *longue durée* of history (Giddens 1981), the autonomous, self-fashioned subject of modernity has been replaced by a mobile and displaced subject formed out of mutative combinations of discourses and a bricolage of signifiers—out of incandescent palimpsests and competing strands of discourses. This model of the new postmodern self as hybrid, splayed, multiple, and syncretic is patterned on the cathedral of capitalism, that sanctuary of consumption where we find a strange convergence of our fragmented identities in the signifying structure of global amusement culture that we know as the shopping mall. The shopping mall self (the self as the rhetorical effect of image value) has become the quintessential model of panic identity in the contemporary United States. With more specific reference to education, the inordinate stress on contractual individualism, achievement in the marketplace, and the politics of consumption have resulted in classrooms where image value supersedes use value and exchange value is the object of fixation. Witness homeboy and homegirl obsession with designer footgear and the workclothes of the hip-hop nation. Witness, too, the desire among young females for waiflike figures displayed in microskirts and crop-tops. Further, social impulses for equality, liberty, and social justice have been flattened by the spellbound subjectivities of talk-radio hosts and video reality until they have become cataleptically rigid. Newspapers announce the "chaos couture" fashion statement of our governor as he tours California's earthquake, flood, and fire damage in what looks to be Crew garb. Fashion designers announce special bulletproof fashion lines for elementary school children, but few are concerned with the violence in schools and the condition of students' and teachers' lives in schools. We believe that the emphasis on style is considerably influenced by a shift of significant cultural practices from the sphere of work to that of consumption. This is due, note Lash and Urry (1995), to the separation of the increasingly reflexive service class and the skilled working class from the so-called underclass. Citing W. J. Wilson, Lash and Urry claim there exists

> the virtual and rapid disappearance of the semi-skilled, unionized and reasonably paid manual jobs that ghetto males previously filled. And the same applies in the white underclass ghettoes of many public housing estates in North America and Europe. In this there is a displacement of reflexivity from production to consumption, in which personality is invested in clothing styles, sport, dance, music, recreational drugs and borderline criminal activities such as "ramraiding." In fact the American ghetto poor have to a degree set the parameters for the popular-cultural lifestyle of the white middle classes. (1995, 57)

For those, like us, who live in Los Angeles, it is certainly no exaggeration to proclaim that some American youth live in a constant state of emergency, in the neighborhood and in the school. Michael Taussig writes that states of emergency are characterized by "the apparent normality of the abnormal" (1992, 13). Echoing Walter Benjamin, Taussig writes that "in the state of emergency which is not the exception but the rule, every possibility is a fact" (34). For instance, it is possible to be a healthy, intelligent, and creative teenager growing up in East or South Central Los Angeles and yet have a life expectancy of eighteen. Similarly, to graduate from a high school can sometimes promise you little more than a life of chronic unemployment and poverty.

The national public climate is not hospitable to the poverty-stricken. In fact, moralizing critiques of U.S. consumer society have taken on racist and xenophobic forms. New Right constituencies such as the National Rifle Association and Republican leaders are influencing both the way that American identity is being diffused through the capillary powers of the megastate and the manner in which our structures of expectation are being defined by promotional culture.

In a social order of corporate decisionmaking where the quest for empire and markets is rationalized as national "defense," is it so surprising that violence has become the coin of the realm? Youth inhabit a media-generated community of memory that, ironically, is forged out of the empty presence of commodity culture, out of the ruins of our present-day social amnesia, out of the slogans, signs, headlines, and sound bytes that structure identity around the quest for global market superiority. Youth are building their communities out of figural traces, fading signs, and impotent public symbols that reflect and reproduce the dissolution of our shared traditions and moral economies.

In a society bereft of decent jobs and hope for a better future, is it surprising that youth who are marginalized by race, class, gender, and sexuality are centralizing themselves through violence—a violence that has become the new labor power of the excluded, a violence that helps youth to define themselves in a world of radical undecidability and plurality? How can we condemn acts of violence when we celebrate, sexualize, and racialize such acts through the media and when we teach our children to valorize and thrillingly emulate them? When the right is mobilizing young people through "Latinophobia" (Proposition 187) and fear of the black planet (anti-affirmative-action initiatives)?

In a society in which the reality of daily life is hidden behind the pacifying and fetishistic lure of commodity satisfaction, is it so surprising that a president who suggests that military-style assault weapons be banned in our streets is denounced as a "radical" who is overturning his inaugural oath? Instead, we point out how the Christian right refuses to link its personal perspectives to the discourses and social practices that give rise to them and how the right links the breakdown of values to the criminalization of minority youth and yet, at the same time, avoids linking crime and violence to the disembedding of the economy, educational tracking, deindustrialization, disinvestment, economic polarization, residential segregation, gentrification, retrograde fiscal responsibility, the privatization of education and the abandonment of public schools. Conservative discourses attempting to address violence rely on the palpable erasure of the link among violence and capitalist social relations (Carlson 1992). Are we too afraid of offending big business to make this claim?

Moralizing critiques of U.S. consumer society and its location within international circuits of debt and consumption have taken on racist and xenophobic forms in the 1990s. The past decade has witnessed unprecedented levels of struggle over the meaning and deployment of racial "difference," culminating in the recent passage of a blatant antiimmigration, antipoor, anti-Latino legislative initiative (Proposition 187) in California. The measure is designed to restrict public schooling, welfare, and nonemergency medical services to those persons who are unable to prove their legal immigration or nationality status in the United States.

The passing of Proposition 187 has served to create a new phalanx of right-wing folk heroes and to spark other New Right initiatives on a series of antiimmigrant, anti-affirmative-action, pro-family-values flanks. Positioned to abolish all "race and gender preferences" and to challenge the linguistic and cultural diversity of the state, proponents of the initiatives blatantly expose their us-them agenda by proclaiming, as one leader did: "It boils down to this: Do we want to retain control of the Southwest more than the Mexicans want to take it from us?" While the initiative by some Proposition 187 backers to abolish the taxing authority of the federal government, to restrict citizenship to people "born of an American," and to strip citizenship rights from foreign nationals appears to be outrageous in the extreme, it appears less so when one considers the catalyzing effect such groups and local initiatives have in the New Right's larger national agenda: They demonize people of different cultures, increase the power and privilege of monied interests, and placate the middle class. This historical moment signals not only the resurfacing of fascism but also the complete villainization of the Latino/a immigrant in a manner so ferocious that even the most militant and cynical Latinos have been caught unprepared. What is at hand is not simply a further step backward in what has been the sad but steady erosion of the ground won by decades of civil rights activism but rather the triumph of cultural apartheid and the inquisition of the colonial mind. Within educational settings, the victory of Proposition 187 appears to have legitimized assaults on the Latino population and spawned new criticisms of multiculturalism. These assaults are tied to rapidly changing demographics. In California, the K-12 student population projected by the year 2004–2005 will be much more ethnically and racially diverse than the present population. According to a report of the Graduate

School of Education and Information Studies, University of California, Los Angeles, in 1991–1992, K-12 minority students (including African Americans, Native Americans, Asians, Filipinos, and Chicanos/ Latinos) constituted about 55.5 percent of enrollments; by 2004–2005 they will likely be over 69 percent of the K-12 population. The diverse Chicano/ Latino population will reach about 49 percent (1995). These projected demographic shifts call for a powerful shift in multicultural education— a shift to a more critical and revolutionary form of multicultural education.

Thus, we find the Proposition 187 legislation morally repulsive, especially in light of the current way the U.S. economy already exploits Mexican workers both in the United States and in Mexico. Consider the case of the *maquiladora* industry, which has been bolstered by "*la crisis*" (the decline in the Mexican standard of living, the falling of oil prices, Mexico's increasing foreign debt, and the devaluation of the peso). Officially described as "production sharing," the *maquiladora* industry involves U.S.-owned factories located in Mexico near the U.S.-Mexico border. In these factories, workers are ruthlessly exploited and paid slave wages, and environmental controls are all but abandoned. According to Deborah Gewertz and Frederick Errington, the agency of the workers "is sharply circumscribed by a world system in which power is unequally distributed and the economic interests of some sharply constrain, at least in broad outline, the destinies of others" (1993, 648).

The conditions that we have too briefly sketched make the possibility of participating in a critical multicultural education increasingly difficult. In the context of these changing demographics, a rising tide of xenophobia, and increasing resistance to the diversification of the classroom, the school, the workplace, and the surrounding communities, we have found that the deskilling of urban students becomes more commonplace as more reform-oriented curricula are replaced by more traditional monologic forms of instruction. These more restricted forms of learning, characterized by rigid hierarchies, tightly managed participation structures, and skill and drill activities, have become more deeply embedded in the culture of the urban classroom.

While we clearly acknowledge that in many ways such classrooms typify schooling practices since the beginnings of the educational state in the late nineteenth century, our six years of ethnographic studies in both urban and suburban schools vividly illustrate that all teacher-fronted or recitational classrooms are not created equally (Gutierrez 1992, 1993; Gutierrez and Larson 1994; Gutierrez, Rymes, and Larson 1995). In particular, by examining the social architecture of the classroom, its discourses, and its normative practices, our studies reveal that the degree of control and micromanagement of learning is intensified in the urban classroom. Further, we have learned how the social organization of the classroom mediates learning, power, and identity. Moreover, we have learned how the social organization of learning privileges the knowledges, discourses, and social practices of some and reauthors others (Gutierrez, Stone, and Larson, in press). In most classrooms, what counts as learning and who has access to this learning is determined by the values and social practices of the local culture and the larger society and by the particular instantiations of beliefs and practices evident in the social spaces of the classroom. Thus, these analyses show that who gets to learn and what is learned are connected to the sociocultural practices of the larger community, as well as the social practices of the schools. Our studies also reveal that power lies in the constructed social relationships. These analyses help illuminate how these arrangements are related in essential ways to what kinds of knowledge and norms children will appropriate and develop in the classroom and, ultimately, how this socialization process influences the trajectory of later schooling experiences.

By drawing on poststructuralist and language socialization theories and methodologies—the history and production of discursive practices in the classroom, the school, and the larger community—we provide the interpretative backdrop for our analysis. Our own studies are revealing (albeit provisionally, since the research is still ongoing) that the urban classroom, in so many cases, has become a site in which the struggle for control best characterizes the everyday practices of the classroom. Rather than illustrate in detail how this control is constructed in moment-to-moment interactions, in this chapter we want to make a case for, among other things, understanding normative schooling practices observed in urban schools from the broader context of the state (see Gutierrez 1993; Gutierrez, Larson, and Kreuter 1995; and Gutierrez, Stone, and Larson in press for a more elaborated discussion of how knowledge and identity in urban classrooms are discursively constructed).

In the case of California, as we have articulated, the state has become openly hostile to the notion of diversity. Let us more specifically examine the consequences or impact these state initiatives have in their local and particular instantiations. There are a number of schools located in predominantly Anglo neighborhoods that are populated by largely Latino/a and/or African American students rather than neighborhood children. Consider the case of a research site in one of our studies—a traditional urban middle school located in a conservative, predominantly white, middle-class neighborhood. The makeup of the school's student population, as in so many public schools in Los Angeles, has dramatically shifted since the late 1970s. Although the school was once predominantly Anglo and middle-class, its students are now nearly 80 percent African American and Latino/a. There have not been comparable changes in the school's teaching staff.

Ethnographic data including teacher, student, and administrator interviews and videotaped classroom instruction revealed that the school is at a critical transition point, experiencing tremendous conflict between maintaining social order, that is, ensuring, it believes, the appropriate socialization of its new student clientele, and educating them. Incidents of violence and crime and, more often, the perceived potential violence among its very poor and urban student population heighten the importance of safety in this school community. Reinforced by the local community's high degree of intolerance—its apparent hostility toward the changing school population and its fearfulness regarding the effects of the transient population on the neighborhood—the school vigorously tries to contain its students both within and outside the school. The influx of outsiders to this relatively homogenous neighborhood is almost imperceptible except for the caravan of yellow school buses that transport the students and the students' late afternoon trek to the city bus stop. Additionally, the underpreparedness of the current school staff to meet the social and academic needs of its diverse student population creates a perceived need for absolute control—a perception that serves only to exacerbate racial tension and both students' and teachers' feelings of alienation and mistrust (Gutierrez, Larson and Kreuter 1995).

We argue that this need to control and to "socialize" this new population of students is linked to the exploitative appropriation of labor and the exploitation of racialized and gendered groups. This is significant in that in many Los Angeles schools, nearly 100 percent of the students are immigrants who are both linguistically and culturally different.

We have found that in many classrooms in schools and school districts with bulging and increasingly diverse student populations and meager budgets, many overcommitted, undersupported, and often underprepared teachers are seduced into "Mcversions" of "Mcteaching," that is, a fast-food-like delivery of monologic, monolithic, and monocultural understandings of teaching and learning (Gutierrez and Larson 1994). The urban curricula, then, are the instantiations of the beliefs and values of the school and local and larger communities as they are articulated hegemonically in relation to broader social and cultural logics and economic relations.

The significance of these various studies is that they point clearly to the power schooling institutions have to create processes of knowledge construction through rigid structures of learning that limit students' opportunities to offer and critique their own perspectives and knowledge.

This is precisely how students are pushed out of schools, that is, by being continually marginalized. We do not, however, want to suggest a glorification of the "marginalized" student. Instead, in our work we acknowledge our "partial perspective" and also offer the value of examining and presenting the subjugated perspective as a means of critiquing classroom research and, ultimately, reform efforts that rarely account for this perspective, its social construction, and its relation to larger structures.

As students experience increased violence and face escalating threats to their education (e.g., Proposition 187), their right to receive health care services and meals at school, and the opportunity to become biliterate, they often must negotiate their way through an increasingly hostile sociocultural terrain within the local and the larger community. In such settings, the transcendent or dominant scripts of the larger society, that is, racism and sexism, are rarely disconnected from the everyday lives of students in urban classrooms. As researchers, we continue the struggle to better understand these connections.

Specifically, we are suggesting that these relations between the transcendent scripts and everyday classroom practices, that is, "between the large and the little" (Geertz 1995) be explored to a greater degree than at present in classroom-based ethnographic research in which there is a concerted attempt on the part of the researcher to address the local instantiation of larger vectors of power and social hierarchies.

Classroom ethnographic research should also be concerned with the relationship of schooling to the local community and, thus, both local and distal power relations. And while critical poststructuralist ethnography calls for a reconceptualization of culture as a field of discourse that is implicated in relations of power and constituted by normative understandings, and a recognition of the complexity of social relations and the researcher's socially determined position within the research she is attempting to describe, often little attention is given to microstructures of power in terms of their linkage to a more globalized political economy with its concomitant informalization and flexibilization, structural adjustment, privatization, and deregulation.

Creating Pedagogical Research as Social Practice

We wish to comment on some of our ongoing research in Los Angeles as a way of suggesting some possible directions that urban ethnography might take. We have not presented our research in detail as much as summarized some of our main findings. We offer our observations not to make a case for our own analysis of schooling but rather to serve as a backdrop against which we will sketch a critical commentary on urban schooling, one that we think points to a pressing need at this present historical conjuncture. In doing so, we do not exempt our own research from an inability (rather than an unwillingness) to make the necessary theoretical and empirical connections to the embeddedness of our schools and communities in an interconnected global system and global ethnoscapes. We are still in the process of searching for systematic ways of connecting the analysis of classrooms to larger systems of cultural and economic mediations. In this chapter, we do not claim to have moved sufficiently beyond stating the enormity of the problem that faces our own research. But we believe that by sketching the dimensions of such a problem, we will encourage researchers and teachers to consider developing methodologies and pedagogical practices able to address some of our concerns, as we attempt to do the same.

Our classroom investigations have examined the manner in which power and social relations and the resulting curriculum are established in local and moment-to-moment interactions through the micropolitics of the classrooms. Our present goal is to better understand these interactions in terms of larger social and economic relations. By locating the discussion of the local construction of power and identity within a larger framework of poststructuralist (Bourdieu 1977, 1991; Bourdieu, Passeron, and de Saint Martin 1994); Foucault 1977) and sociocultural (Gutierrez, Rymes, and Larson 1995; Ochs, Taylor, Rudolph, and Smith 1992) theories, the relations among discursive practices, power, and the production of agency can be better understood. Identity, as we are using the term, follows Laclau and Mouffe's nonessentialist perspective, which centers around a Hegelian-inspired dialectic of continuity and negation (Laclau and Mouffe 1985; Stone 1994). In other words, racial and ethnic identities take into account the continuity of perceptions about race and ethnicity in contemporary temporal and spacial contexts, as well as their differences with respect to class and gender (Stone 1994).

Rethinking Urban Pedagogy

While the pedagogy of many of the urban, multicultural, and multilingual classrooms described in our research does indeed reflect what we believe constitutes some of the normative practices of urban classroom life, we do encounter very different classroom communities in which both teachers and students resist the construction of the traditional teacher-student script (Gutierrez, Rymes, and Larson 1995). In these very different communities, a new pedagogical space is created in which the social construction of the identities of student and teacher differ from the roles and relationships constructed, for example, in the liberal humanist classroom. The temporary and situated asymmetries in these new classrooms reflect the necessary social and pedagogical relationships upon which an emancipatory pedagogy is grounded: social, spatial, and epistemological arrangements in which traditional categories of knowledge and discursive practices are radically transformed.

We want to make clear, however, that our emphasis on co-construction, dialogism, multiculturalism, and the heteroglossic curriculum is more than arguing for a space of engaging in democratic discussion based on a plurality of perspectives. For this would be to endorse a pedagogy of liberal humanism we take to be bankrupt. Liberal humanistic or "democratic" classrooms too often are self-validating, totalizing, and referential systems that domesticate and deflect attention from the irreducible complexity of classrooms and their relationship with the larger structures of economic privilege both locally and globally. These ellipses provoked by a lack of attention to larger economic and historical relations reduce "conflict" to subjectively defined power relations connected to issues of diversity and equality. In the liberal humanistic classroom, politics is occluded by neutralizing the contradictory relations between the stated intentions of democracy and its actual outcomes.

We challenge the epistemological idealism that does not recognize that dialogic pedagogy, in order to be emancipatory, should take into account the fact that such arrangements may still privilege certain groups. In our view, the liberal humanist emphasis in pedagogy, that is, its emphasis on dialogue, democracy, and consensus, often precludes a theory of political agency because the site of liberal pedagogy requires discursive rather than material intervention around issues of equality and reciprocity. Issues of discursive power, then, often take precedence over issues of economic exploitation. Dialogical pedagogy needs to be understood as praxiological and not as equal/intersubjective exchange occurring in an abstract register that is not linked to the realm of material and historical struggle. To help achieve this, we need to ask: What are the extralinguistic determinations and overdeterminations surrounding the classroom logics of signification?

Dialogue is dialectically bound; it is related to social, political, cultural, and gendered relations. While critical pedagogy has no ideal-typical essence, it should be grounded in a conception of the sociality of language that is associated with the discursive realm but is also situated outside of it in the arena of class struggle and power relations. Language is not just a transparent reflection of the social but rather refracts the social, and since language is fundamental to dialogue, it can be understood as informed by a multiplicity of material interests. We should be careful not to be seduced into Richard Rorty's universal conversation, where we can conveniently avoid examining the extralinguistic contexts of dialogue that are connected to the cultural logics of imperialism and where all contradictions will be resolved and the global subject will be miraculously transformed into a straight, Protestant, white American.

Moreover, too often dialogical research and pedagogy remain a formal *comprador* strategy for legitimating the established order. For the most part, the micropractices of classroom pedagogy can be seen as linked to a larger agenda that orients the curriculum toward business and industry imperatives—a relationship that reflects a human capital perspective in which knowledge is adjusted to the requirements of the marketplace. Schools, in this instance, simply become subsectors of the economy. Further, dialogical pedagogy in and of itself is neither necessarily disempowering nor transformative in nature if not positioned to challenge larger social, cultural, and economic relations and practices that exploit some and privilege others.

Dialogue is also a term that we wish to employ to look at how we view social interaction both in the classroom and in the workings of the larger society. The problem with the term "dialogue" is that it implies concord and not relations of inequality, violence, and domination. We are using the term after Bakhtin (Bakhtin 1981, 1986) to include but also point beyond the concept of linguistic exchange, and we are also using it more in relation to material, economic, and political interactions. Dominant grammars, as we see them, are grounded in modes of production and systems of power. Rather than viewing such grammars within a materialist dialectic, we emphasize a dialogical depiction of structures of power as shifting, fluid, and ongoing—structures that do not privilege a temporal hierarchy of systems but rather systems as they are made and remade within the context of specific geopolitical and local shifts.

What is needed in school settings, then, is radical shifts in what counts as knowledge and what counts as learning—shifts that allow disruptive and critical forms of pedagogy to emerge. As has been argued elsewhere (Gutierrez, Rymes, and Larson, 1995), reconceptualizing the curriculum as social heteroglossia can help reposition the teacher and student into roles of critical agents in the service of transforming the local and larger educational, sociocultural, and political terrain. Developing a curriculum with an orientation toward critical and feminist pedagogies will broaden the initiatives of school and social reform.

What we wish to underscore is that recognition of the self as a discursively positioned agent—whether student, teacher, or administrator—has too often occurred at the expense of a socially and situated praxis that breaks free from the "text" of identity in order to situate identity within larger sociodiscursive, prediscursive, and material relations of power and privilege linked to economic forces. Local meaning relations that are copatterned—in classrooms, for instance—constitute the semiotic resources through which global sociocultural relations are assembled and enacted. So we need to ask: How are social agents bound to certain overdetermined intersections of meanings and practices, to some sociodiscursive situated practices rather than to others? How are certain social meaning-making practices and systems of intelligibility naturalized?

Most approaches to school analysis that examine linguistic exchange turn out to be antimaterialist, nominalistic, atomistic, antidialectical, and differentialist precisely because they localize power at the microlevel of pedagogical exchange via processes of signification rather than situating meaning making as a form of social practice or a mode of social action. We have to raise the question: How are patterns of interaction that encode relations of power and domination in the social structure linked to the limitations of the meaningful choices available to social agents in specific social contexts? How are discursive practices that are situated in classroom exchanges (among teachers, students, and administrators) distributed, ordered, and controlled within given discursive formations? How are social meanings enacted and reproduced within the enunciative fields of classroom life in ways that favor dominant social patternings and copatternings of relationships, legitimize certain truth claims, regulate specific knowledge-power relations, and provide differential access to meanings and interpretations? Critical ethnography, as we conceive it, can assist educators to see the lives of their students against the grain of the cultural obvious and reanimate and renarrate their stories otherwise. As such, critical ethnography can help educators understand how students' own historical positions within dominant knowledge systems of intelligibility influence whether such knowledges will be respected or rejected, accepted or refuted.

As critical educators, we further can pose the challenge as follows: Who is doing what to whom in this specific enunciative field, in this agonistic arena of discourse, in this ensemble of intertextual relations known as the classroom? What social relations are being reproduced or challenged by the iteration and enactment of pedagogical rules, practices, strategies, and interpretations? As a result, who has access to certain voices and the power to modulate their semantic registers, and who is in a position to challenge hegemonic knowledge-power relations? As with all urgent questions, they are far easier to pose than to answer.

The social agent—whether teacher or student—is more than a passive effect of discourse. The fact that the individual is constituted in and through social meaning-making practices suggests that we can develop immanent criteria for social action grounded not in metaphysical assumptions but rather in a historical materialist project of social transformation. Such a project is linked to a neomaterialist framework of social transformation that offers a dialectical duality of the material (prediscursive) and the social semiotic (discursive) dimensions of social reality (Thibault 1991, 245). Thibault argues that in a neomaterialist social semiotic theory, "systems of relations are changed and/or maintained on the basis of the constant articulation, disarticulation, and rearticulation of the relations both between systems of social meaning making practices and between the prediscursive and the discursive" (242). As social agents of change, we might follow Thibault in "construct[ing] a self-reflexive praxis that can specify the local and global connections and disjunctions among interaction subsystems and that can articulate intelligent and responsible hypotheses about where, when, and how to intervene in patterned social meaning making on any given level in the social semiotic system" (1991, 244).

New patterns of global interconnections and forms of communication require corresponding forms of analytic attention in our research. Unfortunately, educational ethnographers have only begun to see the necessary connections among disciplinary strategies, institutional structures, and discursive conventions—partly, we believe, for two reasons. The current language of ethnographic practice is generally too microfocused and does not consider the social formations of cultural practices that are instantiated in the everyday practices of schools. But just as important, materialist social theory itself has retreated from a consideration of systematic analysis that takes seriously the totalizing discourses of patriarchal late capitalism. As materialist feminists have pointed out, even in much of materialist feminism, identity is understood as structured by the ambivalence of the signifier rather than by the fact that profits and power under capitalism serve the few through the appropriation of collectively produced surplus value (Hennessy 1993). Furthermore, long-term ethnographic studies in urban Los Angeles schools have helped us better understand that despite the ubiquitousness of the traditional teacher script,[1] even the hegemony of monolithic, monocultural, and monologic instruction can be challenged (Gutierrez 1992; Gutierrez and Larson 1994; Gutierrez, Rymes, and Larson 1995). In the everyday life of urban classrooms, students and many teachers are challenging the transcendent scripts that attempt to control, regulate, and disempower students, teachers, and local communities. These counterscripts (Gutierrez, Rymes, and Larson 1995) serve to illustrate the social construction of power and agency and the possibility for a critical education—even in the context of national and local assaults on progressive education.

The local transformation of schools and classrooms will help rupture the traditional hierarchies and rearrange the social and power relations that historically are designed to exclude teachers (who have been predominantly women), students, and families from the conversations about school reform (Carlson 1992). By instantiating a curriculum of social practice, a heteroglossic and critical pedagogy informed by the local and multiple knowledges of the participants and the employment of a sustained critique of capitalist social relations, the construction of very different communities of practice in schools and the transformation of urban schooling become possible.

The Politics of Multiculturalism and Citizenship

Our classroom investigations and discussions with urban educators in Los Angeles have also provoked us to rethink the issue of multicultural education. We have been distressed by the racial segregation that we see throughout the city at large, as well as in school playgrounds and lunchrooms. We link some of this to the politics of enforced assimilation reflected in the Proposition 187 legislation; the resurgent English Only movement; assaults on bilingual education in Republican legislation and by Republican spokespersons; the persistence of academic tracking; the Latinophobic, antiimmigration sentiment that has been growing since the early 1980s; deindustrialization; and the emergence of ethnic and racial movements that are demanding recognition. One also needs to view multiculturalism in terms of the larger picture, that is, from the reference point of the new world system of large-scale and continuous emigration flows, subaltern and transient cultures, stateless corporations, and the postindustrial labor force of women, racial minorities, and immigrants from previously peripheral nations (Zaretsky 1995).

As a means of countering nationalist and essentialist identity formations and those linked to the idea of the monolithic, autonomous self, the work of McLaren (1995), Anzaldúa (1987), and others has stressed the importance of hybridity and border-crossing in the construction of *mestizaje* identity. *Mestizaje* identity—*mestissage, creolite,* or transcultural identity—has been formulated as a mode of self-fashioning appropriate to the new globalization of culture.

The idea of border-crossing also fits well with the emphasis on the internationalization and deethnocentrization of sociology itself, not to mention the importance of "glocalization," or the recognition that the local is to a large extent constructed on a trans- or superlocal basis (Robertson 1995) and is a micromanifestation of the global (Balibar 1991). *Mestizaje* identity is meant to be a self-reflexive identity capable of rupturing the facile legitimization of "authentic" national identities through an articulation of a subject who is conjectural, who is a relational part of an ongoing negotiated connection to the larger society, who is interpolated by multiple subject positionings. Such identity formation represents a flight from the infantilization and displacement of the indigene; an unsettling of the circumscribed, stable, or entrenched subjective identifications authored and authorized by the dominant culture; and a movement toward the construction of a social *imaginaire* where new social relations can come into being (McLaren 1995). Pieterse notes that when examining the construction of *mestizaje* identity or hybridity, we need always to pay attention to the terms of the cultural mixing and the conditions surrounding the cultural mélange. In short, through our various stances as comparativists, we believe we should acquire a consciousness of local and global relations and how they influence *espace métisse*. For instance, while *mestizaje* identity points to ways of destabilizing isolationist narratives of nationalism, racism, and cultural chauvinism that fetishize an idealized historical past and valorize social activism, it also has an assimilationist inflection in Latin America, referring to a gradual whitening of the population and culture and the reproduction of elite European ideologies (see Pieterse 1995, 54). Along with Lionnet, we suggest that assimilation is partly a myth even though "the more powerful system does incorporate elements of the weaker one, often to the point where certain of its patterns and practices become indistinguishable from those of the imported or inferior culture" (1995, 9). She notes, for instance, after Anthony Appiah, that there is no U.S. culture without African roots, but this fact has not yet become a commonly accepted premise. We would argue the same about Latino culture. Educational researchers, we believe, do not have a sufficient understanding of the reciprocal influence of cultural contact; how, for instance, African American and Latino culture has shaped Western culture and how, especially in the border zones of the popular, cultural elements interact and are changed.

The important lesson here for educators is that the assimilated are rarely, if ever, passive recipients of the culture of domination. For instance, some of our research involves an attempt to see how racial minorities are influencing the dominant school culture and are creating sites of instability in the fabric of the dominant hegemony. In order to fully understand this process, educational researchers should explore with more vigilance cultures of whiteness, and see whiteness as an attribute of ethnicity. How, for instance, have constructions of white ethnicity been influenced by cultural contact with people of color? This is an important direction that we believe needs to be taken in educational research. Part of the problem, however, is the tendency of researchers to orientalize the presentation of the other, in other words, to present the other in essentialized forms as absolutely different from the West; equally as problematic is the process of occidentalism, which refers to the idea that anthropologists' views of the West are frequently central to their exposition of the other. In this process, the knowledge of the other is produced in dialectical opposition with knowledge of the West (Gewertz and Errington 1993). We occidentalize others by misinterpreting who we are, and we orientalize by constructing the other in reified terms as we fail to recognize the ways in which self and other are both caught up in dialectically reinitiating world systems.

The problem, as we see it, with the so-called proliferation of new tribalisms and exclusionist, militant, and separatist identities that we are witnessing on both global and local fronts (not to mention in our classrooms!) is that they deploy the same language as the inclusionist cultural discourses of forced assimilation (Bauman 1995). Bauman writes: "The cultural discourse, once the domain of the liberal, assimilationist *inclusivist* strategy, has been 'colonized' by the *exclusivist* ideology, and the use of traditional 'culturalist' vocabulary no more guarantees the subversion of exclusivist strategy. As Julia Kristeva warned, for the first time in history we are doomed to live with our differences 'without any superior totality which embraces and transcends our particularities'" (1995, 255).

McLaren (1995) has written at length about the attempt to secure such ethical and political totalities, which can be unifying without dominating, and we do not wish to rehearse such arguments here. We wish only to remind the reader of what we consider to be a central task in the struggle toward a critical multiculturalism: to constantly remind ourselves that cultural authenticity—whether we are referring to the melting-pot vision of the advocates of a common culture or to the pan-national identities of the Afrocentric and Chicano movements—does not precede rationality as a form of transcendental essence. Bauman writes that

> traditions do not "exist" by themselves and independently of what we think and do; they are daily reinvented by our dedication, our selective memory and selective seeing, our behaving "as if" they defined our conduct. The allegedly "primordial" communities are *postulated*; and the meaning of their being "real" is that many people, in unison, follow that postulate. The call to give the "community of belonging" our prime and undivided loyalty, the demand to consider ourselves community members first, and all the rest later, is precisely the way to make community a "reality," to split the larger society into little enclaves which eye each other with suspicion and keep their distance from each other. And because these communities, unlike modern nations in the coercive and educational institutions of the nation-state, do not have many legs to stand on except the copying and replicating of our individual loyalties, they require in order to exist an unusually intense emotional dedication and shrill, high-pitched, vociferous and spectacular declarations of faith; and they scent in the half-hearted, lukewarm and undecided fringes the most mortal of dangers. (1995, 276–277)

If all communities are socially constructed and pragmatically lived engagements, then for us the task is to knit such communities together under the challenge of ethical solidarity with the oppressed. McLaren (1995) has used the writings of Emmanuel Lévinas to emphasize the primacy of ethics over epistemology in creating a critical multiculturalism. Bauman underscores a similar position in the following passage:

> To take a moral stance means to assume responsibility for the Other; to act on the assumption that the well-being of the Other is a precious thing calling for my effort to preserve and enhance it, that whatever I do or do not do affects it, that if I have not done it it might not be done at all, and that even if others do or can do it this does not cancel my responsibility for doing it myself. . . . As the greatest ethical philosopher of our century, Emmanuel Lévinas, puts it—morality means *being-for* (not merely being-aside or even being-with) the Other. And this being-for is unconditional (that is, if it is *to be moral*, not merely *contractual*)—it does not depend on what the Other is, or does, whether s/he deserves my care and whether s/he repays in kind. One cannot conceive of an argument that could justify the renunciation of moral responsibility—putting it into cold storage, lending or pawning it. And one cannot imagine a point of which one could say with any sort of moral right: I have done my share, and here my responsibility ends. (1995, 267–268)

The challenge to us as educators is to develop a concept of unity and difference that reconfigures the meaning of difference as *political mobilization* rather than cultural authenticity. Manning Marable's articulation of the concept of blackness comes close to the idea of political mobilization to which we are referring, and which we believe can constitute the defining moment of not only a critical multiculturalism but critical education in general:

> Black and white progressive activists must revive the traditions and tactics of nonelectoral political protest. This requires new institutions of creative resistance. For example, "freedom schools," open multiracial academies held during late afternoons, and on weekends for secondary school and college students, could offer a public protest curriculum. Learning how to organize street demonstrations, selective buying campaigns, civil disobedience, and reading about the personalities and history of American protest, would help to build a radical consciousness among this generation of youth. (1996, 265).

Moving Beyond a Liberal Postmodernist Politics

Emancipatory pedagogies require that our practice as researchers and as pedagogues needs to be identified as transpiring within a systemic entity known as global capitalism. Educators, especially, can politicize their readers against the "comfort zones" that entrap us in liberal humanist pedagogies that appear to redress the deep social ruptures so evident in educational contexts. This current historical moment refracts through a series of unstable standpoints from which to frame our struggle as educators and cultural workers. We are called to examine how we, as educators, have been invented by Western culture within the process of colonization and the formation of Eurocentrism. It is a time that demands educators to construct a countermemory, a counterdiscourse or counterscript, a counterpraxis of liberation.

In the case of Los Angeles, our emphasis on critical multiculturalism should not be confused with a call for a new centrism or subaltern but instead centers around an attempt not only to challenge our strategies of representation and the politics of our ethnicities but to dismantle the ineffable structures of power and violence that pervade the politics of both the public and the popular, that are inextricably bound up with global economic developments, and that form the structural unconscious of the United States.[2] What is essential for educators in this locus of struggle is to dismantle the discourses of power and privilege and social practices that have epistemically mutated into a new and terrifying form of xenophobic nationalism in which there is but one universal subject of history—the white, Anglo, heterosexual male of bourgeois privilege. Such a dilemma points to a necessary displacement of the United States as the center of analysis and the development of a more inclusive, global perspective, one that, as Therborn (1995) points out, needs to be decentered and de-Westernized. It suggests, too, that as critical educators for social justice, we can no longer advance our view of what it means to be American on the graveyards of other people's cultures under the banner of Cartesian imperialism—"I invade you, therefore you exist." Nor should we view ourselves as disinterested chroniclers, as detached entertainers, as agents who operate in a realm of eclectic idealism outside the messy web of ethics and politics.

In such social circumstances, we as critical researchers should move beyond a research agenda that simply celebrates liberal pluralism—because such a pluralism has an ideological center of gravity that rarely ever gets defined for what it is. This is the same pluralistic society that is paying its workers in underdeveloped countries salaries that amount to little more than slave wages—not to mention the *maquiladora* industry and its own sweatshops in Los Angeles, New York, and elsewhere. It is the same system that calls for the privatization and corporatization of education and signals the end of public education as we know it. Further, we should address not only the discursive constructions of race but also economic exploitation and the manner in which such forms of ethnicity are structurally *imbricated* and intertwined in the antinomic configuration of flexible transnational capitalism. In this way, educators can participate not only in analyzing our cultural and social present and decolonizing the Euro-American mind but in effectively organizing our responses to and encounters with the changing economic and cultural world.

Decades of social and historical amnesia have brought many educational researchers to an ideological impasse of such proportions that critical ethnography has been reduced and domesticated into rhetorical performances, textual strategies that avoid the possibility of challenging in any serious manner the social division of labor. Today the solitary worker is laboring under worsening conditions due to drastic shifts in global markets and the reterritorialization of urban life. Consider, for instance, the spacial strategy in the urban planning of cities such as Los Angeles, which more and more are resembling Third World cities. We are referring here to the disintegration of the public sphere, social violence, fortified enclosures, and deliberate sociospacial strategies of urban enclavization and gated communities (Davis 1990). Urban spaces operate as functional totalities organized by socioeconomic, disciplinary, and monocultural discourses and practices such that the inhabitants of non-Anglo communities remain constantly under siege. In the fragmentary postmodern city, the absence of community has led to a new decadentism and narcissistic affirmation of the self. Educators have not adequately provided our students with the tools of social and cultural analysis necessary to permit them to answer the questions raised by Giroux, Aronowitz (Aronowitz and DiFazio 1994), Apple (Apple 1993; Apple and Weiss 1983), and other critical educators: "Who am I when I am participating in this society? What is it about myself that I no longer want to be? What can I do to change the social conditions that have produced the identity upon which my dreams and desires hinge?"[3]

One need only reflect upon the monologic and monolithic pedagogies in the technologies and apparatuses of social regulation, and the transcendent scripts of normative behavior discussed earlier, to understand that the very process of becoming "literate" and "educated" is linked often to simply following orders and participating in practice with few opportunities for critical engagement with social reality. We are not arguing that students do not have greater general access to textual practices but that social control in schools takes on different forms and registers different deployments and effects given the historical, cultural, and geographical specificities linked to larger global practices. Much of this has to do with the species of liberation that undergirds the new postmodern state. Civil society is reduced to merely an administrative mechanism (Hardt and Negri 1994). The problem with the politics of liberalism and the postmodern state has been analyzed by Hardt and Negri and can be summarized as follows: The order and harmony and equilibrium of the system are achieved by excluding points of social conflict and insulating the system from social contents; tolerance means indifference to the determinations of social being and to the avoidance of social antagonisms; questions of labor, production, gender difference, racial difference, sexual orientation, desire, and value are discarded because they are considered personal, not political; the political system is based on absolute contingency rather than material determinations; society is self-referential and premised on *feasibility,* not desirability.

In this view, liberal society is reduced to a "technical calculus of force" emptied of the "subjective field of social conflict." The postmodern state organizes the separation of civil society from the state, pretending that this separation does not exist. The postmodern state also goes beyond the modern state's production of commodities through the exploitation of labor and through economic planning and regulation. It now only concerns itself only with the reproduction of the state and capital as *purely autonomous powers of social control.*

It should be clear by now that throughout these pages we have largely been advancing an ethical argument. Following Bauman (1995), we advance the idea that late capitalism has advanced the logic of procedural rationality to the point that ethics has now been cleaved from the domain of social and economic justice. Postmodern bureaucratic and business life has brought about the deregulation not only of markets but also of hopes and dreams. Business ethics names certain actions as imperative and others as neutral or nonmoral issues, based on sound "business sense." Good business sense means indifference to anything not related to the instrumental task of increasing profits. Bauman writes:

> To make "business sense" . . . assets must be allocated to the highest bidder—not to those who may need them most, but to those who are prepared to give most in exchange. Who the highest bidder is, what are his credentials and entitlements (except his solvency, of course), should not matter, lest the resources be not put to the best use. In business there are no friends and no neighbours (though "good commercial sense" prompts one to pretend that there are). It helps if the partner in a transaction is a complete stranger and remains such, since only then may instrumental rationality gain the uncontested ascendancy it needs; knowing too much of her or him may—who knows?—beget a personal, emotional relationship, which will inevitably confuse and becloud the judgment. (1995, 262)

Bauman adds, "Bureaucracy strangles or criminalizes moral impulses; business merely pushes them aside" (1995, 264). We found this to be the case when in 1995 it became illegal for teachers to hold meetings about proposition 187 in their own schools. The bureaucratic mechanisms that supported Proposition 187, which was ostensibly an economic strategy to reclaim jobs for "real" Americans, managed to control the terms of debate, squeezing out most opposition to it in terms of its ethical implications. Part of the problem, then, faced by teachers is the logic of bureaucratic control based on a procedural ethics. Bauman describes this ethics in terms of two characteristics, responsibility-floating and adiaphorization. The former refers to following the rules faithfully and doing what is asked by one's superiors. The individual is not to be held responsible for the effects of his or her actions. The latter refers to the declaration that most things that members of organizations are expected to do when in service are exempt from moral evaluation—they are neither good nor bad, only correct or incorrect. Duties are judged only by their procedural correctness. Consequently, writes Bauman,

> business interests cannot easily be squared with the sense of responsibility for the welfare and well-being of those who may find themselves affected by the business pursuit of greatest effects. In business language, "rationalization" means more often than not laying off people who used to derive their livelihood from serving the business task before. They are now "redundant," because a more effective way to use the assets has been found—and their past services do not count for much: each business transaction, to be truly rational, must start from scratch, forgetting past merits and debts of gratitude. Business rationality shirks responsibility for its own consequences, and this is another mortal blow to the influence of moral considerations. (1995, 264)

We argue, then, that the struggle for liberatory education cannot be won without changes in the larger social order and the realm of ethical commitment. Since we may be seen as overly disparaging textual exegesis, we wish to emphasize that the discursive aspects of our identities are indeed important. How we mark the boundaries of our ethnicities and racial identifications and representations does draw needed critical attention to the scribal power of dominant narratives and helps us both focus on and demobilize the neocolonial system that energizes our collective values as a citizenry. Yet how we identify ourselves collectively, across differences as a totality, is equally important. Bauman argues persuasively that we are in error as long as we continue to see the increase in individual moral autonomy and collective state responsibility as a contradiction in terms. Rather, we recognize "the intimate connection (not contradiction!) between the autonomous, morally self-sustained and self-governed (therefore, often unruly, unwieldy and awkward) citizen and a fully fledged, self-reflective and self-correcting political community. They can only come together; neither is thinkable without the other" (Bauman 1995, 287).

Consider Bauman's further comments:

> The space we co-habit may be well—consensually—structured; in such a space, in which many things vital to the life of each of us (transport, schools, surgeries, media of communication) are *shared*, we may see each other as

conditions, rather than obstacles, to our collective as well as individual well-being. Much as the fragmented and discontinuous life promotes the waning of moral impulses, a shared life of continuous and multi-faceted relationships would reinvigorate moral responsibilities and awaken the urge to shoulder the task of managing—now truly common—affairs. Much as the life of episodes and the politics reduced to crisis-management prompt the exit from politics, the sharing of responsibilities would go a long way towards helping citizens to recover the voices they lost or stopped trying to make audible. As Steven Connor put it, "it is only in the absolute putting of the 'we' at risk that we realize the possibilities of our humanity." (1995, 284)

Consequently, given the changing demographic realities within the United States, we take the position that it is our collective ethical responsibility as a nation of immigrants to argue for a multicultural as well as biliterate/bicultural education. These educational policies and practices should be given priority, especially at a time of progressive deindustrialization when jobs are scarce and workplaces are downsizing. Further, there needs to be a renewed commitment to public education and an attempt to slow down the rush to privatization. Higher education must become a right rather than a privilege, and democratic access to higher education must be won. This access needs to be followed by "a national guaranteed income that is equal to the historical level of material culture" (Aronowitz and DiFazio 1994, 353). In addition, there needs to be a renewed commitment to instituting arts curricula as well as science programs as artisanship and lifelong learning become available for people of all classes. This is not the same thing, argue Aronowitz and DiFazio, as proposing a new cultural aestheticism in the name of ethical renewal; rather, any new emphasis on ethical renewal needs to bring to the equation the project of social and economic justice. The central insight here is profoundly Marxist: Citizenship through schooling means very little in terms of the project of social justice so long as the subject of history (the student as citizen) remains mystified in terms of the way power is inscribed in relations of domination and exploitation; that is, as long as the subject of history remains mystified by religious, ethical dogmatism and an instrumental-rational system of intelligibility that confuses agency with the politics of capitalist social relations. As Aronowitz and DiFazio argue, active citizenship in the form of self-governance and autonomous agency is impossible without material preconditions, and that means the creation of economic equality on a national level. Without emancipation from labor, the citizen as historical agent for social justice will serve as just another trompe l'oeil for the ideology of the free market. And when that happens, global capitalism will have transformed itself into human nature. Progressive and conservative initiatives on school reform will collapse into the logic of capital such that they are indistinguishable. But to a large extent, hasn't this already happened?

Notes

1. The construction of the classroom community is observed in the participation structures, discourse, and spatial arrangements of everyday life in the classroom. Scripts, or what come to be the normative patterns of the classroom over time, represent orientations that members come to expect after repeated interactions in contexts constructed both locally and over time. There are, of course, multiple scripts in the classroom; yet the normative script is most often the teacher script or orientation. See Gutierrez (1993) for more discussion on script.

2. See Paul Virilio (1986) for an excellent analysis of globilization, speed, and technology.

3. For an analysis of this process in the context of schooling, see Peter McLaren (1993, 1994, 1995), Giroux and McLaren (1989, 1994), and McLaren and Lankshear (1994).

References

Anzaldúa, G. (1987). *Borderlands/La Frontera: The New Mestiza*. San Francisco: Spinsters/Aunt Lute.

Apple, M. (1993). *Official Knowledge: Democratic Education in a Conservative Age*. New York: Routledge.

Apple, M., and Weis, L. (1983). *Ideology and Practice in Schooling*. Philadelphia: Temple University Press.

Aronowitz, S., and DiFazio, W. (1994). *The Jobless Future: Sci-Tech and the Dogma of Work*. Minneapolis: University of Minnesota Press.

Bakhtin, M. M. (1981). *The Dialogic Imagination*. Ed. M. Holquist; trans. M. Holquist and C. Emerson. Austin: University of Texas Press.

Bakhtin, M. M. (1986). *Speech Genres and Other Late Essays*. Ed. C. Emerson and M. Holquist; trans. V. W. McGee. Austin: University of Texas Press.

Balibar, E. (1991). "Es Gibt Keinen Staat in Europa: Racism and Politics in Europe Today." *New Left Review* 186, March-April.

Bauman, Zygmunt. (1995). *Life in Fragments: Essays in Postmodern Morality*. Oxford and Cambridge: Blackwell.

Bogue, Ronald. (1989). *Deleuze and Guattari*. London and New York: Routledge.

Bourdieu, P. (1977). *Outline of a Theory of Practice*. Trans. Richard Nice. Cambridge: Cambridge University Press.

Bourdieu, P. (1991). "Epilogue: On the Possibility of a Field of World Sociology." Trans. L. Wacquant. In P. Bourdieu and J. Coleman, eds., *Social Theory for a Changing Society*. Boulder: Westview Press.

Bourdieu, P., Passeron, J. C., and de Saint Martin, M. (1994). *Academic Discourse: Linguistic Misunderstanding and Professorial Power*. Stanford: Stanford University Press.

Brosio, R. A. (1993). "Capitalism's Emerging World Order: The Continuing Need for Theory and Brave Action by Citizen-Educators." *Educational Theory* 44(4), 467–482.

Carlson, D. (1992). *Teachers and Crisis: Urban School Reform and Teachers' Work Cultures.* New York and London: Routledge.

Davis, M. (1990). *City of Quartz.* London and New York: Verso.

Foucault, M. (1977). *Discipline and Punish: The Birth of a Prison.* Trans. A. Sheridan. London: Allen Lane.

Freire, P., and Macedo, D. (1987). *Literacy: Reading the Word and the World.* South Hadley, MA: Bergin and Garvey.

Geertz, C. (1995). *After the Fact; Two Countries, Four Decades, One Anthropologist.* Cambridge: Harvard University Press.

Gewertz, Deborah, and Errington, Frederick. (1993). "We Think, Therefore They Are? On Occidentalizing the World." In Amy Kaplan and Donald E. Pease, eds., *Cultures of United States Imperialism* (635–655). Durham and London: Duke University Press.

Giddens, A. (1981). *A Contemporary Critique of Historical Materialism.* London: Macmillan.

Giroux, Henry, and McLaren, Peter, eds. (1989). *Critical Pedagogy, the State, and Cultural Struggle.* Albany: State University of New York Press.

Giroux, Henry, and McLaren, Peter, eds. (1994). *Between Borders.* New York and London: Routledge.

Gutierrez, K. (1992). "A Comparison of Instructional Contexts in Writing: Process Classrooms with Latino Children." *Education and Urban Society* 24, 244–252.

Gutierrez, K. (1993). "How Talk, Context, and Script Shape Contexts for Learning: A Cross Case Comparison of Journal Sharing." *Linguistics in Education* 5, 335–365.

Gutierrez, K., and Larson, J. (1994). "Language Borders: Recitation as Hegemonic Discourse." *International Journal of Educational Reform* 3(1), 22–36.

Gutierrez, K., Larson, J., and Kreuter, B. (1995). "Cultural Tensions in the Scripted Classroom: The Value of the Subjugated Perspective." *Urban Education* 29(4), 410–442.

Gutierrez, K., Larson, J., and Kreuter, B. (in press). "Constructing Classrooms as Communities of Learners." In P. Smagorinsky, ed., *Culture and Literacy: Bridging the Gap Between Community and Classroom.* Urbana, IL: National Council of Teachers of English.

Gutierrez, K., Rymes, B., and Larson, J. (1995). "Script, Counterscript, and Underlife in the Classroom: James Brown v. the Board of Education." *Harvard Educational Review* 65(3), 445–471.

Hardt, M., and Negri, A. (1994). *Labor of Dionysus: A Critique of the State Form.* Minneapolis and London: Univerity of Minnesota Press.

Hennessy, R. (1993). *Materialist Feminism and the Politics of Discourse.* London and New York: Routledge.

hooks, bell. (1994). *Outlaw Culture: Resisting Representations.* New York: Routledge.

Laclau, E., and Mouffe, C. (1985). *Hegemony and Socialist Strategy: Towards a Radical Democratic Politics.* London: Verso.

Lankshear, C., and McLaren, P., eds. (1993). *Critical Literacy: Politics, Praxis and the Postmodern.* Albany: State University of New York Press.

Lash, Scott, and Urry, John. (1994). *Economies of Signs and Space.* Thousand Oaks, CA, and London: Sage.

Lionett, Françoise. (1995). *Postcolonial Representations: Women, Literature, Identity.* Ithaca and London: Cornell University Press.

McLaren, P. (1993). *Schooling as Ritual Performance: Towards a Political Economy of Educational Symbols and Gestures,* 2nd ed. New York: Routledge and Kegan Paul.

McLaren, P. (1994). *Life in Schools: An Introduction to Critical Pedagogy in the Foundations of Education,* 2nd ed. New York: Longman.

McLaren, P. (1995). *Critical Pedagogy and Predatory Culture: Oppositional Politics in a Postmodern Era.* London and New York: Routledge.

McLaren, Peter, and Lankshear, Colin, eds. (1994). *Politics of Liberation.* London and New York: Routledge.

Marable, Manning. (1996). *Speaking Truth to Power: Essays on Race, Resistance, and Radicalism.* Boulder, CO: Westview Press.

Ochs, E., Taylor, C., Rudolph, D., and Smith, R. (1992). "Storytelling as a Theory-Building Activity." *Discourse Processes* 15, 37–72.

Pieterse, Jan Nederveen. (1995). "Globalization as Hybridization." In Mike Featherstone, Scott Lash, and Roland Robertson, eds., *Global Modernities* (45–68). Thousand Oaks, CA, and London: Sage.

Robertson, R. (1995). "Glocalization: Time-Space and Homogeneity-Heterogeneity." In Mike Featherstone, Scott Lash, and Roland Robertson, eds., *Global Modernities.* Thousand Oaks, CA, and London: Sage.

Rosenau, J. N. (1990). *Turbulence in World Politics.* Brighton: Harvester.

Stone, J. (1994). "The Phenomenological Roots of the Radical Democracy/Marxism Debate." *Rethinking Marxism* 7(1), 99–115.

Sunker, Heinz. (1994). "America as a Violent Society." Paper delivered at the University of Connecticut at Hartford, April 7.

Taussig, Michael. (1992). *The Nervous System.* New York: Routledge.

Therborn, Goran. (1995). "Routes to/through Modernity." In Mike Feathertone, Scott Lash, and Roland Robertson, eds., *Global Modernities* (124–139). Thousand Oaks, CA, and London: Sage.

Thibault, Paul J. (1991). *Social Semiotics as Praxis.* Minneapolis: University of Minnesota Press.

University of California Graduate School of Education and Information Studies. (1995). *Center X: Mission and Strategies.* Los Angeles: UCLA.

Virilio, Paul. (1986). "The State of Emergency." In *Speed and Politics* (133–151). New York: Semiotext(e).

Walkerdine, V. (1990). *Schoolgirl Fictions.* New York: Verso.

Walkerdine, V. (1992). "Progressive Pedagogy and Political Struggle." In C. Luke and J. Gore, eds., *Feminisms and Critical Pedagogy.* New York: Routledge.

Walkerdine, V. (1994). "Femininity as Performance." In L. Stone, ed., *The Education Feminism Reader.* New York: Routledge.

Willis, Paul. (1977). *Learning to Labour: How Working Class Kids Get Working Class Jobs.* Aldershot, England: Gower.

Zaretsky, E. (1995). "The Birth of Identity Politics in the 1960s: Psychoanalysis and the Public/Private Discussion." In Mike Featherstone, Scott Lash, and Roland Robertson, eds., *Global Modernities* (244–259). Thousand Oaks, CA, and London: Sage.

7

Provisional Utopias in a Postcolonial World: An Interview with Peter McLaren

Gert Biesta and Siebren Miedema

In 1980 you published your first book, Cries from the Corridor, *in which you document your experiences as a elementary school teacher in one of Toronto's 'inner-city' suburbs. Although it became a best-seller in Canada, it was a highly controversial book. Looking back in 1989, you acknowledged that you had failed to see 'how all of it was related to the larger socioeconomic context and technologies of power in a wider society'* (Life in Schools, *p. viii). Can you tell us something about the background of that book and also about your own background and the way in which you encountered critical pedagogy?*

When I entered graduate school I had been an elementary classroom teacher who had a keen interest in writing and art. My background was working-class early in my life until my father landed up in a managerial job. My new-found middle-class life was decidedly 1960s bohemian: it gave me rich if not dangerously self-indulgent encounters with revolutionary politics, the world of avant-garde art and literature; studies in theology and philosophy; counter-cultural lifestyles; the poetry of Dylan Thomas; the aesthetics of madness; historical and contemporary narratives of romantic love; spiritual journeys involving the occult and mysticism; and flirtations with experimental music and an appreciation for Chicago-style and Mississippi Delta blues which remains to this day. But what moved me unsentimentally were the writings of Che Guevara and Malcolm X who wrote piquantly about revolution and the necessity for it. I became involved in radical political groups but at a time when I didn't adequately understand the implications of my involvement and had little theoretical grasp of the local, national, and world-political events that surrounded me and shaped the contours of my subjectivity, folding the social into my perception of the world.

At this time I knew virtually nothing about the politics of knowledge—knowing as a political act, a form of ethical address and revolutionary commitment. I became introduced to critical pedagogy at a relatively late date (in the early 1980s), as a doctoral candidate in the *Ontario Institute for Studies in Education, University of Toronto.* This was shortly after I attended a summer semiotic institute and had the good fortune of studying under Michel Foucault and Umberto Eco—a short few weeks that changed forever the direction of my scholarship, my practice of the self, my revolutionary politics.

In the mid 1970's, I had decided to pursue the career of an elementary school teacher as a means of focusing my interest in self and social transformation. I found myself teaching in some of the toughest inner-city schools in Toronto at that time, schools which were beginning to be introduced to diverse populations of students from all different parts of the world. In one of the schools in which I was teaching, there were approximately thirty-five different nationalities, literally from all over the globe. The challenge at that time for me was to find a way of approaching my pedagogical mission in a way that could best serve the interests of this diverse population. Having been trained as a teacher within a humanistic tradition, from within a very personalistic, positivistic, Cartesian perspective of teacher identity, I saw it as my ethical responsibility to transform and shape the lives of these economically disadvantaged and marginalized groups. Bathed by the effulgences of liberal humanist discourse, I really was intent upon not so much empowering disadvantaged students to speak their own voices but empowering them so that they could communicate to me—so that they could expunge my own liberal guilt and bourgeois alienation. So the task was cast very instrumental and formulaic terms: give them enough attention, and respect, and through techniques gleaned from personalistic psychology I would be able to improve their self-image and forge within them an optimism of the will that would enable them to challenge the growing obstacles to their achievement in North American society.

It wasn't until I wrote the book about my experiences, and the book became a national best-seller, that I found myself embroiled in a national public debate over new Canadian immigration in the schools. The book was theoretically underdeveloped and this was partly intentional and partly due to the fact that I wrote the book years before my seminars with Michel Foucault in Toronto in 1980 or my collisions with the writings of Marx, Lukács, Adorno, Horkeimer, Benjamin, Antonio Negri, Habermas, Althusser, or Freire. Advised by a famous newspaper journalist not to editorialize but to simply describe my personal experiences in the inner city (which was premised on the notion that description was a transparent access to the real), I just wrote my experiences in a rather journalistic fashion. At that time, I chose not to establish a theoretical or political context for the book, feeling that simply my descriptions would be enough to alert the Canadian public to the changing populations in our schools. The implicit message was a rather commonplace liberal one, having not developed the commitment to Marxism that has marked my work since that time. It went something like this: We as a society are failing immigrant students because of our historical amnesia surrounding democracy and social justice and our growing xenophobia as a nation. We need a renewed commitment to immigrant students who will become the next generation of Canadians so we need to give them the material and intellectual resources to lead our country. It sounds quite a bit left liberal to me now.

I took a leave of absence from teaching to pursue doctoral studies shortly after my diary was published, and at that time I became sensitive to criticisms from the radical left: that my book simply mirrored a kind of liberal, individualistic ideology, in that the assumptions upon which my book was based, were generally located within a kind of Eurocentric intellectual tradition, in which the political and the pedagogical were not sufficiently connected in terms of the relation between capital and labor and in which the ideological presuppositions of the book (which were largely grounded in a bourgeois humanistic tradition) remained clouded and masked. Even to myself as the author. So it was only in the early 1980s that I discovered that there was indeed a tradition in North America to which I gave the name "the critical education tradition."

Can you tell us what this tradition looked like in the early 1980s? Which were the dominant positions in North America at that time, and how did you relate your own work to these positions?

There was work coming from England on the sociology of knowledge; there was the Marxist structuralism of Basil Bernstein; there were debates among British symbolic interactionists, neo-Weberians, and Marxist ethnographers, there was the Birmingham School of Contemporary Cultural Studies, there were educators such as Giroux who were interested in the Frankfurt School; there were educators influenced by the social reconstructionists such as John Dewey and George Counts and those who called themselves curriculum reconceptualists. You could see the beginnings of trans-disciplinary approaches—existential phenomenology, critical hermeneutics, the work of Gadamer and Habermas became popular, and then there was the influence of the ethnomethodologists and the symbolic anthropologists.

The theoretical center of gravity in those days one could loosely describe as a political economy approach developed by Michael Apple. And from the Birmingham Center the look began to take on a more ethnographic/phenomenological kind of focus with an emphasis on a Gramscian-inspired cultural Marxism.

And after that?

I think that after Willis' work, *Learning to Labor,* we have witnessed here in the United States a lessening in influence of British scholarship on schooling. However, we have seen the growing popularity of writers such as Stuart Hall, Angela McRobbie, Paul Gilroy, Kobena Mercer, James Donald, John Thompson, Raymond Williams, and some others. I think that the major developments in critical education in the U.S. over the last five or six, seven years have been dominated by American writers: the critique of the reproduction model, with the focus on resistance, which has been largely Henry Giroux's important contribution and which certainly inspired some of my own work on resistance. And then came the current focus on feminist pedagogy and the debates over identity politics and multiculturalism, postmodernism and postcolonialism. We are, however, witnessing the growing influence of the writings of Derrida, Foucault and Lyotard on U.S. critical educationalists. Critical pedagogy spans all of these debates and has become a fertile topic not only in education but in departments of composition writing and literature. There is tremendous interest outside of education in the work of Freire, for instance. Cultural studies—for example, media literacy—is growing in interest among educators and here the British are still very influential, especially writers such as James Carey, Stuart Hall and Paul Gilroy.

My own work resembles very little the standard patterns and developments that have occurred in educational theory. I continue to stray rather far from the frontiers of the acceptable. I seem always on a collision course with acceptability. I have remained outside of the mainstream, in the margins, in the folds of legitimacy or even credibility by normative standards. I think radical intellectuals work better in the borderlands, between worlds. After my first book was criticized for being theoretically underdeveloped—it was more the case of being theoretically absent—I entered a time of theoretical exploration that I would liken to a feeding frenzy of a wild animal; where my writing became hallucinatory, a conceptual cartography of intensities and desires. It was a time of personal turbulence. I sat rather awkwardly in hegemony. A restless sadness overcame me on a rather permanent basis. Staring into the puddles of memories of earlier times—times that I spent as a student activist—critical educational theory seemed so disconnected from real issues of class exploitation, patriarchy, and formations and disciplined mobilizations of white supremacy. The suffering at the level of everyday life of so many people was a concrete, material fact that I refused to allow to be abstracted away by the formal components of a research agenda or the collectible ephemera of hard data. In fact, the concreteness—the corporeality of suffering—was to become the central core of my work. Action research began to figure prominently in my own projects. It is difficult to pinpoint exactly what I was doing because when I started writing as a criticalist I was also very interested in the avant garde art movement in North America—an interest considered too bourgeois for my fellow working-class intellectuals. I was also interested in poststructuralism and the writings of Lacan. And I also became very interested in Gregory Bateson, and eventually social semiotics and the work of Bakhtin, Volosinov, Peirce and Greimas and understanding culture in terms of its systems of signs and symbols and rituals.

That was your dissertation project which became Schooling as a Ritual Performance. *How was it received, especially in the critical education tradition?*

Although it sold modestly, it did receive excellent reviews for the most part. Some colleagues have told me it's become a "cult" text—whatever that means. It has just been released in a new expanded edition. In this edition Colin Lankshear tries to explain why the book captured only a small and select number of readers, and why it didn't receive more widespread attention. I think the language and theoretical questions that I was raising at that time left American readers somewhat perplexed. It was a direction that was so different from the standard leftist ethnography that emphasized a political economy approach, it was not readily picked up as a class text. Readers found the theory very dense and the language too literary. Mainstream journals tried to shut me out.

I have tried to develop further the approach that I had taken in that book—a book which, to this day, I would still say is among my best work. I felt that anthropology in North America needed to be revitalized in terms of attending to relations of power and its relationship to regimes of discourse and larger economies of power and privilege linked to class struggle, so I decided to release the book with a new coda which addressed some of these new concerns. I grew to admire the work of James Clifford, the Comaroffs, and Patricia Tinciento Clough.

In 1985 you moved to Miami University, Oxford, Ohio, where Henry Giroux was already working. Did that have any influence on your work?

Yes. I think that coming to Miami in 1985 was an important time for me because it enabled me to work much more closely in the neo-Marxist tradition of Henry's work, and become much more familiar with the work of pragmatists such as Dewey, with whom Henry was familiar. Not to mention the work of Paulo Freire, with whose work I was already intimately involved. But at the same time, I had the space there to chart a very individual course to my work. One interest took me in the direction of liberation theology, which I felt had a great deal to offer critical pedagogy. The other was the writers on postmodernism and anti-foundationalism as well as cultural theorists such as bell hooks and Cornel West. I think my book *Life in Schools* definitely shows some of Henry's early influence but after that project I developed a different approach to my intellectual work that, to this day, is constantly changing. Which might be a problem because some critics find it hard to locate it in any one field. The same is true of Henry—he's always on the move intellectually—and that is one of many things I admire about him.

How do you see the relevancy of liberation theology for critical pedagogy?

The relevancy of political theology for critical pedagogy has to do with what it has to say about our situatedness in structures of power, in economies of privilege in the contemporary North-American context and elsewhere. In fact, it locates agency within a larger context, within a global perspective. I believe it helps us offer a preferential option for the oppressed, for the wretched of the earth, for the immiserated and the downtrodden. It helps us to engage our humanity in a way that takes us out of our own self-interest, in a way that speaks to the necessity of humility, of compassion, of radical love. And so I began to draw upon some of the work being done in political theology in my own work of critical pedagogy.

How about post-modernism?

I have some doubts about many of the attempts to formulate a postmodern pedagogy. What concerns me is the way that it often forgets about material conditions of exploitation. The unsaid surrounding some postmodern projects, more specifically the ludic varieties—those that locate difference in the realm of the superstructure as a form of tropic excess, the irrepressible heterogeneity of discourse or the uncontainable condition of signification—is the retreat into a fashionable apostasy where material conditions associated with the relations between capital and labor are occluded, where human suffering is treated solely or mainly as a text to unpack or a discourse to uncoil. The problem isn't just the stability of the social system brought about by the unrepresentability or the excess of signs, but rather the antagonisms that shape the struggle between capital and labor. Signs and significations are historically rooted and ideologically connected. I am, more and more, returning to my

Marxist roots. While locating and situating the subject within the textual morass in which ludic postmodernists have buried it, critical postmodernists or resistance postmodernists such as Teresa Ebert are attempting to locate the subject not as simply a series of positions within discursive formations or as ruptures within the unitary cohesiveness of the autonomous ego—as in Donna Haraway's 'infidel heteroglossia'—but as significations that have become relatively fixed within specific historical determinations and the material relations of race, class and gender struggle. Postmodern social theory has provided some wonderful opportunities to develop a kind of radical contextualism—a way of interrogating social relations and analyzing how these relations are implicated in forms of subjectivity and agency. I have, for instance, found those who write under the sign of postmodernism to be very helpful in my current project of interrogating the positivistic reductionism of identity within the labyrinthine profusion of contemporary cultural politics and in analyzing sets of relations between principles and practices of pluralism within the context of trying to develop what I call 'critical multiculturalism'—a polyvocal and insurgent multiculturalism that sets out programmatically to challenge the suffocating, assimilative discourses and social practices of the nation state, the increasing call for social standardization, and the homogeneity that characterizes the growing cultural conservativism; it's a multiculturalism that attempts to resist cultural hegemony, monoculturalism, and capitalist exploitation in its many guises. U.S. culture has disintegrated into a culture of everyday terror in which people live barricaded against the threat of the Other. The serial killer is now the last American hero, the last person who can act, who can take charge of life. It is a sad commentary on civilization and definitely, for me, rebukes the myth of progress. How has this all come about? How are social norms arrived at and enforced? That's what I'm trying to figure out.

I think the reason that the topic of post-colonialism has become so important, at least for me, is because we find ourselves now more enmeshed in global systems of exploitation. And we are seeing the centres and the margins shifting locations as new resistances to new antagonisms occur.

What would this post-colonial sensitivity imply for education, i.e., how would you define 'post-colonial pedagogy'?

By post-colonial pedagogy I refer to the importance of making problematic pedagogical discourses in light of the current movement or trajectory towards global capitalism and the narratives or cultural logic associated with and resulting from the break-up of all imperialisms based on nation states. Now post-colonial pedagogy as I am using it is a pedagogy of anti-imperialism, of anti-colonialism, of anti-racism, of anti-homophobia; a pedagogy which challenges the very categories through which the history of the colonized has been written. I am certainly talking about not simply colonial countries, but also about groups who have been colonized in this country. It's about the wreckage of democracy and the lust to rebuild it but to build it differently by understanding difference in a different way—not as 'deviance', not as 'primitive' or within the narrow narrative of evolutionism. So that in fact this notion of post-colonialism in my mind challenges global transnational capitalism as a kind of Euro-American success story or tale of progress, and specifically challenges the way that Anglo-European discourses have split off the 'other', and have banished and romanticized difference in a politically and ethically disabling manner. So that is the kind of context I am trying to use in terms of situating my description of post-colonialism.

How does this relate to post-modernism?

Post-modernism refers at once, I think, to a sensibility. It is wrong to suggest a categorical divide between modernism and postmodernism. I use the term heuristically to refer to social relations, their cultural logics, and how they have changed with the global disorganization of capital, but also to a mode of social analysis. I think that the term 'postmodern condition' refers to the specific society that people like Jean Beaudrillard have been talking about, you know, the society of the simulacra, the society of the spectacle (Debord), of copies without the originals, of bodies without organs (Deleuze and Guattari). Additionally it refers to the power of the incursion of the image, the preponderance of the image in the construction of media knowledges, and the emphasis on image management, on technocapitalism, on video justice. I really do believe that we live in a society now that is based on the management and articulation of moods. But we need to remember that our affective investment in material objects or consumer fetishes is related to relations of production and a politics of consumption that must be geo-politically and contextually specific. We no longer live in a society of goals, one that is goal-centered. I think that was a society that was predominantly a print-oriented society linked to industrial capitalism in specific ways. Now I think with the advent of the kind of interactive and sophisticated media machinery within the culture industry, and the economic practices of flexible specialization, we are more concerned with roles, living out roles, than we are with fulfilling goals. I realize I'm over-simplifying here, of course. But I think we can say that we have a generation of young people who have been raised and largely socialized by systems of intelligibility that are linked to the exigencies of their class and gender subalternatives but also to the culture industry's production of subjectivity and agency through electronic media. Now the important issue to remember is that while the new postindustrial realities—new social and cultural relations—brought about by deindustrialization have altered the traditional modes of production there never the less still exists, as Teresa Ebert and others have argued, the objective reality of the extraction of surplus labor. Manufacturing productivity hasn't ceased on a global basis; the industrial working class is alive and well. Profit and greed haven't ceased to be a prominent factor in the global marketplace. Living labor is still expropriated and if you don't believe me come to east L.A. and talk to members of the International Lady's Garment Workers Union. The Latino *costureras* will tell you stories. . . . Emancipating these workers from discrimination and relations of oppression due to the subjectivities produced by contradictions within texts of identity is admirable but in response to such a critique the capitalist system will just shift the site of its exploitative operations somewhere else, as Teresa Ebert notes throughout her work; the goal should be an end to capitalist exploitation so that, in Ebert's words, we can meet the needs of all people: 'from each according to her ability, to each according to her needs.'

How, then, would you judge the political consequences of post-modernism? Doesn't it seem as if post-modernism has quite strong depoliticizing effects?

We are not well placed as alienated beings within postmodernism to track the traces of an imperceptible and frighteningly incomprehensible future; nor are we better placed to study the present. We have been exiled into a post-human hyperreality—into a condition the dimensions of which we fail to recognize and are too fearful to fully understand. We are not passive agents as some critics suggest but we are nauseatingly active agents of ignorance. We try hard—in a desperate attempt to hold on to some semblance of sanity—to ignore the completeness of our complicitousness in relations of domination and subjection. To my mind, the post-modern era is an era where democracy becomes historically subverted by capitalism to a greater extent than ever before, where values become a trick of fiction and radically incommensurable. Subjectivities are not co-temporal with, determined by, or homologous to their integration through information circuits and new forms of technology into the world market, but they are greatly shaped by such integration. We no longer live in a world of authenticity—of the unimpeachably accurate transparency of language—but rather a world of complex mediations, of rhetoricity. All meanings are deferred endlessly. One sign refers to, not an original referent or source but to another sign. And that sign then refers to another sign. And to another sign ad infinitum. So that one finds it very difficult to begin to justify one's project on a kind of transcendental platform, an ethical platform, because one finds as one deconstructs one's reference that there is an infinite regression. So I think it is very difficult now to situate our projects within master narratives, within grand narratives, within teleological narratives, such as the Marxian master narrative of the classless society, or the bourgeois, Euro-American and patriarchal narrative of the enlightenment. As Ebert and so many others have correctly observed, the problem with postmodernist reformism is that it attempts to contest domination and authoritarianism in its many guises at the level of cultural autonomy rather than in its determinate and causal relation to economic exploitation and imperialism which is ceaselessly and convulsively on the rise at a global level. And, ironically, the concept of the body—which is articulated as a non-discursive and material site than can resist oppression—is made a transcendent site that is able to escape the social contradictions arising out of the relations of production. But mostly postmodernists concern themselves with immanent critique—contradictions that occur within the texts-in-themselves. Yet they forget—as Marxists do not—that differences within any text need to be situated within the struggle over race, class, and gender inequalities that are produced by the social division of labor. Postmodernists see this as a form of class reductionism. Consequently, they are more likely to privilege the transformation of individual consciousness over collective praxis.

Would there be a place for a concept like 'democracy'—after all an influential notion in the critical education tradition—in your discourse?

I have a strong affiliation with Latin-American groups. And for many of my compañeros and compañeras and colleagues in the university, to evoke the term democracy is evoking the kiss of death. Democracy for them is simply a smokescreen for exploitation. It is a smokescreen for creating a dependency economy. There is an old saying in Mexico that when the United States sneezes, Mexico gets pneumonia. So to evoke the term democracy is to draw attention to a legacy of pain and bloodshed, and therefore I am very self-conscious in using the term because it must always take into consideration its global implications.

But yes, democracy is a very important concept in my work. Democracy in this country has become almost synonymous with capitalism, and unrestricted and unregulated capitalism at that. This is very frightening. One has to always be very specific when one articulates what we mean by the radical imaginary, what we mean by radical democracy, critical democracy, critical socialist democracy. But yes, one needs a referent for resistance, one needs a referent for the project of liberation, and, so when I talk about contingent utopia, I am trying to evoke the idea that while the social can never be closed, and while the democratic project must always be re-invoked and re-invented and re-territorial-

ized given the contextual specificity of the sphere in which one is operating, the transnational flows of corporate capital continue and need to
be reckoned with. We can't do this within an identity politics alone or a
politics of the body. I could evoke as a universal principle the right for
every individual to pursue one's own self-autonomy as a social agent for
the purpose of diminishing needless human suffering. But that only
makes sense, that universal evocation, in the specific context of those
groups who are willing to take up the challenge. We cannot escape the
paradox that democracy is founded upon its own constitutive impossibility, as some post-structuralists such as Ernesto Laclau would argue.

One of the criticisms to your idea of a contingent utopia might be that it is
romantic, sentimental, old-fashioned, and out of date.

I like the way Iris Marion Young talks about democracy in relation to
this idea. We need to move beyond mere interest-based and deliberative
forms of democracy and embrace a form of communicative democracy
or discursive democracy. In other words, interest-based democracy—in
which one's individual interests and preferences are expressed in a
vote—doesn't put any pressure on individuals to dialogue over issues.
Deliberative democracy is preferable because it is grounded in the
Habermasian idea of the force of the better argument. The question that
I want to raise is: How can we have democracy based on dialogical delib-
eration when we are in the midst of postmodern video democracy (such
as the O.J. Simpson trial) in which justice is meted out according to im-
age-effect, within economies of affect that permit the rich to hire the
best image management? Communicative democracy, Young notes, is
located within a communicative ethics that includes standpoints of the
concrete and generalized other. It is based largely upon the transformation of people's preferences and an openness to persuasion. Just norms
in this case are arrived at freely and by maximizing the available social
knowledge. Social understanding, Young points out, occurs from a multiplicity of social locations, from the standpoint epistemologies of the
oppressed and immiserated. In this way we can see how majoritarian
democratic procedures actually perpetuate injustice with respect to the
oppressed. The oppressed are denied the available social and political
resources. Take certain strands of postmodern thinking that reveal an
uncompromising distaste for the masses, that reveal a form of highbrow
anti-bourgeois posing, that is reduced in the last instance to a form of
self-congratulatory vanguardism. We need to take a close look at those
cynical strands of postmodernism. Is my approach simply an inverse of
this? Is it simply a means of offering a facile counterlogic to this dry cynicism of postmodernism? The end of the master narratives, does it instill
a false optimism? Is it simply a discourse that infects and inflames the

spirit much like an evangelist might attempt to do? Yes, I have heard all of these criticisms. Usually the diehard empiricists who decry my work as the evocations of a cultlike rhetorical evangelism launch these specious attacks. And I reject them because the romantics—and when I think of the romantics of course I am thinking of the romantic poets, Walt Whitman for instance, or Shelley, Byron, or Wordsworth—the romantics really were not invoking a transcendental referent but rather positing humankind as the source of transformation. To a certain extent there may be a slight romantic strain to my work in the sense that there exists a radical belief in and preoccupation with humankind, as opposed to some abstract master signifier that can work in everyone's interest and in a uniform way.

Talking about language and about human agency: There is a trend within post-modernism to be quite fatalistic about human agency, as—so it is argued—the omnipresence of discourse is thought to have dissolved the whole idea of agency. What is your opinion about this, and how would you relate this to pedagogy?

Well, there is a sense that we are all predetermined by language. Bakhtin talks about language as always being overpopulated by someone else's meaning. Of course, that is quite true; we don't invent languages in a context free of economic and social relations. We don't inherit languages outside of history. And we exist as part of certain discourse communities. But for me that doesn't have to be an excuse for abdicating to the status quo. For me the notion that we create ourselves, through discourse (although always in conditions not of our own making) gives me a sense of hope that we can engage in what Foucault calls the practice of the self. Of course, we are positioned as subjects by the discourses that we appropriate and we use in our research projects, in our daily existence. And these discourses are always mediated by larger productive relations of power and profit and surplus labor—something Foucault did not emphasize enough. But those discourses don't simply constrain. They also enable. And one is always trying to locate the ethical and moral centre of gravity within the discourses that one uses. One can never talk about the self in isolation from the other. Or the other in isolation from the antagonisms brought on by race, gender or class relations. So that in fact when I talk about empowerment, I never talk about self-empowerment. I am always very careful to ground it in the concept of social empowerment. That unless my brothers and sisters are also empowered, I am not empowered. And so that the notion of empowerment is always finally grounded in the notion of collective solidarity. It is not simply grounded in the notion of consensus because a democracy where everybody consents is no longer a democracy but a form of fascism. As a critical educator I am committed to creating new zones of possibility in my classroom, new spaces where democratic social relations can be struggled over as students learn to situate their own identities critically within, for instance, today's politics of commodity fetishism produced by global consumerism, in order to develop new forms of collective agency that escape the pitfalls of a unified revolutionary subject. But this means very little outside of the struggle to make active alliances with new social movements dedicated to liberate people from the material basis of their suffering.

What would this mean for your own activities as a critical pedagogue, as a teacher and researcher working in academia? How would your situate yourself and how would you situate your language?

With respect to language, the first thing to be acknowledged is that the language I use is an evocatory language. Language is not simply a medium through which ideas are expressed, but language in itself is constituent of the reality one is attempting to describe. Tony Morrison remarked that 'Language is not a substitute for experiences but arches to the place where meaning lies.' All discourse is implicated in the construction of the common good, or the lack of constructing a common good, and there is not simply one common good. There are many common goods. There is no epistemologically pure language. There are multiple languages. Which enable students to see the relations among their own experiences, their own identities, and the relations of profit and production which shape their lives. So that all discourse is a form of advocacy. It cannot be otherwise. The question then is: Are we prepared to acknowledge the potential social effects of the languages we choose to use to engage the world, as teachers, as intellectuals, as cultural workers?

Concerning my own role as a teacher and a researcher, I would like to stress that there is no neutral zone of articulation for me to exist in, other than the critical perspective. I will always narrate the contingency of my own perspective, and in doing so I will help students to gain some purchase on the contingency and partiality of their perspectives, but I will always speak from a politics of self-disclosure. I will always speak from a politics of acknowledging and naming: naming oppression, naming violence, including the possibility of violence in my own perspective, and trying to alert students to the dangers within my own discourse, so that they can begin to critique my position. I want to teach, after all, and not indoctrinate. But at the same time I need to emphasize that pedagogically there is no safe preserve. There is no safety-net. There are no guarantees for peace and tranquility. I want to challenge students to be able to ask the following: How is it that I became what the world has made of me? What is it that the world has made of me that I reject about myself? What is it that the world has made of me that, under present conditions, I can never escape? What is it about you—the Other—that decides the meaning of me? How is who I am conceived of in advance of my asking the question: Who am I? Am I more than an empty form filled out by your fantasy? What accounts for the fact that I can resist the world's symbolization of myself? What is it about myself that always escapes my understanding? What is it about my existence that always escapes meaning? These questions pose the initial struggle for us. But I am afraid that the answers to such questions must propel us to the streets in a struggle. The stakes are too high for it to be otherwise. And that is the answer to why I remain a revolutionary.

8

Unthinking Whiteness, Rethinking Democracy: Critical Citizenship in Gringolandia

To the memory of Emiliano Zapata, el lider campesino necho mártir en 1917 and El Ejército Zapatista de Liberacíon Nacional. Also dedicated to the memory of environmental activist and revolutionary Judi Bari.

A given society is racist or it is not.
—Frantz Fanon, *Black Skin, White Masks*

All forms of exploitation resemble one another. They all seek the source of their necessity in some edict of a Biblical nature. All forms of exploitation are identical because all of them are applied against the same "object": man. When one tries to examine the structure of this or that form of exploitation from an abstract point of view, one simply turns one's back on the major, basic problem, which is that of restoring man to his proper place.
—Frantz Fanon, *Black Skin, White Masks*

Don't mourn. Organize!
—Joe Hill, 1915

Capitalism's Incompatibility with Democracy

This chapter is an attempt to link—albeit provisionally and quite modestly—what is occurring in our cities and inside our schools to structures of imperialism and advanced capitalism that appear to be intractably globalized. It is simultaneously an effort to put forward a series of pronouncements and questions. In Paulo Freire's terms, it is an exercise in problem-posing rather than answer-giving.

I shall discuss critical pedagogy in three basic contexts: the internationalization of capital and labor markets, critical multiculturalism and the abolition of whiteness, and the development of the "ethical self" and critical citizen. In my view, these three contexts mutually inform one another in important ways. I argue that we cannot sufficiently understand our purpose and role as ethical agents and cultural workers without first examining critically how both we and our students are shaped and informed by current characteristics of late capitalism, how late capitalism shapes and is shaped by global cultures (including cultures within the United States), and how capital and culture are connected to the formal and informal practices of citizenship. My commentary unhesitatingly assumes the position that critical citizenship must be directed toward the creation of self-consciously ethical subjects of history and should be redistributive of society's material wealth and resources.

The specific struggle that I wish to address is that of choosing against whiteness. Yet is it possible for us to choose against whiteness given that, historically, the practice of whiteness has brought about such a devastating denial, disassembly, and destruction of other races? One would think that such a choice against whiteness would be morally self-evident. However, precisely because whiteness is so pervasive, it remains difficult to identify, to challenge, and to separate from our daily lives. My message is that we must create a new public sphere where the practice of whiteness is not only identified and analyzed but also contested and destroyed. For choosing against whiteness is the hope and promise of the future.

Most school systems now live in pathetic prostration to the capitalist marketplace and in the thrall of the new technocapitalist social order. We are everywhere witnessing the progressive enlargement of the capitalist economic domain. Everything has been turned into a commodity, including curricula, courses, instructional materials, lifestyles, and belief systems. The economy is impinging on people's lives today more than at any other time in history, largely as a result of economic transactions occurring through mass communications. In fact, television has colonized even our most private thoughts, suturing them to the cultural logic of the marketplace. Bureaucracy has increased and has become more interventionary and has created conditions for transnational corporations to thrive. Market democracy has spawned market justice for the rich. Moneyed interests prevail over the construction of an ethical identity.

Capitalism is traversed by the irrational and exists at the level of insanity, and this state of dementia is infecting the globe. I want to be clear about this. Capitalism nourishes political forms of repression in the way it organizes power through rituals in schools, in the workplace, in churches. It unites private desire and fantasy with economic infrastructure. Postmodern culture provides another, smoother way of facilitating the marriage of time and money. The church was able to invent the idea of international power in the Middle Ages; capitalism has emerged as the magnificent new religious order with more converts than the church. Its cultlike "get rich" hysteria is of the same order of fanaticism as that of Heaven's Gate or Order of the Solar Temple. Old forms of capitalist production, as well as former relations of production, are disappearing, including the class system of classical capitalism. We have now entered the world of commodity forms that function as purchasing power through instantaneous telematic transactions. We live in a digital economy of information and data and superprofits.

Technocapitalism operates through financial transactions undertaken through cyberspace technologies. These technologies efface the contradictions of labor and power; they create a reaction formation against materiality, a kind of packaged sublimity and secular morphology in which the world is reduced to one's subjective constellation of ideas. Here, the realities of pain and suffering no longer exist. Capital subordinates and coordinates all forms of subjectivities within late capitalist culture, creating forms of citizenship supinely weak yet falsely presumed to possess growing autonomy and democratic self-determination. Capitalism has become the most powerful arbiter of our new technodemocracy. It is intimately tied to the resurgent racism we are presently witnessing throughout the country. It is a racism made respectable through its legitimization by politicians who, after the collapse of the Cold War, are turning the immigrant into the new hated "other."

Consider the comments made by Boston University president John Silber during his campaign for governor of Massachusetts in 1990: "Why has Massachusetts suddenly become so popular for people who are accustomed to living in a tropical climate? Amazing. There has got to be a welfare magnet going on here, and right now I am making a study to find out what that magnet is. . . . Why should Lowell be the Cambodian capital of America?" (*Boston Globe* 1990, cited in Macedo and Bartolome, forthcoming).

Donaldo Macedo and Lilia Bartolome (forthcoming) point out that if Silber had conducted such a study he would have soon learned that the majority of Lowell's welfare recipients are white Americans. He would also have discovered that the Asian community is a powerful economic force greatly needed after the flight of jobs and capital out of Lowell.

Current species of consumer capitalism are all about low growth, low wages, and high profits. We live at a juncture of "fast capitalism"; deindustrialization; mass migrations; union-bashing; economic dislocation; the progressive deregulation of national economies; wide-scale unemployment resulting in part from a declining importance of the national economy as an unitary, cohesive category; and a transition to a post-

Fordist phase of capitalism. It is an era consisting of large-scale dias-poric migrations of oppressed peoples, the racialization of spatial recon-figurations resulting from global flows of populations, and incoherences in public narratives of nationalism. Wealth is being transferred from the poor to the rich while the state protects its social and economic prac-tices. There has been a powerful decline in real wages for the vast major-ity of the working population with high levels of un- and underemploy-ment in many of the so-called industrial economies. The contemporary two-parent family with two children has added numerous hours per week outside the home. Blue-collar workers will be nearly obsolete in several decades, and 90 percent of job loss is occurring as part of tech-nological replacement; white-collar service-sector jobs are also on the decline. Business after-tax profit rates continue to grow not as a result of profitability or investment but as a result of declining wages. The rich see their tax bills fall and CEOs now earn approximately 170 times more than the average worker. The agonies and sufferings of the oppressed, whose memories and voices we have buried in the sealed vaults of this country's structural unconscious, continue to haunt us. What's worse, we can see within the context of globalization that some areas of the world are depressingly becoming holograms of the United States.

Jeff Sachs of Harvard University, noted economist and principal archi-tect of the economic transition for the former communist region of East-ern Europe and the USSR, labeled the "shock therapy model," has been assisting the United States in reorganizing the political balance of power across the entire continent. Sachs is masterminding the transformation of the old Soviet command economy. Leading the charge for globalized capitalism, Sachs is helping the United States accomplish such a daunt-ing challenge through the exclusion of Russia from a reorganized Eu-rope and through working for the absorption of East-Central Europe into the Western sphere, creating a European community institutional order along the lines of a U.S.-crafted neoliberal zone. Years ago such global behavior had a name—imperialism. Today it is known under the rubric of global democratization.

The fall of communism in the former Soviet Union is still being cele-brated in the United States by self-righteous bourgeois columnists in newspapers such as the *Los Angeles Times*. We read that in order to get work, young Russian women who want to be secretaries, accountants, and would-be managers are having to describe their physical attributes in job-wanted advertisements, to include their breast and hip measure-ments on their job applications, and to squeeze into tight miniskirts and high heels and prance around hotel ballrooms at Western-style job fairs. This is what the *Times* calls the "wild side" of the job hunt in Russia, making unemployment seem almost thrilling and definitely sexy. While mildly lamenting the sexism and unemployment situation, columnist

Stephanie Simon calls the former Soviet system that made unemployment a crime and résumés unnecessary a "cushy system" (1996, 1). The current unemployment problem is reduced to the failure of Russians in writing effective résumés, developing job-interview skills, and creating enough placement services. The answer to the unemployment problem offered by the *Times* is that the unemployed need to "network to the hilt." Capitalism itself is never criticized. What is blamed for Russian economic malaise is the stubborn and woeful inability of Russians to adjust to that necessary and inevitable transition toward a capitalist system. Of course, the failure of new levels of economic growth, productivity, job creation, and living standards to materialize cannot seriously be linked to the lousy résumés of unemployed Russians but rather to the guiding ideology of the World Bank and International Monetary Fund, which want as little government intervention and as few social programs as possible during the present period of economic shock therapy. Very few newspaper articles link the 42 percent rise in the 1992 Russian murder rate (and the additional 27 percent in 1993) (Boggs 1995), along with rising drug and alcohol addiction, mental illness, and suicide, to shock therapy capitalism. Carl Boggs, columnist for an alternative Los Angeles newspaper, describes the situation in Russia thus:

> Under the rubric of "democracy," the real actors in this process were to be the mechanisms of global capitalism—not the Russian (or Polish or Hungarian) people. Not only was shock therapy too abrupt and too authoritarian, it was much too capitalist. The established planning and welfare structures were largely junked, plunging the country into chaos and stripping it of its ability to carry out any developmental policies. Thus the new order, such as it was, lacked any semblance of coherence and legitimacy. The transition from state to private enterprise had no social basis: the only people with large amounts of capital were either foreign investors looking to make a quick fortune or homegrown mafiosi and black marketers, none of whom had much interest in long-term social goals. The old Communist guarantees (inadequate and bureaucratic as they were)—of work, decent public services, and orderly social life—simply vanished. The economy was ransacked. The significant gains in political and cultural freedom presided over first by Gorbachev and then by Yeltsin were essentially ransomed at the altar of shock therapy. (1995, 8)

Of course the model democracy, that of the United States, is not without its serious challenges in Americanizing the globe. In a recent cover story in the *Los Angeles Times*, Nora Zamichow describes the role of the U.S. military in Bosnia by quoting Captain Bob Rector of the U.S. Army's civil affairs division, who notes that, for the young officers, "it's like a cavalry mission from the 1800s and they're taming the Wild Wild West" (1996, 1). There was no recognition by Captain Rector that the taming of the Wild Wild West historically included the extermination of hundreds of thousands of native peoples and the enslavement and exploitation of others. Captain James "J.J." Love, touring Bosnian trenches, declares: "I swear to God, it's like touring a civil war battlefield" (Zamichow 1996, 10). Apparently the U.S. military can't escape the powerful and popular U.S. mythology surrounding its own history, a mythology that supports the conviction that Americans are a singular species of humanity attempting to mediate between more primitive parties.

Consider some remarks made closer to home—on Capitol Hill, to be exact—by Riordan Roett, an authority on Mexico who serves as a consultant for the Chase Bank. Roett's advice to the Institutional Revolutionary Party—Mexico's ruling party—to facilitate the NAFTA agreement and stimulate its economy was reported in *Time* magazine: "The Mexican government, still reeling from the peso crisis, must 'eliminate' the opposition in the rebellious southern state of Chiapas ... and should 'consider carefully whether or not to allow opposition victories [even] if fairly won at the ballot box.' And indeed, President Ernesto Zedillo's soldiers rolled into Chiapas last Thursday to crack down on the rebels and arrest their leaders as criminals" (*Time* 1995, 9). Roett's remarks echo the official U.S. ideological disposition toward Mexico and other Third World countries, where not only bankers but also the Central Intelligence Agency have played central roles in attempting to destabilize regimes considered inhospitable to U.S. economic interests.

Noam Chomsky (1996) argues that capitalism requires privatizing profit but socializing cost and risk. In the United States, many politicians want money to be controlled by the states, not the federal government. But lack of federal regulations only helps the private sector use the money for its own interests, and the average citizen is even further exploited.

All too often schools are serving the interests of the capitalist social order, which is designed to serve the rich (Darder, 1992). It has been a standard insight of critical educators for decades that schools reproduce class interests (although not without resistance). They do this, for instance, by producing particular ideologies such as individualism and consumerism; by promoting certain character structures that respond to personal responsibility rather than collective responsibility; and by producing creative thinkers and using such creativity more often that not in the service of the entrepreneurial spirit rather than in the service of equality and social justice. I want to argue that capitalist relations, while powerful, are not overdetermining in the last instance such that individuals and groups are reduced to the simple reflexes of moneyed interests. Critical class consciousness is possible and necessary, and critical pedagogy is one means to facilitate it.

If corporate ownership is more globally situated and consolidated, and the means of exploitation more sophisticated, is there any hope for the development of a critical class consciousness in sites such as public schools? For years I have been arguing that we need to rethink class struggle in cultural terms as well as economic terms. But I have never suggested that we forget the production system, the social division of labor, or the social relations of production or consumption. Rather, I have suggested that we expand our understanding of class in ways that broaden the concept of class as only material production.

Stanley Aronowitz and William DiFazio (1994) have developed the idea of class in ways that are worth repeating. They note, for instance, that class identities are contextually specific and multidimensional, especially in this era of globalization in which ownership is highly centralized in a tightly organized transnational corporate system but where production has been radically deterritorialized. Class, therefore, "is operative in the multiple relations of economic, political, and cultural power that together constitute the ruling systems of production and *reproduction* of goods, services, and knowledge" (231).

What we need to grasp here is the idea that individuals and groups are differentially located within overlapping power systems and it is in the context of such differential locations that we need to understand and problematize class struggle. In other words, the cultural and social aspects of class need to be understood. We still need to consider individuals to be living, breathing, subjects of history who possess some relative autonomy rather than dismissing them as simply the inventions of discourse or the offspring of discursive formations. Social classes are more than individual actors, they are formations that struggle for and over power; they are historical struggles for specific forms of life (Aronowitz and DiFazio 1994). Class has not so much to do with individual assets or lack of them. As Aronowitz and DiFazio point out, it is not a question of using distribution-centered class analysis against production-centered analyses or of positing the capitalist market as the independent variable and cultural and collective relations as dependent variables determined in the last instance by the marketplace. Doing so misses my point about agency. Class structure influences but does not irrevocably determine class consciousness. Knowledge and culture possess a relative autonomy through which critical agency can be produced. Class must be seen as a conscious struggle for specific forms of community. As Aronowitz and DiFazio note, "Class relations are social relations. But social relations are not governed by systematic economic relations. They are overdetermined, but not by economics. Class relations are not limited only to the social relations of the labor process; they continue outside the labor process as well. They occur in all aspects of everyday life . . . the question is, how do social actions produce class culture, which is necessary and indispensable if class struggle is going to occur?" (292–293).

Class, race, gender, and sexual orientation are mutually determining sets of social relations and practices, and not all of these sets of social relations are subordinate to moneyed capital. Aronowitz and DiFazio maintain that class is "a social movement" that is engaged in a "struggle to transform its own cultural representation and formulate a new cultural representation of class, work, and power" (1994, 297). This is not, of course, to deny the growing proletarianization of workers as well as members of the "new class" of intellectual and cultural workers. Neither is it to deny that class struggle is important and imperative within a revolutionary multicultural project. In fact, as I have argued throughout this book, the struggle for a revolutionary socialism is the preeminent struggle of our time. While not all social relations are subordinate to capital or overdetermined by economic relations, most social relations constitutive of racialized and gendered identities are considerably shaped by the social division of labor and the social relations of production. Capitalism is an overarching totality that is dropping out of sight in many analyses undertaken by poststructuralists and postmodernists. This can only have dire consequences for a rejuvenated leftist struggle. I agree with Ellen Meiksins Wood that "at the very heart of the new pluralism is a failure to confront (and often an explicate denial of) the overarching totality of capitalism as a social system, which is constituted by class exploitation but which shapes all 'identities' and social relations" (1995, 260).

I maintain that we need to move beyond formal equity by way of legal principles and political procedures (as in the case of the new pluralism) by struggling to transform global capitalist society. This challenge would seem ludicrous to the new pluralists who view capitalism as having identities and social relations that are irrevocably fragmented and pulverized into an endless plurality of competing interests and heterogeneous lifestyles. Such a view ignores the ways in which commodities create a powerful global homogeneity, and it disables our capacity to both recognize and resist the unifying cohesiveness of capitalist relations and overarching structures of coercion that inscribe identities within the abstract and exploitative requirements of the market.

What does ethics have to do with global capitalism and the concept of class as collective agency and struggle? In order to answer this question I will turn to the work of sociologist Zygmunt Bauman (1992) with specific reference to his reflections on postmodernity. I want to connect Bauman's commentary about mortality and immortality to the theme of the construction of identity within current circuits and flows of transnational capitalism.

Bauman's central premise is that modernity was preoccupied with the deconstruction of mortality, whereas postmodernity is preoccupied with the deconstruction of immortality. The age of modernity constructed the present as having no value outside of reason and, furthermore, constructed it within the framework of a project whose value, legitimacy, and authenticity resided in judgment drawn from the future. The modernist present, in other words, delayed its own fulfillment, projecting it instead teleologically into the "not-yet." The age of modernity or Enlightenment (which some would argue has not been abandoned) deconstructed or unsettled the idea of mortality, or death, by transforming death into a series of temporary afflictions that can be overcome (through modern medicine, technology, progress, etc.). In current postmodern times, however, we no longer live within the telic, linear project of creating a better future because the future is accepted as having already arrived and therefore is as fully erasable as the present or the past.

According to Bauman, each moment in postmodernity flows into the next, and the orphans of modernity (I think of the young people in the movies *Kids* and *Welcome to the Dollhouse*) presently occupy the existential condition of nomadic, transient, or evanescent immortality. Whereas the inhabitants of modernity lived within the project such that the present was meaningless unless it was lived in deference to and in the service of the future, postmodernity creates identities that are motivated by roles rather than by future-oriented goals. Modern pilgrims who possessed *connexity* in relation to the time and space of the everyday have given way to postmodern nomads who betray a *disconnexity* of the time/space canvas upon which modern pilgrims plotted their life plans. The postmodern nomad lives moment to moment in an ex post facto sense, that is, lives always already in retrospect or in relation to the "now."

Postmodern nomads live their lives in the contingency of a present in which the future self-destructs into an infinite repetition of the same. The only variable that matters is intensity. The past and future have, in this sense, no claim on the present because simultaneity has replaced history. Life becomes a series of "self-canceling determinations" (Bauman 1992, 169). Postmodern culture decomposes eternity and transforms history into "the right to be recorded" on videotape, film, radio, or in newspaper or magazine articles. Access to historicity is accorded the utmost importance. We disturbingly witness "prime-time" serial killers, wife-beaters, butchers of human flesh, and torturers who eat their victims and keep body parts as fetish objects; these actors enjoy as much currency in our collective historical narrative as do poets, scholars, or saints (I am thinking of themes of the movies *Natural Born Killers* and *Pulp Fiction* and women and men who fall in love with assassins and murderers). Major lawbreakers can become millionaires by selling their stories to television or the film industry. The notorious atrocities of Republika Srpska, its war crimes and practices of ethnic cleansing, were tolerated in the West because they were directed against Muslims. But the same cultural logic can be seen here in the United States in the practices of class warfare and institutional racism

that prohibit access to equality and social justice for people of color—
an access that should be the birthright of all U.S. citizens.

Bauman reports that the most postmodern of games is "the great
twentieth century institution of the quiz," in which the past is instantly
recoverable and in a state of "perpetual resurrection" (1992, 171). Ma-
hatma Ghandi or Martin Luther King carry no more prestige value by
postmodern standards than Jeffrey Dahmer or Ted Bundy. Andy Warhol
was already grasping this phenomenon when he noted that everyone
will one day become a celebrity for fifteen minutes. In the era of postmodernity nothing disappears through death; death is always overcome
and is replaced by the fractal moment of dispersion. Even in the worst-
case scenarios, death can always be put on temporary hold. According
to Bauman, "In the world in which *disappearing* has replaced the dying,
immortality dissolves in the melancholy of presence, in the monotony
of endless *repetition*" (175). Repetition has replaced representation because now everything is mass-produced and it is impossible to discern
what is original. Singularity has dissolved into reassemblances. Nothing,
therefore, is real. In theoretical terms, the signifier has no real referent
and can be found referring to another signifier ad infinitum. In the postmodern world of unlimited semiosis, all signs are autocopulating; they
create no meaning outside of their own self-evidence. They stand for
nothing but themselves. In Bauman's terms, "there is no division among
things that mean and things that are meant" (183). Everything is fiction,
and life is as good as the media wants it to be. Welcome, brother and sister educators, to what I call "predatory culture" (McLaren 1995).

Whereas the modern world was ruled by the law, postmodernity is
guided by the rule. Laws suggest right and wrong, good and evil, oppressors and oppressed. Rules simply describe how the game is played, and
one need not worry about the rules when there is an infinite number of
games to play. There is nothing outside of the game. While you might
choose to exit a game, you are always constructed by another game. If you
are troubled by the thought of hungry and homeless people or reports of
torture, imperialist invasions, or oppressive politics or laws, just quickly
leave that game and play another. It's that simple. Or is it? Postmodernism
does emphasize communities but, as Bauman notes, "The *sociality* of the
postmodern community does not require sociability" (1992, 198).

Built into the structure of everyday postmodern life is a deferral of
death; objects do not die but are merely discarded and then replaced by
newer, more trend-setting, sophisticated, and expensive commodities.
Familiar, trustworthy objects are undermined by the creation of infinitely
new possibilities for prestige capacity and status distinction. We are being
programmed by image managers and marketing firms for desirable citizenship conduct (which is the same as consumer conduct), and it doesn't

take much: just enough time to detract us from our present thoughts so that we can process a commercial message. Even after a single moment of attention to a commercial message, the ground is prepared and the semiotic manure spread for a reforging of the same message, for endless repetition. This is the postmodernist sublime. Are we having fun yet? Postmodernism has surrendered the self-reflexive subject.

It is the conceit of postmodern dream-makers that they can turn the world into a factory for immortality through endless television reruns. We can witness people being blown up by bombs and rockets, rebels being killed by government forces in Chiapas, and resign ourselves to inertia. It's all a fiction anyway. And then we, as academics, can invest our time in debating whether to write the obituary of philosophy. After all, in a world without history or future, who needs philosophy? The postmodern moment is autocopulatory; it has already reproduced itself forever. It cannibalizes itself as soon as it is born so that it can recreate the same moment again, over and over.

Let me try to expand upon what I have just said, this time in the context of talking about democracy and citizenship. We live at a time of what James Holston and Arjun Appadurai (1996) call liberal procedural justice or the liberal compact. Yet within postmodern conditions, where the disparity among the rich and poor has grown so frighteningly and dangerously wide, oppressed peoples and even the middle class no longer believe in the democratic vision of shared goals. Everybody sees through the hoax. People are just out to get as much as they can get, to acquire as much purchasing power as possible. We can refer to this as the devaluation of citizenship membership in the nation-state or the death of the American dream. In cities known for their urban sprawl, such as Los Angeles, people are barricading themselves in fortress communities where numerous urban incorporations have been able to operate with the sanction of local governments and implant zoning regulations to keep "outsiders" away from their communities. Witness the increasing emphasis on the growth of private security forces and, for that matter, the privatization of everything still considered public.

As I pointed out earlier, the transnationalization and globalization of capital has created a new dynamics of inequality and a new criminalization of poor and marginalized communities. There exists a new asymmetry within relations of power and privilege. The liberal compact of shared values and active citizenship participation toward a common good is in crisis due to this "unprecedented growth of economic and social inequalities during the last few decades" (Holston and Appadurai 1996, 192).

Let me now rehearse the argument made by Appadurai and Holston (1996). The current postmodern social imaginary operates as a priority of right over good. This is a process of liberal democracy based not on constitutive or substantive ends but on procedural justice. Procedural justice permits the same principles of justice to regulate each and every individual in the same way. No specific content—or no particular interests—are subscribed to by the res publica. Individual ends can point to almost any interest whatsoever as long as it is officially within the law. In this sense, the liberal compact of shared commitment gives a lie to the concept of community upon which it depends because, as Holston and Appadurai (1996) point out, its lack of moral vision—its content-free aspect—precludes the sense of "prior affiliation" and "shared allegiance" that the liberal compact requires. They write: "Procedural liberalism leaves citizens more entangled in obligations they do not choose and less attached to common identifications that would render these obligations not just bearable but even virtuous" (193). In advanced capitalist contexts, procedural liberalism produces not active, self-reflexive citizens but passive subjects of history. Procedural liberal democracy is to some extent a prophylaxis to liberation.

Procedural liberalism is officially proclaimed to be difference-neutral and universal but is predicated upon group membership in which the white, heterosexual Anglo male of property is the prime signifier. As Bauman (1992) has written:

> The West-European-born modern civilization had won the right to narrate the history of the world; the right which until quite recently it enjoyed and practiced unchallenged. (It is today challenged all over the place—by the once "weaker" sex, by ethnic groups denied their language and by aborigines denied their land—but this challenge can easily be taken in its stride by a society not any more excessively worried with immortality.) The right to tell history was gained by force, but the superior killing potential of guns was interpreted as the superiority of Western reason and form of life, so that its practical impact could be in good conscience taken for the clinching argument, if one was needed, on behalf of the peak historical position on which the gun-carriers were perched. (120)

Noam Chomsky has put forward convincing arguments claiming that what government officials within a procedural democracy fear the most—from conservatives to liberals—is "the crisis of democracy." This "crisis" refers to popular democracy by the people. Government officials fear democracy as a problem that must be eliminated because they believe that the ignorant masses will make decisions that will force the government to be more responsible to the people and less responsive to moneyed interests. The answer to this crisis, as Chomsky persuasively suggests, is "the manufacture of consent"—that is, reducing the masses to obedient, passive subjects and keeping power in the hands of an elite class that is able to manage the people through sophisticated forms of public relations. Chomsky proclaims that in this context government officials provide the people with the means of ratifying decisions that other people have already made, they eliminate the means whereby people can educate themselves and organize themselves, and they find ways to engineer the decisionmaking while giving the public the appearance that it is in control. That's not too difficult when those who have the freedom to persuade or convince others of their opinion are the moneyed interests who own and run the public relations industry. Democracy—procedural democracy—is the power to manufacture agreement in a way that enables moneyed interests to further maximize their advantage at the expense of most of the population, who, as I have noted, are growing poorer.

Displaced in the practice of procedural liberalism is a politics of difference, that is, difference-specific democracy. In fact, difference-neutral or procedural democracy actually amounts to little more than an ideology and practice of discrimination. Just as those who espouse a difference-neutral democracy often decry affirmative action on the basis of promoting a "color-blind" society, we can see the destruction of affirmative action (from the difference-specific perspective) as largely the practice of affirmative action on behalf of white, Anglo, heterosexual males of privilege.

Why do we, as educators, wittingly and unwittingly advance our views about what it means to be an American on the graveyards of other people's cultures, values, and social practices? Marginalized minority groups, the economically disenfranchised, and those under assault from the English Only movement's policies of linguistic apartheid, the colonialist *pronunciamientos* in Propositions 187 and 209, and generous offerings of Latinophobia and an extralegalization of justice will often argue for a difference-specific form of citizenship that recognizes their inalienable right to retain, honor, and nurture their unique, specific identities. From their perspective, they have only *formal* rights, not substantive rights. Consequently, they argue for equal opportunity on the basis of a politics of difference. And while there can be problems with difference-specific claims for citizenship (e.g., defining identities in a narrow, militantly particularistic, or essentialist way), critical educators need to constantly struggle around the issue of naming and defining democracy in ways that unsettle and destabilize Eurocentric and white supremacist forms of procedural, difference-neutral citizenship based on the liberal compact as the telic point of history and civilization.

Critical educators must first recognize that democracy exists in a state of paradox, that it has no universal vision of the common good; democracy does, however, enable particular struggles to determine how it should be defined. The nature of such struggles is what critical pedagogy should be all about. A difference-specific democracy is always relational and never pure; it is always temporary, historically conditional, and contradictorily mediated according to the shifting standpoints of its citizens and their changing circumstances. Here we can follow Ernesto Laclau in understanding the foundation of democracy to be its own constitutive lack, its own impossibility. Proponents of difference-specific democracy are correct in arguing for the detranscendentalizing of universality and the decentering of Eurocentrism and in so doing differentiating between universal Western selves and the particular lived experiences of concrete social actors, such as the experiences of our Chicana/o sisters and brothers here in the Southwest. Critical educators need to ask: How do democratic institutions such as schools *restrict* the universalism of our shared political ideals by legitimizing only or mainly white Anglo perspectives? How are students turned into identities without properties, without contents, stripped and denuded of their ethnic and cultural particularities in order to become raised to the abstract level of the universal American citizen? What are the rights, for instance, of the undocumented worker? Have they been reduced simply to their market worth? In this case, what does entitlement mean?

Racism and the exploitation of peoples considered to be ontologically inferior to Euro-Americans have always been historical allies to the white supremacist, capitalist, and patriarchal hegemony that characterizes the United States. Procedural, difference-neutral democracy does little to challenge the taken-for-granted white privilege that undergirds it. The non–Euro-American world produced by discourses or "regimes of truth" (that include multiform texts, linguistic practices, and representations) is an ethnocentric projection and the result of assigning to the Other values married to the narcissism and arrogance of the colonial mind. It has been engendered by a militantly systematized hierarchization of values and social, cultural, and economic practices of inferiorization, exclusion, peripheralization, and discrimination that have found a safe, institutional home in our schools. Here, whiteness (*gabachismo*) remains the uncontested, implacable marker against which the non–Anglo-American is judged, often leading to a process of *engabachamiento*, in which marginalized groups are forced to act white in order to succeed. (Of course, *engabachamiento* is a discursive relay of sorts—"white but not quite": Latino/as are never really accepted as white because paranoid fantasies about the Latin other on the part of whites keep Latino/as peripheralized and on the cultural and economic sidelines.)

Hypocritical whites, often singing the praises of *mestizaje* consciousness, refuse to create the conditions whereby the *mestizo* can be politically empowered. The structural ambivalence of the term "mestizo" erroneously implies that border-crossing (the creation of *mestizaje* consciousness through the crossing of cultural, social, and political borders) poses the same challenges for whites as it does for people of color. Yet as some Chicana/o groups in California have expressed: "We didn't cross the border; the border crossed us."

What kind of optics of representation frames the Chicano/a student while at the same time denying permission to contribute a verse to the ongoing play of life, a play whose topology regrettably celebrates the civilizational narratives of empire, late-capitalist cultural formations, and the tropes of the Western unconscious?

I am currently a citizen of a country that supplies the United States with a substantial number of undocumented workers—Canada. But you don't see the U.S. government militarizing its northern border. I don't have to be too concerned about harassment from *la migra* if California's Propositions 187 or 209 someday take effect. Consider the vehemently racist comments directed against Mexican and other immigrants of color by Pat Buchanan, a recent Republican candidate for the U.S. presidency: "If British subjects, fleeing a depression, were pouring into this country through Canada, there would be few alarms. The central objection to the present flood of illegals is they are not English-speaking white people from Western Europe; they are Spanish-speaking brown and black people from Mexico, Latin America and the Caribbean" (Bradlee 1996, 1, 12).

I would ask you to consider Buchanan's remarks along with John Silber's earlier comments in light of U.S. history. I offer some comments made by Abraham Lincoln during a speech made in southern Illinois in 1858:

> "I am not," he told his audience, "nor ever have been, in favor of bringing about in any way the social or political equality of the white and black races. . . . I will say in addition that there is a physical difference between the white and black races which, I suppose, will forever forbid the two races living together upon terms of social and political equality; and in as much as they cannot so live, that while they do remain together there must be a position of the superiors and the inferiors; and that I, as much as any other man, am in favor of the superior being assigned to the white man." (cited in Zinn 1970, 148)

Another United States hero, Benjamin Franklin, wrote: "Why increase the Sons of *Africa*, by planting them in *America*, where we have so fair an Opportunity, by excluding all Blacks and Tawneys, of increasing the lovely White and Red?" (cited in Perea 1995, 973).

Or consider the views of Thomas Jefferson, who was concerned about the presence of Africans in America and referred to them as an impure "blot" on the purity of the land. "It is impossible not to look forward to distant times, when our rapid multiplication will expand itself . . . & cover the whole northern, if not the southern continent, with a people speaking the same language, governed in similar forms and by similar laws; *nor can we contemplate with satisfaction either blot or mixture on that surface*" (cited in Perea 1995, 974). Armed with a Protestant Hebralism, an Augustinian conviction, a Spartan virtue of service to the public sphere, an antinomian iconoclasm, a classical republicanist image of liberty and civic virtue, and models of character development founded on Lycurgus, Cato the Elder, and Calvin, Jefferson hid his racism under the higher calling of establishing God's New Jerusalem on the golden soil of America (Murphy 1996).

Not only was Thomas Jefferson a mean-spirited racist and slave owner, he also can be arguably considered the central ideological founder of American apartheid. He advocated an approach to democracy, inspired by a mystical reading of the French Revolution, that justified mass slaughter in the name of liberty and justice for whites only. It is perhaps no coincidence that when Timothy McVeigh was arrested driving away from Oklahoma City on the day the Federal Building was bombed, he was wearing a T-shirt that bore the celebrated words of Jefferson: "The tree of liberty must be refreshed from time to time by the blood of patriots and tyrants." Although Jefferson eventually favored the abolition of slavery, he unhesitatingly called for the banishment of free blacks from the United States, since he believed that "nature, habit, opinion has drawn indelible lines of distinction" between white people and black people such that they "cannot live in the same government" (O'Brien 1996, 57).

Although Jefferson preached against slavery, he had one of his many slaves, James Hubbard, severely flogged for escaping. In addition, he proposed an amendment to the Virginia legal code that would ban free blacks from coming to Virginia of their own accord or taking up residence for more than a year. His amendment was rejected by his contemporaries as being too severe. Jefferson had even proposed that white women who had children by black fathers were to be ordered out of Virginia within a year of the child's birth. Failure to leave the state would place these women "out of the protection of the law," which meant, of course, that they could be lynched. Jefferson also suggested that the government purchase newborn slaves from their owners and pay for their maintenance until the children were old enough to find jobs. They would work up to their date of deportation to Santo Domingo (O'Brien 1996). Fortunately, these other suggestions were also rejected by his contemporaries.

Not to be outdone in the racist department, we have Senator John Calhoun, speaking on the Senate floor in 1848, where he opposed annexation by the United States of land belonging to Mexico on the grounds of preserving a homogeneous white nation: "I know further, sir, that we have never dreamt of incorporating into our Union any but the Caucasian race—the free white race. To incorporate Mexico, would be the very first instance of the kind of incorporating an Indian race; . . . I protest against such a union as that! *Ours, sir, is the Government of a white race*" (cited in Perea 1995, 976)

Compare the ideological logic behind California's Proposition 187 with the statements provided by Calhoun, Jefferson, Franklin, Buchanan, and Silber. Compare, too, Proposition 187's logic to that of its precursor—California's 1855 "Greaser Act." The Greaser Act was an antiloitering law that applied to "all persons who are commonly known as 'Greasers,' or the issue of Spanish and Indian blood . . . and who go armed and are not peaceable and quiet persons" (cited in López 1996, 145).

This is the same racist logic that fueled David Duke's 1992 comments: "Immigrants 'mongrelize' our culture and dilute our values" (cited in López, 143). More recent comments made by Duke, in California in 1996, were in support of Proposition 209, an anti–affirmative-action effort to create a "color-blind" society. The proposition was orchestrated by Ward Connerly, an African American who is currently a University of California regent and chairman of the Proposition 209 initiative. In addition to accusing minority men of raping white women "by the thousands" and claiming that black New Orleans police officers rape and kill local citizens, Duke remarked: "I don't want California to look like Mexico. . . . I don't want to have their pollution. I don't want the corruption. I don't want their disease. I don't want their superstition. I don't want us to look like that country. If we continue this alien invasion, we will be like Mexico" (Bernstein 1996, A14).

Duke reflects a perspective that hasn't changed since the days of the zoot-suit massacre and operation wetback or those days when public Los Angeles swimming pools were frequently drained by whites after they were used by Mexican Americans. It is a perspective also shared by the British extreme right, which sexualizes racism in order to "generate fear among women and masculine protectiveness among men" in relation to the presence of black men in British inner cities (Rattansi 1994, 63). Such perspectives connote earlier ideas of the Empire as a dangerous place where white women need protection (Rattansi, 63). One example is a story that appeared in the National Front youth newspaper *Bulldog*. The story was titled "Black Pimps Force White Girls into Prostitution" and exhorted, "White Man! You Have a Duty to Protect Your Race, Homeland and Family" (63). Of course, this fear of the rape of the white woman is not projected solely onto the African American male. Underwriting Duke's comments on Mexico, for instance, was the image of the

Mexican as rapist and beast. In his discussion of the relationship between San Diegans and Tijuanenses, Ramón Gutiérrez describes how Tijuana—"as a place of unruly and transgressive bodies" (1996, 256)—has become fixed in the American psyche. He reports that "Tijuana first developed as an escape valve for the sexually repressed and regulated American Protestant social body of San Diego" (255). He writes that "the international boundary between Mexico and the United States has long been imagined as a border that separates a pure from an impure body, a virtuous body from a sinful one, a monogamous conjugal body regulated by the law of marriage from a criminal body given to fornication, adultery, prostitution, bestiality and sodomy" (255–256).

The United States is constructed as a country governed by nature and the law; such codes of civility that regulate kinship and the body are thought not to exist in Mexico, where only unregulated desire and criminality exist to menace all who come into contact with Mexicans. The image of the undocumented worker as an illegal alien, as a "migrant" living in squalor, spreading disease, raping white women, extorting lunch money from white schoolchildren, creating squatter communities, hanging out in shopping centers, and forcing Anglo schools to adopt bilingual education programs to accommodate the offspring of criminals and to appease the foreigner living illegally on U.S. soil has served to identify Mexicans with dirt, filth, and unnatural acts while symbolically constructing Euro-American citizens as pure, law-abiding, and living in harmony with God's natural law (Gutiérrez 1996).

One of the nation's relatively unblemished heroes of history is Woodrow Wilson. Many U.S. citizens have little, if any, knowledge about Wilson's Palmer raids against left-wing unions, his segregation of the federal government, and his military interventions in Mexico (eleven times beginning in 1914) and in Haiti in 1915, the Dominican Republic in 1916, Cuba in 1917, and Panama in 1918. Wilson also maintained forces in Nicaragua (Loewen 1995, 23). Wilson was an unrepentant white supremacist who believed that black people were inferior to white people. In fact, Wilson ordered that black and white workers in federal government jobs be segregated. Wilson vetoed a clause on racial equality in the Covenant of the League of Nations. Wilson's wife told "darky" stories in cabinet meetings, and Wilson's administration drafted a legislative program designed to curtail the civil rights of African Americans. Congress refused to pass it. However, Wilson did manage to appoint southern whites to offices traditionally given to blacks (Lowen 1995).

President Warren G. Harding was inducted into the Ku Klux Klan in a ceremony at the White House (Loewen 1995). How many students can boast knowledge of this event? How can U.S. history books cover up these events, and hundreds of others, including the 1921 race riot in

Tulsa, Oklahoma, in which whites dropped dynamite from an airplane onto a black community, destroying 1,000 homes and killing 75 people (Loewen 1995, 165)?

How can we forget the evils of slavery, including the 10,000 Native Americans shipped from Charleston, South Carolina, to the West Indies (in one year) in exchange for black slaves? Must we forget that the United States is a country conceived in slavery and baptized in racism?

The Protocols of the Learned Elders of Zion was an influential book for another American hero, Henry Ford. His newspaper ran a series of anti-Semitic articles in the 1920s that were made available to the public in book form under the title *The International Jew*. In this particular sense the United States is not "post-Fordist" at all. Within many right-wing Christian movements, members fervently believe that white people are the true Israelites, that blacks are subhuman, and that Jews are the issue of Satan. The organization known as Christian Identity is linked to British Israelism, which began as a white supremacist Protestant organization in Victorian England. White Europeans were believed to be the twelve lost tribes of Israel. Like many postmillennial religions, Christian Identity proclaims that God gave the constitution of the United States to the white Christian Founding Fathers and that only white Christian men can be true sovereign citizens of the republic. Identity followers are set to destroy the "Beast"—the government of the United States, in order to hasten forth Armageddon (Southern Poverty Law Center 1996). Members of Pat Robertson's Christian Coalition are aligned with the Patriot movement. This movement wants to establish God's law on earth, which in the view of some of the members calls for the execution of homosexuals, adulterers, juvenile delinquents, and blasphemers (Southern Poverty Law Center 1996). During the Persian Gulf War, over 7,000 white U.S. soldiers were sent letters from neo-Nazi skinheads, urging them not to fight for Israel. Some of these letters were signed by a "racially pure white woman" and called on white GIs to return home and father white children in order to ensure the survival of the white race (Novick 1995).

Buchanan, Duke, Silber, Pete Wilson, and countless other conservative politicians currently enjoying considerable popularity among growing sectors of the U.S. population owe a great deal to the racist perspectives they inherited from historical figures such as Jefferson, Franklin, and Lincoln—figures who have been sanctified and hagiographied in the larger political culture. It appears that it is as patriotic now for white people to proclaim racist sentiments as it was 150 years ago. Today, however, one has to camouflage one's racism in deceptive and sophisticated ways by hiding it in a call for family values, a common culture of decency, and a "color-blind" society, but the racist formations underwriting such a call are clearly in evidence to the discerning cultural critic.

Of course, the populist and nativist sentiments expressed by Buchanan (and reflected in the resurgence of racist groups such as the Order, Posse Comitatus, the Ku Klux Klan, White Aryan Resistance, Aryan Nations, Christian Identity, Gun Owners of America, and various militia movements) are on the rise in the United States. What he and others like him appear to be saying is that undocumented British subjects (whose countrymen invaded the North American continent and stole it from the native inhabitants) would represent a less serious immigrant problem than those groups (such as Mexicans) who had their land stolen from them by the U.S. military (which some Mexicans still consider an "occupying force"). The real "illegal" in this case is Patrick Buchanan himself; his repugnant white supremacist and neoliberal ideology prohibits him from critically examining the economic and sociocultural forces surrounding recent diasporic movements affecting the United States. He remorselessly retires the identities of people of color before they have the opportunity to become established. The Latinophobic perspective of Buchanan and other white supremacists symbolically decapitates the immigrant and ultimately works to decenter and demonize the efforts of immigrants to maintain their dignity though identitarian forms of thinking and belonging. Shohat and Stam (1994) remark that "multicultural bellies, full of tacos, falafel, and chow mein, are sometimes accompanied by monocultural minds" (21). It is the monolithic, monocultural perspective of the white Anglo majority population that is responsible, in large part, for the current state of Latinophobia and the demonization of people of color in general.

Recent scapegoating has been unparalleled in its acrimony and scope of blame. It can be seen in the example of southeastern Klan groups trying to create all-white trade unions or in the operation of rogue border patrols designed to catch (and sometimes torture and kill) undocumented Mexican workers or in the efforts of Bruder Schweigen, American Spring, SPIKE, Stop Immigration Now, Americans for Border Control, White Aryan Resistance, the Stompers, the Populist Party, the Liberty Lobby, the English Only movement, American Immigrant Reform, English First, Students for America, U.S. English, and the Federation for American Immigration Reform. Or it can be witnessed in the "stealth candidate" tactics of Pat Robertson's Christian Coalition. The World Wide Web site of the Carolinian Lords of the Caucasus features an image of a burning cross. Broad stratas of the population are being mobilized by these groups, which continue their war against leftist organizations of all stripes, such as the United Farm Workers Union, eco-feminist groups, gay and lesbian groups, Chicano/a activists, African American resistance groups, Asian activists, Native American groups, and radical educational organizations. Here in California the police and

La Migra are feared nearly as much as these vigilante groups for reasons that, in recent years, have gained national exposure.

I suspect that many educators remain unaware of the fact that U.S. English is linked to the Federation for American Immigration Reform (FAIR) and has bankrolled Americans for Border Control. FAIR is financially supported by the Pioneer Fund, dedicated to eugenics and white racial superiority. Pioneer was created in the 1930s to support Hitler's theories of "Aryan superiority" and the Nazi program of forced sterilization of undesirables. In the 1970s, Pioneer funded the genetic research of William Schockley and Arthur Jensen and supported their claims that blacks have hereditarily lower IQ scores than whites (Novik 1995). Jensen served on the advisory board of *Neue Anthropologie*, a German neo-Nazi publication, and his work paved the way for studies like the recent *The Bell Curve*. U.S. English is also supported by Cordelia Scaife May, an heiress to the Mellon family fortune who also sponsored, through her Laurel Foundation, the futuristic fantasy *The Camp of Saints*, a book that depicts Third World immigrants invading Europe and destroying its foundations of civilization. This book was required reading among staffers at U.S. English (Novik 1995).

English First is an organization underwritten by an equally insidious white supremacy. Its founder, Larry Pratt, is a former Virginia legislator and officer of the Council on Inter-American Security (CIS). The CIS authored much of Ronald Reagan's and George Bush's Latin American policy. Pratt also heads Gun Owners of America and has steered the CIS toward a position that equates bilingual education and services with terrorism. The CIS describes the Indian ancestors of Latinos as "uncivilized barbaric squatters" with "a penchant for grotesque human sacrifices, cannibalism, and kidnapping women" (Novik 1995, 189). Not surprisingly, the CIS has major ties to the Reverend Sun Myung Moon's Unification Church and boasts Pat Buchanan as a member.

U.S. English and English First have jointly funded LEAD (Learning English Advocates Drive), a parent group that opposes bilingual education and that has tried to conscript the support of the United Teachers of Los Angeles to oppose bilingual education.

Unthinking Whiteness, Rearticulating Diasporic Praxis

Now, this is the road that White Men tread
When they go to clean a land—Iron underfoot and the vine overhead
And the deep on either hand.
We have trod that road—and a wet and windy road—
   Our chosen star for guide.

Oh, well for the world when the White Men tread
Their highway side by side!
—**Rudyard Kipling (cited in Said 1985, 226)**

Who can deny that the use of gunpowder against pagans is the burning of incense to
our Lord.
—**Oviedo, a governor of the settlement at Hispaniola (cited in Todorov 1984, 151)**

In 1996, the following article appeared in *Crosscurrents:*

It was not until March 2, 1996, that the mystery surrounding Ly's murder ended. That day, police arrested Gunner Lindberg, age twenty-one, and Dominic Christopher, age seventeen, after discovering a letter that Lindberg had written to a former prison inmate in New Mexico. The letter contained graphic details about the murder, as well as the writer's apparent insolence about the whole incident. Sandwiched between birthday plans, news about a friend's baby, and talk about the need for a new tattoo was this boastful account of what happened the night of January 29:

"Oh, I killed a jap a while ago. I stabbed him to death at Tustin High School. I walked up to him; Dominic was with me and I seen this guy rollerblading and I had a knife. We walked in the tennis court where he was; I walked up to him. Dominic was right there; I walked right up to him and he was scared; I looked at him said, 'Oh I thought I knew you,' and he got happy that he wasn't gonna get jumped. Then I hit him . . .

"I pulled the knife out, a butcher knife, and he said 'no,' then I put the knife to his throat and asked him, 'Do you have a car?' And he grabbed my hand that I had the knife in and looked at me, trying to get a description of me, so I stomped on his head 3 times and each time said, 'Stop looking at me,' then he was kinda knocked out, dazed, then I stabbed him in the side about 7 or 8 times; he rolled over a little, so I stabbed his back out 18 or 19 times, then he lay flat and I slit one side of his throat on his jugular vein. Oh, the sounds the guy was making were like, 'Uhhh.' Then Dominic said, 'do it again,' and I said, 'I already did, Dude. Ya, do it again,' so I cut his other jugular vein and Dominic said, 'Kill him, do it again' and I said 'he's already dead.' Dominic said, 'Stab him in the heart.' So I stabbed him about 20 or 21 times in the heart. . . .

"Then I wanted to go back and look, so we did and he was dying just then, taking in some bloody gasps of air so I nudged his face with my shoe a few times, then I told Dominic to kick him, so he kicked the f___ out of his face and he still has blood on his shoes all over . . . then I ditched the knife, after wiping it clean on the side of the 5 freeway . . . here's the clippings from the newspaper . . . we were on all the channels." ("Grisly Account of Ly Killing Believed Penned by Suspect," *Los Angeles Times* Orange County Edition, March 7, 1996).

Was there racial motivation behind the crime? White supremacist paraphernalia were found at Lindberg's and Christopher's home. (Mai Pham, "Former UCLA Student Leader Murdered in Hate Crime," *Crosscurrents* [Fall/Winter 1996], 11)

The concept of whiteness became lodged in the discursive crucible of colonial identity by the early 1860s. Whiteness at that time had become a marker for measuring inferior and superior races. Interestingly, Genghis Khan, Attila the Hun, and Confucius were at this time considered "white." Blackness was evaluated positively in European iconography from the twelfth to the fifteenth centuries, but after the seventeenth century and the rise of European colonialism, blackness became conveniently linked to inferiority (Cashmore 1996). For instance, during the sixteenth and seventeenth centuries, blood purity (*limpieza de sangre*) became raised to a metaphysical—perhaps even sacerdotal—status, as it became a principle used to peripheralize Indians, Moors, and Jews. Blackness was not immediately associated with slavery. In the United States, the humanistic image of Africans created by the abolitionist movement was soon countered by new types of racial signification in which white skin was identified with racial superiority. Poor Europeans were sometimes indentured and were in some sense de facto slaves. They occupied the same economic categories as African slaves and were held in equal contempt by the lords of the plantation and legislatures (Cashmore 1996). So poor Europeans were invited to align themselves with the plantocracy as "white" in order to avoid the most severe forms of bondage. This strategy helped plantation owners form a stronger social control apparatus; hegemony was achieved by offering "race privileges" to poor whites as acknowledgment of their loyalty to the colonial land (Cashmore 1996).

By the early twentieth century, European maritime empires controlled over half the land (72 million square kilometers) and a third of the world's population (560 million people). Seventy-five million Africans died during the centuries-long transatlantic slave trade (West 1993). The logics of empire are still with us, bound to the fabric of our daily being-in-the-world, woven into our posture toward others, connected to the muscles of our eyes, dipped in the chemical relations that excite and calm us, structured into the language of our perceptions. We cannot will our racist logics away. We need to work hard to eradicate them. We need to struggle with a formidable resolve in order to overcome what we are afraid to confirm exists, let alone to confront it, in the battleground of our souls.

Cornel West has identified three white supremacist logics: the Judeo-Christian racist logic, the scientific racist logic, and the psychosexual racist logic. The Judeo-Christian racist logic is reflected in the biblical story of Ham, son of Noah, who in failing to cover Noah's nakedness, had his progeny blackened by God. In this logic, unruly behavior and catholic rebellion are linked to racist practices. The "scientific" racist logic is identified with the evaluation of physical bodies in light of Greco-Roman standards. Within this logic racist practices are identified with physical ugliness, cultural deficiency, and intellectual inferiority. They psychosexual racist logic identifies black people with Western sexual discourses associated with sexual prowess, lust, dirt, and subordination. A serious question is raised by West's typology in relation to the construction of whiteness: What are the historically concrete and sociologically specific ways that white supremacist discourses are guided by Western philosophies of identity and universality and capitalist relations of production and consumption? West has located racist practices in the commentaries by the church fathers on the Song of Solomon and the Ywain narratives in medieval Brittany, to name just a few historical sources. West has also observed that human bodies were classified according to skin color as early as 1684 (before the rise of modern capitalism) by French physician François Bernier. The famous eighteenth-century naturalist Carolus Linnaeus produced the first major written account of racial division in *Natural System* (1735). White supremacy is linked to the way culture is problematized and defined. As we have seen, theories of culture are themselves by-products of and symptoms of theorists' relation to an ongoing global struggle over issues of social class.

George Lipsitz (1995) argues that understanding the destructive quality of white identity requires what Walter Benjamin termed "presence of mind" or "an abstract of the future, and precise awareness of the present moment more decisive than foreknowledge of the most distant events" (1995, 370). Noting that "race" is not merely a "cultural construct" but a construct that has "sinister structural causes and consequences," Lipsitz argues that from colonial times to the present there have existed systematic efforts "to create a possessive investment in whiteness for European Americans" (371). Identifying what he calls a new form of racism embedded in "the putatively race-neutral liberal social democratic reforms of the past five decades" (371), Lipsitz asserts that the possessive investment in whiteness can be seen in legacies of socialization bequeathed to U.S. citizens by federal, state, and local policies toward African Americans, Native Americans, Mexican Americans, Asian Americans, "and other groups designated by whites as 'racially other.'"

Lipsitz impressively covers a great deal of historical ground in his discussion of white privilege—from colonial legal systems and racialized chattel slavery to contemporary efforts at urban renewal and highway construction that victimized mainly minority neighborhoods. For instance, Lipsitz tells us that while blacks in Houston, Texas, make up a little more than one-quarter of the local population, more than 75 percent of municipal garbage incinerators and 100 percent of city-owned garbage dumps are located in black neighborhoods. Lipsitz reports that in response to 1,177 toxic waste cases, the Environmental Protection

Agency exacted penalties on polluters near the largest white populations that were 500 percent higher than penalties imposed on polluters in minority areas (income did not account for these differences). Not only were penalties for violating all federal environmental laws regarding air, water, and waste pollution in minority communities found to be 46 percent lower than in white communities, minority communities had to wait longer for cleanups, sometimes 42 percent longer than at white sites, and endure a 7 percent greater likelihood of "containment" (walling off a hazardous site) than cleanup. White sites enjoyed treatment and cleanup 22 percent more often than containment.

Urban renewal also favored the rich by constructing luxury housing units and cultural centers, rather than affordable housing for the poor, in order to help cities compete for corporate investment. After providing a long litany of policies and practices infused with institutionalized forms of racism that have persisted over decades—forms that included government subsidies to private sectors, tax breaks for the wealthy, tax increment redevelopment programs, industrial development bonds, tax reforms, and federal housing loan policies—Lipsitz goes on to argue that Americans produce largely cultural explanations for structural social problems. They do so, Lipsitz maintains, because they are "largely ignorant of even the recent history of the possessive investment in whiteness" (1995, 379). For instance, whites are often unaware that nationwide financial institutions receive more money in deposits from black neighborhoods than they invest in them in the form of home mortgage loans. Home lending has thus become a vehicle for the transfer of capital away from black savers and toward white investors. Disturbingly, some polls have revealed that whites believe blacks have the same opportunity to acquire a middle-class life as whites. At the same time, whites persist in viewing negatively blacks' abilities, work habits, and character.

John Gallagher (1994) has worked as a professor with working-class and middle-class white students at an urban U.S. university. He makes the important point that the efforts of the media and racial politics in general has made whiteness more distinct as a racial category and has prompted whites to see themselves other than "colorless or racially transparent" (166). Unlike other critics who maintain that whiteness is largely invisible to whites themselves, Gallagher maintains that the political and cultural mobilization of racially defined minorities has positioned whites to think about themselves in relation to other racial groups and that the decline of ethnicity among late-generation whites has created an "identity vacuum" that has been, in part, replaced by a radicalized identity. In this milieu, right-wing factions are currently attempting to reconstruct being "white" as a nonracist cultural identity informed by decent citizens trying to preserve their white heritage and by white students trying to create an identity in ways "that do not demonize white as a racial category" (167).

Gallagher argues that "white reconstruction" is occurring "among a sizable part of the white population, particularly among young people" (1994, 168). White males especially feel under assault by nonwhites "even though the 47 percent of white males in the labor force account for almost 92 percent of corporate officers and 88 percent of corporate directors" (169). According to Gallagher, many white students view themselves as being victimized by black racists and used as targets because they are white. They feel further under attack by "university-sanctioned race-based curricula" and "social clubs" such as the NAACP and La Raza. But Gallagher believes that this is a construction of white students' "own racist projections about what blacks think about whites" (171). Feeling that their status is under siege, whites are now constructing their identities in reaction to what they feel to be the "politically correct" challenge to white privilege. Many whites, Gallagher notes, feel that being a minority is actually an asset and advantage in the job market and, furthermore, believe that "what is 'great' for minorities must be a handicap to whites" (176).

Many white students reportedly still "believe the United States is an egalitarian, colorblind society" and thus refuse to define themselves as oppressors or recipients of white privileges. Gallagher found that among college students a legitimate, positive narrative of one's own whiteness was often created by constructing an identity that negated white-oppressor accusations and framed whiteness as a liability. Not only do white students deny U.S. racial history but they believe that their skin color provides them with no benefits. Embracing a color-blind society permits white people to construct ideologies that help them to avoid the issue of racial inequality while simultaneously benefiting from it. The creation or invention of whiteness described by Gallagher suggests that the ways in which the white population "get raced" points to a process that needs to be better understood. White identity needs to be understood as "a reaction to the entrance of historically marginalized racial and ethnic groups into the political arena and the ensuing struggle over social resources" (1994, 183). It appears as if whiteness is beginning to be formed within the context of its own racial logics and essences. Gallagher explains:

> The explicit reinsertion of whiteness into politics is possible only by creating the illusion that being white is no different than belonging to any other racial group in the United States. If that illusion can be maintained, a white identity and white culture modeled on a Disney America theme park, with its purified historic revisionism, will allow whites to reinvent a cultural history that does not evoke such matters as the Ku Klux Klan or Japanese in-

ternment during World War II but instead is synonymous with egalitarianism, rugged individualism, and democracy. (184)

In her article "Whiteness as Property" (1993), Cheryl I. Harris makes the compelling case that within the legal system and within popular reasoning, there exists an assumption that whiteness is a property interest entitled to legal protection. Whiteness as property is essentially the reification in law of expectations of white privilege. Not only has this assumption been supported by systematic white supremacy through the law of slavery and "Jim Crow" laws but also by recent decisions and rationales of the Supreme Court concerning affirmative action. Harris is correct in arguing that white racial identity provides the basis for allocating societal benefits in both public and private spheres. Whiteness as a property of status continues to assist in the reproduction of the existing system of racial classification and stratification that protects the socially entrenched white power elite. According to Harris, rejecting race-conscious remedial measures as unconstitutional under the equal-protection clause of the Fourteenth Amendment "is based on the Court's chronic refusal to dismantle the institutional protection of benefits for whites that have been based on white supremacy and maintained at the expense of Blacks" (1993, 1767).

Current legal definitions of race embrace the norm of color blindness and thus disconnect race from social identity and race consciousness. Within the discourse of color blindness, blackness and whiteness are seen as neutral and apolitical descriptions reflecting skin color and as unrelated to social conditions of domination and subordination and to social attributes such as class, culture, language, and education. In other words, color blindness is a concept that symmetrizes relations of power and privilege and flattens them out so that they appear symmetrical or equivalent. But blackness and whiteness exist symmetrically only as idealized oppositions; in the real world they exist as a dependent hierarchy, with whiteness constraining the social power of blackness by colonizing the definition of what is normal, by institutionalizing a greater allocation of resources for white constituencies, and by maintaining laws that favor whites. According to Harris,

> To define race reductively as simply color, and therefore meaningless is as subordinating as defining race to be scientifically determinative of inherent deficiency. The old definition creates a false linkage between race and inferiority; the new definition denies the real linkage between race and oppression under systematic white supremacy. Distorting and denying reality, both definitions support race subordination. As Neil Gotanda has argued, colorblindness is a form of race subordination in that it denies the historical context of white domination and Black subordination. (1993, 1768)

Affirmation action needs to be understood not through privatizing social inequality through claims of bipolar corrective justice between black and white competitors but rather as an issue of distributive social justice and rights that focuses not on guilt or innocence but on entitlement and fairness.

According to Alex Callinicos (1993), racial differences are invented. Racism occurs when the characteristics that justify discrimination are held to be inherent in the oppressed group. This form of oppression is peculiar to capitalist societies; it arises in the circumstances surrounding industrial capitalism and the attempt to acquire a large labor force. Callinicos points out three main conditions for the existence of racism as outlined by Marx: economic competition among workers; the appeal of racist ideology to white workers; and efforts of the capitalist class to establish and maintain racial divisions among workers. Capital's constantly changing demands for different kinds of labor can be met only through immigration. Callinicos remarks that "racism offers for workers of the oppressing 'race' the imaginary compensation for the exploitation they suffer of belonging to the '*ruling* nation'" (1993, 39).

Callinicos notes how Marx grasped the fact that racial divisions between "native" and immigrant workers could weaken the working class. U.S. politicians take advantage of this division, which the capitalist class understands and manipulates only too well. George Bush, Jesse Helms, Pat Buchanan, Phil Gramm, David Duke, and Pete Wilson have effectively used racism to divide the working class.

At this point you might be asking yourselves: Doesn't racism predate capitalism? Here I agree with Callinicos that the heterophobia associated with precapitalist societies was not the same as modern racism. Precapitalist slave and feudal societies of classical Greece and Rome did not rely on racism to justify the use of slaves. The Greeks and Romans had no theories of white superiority. If they did, that must have been unsettling news to Septimus Severus, Roman emperor from A.D. 193 to 211, who was, many historians claim, a black man. Racism developed at a key turning point in capitalism during the seventeenth and eighteenth centuries of colonial plantations in the New World, where slave labor stolen from Africa was used to produce tobacco, sugar, and cotton for the global consumer market (Callinicos 1993). Callinicos cites Eric Williams, who remarks: "Slavery was not born of racism; rather, racism was the consequence of slavery" (cited in Callinicos 1993, 24). Racism emerged as the ideology of the plantocracy. It began with the class of sugar planters and slave merchants that dominated England's Caribbean colonies. Racism developed out of the "systemic slavery" of the New World. The "natural inferiority" of Africans was used by whites to justify enslaving them. According to Callinicos,

Racism offers white workers the comfort of believing themselves part of the dominant group; it also provides, in times of crisis, a ready made scapegoat, in the shape of the oppressed group. Racism thus gives white workers a particular identity, and one moreover which unites them with white capitalists. We have here, then, a case of the kind of "imagined community" discussed by Benedict Anderson in his influencial analysis of nationalism. (1993, 38)

To abolish racism, we need to abolish global capitalism. Callinicos is very clear on this point.

The educational left has largely failed to address the issue of whiteness and the insecurities that young whites harbor regarding their future during times of diminishing economic expectations. With their "racially coded and divisive rhetoric," neoconservatives may be able to enjoy tremendous success in helping insecure young white populations develop white identity along racist lines. Consider the comments by David Stowe:

The only people nowadays who profess any kind of loyalty to whiteness *qua* whiteness (as opposed to whiteness as an incidental feature of some more specific identity) are Christian Identity types and Ayran Nation diehards. Anecdotal surveys reveal that few white Americans mention whiteness as a quality that they think much about or particularly value. In their day-to-day cultural preferences—food, music, clothing, sports, hairstyles—the great majority of American whites display no particular attachment to white things. There does seem to be a kind of emptiness at the core of whiteness. (1996, 74)

People don't discriminate against groups because they are different but rather the act of discrimination constructs categories of difference that hierarchically locate people as "superior" or "inferior" and then universalize and naturalize such differences. When I refer to whiteness or to the cultural logics of whiteness, I need to qualify what I mean. Here I adopt Ruth Frankenberg's injunction that cultural practices considered to be white need to be seen as contingent, historically produced, and transformable. White culture is not monolithic, and its borders must be understood as malleable and porous. It is the historically specific confluence of economic, geopolitical, and ethnocultural processes. According to Alastair Bonnett (1996), whiteness is neither a discrete entity nor a fixed, asocial category. Rather, it is an "immutable social construction" (98). White identity is an ensemble of discourses, contrapuntal and contradictory. Whiteness—and the meanings attributed to it—are always in a state of flux and fibrillation. Bonnett notes that "even if one ignores the transgressive youth or ethnic borderlands of Western identities, and focuses on the 'center' or 'heartlands' of 'whiteness,' one will discover racialised subjectivities, that, far from being settled and confidant, exhibit a constantly reformulated panic over the meaning of 'whiteness' and the defining presence of 'non-whiteness' within it" (106). According to Frankenberg, white culture is a material and discursive space that "is inflected by nationhood, such that whiteness and Americanness, though by no means coterminous, are profoundly shaped by one another. . . . Similarly, whiteness, masculinity, and femininity are coproducers of one another, in ways that are, in their turn, crosscut by class and by the histories of racism and colonialism" (1993, 233).

Whiteness needs to be seen as *cultural*, as *processual*, and not ontologically different from processes that are nonwhite. It works, as Frankenberg notes, as "an unmarked marker of others' differentness—whiteness not so much void or formlessness as norm" (1993, 198). Whiteness functions through social practices of assimilation and cultural homogenization; whiteness is linked to the expansion of capitalism in the sense that "whiteness signifies the production and consumption of commodities under capitalism" (203). Yet capitalism in the United States needs to be understood as contingently white, since white people participate in maintaining the hegemony of institutions and practices of racial dominance in different ways and to greater or lesser degrees. Ruth Frankenberg identifies the key discursive repertoires of whiteness as follows:

> [First,] modes of naming culture and difference associated with west European colonial expansion; second, elements of "essentialist" racism . . . linked to European colonialism but also critical as rationale for Anglo settler colonialism and segregationism in what is now the USA; third, "assimilationist" or later "color- and power-evasive strategies for thinking through race first articulated in the early decades of this century; and, fourth, . . . "race-cognizant" repertoires that emerged in the latter half of the twentieth century and were linked both to U.S. liberation movements and to broader global struggles for decolonization. (239)

While an entire range of discursive repertoires may come into play, jostling against, superseding, and working in conjunction with each other, white identity is constructed in relation to an individual's personal history, geopolitical situatedness, contextually specific practices, and location in the materiality of the racialized social order. In other words, many factors determine which discursive configurations are at work and the operational modalities present.

Whiteness has no formal content. It works rhetorically by articulating itself out of the semiotic detritus of myths of European superiority. These are myths that are ontologically empty, epistemologically misleading, and morally pernicious in the way that they privilege descendants of Europeans as the truly civilized in contrast to the quaint, exotic, or barbaric character of non-European cultures. Whiteness is a sociohistorical form of consciousness, given birth at the nexus of capitalism, colonial rule, and the emergent relationships among dominant and subordinate groups. Whiteness operates by means of its constitution as a universalizing authority by which the hegemonic white bourgeois subject appropriates the right to speak on behalf of everyone who is nonwhite while denying voice and agency to these others in the name of civilized humankind. Whiteness constitutes and demarcates ideas, feelings, knowledge, social practices, cultural formations, and systems of intelligibility that are identified with or attributed to white people and that are invested in by white people as "white." Whiteness is also a refusal to acknowledge how white people are implicated in certain social relations of privilege and relations of domination and subordination. Whiteness, then, can be considered as a form of social amnesia associated with modes of subjectivity within particular social sites considered to be normative. As a lived domain of meaning, whiteness represents particular social and historical formations that are reproduced through specific discursive and material processes and circuits of desire and power. Whiteness reflects a conflictual sociocultural, sociopolitical, and geopolitical process that animates commonsensical practical action in relationship to dominant social practices and normative ideological productions. Whiteness constitutes the selective tradition of dominant discourses about race, class, gender, and sexuality hegemonically reproduced. Whiteness has become the substance and limit of our common sense articulated as cultural consensus. As an ideological formation transformed into a principle of life, into an ensemble of social relations and practices, whiteness needs to be understood as conjunctural, as a composite social hieroglyph that shifts in denotative and connotative emphasis depending on how its elements are combined and on the contexts in which it operates (Haymes, 1995).

Whiteness is not a pregiven, unified ideological formation but is a multifaceted collective phenomenon resulting from the relationship between the self and the ideological discourses, which are constructed out of the surrounding local and global cultural terrain. Whiteness is fundamentally Euro- or Western-centric in its episteme, as it is articulated in complicity with the pervasively imperializing logic of empire. Whiteness in the United States can be understood largely through the social consequences it provides for those who are considered to be nonwhite. Such consequences can be seen in the criminal justice system, in prisons, in schools, and in the boardrooms of corporations such as Texaco. It can be defined in relation to immigration practices and social policies and practices of sexism, racism, and nationalism. It can be seen historically in widespread acts of imperialism and genocide and can be linked to an erotic economy of "excess." Eric Lott writes:

In rationalized Western societies, becoming "white" and male seems to depend upon the remanding of enjoyment, the body, and aptitude for pleasure. It is the other who is always putatively "excessive" in this respect, whether through exotic food, strange and noisy music, outlandish bodily exhibitions, or unremitting sexual appetite. Whites in fact organize their own enjoyment through the other, Slavoj Zizek has written, and access pleasure precisely by fantasizing about the other's "special" pleasure. Hatred of the other arises from the necessary hatred of one's own excess; ascribing this excess to the "degraded" other and indulging it—by imaging, incorporating, or impersonating the other—one conveniently and surreptitiously takes and disavows pleasure at one and the same time. This is the mixed erotic economy, what Homi Bhabha terms the "ambivalence," of American whiteness. (1993, 482)

Whiteness is a type of articulatory practice that can be located in the convergence of colonialism, capitalism, and subject formation. It both fixes and sustains discursive regimes that represent self and "other"; that is, whiteness represents a regime of differences that produces and racializes an abject other. In other words, whiteness is a discursive regime that enables real effects to take place. Whiteness displaces blackness and brownness—specific forms of nonwhiteness—into signifiers of deviance and criminality within social, cultural, cognitive, and political contexts. White subjects discursively construct identity through producing, naming, "bounding," and marginalizing a range of others (Frankenberg 1993, 193).

Whiteness constitutes unmarked (Euro-American male) practices that have negative effects on and consequences for those who do not participate in them. Inflected by nationhood, whiteness can be considered an ensemble of discursive practices constantly in the process of being constructed, negotiated, and changed. Yet it functions to instantiate a structured exclusion of certain groups from social arenas of normativity. Coco Fusco remarks: "To raise the specter of racism in the here and now, to suggest that despite their political beliefs and sexual preferences, white people operate within, and benefit from, white supremacist social structures is still tantamount to a declaration of war" (1995, 76).

Whiteness is not only mythopoetical in the sense that it constructs a totality of illusions formed around the ontological superiority of the Euro-American subject, it is also metastructural in that it connects whiteness across specific differences; it solders fugitive, breakaway discourses and rehegemonizes them. Consumer utopias and global capital flows rearticulate whiteness by means of relational differences (Kincheloe and Steinberg, in press).

Whiteness is dialectically reinitiated across epistemological fissures, contradictions, and oppositions through new regimes of desire that connect the consumption of goods to the everyday logic of Western democracy. The cultural encoding of the typography of whiteness is achieved by remapping Western European identity onto economic transactions, by re-cementing desire to capitalist flows, by concretizing personal history into collective memory linked to place, to a myth of origin. Whiteness offers a safe "home" for those imperiled by the flux of change.

Whiteness can be considered as a conscription of the process of positive self-identification into the service of domination through inscribing identity into an ontoepistemological framework of "us" against "them." For those who are nonwhite, the seduction of whiteness can produce a self-definition that disconnects the subject from his or her history of oppression and struggle, exiling identity into the unmoored, chaotic realm of abject otherness (while tacitly accepting the positioned superiority of the Western subject). Whiteness provides the Euro-American subject with a known boundary that places nothing "off limits" yet provides a fantasy of belongingness. It's not that whiteness signifies preferentially one pole of the white-nonwhite binarism. Rather, whiteness seduces the subject to accept the idea of polarity as the limit-text of identity, as the constitutive foundation of subjectivity.

In his important volume, *Psychoanalytic-Marxism*, Eugene Victor Wolfenstein describes the whiteness of domination as the "one fixed point" of America's many facisms. He argues that whiteness is a social designation and a "history disguised as biology" (1993, 331). Whiteness is also an attribute of language. Wolfenstein claims that "languages have skin colors. There are white nouns and verbs, white grammar and white syntax. In the absence of challenges to linguistic hegemony, indeed, language is white. If you don't speak white you will not be heard, just as when you don't look white you will not be seen" (331).

Describing white racists as "virtuosos of denigration," Wolfenstein maintains that the language of white racism illustrates "a state of war" (1993, 333). Yet the battles are fought through lies and deceit. One such lie is the idea of "color blindness."

Wolfenstein notes that color blindness constitutes more than a matter of conscious deceit:

> White racism is rather a mental disorder, an ocular disease, an opacity of the soul that is articulated with unintended irony in the idea of "color blindness." To be color blind is the highest form of racial false consciousness, a denial of both difference and domination. But one doesn't have to be color blind to be blinded by white racism. . . . Black people see themselves in white mirrors, white people see black people as their own photographic negatives. (1993, 334)

Wolfenstein suggests that two epistemological tasks be undertaken. Black people need to look away from the white mirror; white people need to attempt to see black people as they see themselves and to see themselves as they are seen by other black people. Wolfenstein links white racism to what he terms "epidermal fetishism." Epidermal fetishism reduces people to their skin color and renders them invisible. It is a type of social character that is formed within a process of exchange and circulation. As such, whiteness represents the superego (the standard of social value, self-worth, and morality). Since the ego is affirmatively reflected in the superego, it also must be white. What is therefore repressed is blackness, which "becomes identified with the unwanted or bad parts of the self" (1993, 336).

> At the level of social character, white racism is self-limiting for white people, self-destructive for black people. White people alienate their sensuous potentialities from themselves. They are devitalized and sterilized. Blackness, officially devalued, comes to embody their estranged life and desire. They are able, however, to see themselves reflected in the mirrors of selfhood. But if black people have their selfhood structured by the whitened-out form of social character, they become fundamentally self-negating. Their blackness, hated and despised, must be hidden away. Hair straighteners and skin lighteners testify to the desire to go further and eradicate blackness altogether. (1993, 336–337)

The incorporeal luminescence of whiteness is achieved, according to Wolfenstein, by the subsumption of blackness within whiteness. What cannot be subsumed and digested is excreted. White people both despise and lust after blackness. Wolfenstein describes some forms of interracial romantic heterosexual relationships as epidermally mediated erotic domination, as an epidermalized sexual rebellion against a repressive social morality, and as an epidermally mediated double violation of the oedipal incest taboo. In order to resist epidermal fetishism, oppressed people need a language and a politics of their own.

It is important to recognize that white racism is neither purely systemic nor purely individual. Rather, it is a complex interplay of collective interests and desires. White racism in this instance "becomes a rational means to collective ends" (Wolfenstein 1993, 341) when viewed from the standpoint of ruling-class interests. Yet for the white working class it is irrational and a form of false consciousness. White racism also circumscribes rational action for black people in that they are encouraged to act in terms of their racial rather than class interests.

Whiteness offers coherency and stability in a world in which capital produces regimes of desire linked to commodity utopias where fantasies of omnipotence must find a stable home. Of course, the "them" is always located within the "us." The marginalized are always foundational to the stability of the central actors. The excluded in this case establish the condition of existence of the included. So we find that it is impossible to separate the identities of both oppressor and oppressed. They depend on each other. To resist whiteness means developing a politics of difference. Since we lack the full semantic availability to understand whiteness and to resist it, we need to rethink difference and identity outside of sets of binary oppositions. We need to view identity as coalitional, as collective, as processual, as grounded in the struggle for social justice.

Alistair Bonnett notes that the reified notion of whiteness "enables 'white' people to occupy a privileged location in antiracist debate; they are allowed the luxury of being passive observers, of being altruistically motivated, of knowing that their 'racial' identity might be reviled and lambasted but never actually made slippery, torn open, or, indeed, abolished" (1996, 98). Bonnett further notes: "To dismantle 'blackness' but leave the force it was founded to oppose unchallenged is to display both a political and theoretical naïveté. To subvert 'blackness' without subverting 'whiteness' reproduces and reinforces the 'racial' myths, and the 'racial' dominance, associated with the latter" (99).

Ian F. Haney López's book, *White by Law*, offers a view of white transparency and invisibility that is at odds with Gallagher's thesis that whites are growing more conscious of their whiteness. López cites an incident at a legal feminist conference in which participants were asked to pick two or three words to describe themselves. All of the women of color selected at least one racial term, but not one white woman selected a term referring to her race. This prompted Angela Harris to remark that only white people in this society have the luxury of having no color. An informal study conducted at Harvard Law School underscores Harris's remark. A student interviewer asked ten African Americans and ten white Americans how they identified themselves. Unlike the African Americans, most of the white Americans did not consciously factor in their "whiteness" as a crucial or even tangential part of their identity.

López argues that one is not born white but becomes white "by virtue of the social context in which one finds oneself, to be sure, but also by virtue of the choices one makes" (1996, 190). But how can one born into the culture of whiteness, one who is defined as white, undo that whiteness? López addresses this question in his formulation of whiteness. He locates whiteness in the overlapping of *chance* (e.g., features and ancestry that we have no control over, morphology); *context* (context-specific meanings that are attached to race, the social setting in which races are recognized, constructed, and contested); and *choice* (conscious choices with regard to the morphology and ancestries of social actors) in order to "alter the readability of their identity" (191).

In other words, López maintains that chance and context are not racially determinative. He notes: "Racial choices must always be made from within specific contexts, where the context materially and ideologically circumscribes the range of available choices and also delimits the significance of the act. Nevertheless, these are racial choices, if sometimes only in their overtone or subtext, because they resonate in the complex of meanings associated with race. Given the thorough suffusion of race throughout society, in the daily dance of life we constantly make racially meaningful decisions" (1996, 193).

López's perspective offers real potential, it would seem, for abolishing racism, since it refuses to locate whiteness only as antiracism's "other." I agree with Bonnett when he remarks that "to continue to cast 'whites' as anti-racism's 'other,' as the eternally guilty and/or altruistic observers of 'race' equality work, is to maintain 'white' privilege and undermine the movement's intellectual and practical reach and utility" (1996, 107). In other words, whites need to ask themselves to what extent their identity is a function of their whiteness in the process of their ongoing daily lives and what choices they might make to escape whiteness. López outlines—productively in my view—three steps in dismantling whiteness. They are worth quoting in full: "First, Whites must overcome the omnipresent effects of transparency and of the naturalization of race in order to recognize the many racial aspects of their identity, paying particular attention to the daily acts that draw upon and in turn confirm their whiteness. Second, they must recognize and accept the personal and social consequences of breaking out of a White identity. Third, they must embark on a daily process of choosing against Whiteness" (193).

Of course, the difficulty of taking such steps is partly due to the fact that, as López notes, the unconscious acceptance of a racialized identity is predicated upon a circular definition of the self. It's hard to step outside of whiteness if you are white because of all the social, cultural, and economic privileges that accompany whiteness. Yet whiteness must be dismantled if the United States is to overcome racism. Lipsitz remarks: "Those of us who are 'white' can only become part of the solution if we recognize the degree to which we are already part of the problem—not because of our race, but because of our possessive investment in it" (1995, 384).

The editorial in the book *Race Traitor* puts it thus: "The key to solving the social problems of our age is to abolish the white race. Until that task is accomplished, even partial reform will prove elusive, because white influence permeates every issue in U.S. society, whether domestic or foreign. . . . Race itself is a product of social discrimination; so long as the white race exists, all movements against racism are doomed to fail" (Ignatiev and Garvey 1996, 10).

While we lack the semantic availability to fully capture the meaning and function of whiteness, we can at least describe it as a discursive strategy, articulation, or modality; or we can refer to it perhaps as a form of discursive brokerage, a pattern of negotiation that takes place in conditions generated by specific discursive formations and social relations. Historically, whiteness can be seen as a tattered and bruised progeny of Western colonialism and imperialism.

Whiteness is crisscrossed by numerous social dynamics. It is produced through capitalist social relations or modes of domination. The marker "whiteness" serves as a discursive indicator or social hieroglyph (Cruz 1996)—an "effect" of systematic social relations of which those who are marked as "white" have little conscious understanding. Whiteness, therefore, is socially and historically embedded; it's a form of racialization of identity formation that carries with it a history of social, cultural, and economic relations. Whiteness is unfinalizable, but compared to other ethnic formations, its space for maneuvering in the racialized and genderized permutations of U.S. citizenship is infinitely more vast. The task here for critical educators is to denaturalize whiteness by breaking its codes and the social relations and privileging hierarchies that give such codes normative power. The codification of whiteness as a social hieroglyph associated with civility, rationality, and political advancement is part of inherited social and cultural formations, formations that were given birth after the early capitalist marriage of industrialism and militarism. Whiteness is linked in a fundamental—if not dramatic—way to the racialization of aggression. Inherited categories and classifications that made whiteness the privileged signifier over blackness is a theme I have addressed in "White Terror" (McLaren 1995), and I will not rehearse that argument here.

I think that the relation between whiteness and privilege can be better understood by locating whiteness in the context of what Howard Winant (1994) calls "racial formation" and what David Theo Goldberg (1993) calls "racial modality." A racial modality refers to "a fragile structure of racist exclusions at a space-time conjuncture" that is sustained by the power of socioeconomic interests and the intersection of discursive fields and strategies of representation (Goldberg 1993, 210). Winant defines race as "*a concept that signifies and symbolizes sociopolitical conflicts and interests to different types of human bodies*" (1994, 115). This signals an understanding of race as an everyday phenomenon, one that is historically and socially constructed and is implicated in social structures, identities, and signification systems. The concept of racial formation also addresses the "*expansion and intensification of racial phenomena*" on a global basis (116). Further, it suggests "*a new conception of racial history and racial time*" (my italics, 116). Concerning the latter, then, whiteness can be seen as implicated in the progressive expansion of capitalism throughout the world and the genealogical racial time of

European conquest, what Winant calls an "archetypal *longue durée*: a slow agony of inscription upon the human body, a murder mystery, if you will, but on a genocidal scale. The phenotypical signification of the world's body took place in and through conquest and enslavement, to be sure, but also as an enormous act of expression, of narration" (117).

Whiteness, of course, is also a product of historical time in terms of what Winant calls "contingency," or the contextual specificity of its hegemonic articulations. Whiteness is implicated on a global basis in the internationalization of capital, which is being accompanied by the internationalization of race. We are witnessing growing diasporic movements as former colonial subjects immigrate to the Western metropoles, challenging the majoritarian status of European groups. Winant remarks that we are also witnessing "the rise of 'diasporic' models of blackness, the creation of 'panethnic' communities of Latinos and Asians (in such countries as the United Kingdom and the United States), and the breakdown of borders in both Europe and North America all [which] seem to be hybridizing and racializing previously national policies, cultures and identities" (1994, 118). I would follow Winant in maintaining that the focus of our investigation at this present juncture should be on the racial dimensions of capitalism and the mobilization of white racial antagonisms. Prior to World War II in the United States there existed a well-developed racial ideology, "a caste-based social structure developed to guarantee white workers their racial identity as a signifier of their 'freedom'" (125). White people represented the *Herrenvolk*—a democracy of white males. Winant observes that the *Herrenvolk's* supremacy was seriously eroded during the civil rights era. Of course, the post–civil rights era is another matter altogether. As racial domination gave way to racial hegemony, the task was no longer to subdue the masses of disenfranchised minorities but to accommodate them. The caste-based logic of race was discarded by white folks in favor of an egalitarian politics underwritten by a culture of poverty thesis: People of color should pull themselves up out of the "underclass" through their own initiatives. Consider the recent case in point of the University of California's dismantling of affirmative action, championed by Ward Connerly, a conservative African American UC regent. When reports commissioned by the UC provost projected that the numbers of white and Asian UC undergraduates would markedly grow and numbers of underrepresented minority students would diminish, Connerly responded: "This is the most tacit admission of the extent that we are using race for underrepresented students that one could ever find" (cited in Wallace 1996, 1, 18). Connerly's comment is underwritten by a belief that African American and Latino/a students, for instance, are being given an unfair advantage by affirmative action programs. This presumes that the playing field is now equal and that we have arrived at a point in our society where meritocracy actually exists. It ignores issues of culture, economics, and ideology and how these factors and others work in relation to public institutions and the (re)production of structural racism. Consequently, Connerly is unable to fathom how his position on affirmative action acts in the service of white privilege.

I don't believe in reverse racism, since I don't believe white people have transcended race; nor do I believe that Latino/as or African Americans have acquired a systematic power to dominate whites. Yet along with the editors of *Race Traitor*, I believe in reversing racism by systematically dismantling whiteness. Even so, I am acutely aware that people of color might find troubling the idea that white populations can simply reinvent themselves by making the simple choice of not being white. Of course, this is not what López and others appear to be saying. The choices one makes and the reinvention one aspires to as a race traitor are not "simple"; nor are they easy choices for groups of whites to make. Yet from the perspective of some people of color, offering the choice to white people of opting out of their whiteness could seem to set up an easy path for those who don't want to assume responsibility for their privilege as white people. Indeed, there is certainly cause for concern. David Roediger captures some of this when he remarks: "Whites cannot fully renounce whiteness even if they want to" (1994, 16). Whites are, after all, still accorded the privileges of being white even as they ideologically renounce their whiteness, often with the best of intentions. Yet the potential for nonwhiteness and antiwhite struggle is too important to ignore or dismiss as wishful thinking or associate with a fashionable form of code-switching. Choosing not to be white is not an easy option for white people, not as simple as deciding to make a change in one's wardrobe. To understand the processes involved in the racialization of identity and to consistently choose nonwhiteness is a difficult act of apostasy, for it implies a heightened sense of social criticism and an unwavering commitment to social justice (Roediger 1994). Of course, the question needs to be asked: If we can choose to be nonwhite, then can we choose to be black or brown? Insofar as blackness is a social construction (often "parasitic" on whiteness), I would answer yes.

Theologian James H. Cone, author of *A Black Theology of Liberation*, urges white folks to free themselves from the shackles of their whiteness: "If whites expect to be able to say anything relevant to the self-determination of the black community, it will be necessary for them to destroy their whiteness by becoming members of an oppressed community. Whites will be free only when they become new persons—when their white being has passed away and they are created anew in black being. When this happens, they are no longer white but free" (1986, 97).

I want to be clear that I am not arguing for constructing a positive white identity where whiteness is defined with the best intentions as part of an antiracist and antiimperialist ideology. I argue for a self-consciousness about one's whiteness in terms of recognizing the danger of its transparency but do not advocate celebrating whiteness in any form. Rather, I argue for the disassembly and destruction of whiteness and advocate its rearticulation as a form of critical agency dedicated to struggles in the interests of the oppressed. López notes that "because races are constructed diacritically, celebrating Whiteness arguably requires the denigration of Blackness. Celebrating Whiteness, even with the best of antiracist intentions, seems likely only to entrench the status quo of racial beliefs" (1996, 172). Since white identity is the antonym to the identity of nonwhites, as López maintains, it is a sobering acknowledgment to make that the only positive identification one can offer with respect to whiteness is to call for the disassembly of whiteness and for its eventual destruction. López remarks that "whiteness can only retain its positive meanings through the denial at every turn of the social injustices associated with the rise and persistence of this racial category" (185). The celebration of whiteness in any form is inseverably linked to the peripheralization and demonization of nonwhites. White identity serves implicitly as the positive mirror image to the explicit negative identities imposed on nonwhites (López 1996). Even in the case of white U.S. citizens who claim European American identity as a way of avoiding the white versus nonwhite opposition, such a move is actually based on the double negative of not being nonwhite (López 1996).

But again I would stress that becoming nonwhite is not a "mere" choice but a self-consciously political choice, a spiritual choice, and a critical choice. To choose blackness or brownness merely as a way to escape the stigma of whiteness and avoid responsibility for owning whiteness is still very much an act of whiteness. To choose blackness or brownness as a way of politically disidentifying with white privilege and instead identifying with and participating in the struggles of nonwhite peoples is an act of transgression, a traitorous act that reveals a fidelity to the struggle for justice. Lipsitz sums up the problems and the promise of the abolition of whiteness as follows:

> Neither conservative "free market" policies nor liberal social democratic reforms can solve the "white problem" in America because both of them reinforce the possessive investment in whiteness. But an explicitly antiracist pan-ethnic movement that acknowledges the existence and power of whiteness might make some important changes. Pan-ethnic, antiracist coalitions have a long history in the United States—in the political activism of John Brown, Sojourner Truth, and the Magon brothers, among others— but we also have a rich cultural tradition of pan-ethnic antiracism con-

nected to civil rights activism. . . . Efforts by whites to fight racism, not out of sympathy for someone else but out of a sense of self-respect and simple justice, have never completely disappeared; they remain available as models for the present. (1995, 384)

George Yúdice gives additional substance to Lipsitz's concerns related to coalition-building when he points out some of the limitations of current identity politics: "The very difficulty of imagining a new social order that speaks convincingly to over 70 percent of the population requires critics to go beyond pointing out the injustices and abuses and move on to an agenda that will be more effective in transforming structures. What good is it to fight against white supremacy unless whites themselves join the struggle?" (1995, 268). Stowe echoes a similar sentiment when he writes: "Race treason has its limits as a workable strategy. Consider the economistic language in which it is described. Whites are exhorted to renounce the wages of whiteness, to divest from their possessive investment in whiteness, to sabotage the exchange value of racial privilege. . . . How many social movements have gotten ahead through the renunciation of privilege, though?" (1996, 77).

Yúdice makes a lucid point when he criticizes the journal *Race Traitor* for lacking a notion of political articulation. I agree with him that it is not enough to simply have faith in whites of goodwill to disidentify with their whiteness. He argues that change will not come suddenly as whites rise up against their whiteness. This position ignores that "(1) we are living in a time of diminishing expectations and (2) what binds together a society is an overdetermined configuration or constellation of ideologemes: democracy, individuality, free enterprise, work ethic, upward mobility, and national security are articulated in complex ways that do not simply split apart when any one of them is challenged. Social formations tend to undergo processes of rearticulation, according to Ernesto Laclau, rather than the kind of upheaval that *Race Traitor* seeks" (Yúdice 1995, 271–272).

What is needed, argues Yúdice, is a multicultural politics that is capable of projecting "a new democratic vision that makes sense to the white middle and working classes" (1995, 273). Whites must be interpolated in rearticulating the whiteness of the dominant class. Whites need to "feel solidarity with those who have suffered deprivation as members of subordinated groups" (276). They must be offered more than a rationalized rights discourse. They need to struggle over the interpretation of needs through the proliferation of public spheres in which the struggle for democracy can take place. The key, Yúdice maintains, is to center the struggle for social justice around resource distribution rather than identity: "Shifting the focus of struggle from identity to resource distribution will also make it possible to engage such seemingly nonracial issues as the environment, the military, the military-industrial complex, foreign aid, and free-trade agreements as matters impacting local identities and thus requiring a global politics that works outside of the national frame" (280).

That whiteness was reproduced in the petri dish of European colonialism cannot be disputed, but it is wrong to think of whiteness as an incurable disease. Multiculturalists whose identities depend on whiteness being the static other to antiracist efforts will perhaps resist the abolition of whiteness even though its destruction is their stated aim. We need to transgress the external determinations of white identity, which has brought about the unique conjuncture I have labeled the social hieroglyphics of whiteness, an ensemble of discourses informed, in part, by a perceived lack of ethnicity and also by issues of race, sexual identification, religion, and nation. Since the meanings that suture whiteness to special options denied to other groups within the United States are socially and historically constituted through circuits of investment and exchange, such meanings are mutable and can be transformed, but certainly not by self-willed efforts at refashioning whiteness into a new liturgy of self-critique accompanied by a new white cultural etiquette. Not until the social relations of (re)production and consumption are recognized as class relations linked to whiteness and thus challenged and transformed can new ethnicities emerge capable of eliminating white privilege.

Euro-Americans still constitute the gatekeepers of the white racial order known as the United States. Its *Herrenvolk* democracy of white supremacy remains largely camouflaged under the logic of egalitarianism and meritocracy and the denial of the significance of race expressed by calls to abolish the "color line" through anti-affirmative-action measures. This "color line" is no longer bipolar—black versus white—but rather multipolar; Asians and Latino/as increase their pressure on white majoritarian constituencies in the larger struggle for racial democracy. Winant argues for the elimination of racial discrimination and inequality but emphasizes as well the liberation of racial identity itself. I agree with Winant that this will involve "a reenvisioning of racial politics and a transformation of racial difference" (1994, 169). This means making racial identity a matter of choice rather than an ascription of meaning to phenotype and skin color. Today the racist state still polices the "color line" as it did in the past, but this time by arguing that it is actually created by affirmative action. Important questions that still need to be raised involve the refiguring of whiteness in the context of globalization, diasporic identities, and the increasing dissolution of the nation-state. How might the construction of postnational identities cause us to rethink whiteness?

The Struggle for Democracy

In this final section I will try to raise some of the concerns touched upon by Yúdice in the call for a radical vision of democratic practice. It is a vision that in my view is compatible with the struggle for a socialist democratic imaginary. Universal and particular rights will always be struggled over; they will never be fully compatible. For the critics of the universal there are no universal rights provided by the nation-state, only further exclusion and demonization as the "enemies of America." Paradoxically, if the universal and the particular ever achieve compatibility, democracy will have disappeared and fascism taken its place. And while the practice of justice will always contain contradictions and ambiguities, critical educators still need to ask the tough question: How, for instance, do schools and other institutions restrict the universalisms of our shared political ideals mainly to privileged, white Anglo groups? But in asking the tough questions, critical educators should not subsume the universal quest for liberty and equality into the particular. Rather, the spheres of the universal should be considerably widened, and as this widening occurs, the contents of this universality should be reformulated to include the voices of those already marginalized and excluded (Laclau 1992).

Etienne Balibar reflects a similar idea when he stresses the importance of understanding the social as well as the ideological conditions of democracy:

> If democracy as a system of living traditions finds its expression in both the representation of the governed and the control of those who govern—by a sufficient appropriateness of the representation of the population's interests and ideas and by a sufficient degree of popular control over the controllers themselves—it is never more than a fragile equilibrium between the functions of consensus and the functions of conflict. Ultimately, democracy lies on the inverse excesses of these functions. In this way, democracy depends at least as much upon *fortuna* as upon *virtú*, as much upon favorable circumstances as upon the initiative of the ruling class, the parties, and the citizens. It is essential, if we want to understand history, that we not exaggerate the importance of consensus to the detriment of conflict. (1996, 370)

I want to argue that critical educators need to embrace what Nancy Fraser (1993) calls a "democratic socialist–feminist political imaginary." This imaginary entails, among other things, the following: expanding the vision of a fully social wage; defending the importance of public goods against commodities; challenging the technocratic discourses of the state that reduce citizens to clients and consumers; advocating for the importance of unwaged domestic work and the child-raising labor of women; enlarging the view of entitlement; criticizing "the hyperbolic masculinist-capitalist view that individual 'independence' is normal and desirable while 'dependence' is avoidable and deviant" (21); insisting on a view of public provision as a system of social rights; rejecting the idea of "personal responsibility" and "mutual responsibility" in favor of "social responsibility"; and promoting social solidarity through confronting racism, sexism, homophobia, and class exploitation. We need a sense of shared responsibility without necessarily having to depend upon a shared identity (Darder, 1992).

Broadly speaking, Bauman sees communitarian democracy as community without freedom and liberal democracy as freedom without community. Bauman argues that the liberal concept of difference is "external" to the individual and stands for "the profusion of choices between the ways of being human and living one's life" (1996, 81). For communitarians, however, difference is "internalized" and represents "the refusal, or inability to consider other forms of life as options" (81). Liberal difference has to do with affirming individual freedom; the difference spoken about by communitarians often has to do with the necessity of imposing limits on human freedom. In this latter view, freedom should be exercised in order to choose unfreedom. For communitarians, outcomes of choices need to be understood before the actual choice is made. In contrast, Bauman notes that liberal freedom of choice "has become a major stratifying variable in our multi-dimensionally stratified society" (88). In postmodern/consumer society we are all fated to choose, but there exists a range of realistic choices because resources are needed to make those choices. While individual responsibility for choice is equally distributed, equality disappears, maintains Bauman, when we are considering the means to act on that responsibility: "What the liberal vision of the universal and equally awarded right to choose failed to take account of, is that 'adding freedom of action to the fundamental inequality of social condition will result in inequality yet deeper than before.' What liberal society offers with one hand, it tends to take back with the other; the duty of freedom without the resources that would permit a truly free choice is, for many affected a recipe for life without dignity, filled instead with humiliation and self deprecation" (88).

Scott Lash (1996) argues against some of Bauman's criticisms of communitarian ethics, noting favorably that communitarian ethics has provided a "groundedness" necessary to promote an ethics linked to political collectivity and action. Lash offers some criticisms of the work of Lévinas and his ethical imperative of unconditional responsibility for the other. According to Lévinas, totality must be deconstructed and infinitely embraced. Totality—referring to tradition and contractual individualism and institutions such as law, politics, and history—permits the judgment of the individual as a universal "I." Whatever is left once ontological justification is removed constitutes the ethical moment for Lévinas. The ethical relation is therefore based on an originary, transcendental intersubjectivity prior to language. However, Lash presciently observes that upon closer examination of Lévinas's work, the concrete, particular "I" in its radical singularity and the "other" appear to be both excluded in such an act of judgment. Lash criticizes Lévinas for offering a choice only between a politics of institutions (totality) and a politics of radical difference (infinity) and consequently rejecting a "subinstitutional politics of practice" (94).

Lash maintains that in order for social transformation to take place, the singular "I" must be grounded in a set of political practices. According to Lash, Lévinas might respond that such practices are necessarily "egotistical." Lash maintains that this is not necessarily the case, and on this point I agree with him. It is not mandatory that ethics be world-denying and focus solely on the "event" of the moral relationship between subjectivity and the other (Lash 1996, 94). Lévinas's "event" takes place at every instant of revelation that consciousness encounters its own singularity. Lash reports that the construction of meaning, or the "pretemporal event," of revelation in which consciousness relates to the very act of saying is highly problematic in Lévinas's conceptualization. For instance, the subject in this case is reduced to the signifier that brings about being in the event horizon of the word. Whereas a communitarian ethics would inhere in the world of social life and formations as regulative practices, for Lévinas the ethical relation is constitutive, not regulative, and occurs only when subjectivity turns away from the messiness of social life and toward infinity and the voice of the other (the excluded, the oppressed, the strangers among us) is recognized.

Lash does concede that a communitarian ethics cannot sufficiently address the singularity of the other. Yet still Lash argues that a community-oriented ethics of practice is necessary and can be carefully fashioned so that a space is left open "for the inscrutability of the other's singularity" (1996, 98). Rather than conceiving of the stranger as the featureless other (as in Lévinas's work), Lash argues for an understanding of aspects of the horizon of the other through dialogue. This dialogue would be grounded in diasporic understanding, that is, in communities of practice and the rhythms of shared languages and practices.

In Lash's view, a politics of difference should recognize the singularity of the other through a dialogical praxis, through the overlapping of horizons, and through an ethics of sociality. Lévinas's space of infinity (where subjectivity confronts the face of the other in an economy of being) must be made to extend beyond moral relationships in order to include dimensions of social relationships that exist exterior to totality and that embrace violence and death. Lash correctly points out that the ethical agent lives an infinite temporality that is not an empty eternity but rather one that is peopled and meaningful. He further observes—correctly in my view—that the concepts of patience and suffering in the work of Lévinas do not open up to the world of flesh and body. In Lévinas's ethical universe, pain takes place exterior to forms of social life. I should note, in passing, that Lash's position is reminiscent of my concept of *enfleshment,* in which subjectivity is formed in the temporal archives of the flesh and the historical moments of lived experience (see Mclaren 1995).

According to Lash, Lévinas gives us the polar opposite of the Third Reich's politics of spectacle, of the ethicization of aesthetics. We are offered an *éthique/esthétique* that begins with a subjectivity facing toward infinity. Yet paradoxically, this Lévinsian sublime does not mirror the Kantian sublime and the terror of aesthetic space but rather the ethical space of Kant's *Second Critique*, the realms of pure practical reason of *The Critique of Pure Reason*. Here, Lévinas's figures of singular subjectivity encounter the face of the other in the sphere of reason where ethics becomes the primordial ground of knowledge and of truth. In this view we become our most moral selves when we are the furthest away from the constraints of time and space. I am arguing for a detranscendalized ethics of location grounded in one's situatedness in the messy web of social relations, and the worldliness of space and locality.

In arguing for an ethics grounded in the concrete praxis and situatedness of dialogical relations, we need to turn to the writings of Bakhtin. Bahktin's perspectives can also help to forge an ethics that can take us past some of the limit conditions of Lévinas's position and in doing so bring us closer to a position compatible with that of the concept of "praxis" found in the work of the early Marx (Gardiner 1996, 138; see also the important book on Volosinov and bilingual education by Marcia Moraes [1996]).

The materiality of ethics that is being discussed here, including Bakhtin's notion of multivocality and dialogue, undergirds a concept of revolutionary multiculturalism that I consider to be fundamental to a pedagogy of liberation. The perspective on multiculturalism that I am advancing here I have referred to elsewhere as "critical multiculturalism" (see McLaren 1995), and it bears a strong affinity to what Shohat and Stam (1994) refer to as "polycentric multiculturalism." Polycentric multiculturalism disidentifies with liberal pluralist multiculturalism premised on ethical universals; it is not simply about describing cultural history but about analyzing social power and transforming discourses, institutions, and social practices of privilege. It does not order cultures hierarchically against the invisible norm of whiteness in a liberal swirl of diversity but rejects the idea of a preexisting center. That is, polycentric multiculturalism is articulated "from the margins" and views minoritarian communities "as active, generative participants at the very core of a shared, conflictual history" (Shohat and Stam 1994, 48). It does not view identities as stable or fixed or essentialized but rather as unstable and historically situated. It is reciprocal and dialogical and rejects narrow definitions of identity politics as simply the work of discrete, bounded communities. Accompanied by a strategy of political articulation, critical multiculturalism can be a crucial practice in cutting racism at the joints and working toward a vision of cultural democracy premised on social and economic justice.

Dear brothers and sisters in struggle, I have been slowly leading up to a conclusion. Let me summarize some of the more prescriptive points that follow from my previous discussions. It seems clear to me that we must steadfastly refuse to cut our ties to the lifeworld of our students and the communities in which they live. We must work collectively to try to help our students better understand both what is occurring at the global level of capitalist flows and transactions and how consumer culture within late capitalism is producing marketplace justice for the privileged and poverty for the rest. This means inviting our students to challenge the cultural logics and social relations of late capitalism and how such logics and relations are not only turning individual subjects into servants of transnational regulatory banking institutions and corporations but are also coordinating identities and subjectivities into a cybercitizenship. This cybercitizenship promotes character structures that respond to personal responsibility and the entrepreneurial spirit rather than to collective responsibility and equality and social justice. In other words, we need to provide for our students the conditions for critical consciousness and struggle not only for economic justice (although this is crucial) but also for justice in the political arenas of race, gender, and sexuality.

What can we say about critical pedagogy in light of the contexts I have discussed? Broadly speaking, critical pedagogy is about struggling at the level of the social relations of production for economic justice for all working people. It is also about recreating culture and agency through the practice of criticism and the criticism of practice. I have tried to rescue in this book some undisputably Marxist foundations for critical pedagogy. Of course, much more work needs to be done in the area of pedagogy and class struggle, as unfashionable as this may seem in our current era of "post-Marxism."

"Is critical pedagogy about creating cultural heroes?" a student revolutionary once asked me following a lecture in Jalapa City, Mexico, a few years ago. Let me answer that question as a way of concluding my discussion. In my view, critical pedagogy is not mainly about struggling for cultural values (although values are certainly—fundamentally—important); it is, however, most emphatically about struggling with and for the oppressed. Critical citizenry is not about becoming a cultural hero by serving as a watchdog for family or civic values. Cultural heroes espouse certain values and may even die to defend them. They might even implore others to do the same (Bauman 1992). While cultural heroes fight for cultural values, critical citizens, in contrast, sacrifice themselves for disenfranchised others, and not necessarily for unpopular ideals. Life lived in service to others—rather than in service to abstract values—is one of the few measures that can give life within postmodern Gringolandia revolutionary meaning. Willingness to sacrifice ourselves for others is, as Emmanual Lévinas, Mikhail Bakhtin, and Zygmunt Bauman argue, the only revolutionary way to live amid the debris of existential uncertainty and alienation.

The Struggle for the Ethical Self

I am advocating for the development of the ethical self as a way of living within and challenging the historical present of postmodern culture and transnational capitalism. Of the ethical self, Bauman writes:

> Only in the shape of the ethical self is humanity complete. Only in that shape does it attain the subtle blend and sought-for reconciliation of uniqueness and togetherness. Only when raised to the level of the ethical self, individuality does not mean loneliness, and togetherness does not mean oppression. "Concern for the other, up to the sacrifice, up to the possibility of dying for him; responsibility for the other"—this is, as Lévinas insists, the "otherwise than being," the only exit from what otherwise would be self-enclosed, selfish, lonely, void (and ultimately meaningless) existence. (1992, 201)

I agree with Bauman when he explains that heroes traffic in ideas and die for them whether these happen to be ideas about freedom, justice, race, class, or God. Ethical selves, unlike heroes, die for the dignity of other human beings and for their well-being and in doing so they cannot justify any death or sacrifice *but their own*. Heroes often exhort others to die in the name of a cause (Bauman 1992), whereas ethical selves cannot live at the expense of their responsibility to others.

As Bauman points out, "Death itself becomes a cause for the hero of a cause," whereas for the ethical self, life becomes the cause for those who are willing to die for the dignity and liberation of the other. As critical citizens we need to act as if the elimination of the needless suffering of all others depends upon the day-to-day choices that we make. We must refuse to allow postmodern culture to domesticate the people, to render them useless, and we must struggle to deny contemporary democracy the license to proclaim the people unworthy servants of the common good. That is what is meant by acting critically, and that is the power, promise, and sacrifice of critical pedagogy.

Acting critically also means acting with aesthetic sensibility, since in some fundamental ways aesthetic culture inevitably shapes political culture. Wolfgang Welsch (1996) suggests that relations of plurality, specificity, and partiality—as these operate within the realm of aesthetics—are structurally similar to the way in which they operate in everyday conditions of social life. Consequently, what is needed in contemporary formulations of critical pedagogy is an aesthetically reflexive awareness of difference in which social subjects are sensitized "for basic differences and for the peculiarity and irreducibility of different ways of life" (19). Welsch notes that aesthetically reflective awareness "perceives deviant principles, sees through imperialisms, is allergic to injustice and encourages one to intervene for the rights of the oppressed" (19). For example, Welsch claims that tolerance for difference without aesthetic sensibility is insufficient. He writes:

> The example of tolerance serves to make clear just how dependent political culture is on aesthetic culture. Tolerance without sensibility would be just a bare principle. One imagines a person who has made all of the maxims of tolerance their own, but who in day-to-day life lacks the sensitivity to even notice that the perceptions of others are different in principle and not just subject to some arbitrary lapse, that is, that it's a case not of a deficit as such, but of a cultural difference. A person of this sort would never be embarrassed by so much as having to make use of his tolerance, but rather would incessantly practice imperialisms and oppression with the clearest of consciences and in the securest of beliefs that he's a tolerant person. Sensitivity for differences is then a real condition for tolerance. Perhaps we live in a society which talks too much of tolerance but has too little command of sensitivity. (19)

In fact, I would extend Welsch's example of tolerance by arguing that critical muliculturalism must move beyond tolerance in order to embrace a politics of respect and affirmation. One way of extending Welsch's insights on aesthetic reflection—a project that I do not have time to develop here—would be to follow Paul Trembath (1996) in utilizing Deleuze's work on "affective capacities" in conjunction with a revised Marxian theory of sensuous activity in ways that are compatible with poststructuralist theories of difference and cultural materialism's opposition to the idealization of sense. In other words, we need a new language and politics of the body (McLaren 1995).

The charge that I have leveled at U.S. democracy throughout this chapter is more than an arraignment of American civic-mindedness or national character but speaks to deep-seated structural arrangements prohibitive of equality and social justice. I am drawing attention to the ominous historical moment of citizen abdication of democracy to the powers of capital and to the false prophets of the antigovernment Patriot movement. It is a time of capitulation of government to corporations and of the fundamental incompatibility of unbridled capitalism and democracy. In this historical moment we witness the marriage of dominant cultural life to *engabachamiento*.

I make this charge because the cause of liberation through schooling and other public spheres is too important to be left to narrow-minded educational researchers and pundits. The liberation of our schools is too vital a project to abandon to those who would domesticate critical pedagogy—such as some microethnographers who either neutralize the social relations of production and consumption by ignoring the larger context of capitalism or pretend that it doesn't exist—or to right-wing journalists, conservative talk-show hosts, or conservative or liberal think tanks that seek democracy in our schools in only the most narrow functionalist or procedural sense. There are many arenas of struggle occupied by various groups offering strategies of hope: the EZLN (Ejército Zapatista de Liberación Nacional) in Chiapas; the EPR (Ejército Popular Revolucionario), and PROCUP-PDLP (Partido Revolucionario Obrero Clandestino Unión de Pueblo–Partido de los Pobres) in Oaxaca, Guerrero, and Hidalgo; ecofeminists struggling in southeastern Mexico; educational activists trained at the Centro de Estudios sobre la Universidad UNAM (Universidad Nacional Autonoma de Mexico) in Mexico City; African American urban activists in Detroit; student activists struggling to keep affirmative action in California; Puerto Rican students in Chicago politicizing their community; Nuyoricans struggling for justice in El Barrio; Chicano/a activists in Los Angeles fighting for *la raza*. Which arenas we are called to occupy will depend a great deal on the extent to which we can force democracy to provide for the basic needs of the people. Up to this point the situation is unequivocal: We have failed democracy and it has failed us.

Whites need to do more than remember the history of colonialism as it affected the oppressed; they need to critically re-member such history. As Homi Bhabha (1986, xxiii) reminds us, "Remembering is never a quiet act of introspection or retrospection. It is a painful re-membering, a putting together of the dismembered past to make sense of the trauma of the present." This means piercing the vapors of mystification surrounding the objectification of human relations within bourgeois consciousness in order to construct new forms of subjectivity and agency that operate within a socialist political imaginary.

What I am advocating, dear sisters and brothers in struggle, is a post-colonial multiculturalism that moves beyond the ludic, metrocentric focus on identities as hybrid and hyphenated assemblages of subjectivity that exist alongside or outside of the larger social totality. Postcolonial multiculturalism, as I am articulating the term, takes as its condition of possibility the capitalist world system; it moves beyond a monocultural-ist multiculturalism that fails to address identity formation in a global context and focuses instead on the idea that identities are shifting, changing, overlapping, and historically diverse (Shohat 1995). Multicul-turalism is a politics of difference that is globally interdependent and raises questions about intercommunal alliances and coalitions. Accord-ing to Ella Shohat, intercommunal coalitions are based on historically shaped affinities, and the multicultural theory that underwrites such a coalitionary politics needs "to avoid either falling into essentialist traps or being politically paralyzed by deconstructionist formulations" (1995, 177). Shohat articulates the challenge as follows:

> Rather than ask who can speak, then, we should ask how we can speak to-gether, and more important, how we can move the dialogue forward. How can diverse communities speak in concert? How might we interweave our voices, whether in chorus, in antiphony, in call and response, or in polyphony? What are the modes of collective speech? In this sense, it might be worthwhile to focus less on identity as something one "has," than on identification as something one "does." (1995, 177)

Revolutionary multiculturalism recognizes that the objective struc-tures in which we live, the material relations tied to production in which we are situated, and the determinate conditions that produce us are all reflected in our everyday lived experiences. In other words, lived experi-ences constitute more than subjective values, beliefs, and understand-ings; they are always mediated through ideological configurations of discourse, political economies of power and privilege, and the social di-vision of labor. Revolutionary multiculturalism is a socialist-feminist multiculturalism that challenges those historically sedimented processes through which race, class, and gender identities are produced within capitalist society. Therefore, revolutionary multiculturalism is not limited to transforming attitudinal discrimination but is dedicated to re-constituting the deep structures of political economy, culture, and power in contemporary social arrangements. It is not about reforming capitalist democracy but rather transforming it by cutting at its joints and then rebuilding the social order from the vantage point of the op-pressed.

Revolutionary multiculturalism must not only accommodate the idea of capitalism; it must also advocate a critique of capitalism and a strug-gle against it. The struggle for liberation on the basis of race and gender must not remain detached from anticapitalist struggle. Often the call for diversity and pluralism by the apostles of postmodernism is a surrender to the ideological mystifications of capitalism. The fashionable apostasy of preaching difference from the citadels of postmodernist thought has dissolved resistance into the totalizing power of capitalist exploitation. In this regard, Ellen Meiksins Wood rightly warns: "We should not confuse respect for the plurality of human experience and social struggles with a complete dissolution of historical causality, where there is nothing but diversity, difference and contingency, no unifying structures, no logic of process, no capitalism and therefore no negation of it, no universal project of human emancipation" (1995, 263).

The challenge is to create at the level of everyday life a commitment to solidarity with the oppressed and an identification with past and present struggles against imperialism, against racism, against sexism, against homophobia, against all those practices of unfreedom associated with living in a white supremacist capitalist society. As participants in such a challenge we become agents of history by living the moral commitment to freedom and justice, by maintaining a loyalty to the revolutionary domain of possibility, by speaking truth to power, and by creating a collective voice out of the farthest reaching "we"—one that unites all those who suffer under capitalism, patriarchy, racism, and colonialism throughout the globe.

Through critical pedagogy we can begin to ask questions about how we can live modernity's quest for emancipation within postmodern cultural climates without at the same time being deformed by its sufferings and practices of destruction. We can struggle to fathom how the goals of liberation can be won without dragooning less privileged groups into the service of our unacknowledged capitalist will to power. We need to do more than simply invert relations of power because then the oppressed, newly freed from their bondage, would inevitably recuperate the logic of the oppressor so long as the same system of power informs their identities as emancipated agents. Consequently, we must define liberation from whiteness outside of the particular goals of such a struggle. We must invariably ask: From whiteness to *where*? Addressing such a question will play a crucial role in the struggle for social justice in the decades ahead. And this will be no small task in a world in which the theoretical pirouettes of the postmodern left have replaced a Marxian emphasis on concrete struggle and community activism; where a playful decentering of the signifier has replaced the struggle against oppression; and where the notion of oppression itself has been psychologized to mean anything that happens to be bothering you at the time, like the weeds in your front lawn. In this instance, resistance is co-opted and reduced to a variation of the monolithic theme of procedural democracy.

A revolutionary multiculturalism must begin with an immanent rather than a transcendent critique, revolutionary praxis rather than melioristic reforms. It must engage what Enrique Dussel (1993) calls "the Reason of the Other." The debates over modernity and postmodernity have a different set of valences for *los olvidados* in Latinoamerica, for the peripheralized, for the marginalized, for the wretched of the earth. Dussel writes about this distinction from his Latin American context: "Unlike the postmodernists, we do not propose a critique of reason as such; but we do accept their critique of a violent, coercive, genocidal reason. We do not deny the rational kernel of the universalist rationalism of the Enlightenment, only its irrational moment as sacrificial myth. We do not negate reason, in other words, but the irrationality of the violence generated by the myth of modernity. Against postmodernist irrationalism, we affirm the 'Reason of Other'" (1993, 75).

I wish to present critical pedagogy not as a set of classroom teaching practices but rather position it within a larger political problematic; here critical pedagogy is located as a politically informed disposition and commitment to marginalized others in the service of justice and freedom. Justice is conceptualized in this context from within the spirit of a transformative diasporic consciousness and encompasses issues of class, race, gender, and sexual orientation because all of these ongoing relations inform each other. A critical pedagogy grounded in a rearticulation of whiteness must seek to create a larger context in which it shares values with other struggles. We need, in other words, to fight for each other's differences and not just our own. This stipulates that we must identify a common ground of struggle in which a universality of rights and the common good passes into particular social struggles and then is reinitiated dialectically at a higher level of universality, and so on, without final closure. I am pointing to a nonabsolutist form of cultural politics, one that is never quite free from historically given languages, cultural codes, positionings of time and space, and forms of memory and narration that make political articulation and expression possible in the first place (Rattansi 1994,76). The new political subject that will emerge will be constituted by deessentializing forms of agency and syncretic forms of political consciousness. An example of such syncretic tactics in the realm of music can be seen in the work of Britain's Apache Indian (Stephen Kuper), a Hindu Punjabi who was raised in a multiethnic area of working-class Birmingham. Apache has been voted best newcomer at the British Reggae Industry Awards and is popular among African Caribbean and South Asian diasporic communities, and his work topped the reggae and bhangra charts in 1991 (Bhachu 1996). Similarly, the group PBN—Punjabi by Nature—is a Toronto-based group of Canadian-born South Asians whose music has been influenced by four continents, resulting in what Parminder Bhachu calls a "quadruple diasporic consciousness" (1996, 286). George Lipsitz tells the story of an African man who grew up believing that Pete Seeger was black, because he knew Seeger was a civil rights activist, sang freedom songs, and included Paul Robeson among his personal friends. After coming to the U.S., the man got into an argument over Seeger's ethnicity and was shown a picture of Seeger that showed him to be white. Yet still the man replied: "I know that Pete Seeger is Black . . . why should I change my mind just because I see his face" (1996, p. 409).

Only through a multidimensional approach to agency and a transformation of the human condition created by capitalism can we begin the task of transforming the overwhelming power of transnational capital and truly live as liberated subjects of history.

References

Aronowitz, S., and DiFazio, W. (1994). *The Jobless Future: Sci-Tech and the Dogma of Work*. Minneapolis: University of Minnesota Press.

Balibar, Etienne. (1996). "Is European Citizenship Possible?" *Public Culture* no. 19, 355–376.

Bauman, Zygmunt. (1992). *Mortality, Immortality and Other Life Strategies*. Stanford: Stanford University Press.

Bauman, Zygmunt. (1996). "On Communitarians and Human Freedom, or, How to Square the Circle." *Theory, Culture and Society* 13(2), 79–90.

Bernstein, Sharon. (1996). "Storm Rises over Ex-Klansman in Debate." *Los Angeles Times*, Wednesday, September 11, A3, A14.

Bhabha, Homi. (1986). "Remembering Fanon." Foreword to Frantz Fanon, *Black Skin, White Masks*. London: Pluto Press.

Bhachu, Parminder. (1996). "The Multiple Landscapes of Transnational Asian Women in the Diaspora." In Vered Amit-Talai and Caroline Knowles, eds., *Re-Situating Identities: The Politics of Race, Ethnicity, and Culture* (283–303). Peterborough, Canada, and Essex, London: Broadview Press.

Boggs, C. (1995). "The God Reborn: Pondering the Revival of Russian Communism." *Los Angeles View* 10(20), 8.

Bonnett, Alastair. (1996). "Anti-Racism and the Critique of White Identities." *New Community* 22(1), 97–110.

Boston Globe, January 26, 1990.

Bradlee Jr., B. (1996). "The Buchanan Role: GOP Protagonist." *Boston Sunday Globe*, March 3, 1996, 1, 12.

Cashmore, Ellis. (1996). *Dictionary of Race and Ethnic Relations*, 4th ed. London and New York: Routledge.

Chomsky, Noam. (1996). *Class Warfare: Interviews with David Barsamian*. Monroe, ME: Common Courage Press.

Cone, James H. (1986). *A Black Theology of Liberation*. New York: Orbis Books.

Cruz, Jon. (1996). "From Farce to Tragedy: Reflections on the Reification of Race at Century's End." In Avery Gordon and Christopher Newfield, eds., *Mapping*

Multiculturalism (19–39). Minneapolis and London: University of Minnesota Press.

Darder, Antonia. (1992). *Culture and Power in the Classroom.* South Hadley, MS: Bergin and Garvey.

Dussel, Enrique. (1993). "Eurocentrism and Modernity (Introduction to the Frankfurt Lectures)." *boundary 2* 20(3), 65–77.

Fanon, Frantz. (1967). *Black Skin, White Masks.* New York: Grove Press.

Frankenberg, Ruth. (1993). *The Social Construction of Whiteness: White Women, Race Matters.* Minneapolis: University of Minnesota Press.

Fraser, Nancy. (1993). "Clintonism, Welfare, and the Antisocial Wage: The Emergence of a Neoliberal Political Imaginary." *Rethinking Marxism* 6(1), 9–23.

Fusco, Coco. (1995). *English Is Broken Here: Notes on Cultural Fusion in the Americas.* New York: New Press.

Gallagher, Charles A. (1994). "White Construction in the University." *Socialist Review* 1/2, 165–187.

Gardiner, Michael. (1996). "Alterity and Ethics: A Dialogical Perspective." *Theory, Culture and Society* 13(2), 121–144.

Goldberg, David Theo. (1993). *Racist Culture: Philosophy and the Politics of Meaning.* Cambridge, MA, and Oxford, England: Blackwell.

Gutiérrez, Ramón. (1996). "The Erotic Zone: Sexual Transgression on the U.S.-Mexican Border." In Avery Gordon and Christopher Newfield, eds., *Mapping Multiculturalism.* Minneapolis: University of Minnesota Press.

Harris, Cheryl I. (1993). "Whiteness as Property." *Harvard Law Review* 106(8), 1709–1791.

Haymes, Stephen Nathan. (1995). *Race, Culture, and the City: A Pedagogy for Black Urban Struggle.* Albany: State University of New York Press.

Holston, James, and Appadurai, Arjun. (1996). "Cities and Citizenship." *Public Culture* no. 19, 187–204.

Ignatiev, Noel, and Garvey, John. (1996). *Race Traitor.* New York and London: Routledge.

Kincheloe, Joe, and Steinberg, Shirley. (in press). *Changing Multiculturalism: New Times, New Curriclum.* London: Open University Press.

Laclau, Ernesto. (1992). "Universalism, Particularism, and the Question of Identity." *October* 61, Summer, 83–90.

Lash, Scott. (1996). "Postmodern Ethics: The Missing Ground." *Theory, Culture and Society* 13(2), 91–104.

Lipsitz, George. (1995). "The Possessive Investment in Whiteness: Racialized Social Democracy and the 'White' Problem in American Studies." *American Quarterly* 47(3), 369–387.

Lipsitz, George. (1996). "It's All Wrong, but It's All Right: Creative Misunderstandings in Intercultural Communication." In Avery Gordon and Christopher Newfield, eds., *Mapping Multiculturalism* (403–412). Minneapolis and London: University of Minnesota Press.

Loewen, James W. (1995). *Lies My Teacher Told Me: Everything Your American History Textbook Got Wrong.* New York: Touchstone.

López, Ian F. Haney. (1996). *White by Law.* New York and London: New York University Press.

Lott, Eric. (1903). "White Like Me: Racial Cross-Dressing and the Construction of American Whiteness." In Amy Kaplan and Donald E. Pease, eds., *Cultures of United States Imperialism* (474–498). Durham, NC: Duke University Press.

Macedo, Donald, and Bartolome, Lilia. (forthcoming). "Dancing with Bigotry: The Poisoning of Racial and Ethnic Identities." In Enrique Bartolomé Trueba and Yali Zou, eds., *Ethnic Identity and Power*. Albany: State University of New York Press.

McLaren, Peter. (1995). *Critical Pedagogy and Predatory Culture: Oppositional Politics in a Postmodern Era:* London and New York: Routledge.

Moraes, Marcia. (1996). *Bilingual Education: A Dialogue with the Bakhtin Circle.* Albany: State University of New York Press.

Murphy, Peter. (1996). "Peregrini." *Thesis Eleven* no. 46, 1–32.

Novik, Michael. (1995). *White Lies, White Power: The Fight Against White Supremacy and Reactionary Violence.* Monroe, ME: Common Courage Press.

O'Brien, Conor Cruise. (1996). "Thomas Jefferson: Radical and Racist." *Atlantic Monthly,* October, 53–74.

Perea, Juan, F. (1995). "Los Olvidados: On the Making of Invisible People." *New York University Law Review* 70(4), 965–991.

Rattansi, Ali. (1994). "'Western' Racisms, Ethnicities and Identities in a 'Postmodern' Frame." In Ali Rattansi and Sallie Westwood, eds., *Racism, Modernity and Identity on the Western Front* (403–412). Cambridge and Oxford: Polity Press.

Roediger, David. (1994). *Towards the Abolition of Whiteness.* London and New York: Verso.

Said, Edward. (1985). *Orientalism.* London: Penguin.

Shohat, Ella. (1995). "The Struggle over Representation: Casting, Coalitions, and the Politics of Identification." In Román de la Campa, E. Ann Kaplan, and Michael Sprinker, eds., *Late Imperial Culture* (166–178). London and New York: Verso.

Shohat, Ella, and Stam, Robert. (1994). *Unthinking Eurocentrism: Multiculturalism and the Media.* New York and London: Routledge.

Simon, S. (1996). "Job Hunt's Wild Side in Russia." *Los Angeles Times,* January 2, 1, 9.

Southern Poverty Law Center. (1996). *False Patriots: The Threat of Antigovernment Extremists.* Montgomery, AL: SPLC.

Stowe, David W. (1966). "Uncolored People: The Rise of Whiteness Studies." *Lingua Franca* 6(6), 68–77.

Time. (1995). "Banker to Mexico: 'Go get 'em.'" February 20, 9.

Todorov, Tzventan. (1984). *The Conquest of America: The Question of the Other.* New York: Harper and Row.

Trembath, Paul. (1996). "Aesthetics Without Art or Culture: Toward an Alternative Sense of Materialist Agency." *Strategies* 9/10, 122–151.

Wallace, Amy. (1996). "Less Diversity Seen as UC Preferences End." *Los Angeles Times,* Wednesday, October 2, A1, 18.

Welsch, Wolfgang. (1996). "Aestheticization Processes: Phenomena, Distinctions and Prospects." *Theory, Culture and Society* 13(1), 1–24.

West, Cornel. (1993). *Keeping Faith: Philosophy and Race in America.* New York: Routledge.

Winant, Howard. (1994). *Racial Conditions: Politics, Theory, Comparisons.* Minneapolis and London: University of Minnesota Press.

Wolfenstein, Eugene Victor. (1993). *Psychoanalytic-Marxism: Groundwork.* New York and London: Guilford Press.

Wood, Ellen Meiksins. (1995). *Democracy Against Capitalism: Renewing Historical Materialism.* Cambridge and New York: Cambridge University Press.

Wray, Matt, and Newitz, Annalee, eds. (1997). *White Trash: Race and Class in America.* New York: Routledge.

Yúdice, George. (1995). "Neither Impugning nor Disavowing Whiteness Does a Viable Politics Make: The Limits of Identity Politics." In Christopher Newfield and Ronald Strickland, eds., *After Political Correctness: The Humanities and Society in the 1990s* (255–285). Boulder: Westview Press.

Zamichow, N. (1996). "Captains Courageous Enough Not to Fight." *Los Angeles Times,* January 23, 1, 9–10.

Zinn, Howard. (1970). *The Politics of History.* Boston: Beacon Press.

Epilogue—
Beyond the Threshold of
Liberal Pluralism: Toward
a Revolutionary Democracy

In this brief epilogue I would like to extend some of the ideas that connect the various chapters of this book by focusing on the intersection of the following questions: What kind of political agency is implicitly endorsed in an official politics of inclusion that is undeniably committed to the major tenets of a multicultural democracy: hybridity, difference, and diversity? What is wrong with current conceptions of multicultural democracy?

In addressing this issue it is necessary to situate multicultural education in a larger problematic beyond the politics of inclusion. In so doing I want to make the claim that a multiculturalist pluralism that purports to be inclusive may actually be founded upon discourses and practices of structural exclusion. Further, it is likely to be based on a homogenizing drive grounded in a politics of white, patriarchal, and imperialist capitalism.

Because so many educators are trying to tie multiculturalism to the idea of diversity and liberal democracy, and because to me this is an exceedingly problematic—even dangerous—venture, I would like to make some concluding remarks about the pernicious uses to which diversity can be put, such as its paradoxical consolidation of social relations of domination and exploitation.

Negatively prejudiced by the choice of its constitutive premises, liberal pluralism often reproduces those values it a priori stipulates in its tacit, unstated, metaphysical vision of democracy. A view of a democracy as a terrain where a plurality of voices emerges from the discourse and practices of popular identity need require nothing external to itself in order to account for itself. A democracy built upon an open-ended conversation among many "others" too often is merely self-validating from the very beginning; in its operational circularity and circuitousness it is designed to sanitize and to neutralize its own constitutive properties while purging its ethnos of oppositional views and practices and shaping its premises such that its conclusions are already built into them.

The questions that critical educators need to raise must revolve around the nature and purpose of the narratives that circumscribe the multivocal boundaries of the everyday imagination, that map the discursive and material boundaries of everyday possibility such that the marginalized are seemingly granted permission to narrate their dreams and desires—in putatively autonomous fashion—through an invisible and often paradoxical metanarrative that is always/already reading the world. It is in such a paradoxical setting that the soul of narration can be deformed as autonomous agency is transformed into the lie that the politics of diversity formulates in order to defend itself against the "crime" of recognizing and respecting otherness.

A democracy of diverse subjectivities and dispositions must never be captured in any grand consensus-seeking narrative. The true Civitas Dei is not harmonious but a conflictive clamor of ideas and disagreements. Any democracy built upon consensual narratives of agreement constitutes a form of functionalism that refuses to confront privileging hierarchies and asymmetrical arrangements and relations of power; it falsely presumes that individuals or groups can possess equivalence in the realm of material needs. Further, liberal democracy represses the contingency of its own selection of values, betraying an epistemological idealism in its hidden desire to merge its yearning for connection into a prelapsarian harmony and metaphysical unity.

According to Louise Marcil-Lacoste (1992), pluralism works against the concept of the common good; it sets itself up as a value in itself without regard for context or content. Pluralism as an operational mechanism reduces politics to the instrumentality of management and democracy to a set of procedural rules. Pluralism leads to a sheer conflagration of interest and, notes Marcil-Lacoste, rarely leads to consensus. Pluralism is more concerned with who has the authority to choose than with what is to be done. Revealing a functional bias, pluralism displaces the issue of defining society in terms of substantive narrative choices about social, economic, and political finalities. While pluralism attempts to challenge and refute monism, totalitarianism, dogmatism, and absolutism, it can actually lead to new forms of epistemological and axiological monism, since pluralism actually erodes the pluralities it claims to support. Pluralism suggest that individuals incorporate all values in a single viewpoint and that they must remain equidistant from all dogmas.

As educators, we need to work from our diverse situated knowledges— our partial and contingent subjective standpoints—but in doing so we must ground our forms of inquiry ethically and politically and not merely reduce them to issues and questions of epistemology (Mirón, 1996). In other words, we need to be aware that our "everyday identities"—despite the fact that they may be promoted and produced in contexts that support diversity—are often subtended by macrostructures of power and privilege and produced through expressions of bourgeois self-consciousness disguised as popular discourse produced in the interests of "the people." Absolute autonomy transforms itself within global capitalism into a self-referential intolerance and even hatred of otherness. The oppositional imagination—no matter how it postures amid the throng of the suffering masses—potentially serves as a constant ally of domination and exploitation. We need, therefore, to create a new political culture in which we are encouraged to interrogate the received consensus of American values and to resist hegemonized approaches to ethnic diversity whose narrative telos is necessarily linked to a politics of premature and uncritical unity, consensus, and agreement, to the logic of liberal individualism, to political appeasement, to a stratified and hierarchically ordered polity. For a democracy of consensus is a democracy of neutrality in which undemocratic practices at the level of daily life go depressingly unquestioned and unchallenged. It is to the challenge of creating such a political culture that this book has been directed.

Diversity in and of itself means very little by itself, but if conscripted into the service of a racist state, it could function in an ominous and frightening fashion. Diversity is not something to be struggled over "for its own sake" if the alignments of power relations and trajectories of political forces favor some individuals and groups over others. The production of difference is not as important as the ends to which such differences are put, deployed, or redeployed. We need to understand and engage the political economy of knowledge production so that we can always locate the production of meaning within the struggle over and across class, gender, ethnicity, and sexuality. As the preceding chapters have argued, identity as a form of self-differentiation is relationally constituted within competing discourses that make contradictory demands upon us. Individuals and groups are not discriminated against on the basis of their difference; rather the enunciation of discrimination itself constructs the form and character of "difference" and produces the interpretations by which difference is measured, evaluated, and judged. It is the political economy of such forms of enunciation and the social relations of their production that should concern us here. Since it is undeniably the case that groups are differentially incorporated into U.S. society, we need to take liberal pluralism to task in terms of the inequality of power and control over resources suffered by disadvantaged minority groups. We need to understand how both the official culture and the cultures of the popular coalesce difference and identity within an ideology of liberal humanism and a sovereign enlightenment view of tolerance and inclusion.

When we argue that people who are different from us should be judged according to the standards of their "particular identities," are we not supplying the dominant culture with the ideological alibi it needs to condemn the other as separate from us? Is it not an apology for a de facto differential incorporation of racial collectivities, as social theorist E. San Juan might put it? In this view, a politics of diversity can unwittingly be held to guarantee the production of the labor force and the smooth maintenance of the order of the law. Here, a politics of difference and liberal pluralism acquiesces to the status quo unless it is contingently grounded in and framed by an ethico-political project. When liberal humanists maintain, as they often do, that all groups are serially situated in variegated contexts that together constitute a shared community of values (with some groups doing a better job than others in harmonizing with the social and cultural norms), in my mind they paint a false picture of a society whose hegemonizing drive and sovereign narratives of desire help to sift the best ideas from the worst in order to regulate and accommodate the social in the interests of all.

Class and status hierarchies in the United States are not the benign result of a competition among diverse ethnic norms operating within a neutral marketplace of values and behaviors. Rather, within a late-capitalist political economy, social stratification on the basis of class, race, and ethnicity is not simply discursive or textual. It is fundamentally and irredeemably ideological and material and is tied to dominant hegemonic relations and the ideological-political machinery of state power. When we are infected with the bacillus of postmodernism, everything "appears" only textual. Oppressed groups who live in the internal colonies of the United States—disenfranchised Native Americans, African Americans, Latino/as, Puerto Ricans, and others—understand only too well that they do not live in metaphysical harmony with their oppressors but rather are located in hierarchies of subordination that are inescapably inscribed in political contestation.

The ill-founded notion that democracy requires consensual agreement evokes a society resembling a frozen space of emptiness, a structured and sedimented silence in which power and antagonism disappear. As the preceding chapters strongly suggest, a democracy in which identities are able to sound their voices in a dialogical engagement with otherness is a democracy that is noisy, requiring open disputation within (at least tentatively) agreed-upon frameworks—and utilizing a contrapuntal form of criticism—in order to prevent animosity from seething and spilling over into violence. In addition to a noisy democracy, what is needed is the creation of spaces of identity that thwart the purity of sameness, that point to a narrative space that is nonnarratable, in other words, a narrative space that escapes the linearity and ocularism of Western cultural conceits and tropes. Such a space is one in which group identity is not functional to cultural integration and social consensus. As Parekh (1994, 306) affirms, "Equality implies both sameness and difference, and requires that each of the two should be so defined as to include the other. People should be treated in the same way, but the sameness must take account of their differences. . . . Equality requires a rejection of arbitrary or irrelevant differences and a full recognition of legitimate and relevant differences."

An oppositional multicultural identity should not be conceived of as a nativist glorification of some prelapsarian past. Nor should it consist of the detritus of late capitalism—whatever can be cobbled out of a hyper-real bricolage of discursive offerings that have broken away from our national stockpile of stable meanings. We need not succumb to the postmodern sirens of despair who implore us to celebrate as a form of contemporary virtue the nihilism oozing out of the cracks of our hybrid, splayed, and syncretic subjectivities.

Hybrid identities have become commodified. They are about lifestyle shopping and cultural appropriation. For poststructuralist self-fashioners, to become a border-crosser too often constitutes a voguish way to refuse the harsh reality that capitalism has commodified and cannibalized the entire worlds of nature, leaving us little out of which to fashion our identities other than the excess of exchange value. According to Teresa Brennan (1996, 35), "We console ourselves with myths of hybrids, while living the divide between a speedy fantasy that overlays us, and a natural time that knows it is running out."

The critical pedagogy to which this book speaks poses a concerted challenge to articulations and struggles over identity that we are witnessing within and between groups throughout North America and the rest of the world—in Quebec, Chicago, New York, Los Angeles, Bosnia, Africa. What we are seeing in the particularistic struggles for identity is the reverse of the quest for universality; it is the assertion of a purer singularity in the face of the pressure to be absorbed into an abstract universalism otherwise known as democracy. As Slavoj Žižek, Ernesto Laclau, and others have noted, the paradox of democracy is precisely that we achieve universal status without regard for particular, distinctive characteristics among the citizenry. Citizens in a democracy are stripped culturally and remade as a "constituent lack"—they become subjects without properties or characteristics. In the United States, for instance, you may become part of the melting pot only by subtracting the particular content that makes you unique. Democracy becomes in this process merely a formal link between abstract individuals emptied of their cultural, subjective specificity. In the formal democratic practices of the United States, there is little place for human content, since democracy is fundamentally antihumanistic. The foundation of democracy, notes Žižek, is its own constitutive lack—its own impossibility. Liberal democracy reproduces the paradox of a collective understanding of individualism. Can individualism be the object of a collective investment? Edward O'Neill put it thus: "There is no common language nor any public sphere which is so neutral that it does not already delimit exactly that which it claims not to regulate but merely to preserve. Just as for Wittgenstein what the skeptic says is correct only it cannot be asserted, so the assertion of universal rights is correct, only the language in which it is asserted is never universal but always particular, and so the case must always break down or reach its own limits" (1996, 117).

Democracy therefore implies a cleavage—a split between the abstract, universal citizen who has been melted down—purified—to a glistening bone-whiteness and the bourgeois carrier of particular, "darker," and more sinister interests. Democracy exists only in the thin margin between the public and the private, between private pathology and public morality, between love and its object of desire. The democratic call for universal integration has the effect of subsuming ethnic particularities. The surplus values contained in the leftovers of formal democracy are reflected in the pathological notion of the nation-state.

It is regrettable that within contemporary democratic social life, ethics has been demoted to a figural trace in the interval between the formation of our identities as oppressor and oppressed. Our identities work through discourses of master and slave but are not reducible to them; our identities do not exist prior to discourse, yet discourses cannot fully capture the totality of identity. Discourses of identity are historical and relational and not autonomous and unified. Yet we refuse to link identity to the politics of collective struggle because the race, gender, sexuality, and social class are almost always understood from a perspective that is inherently individualistic. Identities are constantly in the process of differentiation, flux, and contradiction but always open to change and transformation. We must remember that there is nothing about identity formation that precludes identities from becoming coalitionary instead of split off and free-floating.

Žižek (1991) remarks that since it is difficult to organize ourselves as citizens of the world with any real emotional enthusiasm and political agency, we need to search for other structures of enjoyment and desire. Regrettably, in many instances such structures have been and continue to be found in an allegiance to a particular national cause by means of an organization of collective enjoyment through participation in white supremacist myths of nationhood. Žižek argues that in such a context the other always wants to steal our enjoyment, always wants to ruin our "way of life," always has access to some secret, some perverse satisfaction at our expense. From this racist formation, Žižek maintains that the other becomes the workaholic stealing our jobs or the idler living on our labor.

Žižek claims that democracy can be a democracy only of the subject (or the signifier) and not of the object. Enjoyment and fantasy are incommensurable with symbolic law, the big Other. The *object petit à*, the object cause of desire, always manages to escape the network of universal exchange, or universal equalization. The particular local right to enjoyment always subverts and unsettles the universal field of bourgeois equivalent exchange. Žižek points out that the limit of democracy is therefore internal—it resides in its internal antagonism. Because democracy recognizes that its limit is internal—that it is possible only on the basis of its own impossibility—we can perhaps avoid the fate of totalitarianism, which is condemned to invent external enemies such as the immigrant within us. This, perhaps, is the message of the struggle for oppositional identities: to confront the impossible surplus of our dreams and the fundamental impasse of democracy and yet to act as if freedom and justice are possible.

Oppositional subjects of history working within pedagogies of dissent need to open up pedagogical practices from the inside and discover what determines pedagogy itself while remaining outside of pedagogy's control. And to do this means nothing short of waging class struggle against machineries of oppression in all of their various guises and forms. This means making political interventions in the way that we live pedagogically at the level of the everyday. A pedagogy of liberation is a pedagogy that is able to recognize the daily transmutations of capital, to organize the day-to-day resistance of the dominated classes, and to release the liberation project from the bondage of its own inertia and disillusionment. It plays a hinge role in turning individual memories into living enactments of historical, collective memory. This is a message that too often gets lost in the post-Marxist call for radical democracy. Only with a renewed emphasis on and approach to class analysis and struggle can critical pedagogy remain true to its project of liberation. Interventions mainly at the level of cultural *difference* are decidedly not enough and run the risk of reproducing those structures of oppression that critical pedagogy has been historically committed to transform.

Postscript

Orale, loco, no te escames . . . The smell of blood lingers in the air. A regime of madmen watch from the darkness that is preparing to descend. It is a darkness brought by the false promises of neoliberalism and the false hopes of liberal democracy. As hope moves into full retreat throughout the globe, the postmodernists stumble about like weekend drunks, trying to reinvent catharsis in a world where abjection has replaced interpretation, where the signifier has replaced meaning, where spectators have replaced participants. They are trying to construct a Baudrillardian avant-garde, that is, when they are not off shopping in the retro boutiques, buying prints by Frida Kahlo at Westside art fairs, or walking through the mercado Mexicano on Olivera Street (where the *vendedores ambulantes* make them feel so deliciously "Third-worldish"). The only pleasure that remains is the act of forgetting the present. The only option available is the creation of new fictions of identity cut loose from history. The challenge that we face in the approaching millennium cannot be met in this arena of American spectacles. It can be met only in the concrete struggle for history. While our postmodern dilettantes and *soi disant* intelligentsia dine on pasta and smoked salmon at funky restaurants on the West Side, the carnales from Big Hazard and la Eme stroll though the streets of Ramona Gardens near Smokey's wall or disappear down the sidewalks of Estrada Courts. The night descends and it is business as usual in Los Angeles.

South of *la linea*, in Mexico, *vatos locos* from Nezahualcoyotl, powered by La Banda and political fearlessness, walk through streets paved with blood and dreams. It is the stuff of which *corridos* are made.

At a school on the outskirts of San Cristobal de las Casas in Chiapas, students read quotations from the Mexican constitution in Spanish and Tsotsil. Attempting to assimilate the fifty-six native cultures into the republic, the Mexican government has been promoting bilingual education as a means of bringing its indigenous population into the *mestizo* mainstream. But there is a spirit in the making that refuses to succumb to the lure of nationalism, a spirit that is rising up like a great serpent of fire. It is a spirit that refuses to die. The world has seen this spirit before. And capitalism's pinstriped gangsters would do well to tremble before its humble grandeur and to drive their Bentleys out of town before the apocalypse strikes.

References

Brennan, Teresa. (1996). "Why the Time Is Out of Joint: Marx's Political Economy Without the Subject" Part 1. *Strategies* 9/10, 18–37.

Laclau, Ernesto. (1990). *New Reflections on the Revolution of Our Time*. London and New York: Verso.

Marcil-Lacoste, Louise. (1992). "The Paradoxes of Pluralism." In Chantal Mouffe, ed., *Dimensions of Radical Democracy: Pluralism, Citizenship, Community* (128–142). London and New York: Verso.

Mirón, Louis F. (1996). *The Social Construction of Urban Schooling*. Cresskill, NJ: Hampton Press, Inc.

O'Neill, Edward R. (1996). "Making Ideology Perfectly Queer or, How I Stopped Worrying and Learned to Love Ideology." *Strategies*, 9/10, 94–121.

Parekh, B. (1994). "Equality, Fairness and Limits of Diversity." *Innovation* 7(3), 289–308.

San Juan, E. (1992). *Articulations of Power in Ethnic and Racial Studies in the United States*. London: Humanities Press.

Žižek, Slavoj. (1991). *Looking Awry: An Introduction to Jacques Lacan Through Popular Culture*. Cambridge: MIT Press.

Afterword— Multiculturalism: The Fracturing of Cultural Souls

Donaldo Macedo and Lilia I. Bartolomé

Nicolás Guillén's poem "Responde tú" forcibly announces Peter McLaren's new insightful book, *Revolutionary Multiculturalism: Pedagogies of Dissent for the New Millennium* by capturing the ambivalence of our fractured cultural soul yearning to make meaning out of a bittersweet existence in a racist society. In denouncing the horrors of oppression, McLaren skillfully unveils the drama of multiculturalism, which often forces us to live in a borrowed cultural existence—an existence that is almost culturally schizophrenic. That is, being present and yet not visible—being visible and yet not present. It is a process through which we come to know what it means to be at the periphery of the intimate and yet fragile relationship between two cultural worlds coexisting asymmetrically.

Revolutionary Multiculturalism is not only illuminating in that it sheds important light on the ideological mechanisms that shape and maintain our racist social order, it painstakingly moves the discussion of multiculturalism beyond the reductionistic binarism of White vs. Black debate. Peter McLaren not only avoids falling prey to a binaristic approach to race analysis, he differentiates ethnic from racial entities in order to avoid the facile interpretation of these ideological constructs. In other words, McLaren's work avoids the fragmentation of ethnic and racial realities that are part of the social organization and knowledge defined along disciplinary boundaries, i.e., ethnic studies. This fragmentation represents a rupture with ethnic and racial relations, and it propagates an ideology that creates and sustains false dichotomies delineated by ethnic or race disciplinary boundaries. Racism must be treated as an ideological construct that interpenetrates both ethnic and racial realities. An analysis of racism isolated from other social organizations along the lines of ethnicity and culture does little good. Only by means of a process through which the dominant white ideology is deconstructed can we begin to understand the intimate relationships among asymmetrical distribution of power and privilege along different ethnic groups, including lower-class ethnic whites.

What is important to point out is that the analysis of race, ethnicity, or gender as monolithic entities often prevents the understanding that these categories represent interpenetrating realms of a shared dominant ideological foundation. In the case of gender, for example, bell hooks so accurately argues that "sexism, racism, and class exploitation constitute interlocking systems of domination—that sex, race, and class, and not sex alone, determine the nature of any female's identity, status, circumstance, the degree to which she will or will not be dominated, the extent to which she will have the power to dominate."[1]

As it is the case with sex, the same can be argued for race and ethnicity. Thus, as part of a broader struggle to fight oppression of all forms, race and ethnicity need to be understood as both ideological constructs that have historically served the purpose of perpetuating racism, and as political categories that can function to mobilize resistance against white domination. In the latter case, both race and ethnic identities take on positive values as they contribute to the struggle for social justice and the eradication of oppression. As ideological constructs, both race and ethnicity are separated from class and gender issues so as to prevent the understanding of the interconnecting relationships hidden in the dominant white ideology. In other words, we need to avoid the lumping of multiple identities into a monolithic entity such as race or ethnicity. Part of the deconstruction of dominant white ideology involves the understanding of how ethnicity and race interpenetrate each other, a concept that Pepi Leistyna refers to as "Racenicity, a process through which the ideological construction of race has a significant impact on ethnicity."[2] We need to move beyond a discourse that views difference as simply aesthetic or separate categories of analysis. It is important to link difference to questions of power where Whiteness and Blackness, among other characteristics, are treated as political categories that do not exist in a power vacuum. These categories exist in relation to one another mediated always by asymmetrical power relationships. According to Stanley Aronowitz:

> The concept of ethnicity with respect to education expresses two somewhat different characteristics of how issues of inequality are conventionally addressed in the literature. Recently, descriptively, the term has been employed to discuss issues of access and since we have no social scientifically

acceptable discourse of class, ethnicity has become the displacement of this largely unacknowledged aspect of educational access and performance.[3]

The challenge for educators is to interrogate the descriptive nature of the discourse on race and ethnicity so as to unveil the inherent description that hides how "ethnicity has become the displacement" of class. Educators also need to understand how "cultural differences are purged and social practices are reshaped around a racial identity [giving rise to] a hierarchy that subcategorizes while devaluing groups of people that are designated 'racial others,' 'ethnics,' 'outsiders.'"[4]

What makes *Revolutionary Multiculturalism* a must read is that in denuding the complex web of a racist dominant ideology it never falls prey to a form of paralyzing fatalism. On the contrary, *Revolutionary Multiculturalism* is infused by a pedagogy of hope that is informed by tolerance, respect, and solidarity: A pedagogy that rejects the social construction of images that dehumanize the "other"; a pedagogy of hope that points out that in our construction of the "other" we become intimately tied with the "other"; a pedagogy that teaches us that by dehumanizing the "other" we become dehumanized ourselves. In short, we need a pedagogy of hope that guides us toward the critical road of truth, not myths, not lies, toward the reappropriation of our endangered dignity, toward the reclaiming of our humanity. A pedagogy of hope will point us toward a world that is more harmonious, less discriminatory, more just, less dehumanizing, and more humane. A pedagogy of hope will reject our society's policy of hatred, bigotry, and division while celebrating diversity within unity.

Notes

1. bell hooks, *Talking Back* (Boston: South End Press, 1989), p. 22.
2. Pepi Leistyna, "Racenicity: Whitewashing Ethnicity" in Donaldo Macedo (ed.). *Tongue-Tying Multiculturalism.* In progress.
3. Stanley Aronowitz, "Ethnicity and Higher Education in the U.S." *Harvard Educational Review.* Forthcoming. Summer 1997.
4. Pepi Leistyna, "Racenicity: Whitewashing Ethnicity" in Donaldo Macedo (ed.). *Tongue-Tying Multiculturalism.* In progress.

Credits

"Responde tú," by Nicolás Guillén, reprinted by permission of Monthly Review Foundation from *Patria O Muerte! The Great Zoo and Other Poems.* Copyright © 1972 by Marquez.

Sections of the introduction are drawn from "Critical Ethnicities: Afterword," forthcoming in Henry Trueba and Yali Zou, eds., *Ethnic Identity and Power: Cultural Contexts of Political Action in School and Society* (Albany: State University of New York Press).

Chapter 1 originally appeared as Henry A. Giroux and Peter McLaren, "Writing from the Margins: Geographies of Identity, Pedagogy, and Power," *Journal of Education* 174(1), 1992, 7–30. Reprinted with permission of the publisher.

Chapter 2 appeared in an earlier version as "Freirean Pedagogy and Higher Education: The Challenge of Postmodernism and the Politics of Race," *Cultural Critique*, Spring 1996, 151–184. This chapter also appeared in Henry A. Giroux, Colin Lankshear, Peter McLaren, and Michael Peters, *CounterNarratives* (New York and London: Routledge, 1997). Reprinted with permission of the publisher.

Chapter 3 is a revised version of an essay that will appear in Yvonna Lincoln and William Tierney, eds., *Representation and the Text: Reframing the Narrative Voice* (New York: State University of New York Press). Reprinted with permission of the publisher.

Chapter 4 is an expanded version of a chapter that is forthcoming in Michael Peters, ed., *Naming the Multiple: Poststructuralism and Education.* Copyright © 1997 by Bergin and Garvey. Published with permission of Greenwood Publishing Group, Inc., Westport, CT.

A section of Chapter 5 draws from material that appeared in "Gangsta Pedagogy and Ghettocentricity: The Hip-Hop Nation as Counterpublic Sphere," *Suitcase* 1(1,2), 1995, 74–87. Chapter 5 also appeared in an earlier version as "Gangsta Pedagogy and Ghettoethnicity: The Hip-Hop Nation as Counterpublic Sphere," *Socialist Review* 95(2), 1995, 9–56. Reprinted by permission.

Some portions of the first section of Chapter 6 are expanded discussions based on Peter McLaren, "Critical Pedagogy in the Age of Global Capitalism: Some Challenges for the Educational Left," *Australian Journal of Education* 39(1), 5–21; Peter McLaren, "Strategies to Halt Violence Against American Youth: Too Late. Too Soon. A Response to Marian Wright Edelman," *Religious Education* 89(4), 1994, 561–567; and Peter McLaren, "The Educator as Agent of History," *Education Theory* 45(2), 1995, 270–271.

Chapter 7 originally appeared in *Comenius* 15(3), 335–347.

Chapter 8 is based on several presentations that occurred at the University of California–Berkeley and Harvard University. They were developed on subsequent occasions into talks presented in Argentina, Mexico, Germany, Canada, Puerto Rico, and Japan. Sections of this chapter are forthcoming in "Unthinking Whiteness, Rethinking Democracy," in Christine Clark and James O'Donnell, eds., *Becoming White: Owning a Racial Identity* (Albany: State University of New York Press) and *Educational Foundations.*

About the Book and Author

This work by one of North America's leading educational theorists and cultural critics culminates a decade of social analyses that focus on the political economy of schooling, Paulo Freire and literacy education, hip-hop culture, and multicultural education. McLaren also examines the work of Baudrillard as well as Bourdieu's reflexive sociology.

Always in McLaren's work is a profound understanding of the relationship among advanced capitalism, the politics of knowledge, and the formation of identity. One of the central themes of this volume is the relationship between the political and the pedagogical for educators, activists, artists, and other cultural workers. McLaren argues that the central project ahead in the struggle for social justice is not so much the politics of diversity as the global decentering and dismantling of whiteness. This volume also contains an interview with the author.

Peter McLaren is professor of education at the Graduate School of Education and Information Studies, University of California at Los Angeles. His development of a revolutionary politics of liberation has taken him throughout Europe, Latin America, and Southeast Asia, where he is frequently invited to discuss his work. He has written numerous books, articles, and monographs on critical pedagogy, cultural studies, and race relations. His writings have appeared in Spanish, Portuguese, Catalan, French, German, Polish, Hebrew, and Japanese.